Praise for *Animal F...*

"Animals communicate with us on many different sp... ...mal Frequency* is a powerful resource that will enable ...dom and divine essence on a higher level. The guid... ...connect to the frequency of the animal kingdom to l... ...mind to their powerful messages."

—Karen ...

and psychic medium

"*Animal Frequency* opens our minds to both the rich possibility of communicating more easily with our animal friends and to recognizing their powerful symbolic meanings as they appear in our lives. You'll enjoy the personal stories about how animals influence our lives—and begin to pay closer attention to the ways that they show up to bring messages. *Animal Frequency* is a fun reference book to keep on the shelf."

—Debra Moffitt, award-winning author of
Garden of Bliss and *Awake in the World*

"Melissa has given us a wonderful reference to help us tap into the frequency of our incredible animal kingdom. As a practicing psychic, I receive many messages using animals to help me and having this as a go to guide will be a necessary part of my practice! I recommend this book to anyone who is developing or understanding their own intuitive gifts as Melissa has gone above and beyond to help us connect to our animals in a way no other has before—she gives us different, relevant ways to interpret each animal's energy. This book will be one you will want to keep in your collection always!"

—Melanie Barnum, author of *Psychic Vision* and
The Pocket Book of Psychic Development

Animal
Frequency

About the Author

Melissa Alvarez is a best-selling, award-winning author who has written ten books and nearly five hundred articles on self-help, spirituality, and wellness. As a professional intuitive coach, energy worker, spiritual advisor, medium, and animal communicator with more than twenty-five years of experience, Melissa has helped thousands of people bring clarity, joy, and balance into their lives. Melissa teaches others how to connect with their own intuitive nature and how to work with frequency for spiritual growth. She has appeared on numerous radio shows as both a guest and host. Melissa is the author of *365 Ways to Raise Your Frequency* and *Your Psychic Self*. Melissa's books have been translated into Romanian, Russian, Chinese, French, and Czech. She lives in South Florida with her family, dogs, and horses. Visit her online at www.MelissaA.com. *Animal Frequency*® *Oracle Cards* are available at www.AnimalFrequency.com.

Animal Frequency

Identify,
Attune, and
Connect to the
Energy
of
Animals

Melissa Alvarez

Llewellyn Publications
Woodbury, Minnesota

FIRST EDITION
First Printing, 2017

Book design by Donna Burch-Brown
Cover Illustration by Mia Bosna
Cover design by Lisa Novak
Interior illustrations by Wen Hsu

Llewellyn Publications is a registered trademark of Llewellyn Worldwide Ltd.

Animal Frequency is a registered trademark of Melissa Alvarez.

Library of Congress Cataloging-in-Publication Data (Pending)
ISBN: 978-0-7387-4928-0

Llewellyn Worldwide Ltd. does not participate in, endorse, or have any authority or responsibility concerning private business transactions between our authors and the public.

All mail addressed to the author is forwarded, but the publisher cannot, unless specifically instructed by the author, give out an address or phone number.

Any Internet references contained in this work are current at publication time, but the publisher cannot guarantee that a specific location will continue to be maintained. Please refer to the publisher's website for links to authors' websites and other sources.

Llewellyn Publications
A Division of Llewellyn Worldwide Ltd.
2143 Wooddale Drive
Woodbury, MN 55125-2989
www.llewellyn.com

Printed in the United States of America

Other Books by Melissa Alvarez

365 Ways to Raise Your Frequency

Your Psychic Self

Forthcoming Books by Melissa Alvarez

Llewellyn's Little Book of Spirit Animals

Universal Power

Contents

List by Category xiii

Acknowledgments xvii

Introduction 1

The Animal Kingdom 3

Animal Frequency 4

Is Animal Frequency the Same as Animal Communication? 5

The Spiritual World 6

Animal Totems or Spirit Animals? What's the Difference? 7

Not What You Expected? 8

Dream Animals 8

How to Use This Book 10

Using Frequency Connections to Receive Energy Animal Messages 13

Feel the Animal's Frequency 14

Is Your Pet Your Energy Animal? 16

Color and Elemental Meanings 18

Part 1: Wild Animals

Aardvark 20

Alligator (Crocodile) 22

Ant 24

Antelope (Pronghorn) 26

Armadillo 28

Badger 30

Bat 32

Bear 34

Beaver (Muskrat) 36

Bee 38

Beetle 40

Black Panther 42

Blue Jay 44

Boar 46

Buffalo (Bison) 48

Butterfly 50
Catbird 52
Caterpillar (Inchworm) 54
Catfish 56
Centipede (Millipede) 58
Cheetah 60
Chickadee 62
Chipmunk (Ground Squirrel) 64
Clam 66
Cockroach 68
Conch 70
Coral 72
Cougar (Mountain Lion, Puma) 74
Coyote 76
Crab (Crayfish, Lobster) 78
Cricket 80
Deer 82
Dolphin (Porpoise) 84
Dove 86
Dragonfly (Damselfly) 88
Eagle 90
Earthworm 92
Eel 94
Elephant 96
Firefly (Lightning Bug) 98
Flamingo 100
Fly 102
Fox 104
Frog (Toad) 106
Giraffe 108
Gopher (Groundhog, Woodchuck) 110
Grasshopper 112
Grouse 114
Hare 116
Hawk 118

Hippopotamus 120
Hummingbird 122
Jaguar 124
Jellyfish 126
Kangaroo 128
Ladybug (Asian Lady Beetle) 130
Lion 132
Lizard (Gecko) 134
Loon 136
Lynx (Bobcat) 138
Meerkat (Mongoose) 140
Monkey 142
Moose 144
Mouse 146
Narwhal 148
Octopus (Squid) 150
Opossum 152
Orangutan 154
Owl 156
Oyster 158
Panda 160
Parrot (McCaw) 162
Peacock 164
Penguin 166
Porcupine 168
Raccoon 170
Raven (Crow) 172
Rhinoceros 174
Salamander 176
Salmon 178
Scorpion 180
Sea Horse (Sea Dragon) 182
Seal (Sea Lion) 184
Shark 186
Skunk 188

Sloth 190
Snake (Viper) 192
Spider 194
Starfish 196
Stick Insect 198
Stingray 200
Swan 202
Swordfish 204
Tiger 206
Turtle 208
Vulture (Buzzard) 210
Weasel (Maarten, Mink) 212
Whale 214
Wolf 216
Woodpecker 218
Zebra 220

Part 2: Domesticated Animals

Angelfish 224
Camel 226
Canary 228
Carp 230
Cat 232
Cattle (Cow) 234
Chameleon 236
Chicken 238
Chinchilla 240
Cockatiel (Cockatoo, Parakeet) 242
Dog 244
Donkey 246
Duck 248
Ferret 250
Gerbil 252
Goat 254
Goldfish (Koi) 256
Goose 258
Guinea Fowl 260
Guinea Pig (Hamster) 262
Guppy 264
Hedgehog 266
Horse 268
Iguana 270
Llama (Alpaca) 272
Lory (Rainbow) 274
Mule 276
Pig 278
Pigeon 280
Praying Mantis 282
Rabbit 284
Sheep 286
Siamese Fighting Fish (Betta Fish) 288
Silkworm (Silk Moth) 290
Society Finch 292
Squirrel Monkey 294
Sugar Glider 296
Tortoise 298
Turkey 300
Yak 302

Part 3: Mythical Animals

Amarok 306
Amphisbaena 308
Basilisk 310
Bigfoot 312
Bunyip 314
Cadmean Vixen 316
Caladrius 318
Cerastes 320
Cetan 322
Chimera 324

Chupacabra 326
Cockatrice 328
Dragon 330
Erymanthian Boar 332
Gargoyle 334
Gremlin 336
Griffin 338
Hippogriff 340
Hydra of Lerna 342
Jackalope 344
Jersey Devil 346
Jormungand 348
Kelpie 350
Kongamato 352
Kraken 354

Ladon (Python) 356
Loch Ness Monster 358
Nandi Bear 360
Nemean Lion 362
Ogopogo 364
Owlman 366
Pegasus 368
Phoenix 370
Sea-Goat 372
Shisa 374
Sleipnir 376
Stymphalian Bird (Roc) 378
Thunderbird 380
Unicorn 382
White Stag 384

Conclusion 387
Appendix A: Color Meanings 391
Appendix B: Elemental Meanings 395
Bibliography 397

List by Category

Amphibian

Frog (Toad) 106

Salamander 176

Birds

Blue Jay 44

Caladrius 318

Canary 228

Catbird 52

Cetan 322

Chickadee 62

Chicken 238

Cockatiel (Cockatoo, Parakeet) 242

Cockatrice 328

Dove 86

Duck 248

Eagle 90

Flamingo 100

Goose 258

Griffin 338

Grouse 114

Guinea Fowl 260

Hawk 118

Hippogriff 340

Hummingbird 122

Kongamato 352

Loon 136

Lory (Rainbow) 274

Owl 156

Owlman 366

Parrot (McCaw) 162

Peacock 164

Penguin 166

Phoenix 370

Pigeon 280

Raven (Crow) 172

Society Finch 292

Stymphalian Bird (Roc) 378

Swan 202

Thunderbird 380

Turkey 300

Vulture (Buzzard) 210

Woodpecker 218

Canines

Amarok 306

Bunyip 314

Coyote 76

Dog 244

Fox 104

Shisa 374

Wolf 216

Equines

Bunyip 314

Donkey 246

Hippogriff 340

Horse 268

Kelpie 350

Mule 276

Pegasus 368

Sleipnir 376

Unicorn 382

Zebra 220

Felines

Black Panther 42
Cadmean Vixen 316
Cat 232
Cheetah 60
Cougar (Mountain Lion, Puma) 74
Jaguar 124
Lion 132
Lynx (Bobcat) 138
Tiger 206

Fish

Angelfish 224
Carp 230
Catfish 56
Goldfish (Koi) 256
Guppy 264
Kelpie 350
Salmon 178
Siamese Fighting Fish (Betta Fish) 288

Insects

Ant 24
Bee 38
Beetle 40
Butterfly 50
Caterpillar (Inchworm) 54
Centipede (Millipede) 58
Cockroach 68
Cricket 80
Dragonfly (Damselfly) 88
Earthworm 92
Firefly (Lightning Bug) 98
Fly 102

Grasshopper 112
Ladybug (Asian Lady Beetle) 130
Praying Mantis 282
Scorpion 180
Silkworm (Silk Moth) 290
Spider 194
Stick Insect 198

Other Mammals

Aardvark 20
Antelope (Pronghorn) 26
Armadillo 28
Badger 30
Bat 32
Bear 34
Beaver (Muskrat) 36
Bigfoot 312
Boar 46
Buffalo (Bison) 48
Bunyip 314
Camel 226
Cattle (Cow) 234
Chimera 324
Chinchilla 240
Chipmunk (Ground Squirrel) 64
Chupacabra 326
Deer 82
Elephant 96
Erymanthian Boar 332
Ferret 250
Gargoyle 334
Gerbil 252
Giraffe 108
Goat 254

Gopher (Groundhog, Woodchuck) 110
Gremlin 336
Griffin 338
Guinea Pig (Hamster) 262
Hare 116
Hedgehog 266
Hippopotamus 120
Jackalope 344
Jersey Devil 346
Kangaroo 128
Lion 132
Llama (Alpaca) 272
Meerkat (Mongoose) 140
Monkey 142
Moose 144
Mouse 146
Nandi Bear 360
Nemean Lion 362
Opossum 152
Orangutan 154
Panda 160
Pig 278
Porcupine 168
Rabbit 284
Raccoon 170
Rhinoceros 174
Sea-Goat 372
Seal (Sea Lion) 184
Sheep 286
Shisa 374
Skunk 188
Sloth 190
Squirrel Monkey 294
Sugar Glider 296

Weasel (Maarten, Mink) 212
White Stag 384
Yak 302

Other Sea Life

Clam 66
Conch 70
Coral 72
Crab (Crayfish, Lobster) 78
Dolphin (Porpoise) 84
Eel 94
Jellyfish 126
Kraken 354
Loch Ness Monster 358
Narwhal 148
Octopus (Squid) 150
Ogopogo 364
Oyster 158
Sea Horse (Sea Dragon) 182
Sea-Goat 372
Shark 186
Starfish 196
Stingray 200
Swordfish 204
Whale 214

Reptiles

Alligator (Crocodile) 22
Amphisbaena 308
Basilisk 310
Bunyip 314
Cerastes 320
Chameleon 236
Chimera 324

Cockatrice 328

Dragon 330

Griffin 338

Hydra of Lerna 342

Iguana 270

Jormungand 348

Ladon (Python) 356

Lizard (Gecko) 134

Snake (Viper) 192

Tortoise 298

Turtle 208

Acknowledgments

I would like to express my sincerest appreciation to the following:

As always, to my husband, Jorge, and my wonderful kids, Jordan, Jason, Justin, and Jorgie, for your love and belief in me. Without you guys, I wouldn't be me. I love you with all that I am.

My parents, Warren and Nancy McDowell, for allowing me to buy Lady and letting her have April. My first horses were the best gifts in the world. Thanks for never getting mad all of the times that I came home with a stray animal.

Angela Wix, my acquisitions editor, Stephanie Finne, my production editor, for this book, and the board, editorial, art, and marketing departments at Llewellyn Worldwide. You guys are awesome. You make my writing shine and the covers are amazing! Thanks for all that you do.

Dr. Erin Newkirk, DVM (from Reid & Associates)—the best equine repro vet in the world! I can't begin to thank you for everything you do to keep our horses in the best health possible and for all you've taught me over the years. Thanks so much for being you.

Annemette Minor (from Reid & Associates)—the best equine repro vet tech ever! Thanks for all you do in helping our four-legged family and for making me laugh.

Dr. Byron Reid, Dr. Rebecca Adkins, Dr. Alexander Daniel, Dr. Allyson Ripley (intern) and the rest of the team and staff at Reid & Associates. For all you do every day for the equines in your care, including mine.

Celeste Hebets—It's wonderful when animals bring people together and create lasting friendships. I'm so glad Zoltan did that for us.

Mimi Riser—Thanks for all the in-depth discussions about publishing, animals, theories, metaphysics, spirituality, and everything else in between. Who knew that my review of your book would lead to such a long friendship?

Sally Painter—Thanks for always being you, for sharing the signs and messages with me when they appear to you, for insightful revelations of the past, and impressions of the future. They are always appreciated, as are you.

Shawn Wilhelm—Thanks for interesting "what does this mean" intuitive discussions and listening to my endless animal stories.

Victoria Germony—Thanks so much for taking care of the horses while I wrote this book. You are a strong, powerful, and determined woman who will excel in all you do in life. Don't ever let anyone, or anything, hold you back from achieving all you want in life. Learn the lessons and move forward in positivity. I'm so excited for you to start vet tech school. You're going to be amazing! I miss you.

Katherine Smith—What a wonderful addition you are to our equine facility! Thank you for being so great with the horses and for all you do. I'm so happy to have you on the team.

All of the animals I've had the honor of loving through the years. I can't begin to name you all here but there are some who deserve a special mention. Dogs: Bandit, Tinkerbell, Klaskie, Joker, Gypsy, Jinx, Max, Chanel, Irie, Domino. Cats: Chalis, Onyx. Horses: Lady, April, Picasso, Eike, Knight, Zoltan, Zoey, Klaske, Trudy, Nikita, Friesia, Bella, Ce-Ce, Bonita, Kissa, Jitska, Silver, Grasshopper, Madonna. And especially April, my New Forest Pony who followed the ten-year-old me wherever I'd go, even into the basement to lie on the floor and watch *Dark Shadows*, or to my bedroom when Mama and Daddy weren't looking (and until we got caught and had to go back outside). To all of the animals that showed up while I was writing this book (there are way too many to name individually). You have each taught me so much and for that, and you, I am thankful.

Introduction

Thanks for picking up my book today. Before we delve into the subject of animal frequency, let me tell you a little about my connection with animals and why I wrote this book. I grew up on a farm in Southern Virginia surrounded by nature and animals. Like most farmers in the area, we had dogs, cats, hogs, cows, chickens, and horses. There were fish and bullfrogs in the ponds behind our house. Summer evenings were filled with chasing fireflies and listening to the whip-poor-will's lonesome call. Summer nights brought the sounds of the bullfrogs, cicadas, crickets, and other creatures of the night, which often lulled me to sleep with their rhythmic resonance. Morning dawned with the song of the sparrows, meadowlarks, robins, and cardinals. During my childhood, I frequently encountered chinchillas, foxes, deer, snakes, snapping turtles, terrapins, squirrels, rabbits, chipmunks, dogs, cats, pigs, horses, cows, and many other wild and domesticated animals. As a child, it was all I knew. My father even nicknamed me Lizard because I would catch and release the lizards around the barn. Now, as an adult living in Florida, I still catch all the lizards that get in the house and put them back outside, my dad still calls me Lizard from time to time, and I still hold to my childhood memories because that is where my understanding and connection to what I call *animal frequency* and *energy animals* began.

I work with energy from a metaphysical and spiritual perspective. Through energy work, I help people understand their personal vibration, their own unique frequency, and how they can raise it to higher levels. I teach them to understand their intuitive nature and how to recognize their core spiritual essence so they can progress along their spiritual path and learn their chosen lessons in this lifetime. Quite often, at some point along their paths, people recognize the connection we all have with the animal kingdom. They feel drawn to know what animal they are most connected to in this lifetime. For some, the animal connection may begin in childhood, and for others it may occur later in life. In metaphysical circles, the animal that guides you is called a totem, a familiar, a power animal, a spirit animal, or an animal spirit guide, depending upon the person's beliefs. Many books about connecting with animals approach it from a Native American or shaman's point of view and practices. Because I work with energy, I approach the topic from the perspective of energy connections. I call the process *animal frequency* and the animals who appear to you are *energy animals*.

Animal frequency is the distinctive energy vibration that all individual animals possess. When combined with our own unique frequencies, we can communicate with and understand the reason for the animal's presence in our lives. Animal frequency is important to every one of us because, as spiritual beings themselves, animals bring messages that will positively affect your life. In this book, it is my intention to teach you how to connect to a multitude of animals and how to understand these animals when they appear in your life. Connecting to individual animal frequencies enables you to intertwine your frequency with theirs, which leads to a deeper understanding of the specific animal and of your own true spiritual nature.

I wrote this book for two reasons. The first is to honor the animals that have honored me with their presence in my life. The second is so you can learn to connect to the animal kingdom and experience your own spiritual growth during the process. I have tried to make this book a super easy reference in the hopes that you'll use it often. I've also tried to provide new information about the animals from an energy point of view that may not be found in other books because it came from the animals themselves, my own guides, and intuition. The guided imagery section gives you a possible scenario to help you imagine interacting with the animal. That's what this book is about—understanding and connecting frequencies, the energy of spiritual beings—so that's what we'll do.

I hope the animals I've chosen for this book are helpful to you along your path. Animals have always been an important part of my life, and I'm honored to share their messages with you.

The Animal Kingdom

Did you know that more than two million animal species have been discovered by scientists, and there are probably even more that haven't been discovered yet? We share Earth with animals, so it only makes sense that we will have interactions with them during our lives. Maybe you've heard that humans tend to be calmer and live longer when they have pets. The unconditional love of domesticated animals can bring great joy within us through their positive influence. When you connect with animals on a physical, emotional, or spiritual level, you can deepen the experience by also connecting with their frequency, which can enable soul growth within your core essence. You can do this with wild animals as well. While you might not be able to give a wild animal a hug like you would a dog or a cat, you will benefit from their unique frequencies and the messages they bring into your life.

The animal kingdom is classified as a "grouping of all living beings with more or less complex organs, with which they move about and feed themselves." Within the animal kingdom the subgroup of insects and arachnids are described as a "highly diversified grouping of all animal invertebrates" that are "more numerous than all other animal or plant species." Insects are included in *Animal Frequency* because they are considered animals by definition and are part of the animal kingdom.

Animal frequency is easy, rewarding, and allows you tremendous spiritual growth. Once you learn how to intuitively feel the animal's frequency (their unique energy) and understand how to connect with them through pictures, thoughts, and words, you'll be actively using the energy highway between the two of you. Some of the information you'll receive from them will be feelings, sometimes you'll hear words, or you'll see pictures. Other times it will be a clear, concise knowing without explanation when you look into the animal's eyes. But you don't have to be in the presence of the animal to receive messages from it. Often the spirit of the animal will come to you in ways you least expect with messages intended to guide you or so you can help them.

In the history of the world, people have always had a connection with animals. They have been placed on pedestals and worshipped because it was thought their power could bring harmony and peace to mankind if humans communicated with and respected the animal. In our current time, we're experiencing a change in the way we think about animals as a culture. We're becoming more protective of them. At our core we've always known our connection to animals runs deep. Now we're listening to the animals again, just as people did in times past.

Animals are pure, peaceful, and innocent. They don't harbor resentment, drama, or any of the negative emotions humans sometimes experience. They act and react to the situations around them in order to survive. In the wild, they are predators or prey only because they must eat to live. There is balance in their world. By connecting to their frequency you can find balance in your world. They touch us at our core, where our primal instincts live. We can relate to being as wild and free as they are, since we often inhibit these feelings in our daily life.

Animal Frequency

Animal frequency is an animal's energy vibrating within their spiritual being, which is contained within their physical body. With animals, the wisdom of the ages is held within them. They are peaceful and soulful, and they offer lessons that can bring us balance and allow spiritual growth. Animal frequency includes your own personal energy vibration because you too are an animal. The process of connecting human and animal energy during a session is what animal frequency is all about. Each person and animal has a unique energy within their spiritual being. When we incarnate on the earthly plane, this energy is contained within our physical bodies. Your personal frequency can go from low to high and is constantly in flux due to changes in your life. The frequency of animals tends to be more stable because they don't deal with the drama or stress that we do. Our frequency is based on our spiritual selves, but it can be changed, raised, or lowered based on outside influences and our life experiences.

Universal frequency is the overall energy of the universe that is part of us all. As humans, we are connected to the frequency of the human race, but as individuals within the human species we each have our own individual frequency. It's the same for animals. Cats, as a species, have a unique frequency, but the energy of a house cat is different from a mountain lion and two house cats will each have their own unique individual frequencies.

Frequency has layers if we look at it from a universal viewpoint. We can choose to connect our frequency to the frequency of a species of animals or to an individual animal. It is also beneficial to do both because you can learn different things.

Just like we all have intuitive abilities, we all have the ability to identify, attune, and connect with animals using animal frequency. When working with animal frequency, the first thing you have to do is let go of any preconceived notions that animals are inferior beings because they can't speak like we do, or they don't have feelings, aren't smart, or *it's only an animal*. Remember, you're an animal too. Once you can see an animal as a spiritual being like yourself, then you'll easily connect with it.

Is Animal Frequency the Same as Animal Communication?

I'm often asked if animal frequency is the same thing as animal communication. It is comparable, but there are also vast differences. It is similar, when you're first learning how to do it, because you begin the session by communicating with the animal using intuition, telepathy, thoughts, feelings, and accompanying sounds, which is how they communicate with one another. They're incapable of voicing words, so you have to become part of their world. It's different because you're also working with energy at very high vibrational levels using all of your intuitive senses as both you and the animal are connected to the Divine. It's being in a place of knowing without words, pictures, or sound; instead you're surrounded by energy, light, and feelings. It's a different sensation than just doing animal communication—it's more powerful, intimate—and, while you'll receive information from the animals, it happens almost instantaneously and with vivid intensity. It's as if you're sharing a stream of consciousness on a soul level and recognize one another as being part of universal creation. Animal frequency feels like you're sharing pieces of your spiritual essence as your souls connect with one another, rather than just having a conversation. When using animal frequency, I go back and forth between the intense level of animal frequency and the normal levels of animal communication that I work with all of the time. As you practice animal frequency, you'll be able to move from one to the other in an instant.

The Spiritual World

Within the spiritual world of universal frequency, there is ancient wisdom and timeless knowledge that we can access. At our core essence we are all spirit and are all part of this universal frequency. We are beings of energy and light who chose to live in the physical realm in order to learn lessons that will enable us to experience spiritual growth. Because we are made up of energy, our frequencies are able to connect to every aspect of the universe. Animals are also energy and part of universal frequency, just as we are, which allows us to consciously connect to their frequency.

Within the spiritual world you will find your spirit guides, animal spirit guides, departed loved ones, masters, ascended masters, angels, archangels, and God. Each one of these beings is important to your journey in the physical realm, and many of them have agreed, prior to your birth, to assist, protect, and inspire you along the way.

Before we are born into the earthly plane of existence, we make agreements with the people and the animals we will interact with and learn lessons from during our lifetimes. Just as we have spirit guides, angels, and masters to direct us along this path, we also have energy animals that act as our guides. We have some energy animals that are with us for a lifetime and others that come to us when they're needed for a specific message. Some are with us from birth, guiding and directing us, while others come with specific messages when we need them the most and then disappear once the message has been received. Many times energy animals will bring messages from deceased loved ones from the spiritual realm.

Our physical bodies are created to hold our true spiritual self, which is energy, on the earthly plane. Since we are interconnected to all that is, which includes the animal kingdom, we are able to call upon our guides, angels, and masters when needed, so it only makes sense that we can call on animals, too. The animals have chosen to incarnate just as we have. You'll interact with animals on the earthly plane in their physical incarnation and you will also interact with them as guides in their true energy form on the spiritual realm. Regardless of how they appear to you, it is their frequency and messages that are most important and that will assist you.

Purposefully reaching out to your energy animals and acknowledging them when they appear will enable you to become more spiritually enlightened. You will raise your own frequency through these positive connections. This can lead to a more peaceful and balanced feeling within you, which can enable you to heal, become stronger, and feel empowered on your life path.

Animal Totems or Spirit Animals? What's the Difference?

Depending on who you speak to regarding the significance of animal appearances, you'll discover animals are called many different things. Some of these terms include (but are not limited to): totems, guardians, familiars, power animals, protectors, spirit animals, core animals, and spirit animal guides. All of these terms basically mean the same thing (except for one big difference) depending on the belief system they originated from, and it can get confusing at times. What's the big difference? Most people believe that animal spirit guides choose you and you choose your animal totems.

To me they are all spirit guides, so my preference is to use the term *energy animals* because we're connecting our energy with theirs. I have found that even though spirit animals choose you, and can be unpredictable in their appearances, you can still call upon them in times of need because of the special energy connection the two of you share. You can call on totems too, so for me it is easier and less confusing to call all of them energy animals. This also includes mythical beings, so don't be surprised if you encounter a unicorn or a griffin on your journey.

You have many energy animals that only visit you when they have an important message to share. You have others that are with you for your entire lifetime and align their frequency with yours to strengthen and empower you. Some come to help you make tough decisions and then leave. Others test you so you learn, grow, and change to reflect your true spiritual essence. Energy animals will guide you, advise you, protect you, and impart their skills upon you. All you have to do is be aware of them, ask for their help, be attentive to their answers, and honor their assistance. You can call them to you by wearing jewelry featuring the animal, by keeping a picture of the animal close by so you can see it often, or by putting a picture of the animal as a screen saver on your computer. You can also think of the animal several times a day, do research on it, and connect to its frequency in order to obtain the most knowledge and aid from it. Energy animals can appear to you in their physical form, through the media, in the shape of a cloud, as a word, or in any other manner that will help you receive their message.

You can also reverse this so you intentionally align your frequency with energy animals as you seek out the connection to their qualities instead of waiting for them to connect to you. This will raise your own frequency to that of the animal because energy connections can be miraculous and cause change in the lower energy, bringing it up to the level of the higher energy. When you ask an energy animal for help, that animal will work for you to deliver what is needed for your greatest good so you are able to progress forward on your own spiritual journey in a positive light. Trust that the animal is working for your higher self.

Some energy animals will reveal themselves to you and present you with a situation where you will learn a life lesson. They just show you the lesson you need to learn by appearing in your life for a short time and then they vanish. You'll wonder what their presence means because there is an intuitive awakening at a soul level associated with the appearance of these energy animals. Their individual characteristics will prove to be powerful to you on your path. They make you feel drawn to them so you notice them and don't put their appearance up to just another bird flying by or rabbit in your yard. Their energy feels different, it's arresting, and you're unable to ignore their presence when they appear. They can project themselves into your thoughts so you're thinking about them, wondering what it means when they're around, until you go look it up in a book like this one to see what their presence in your life could mean. It's at that point when you'll probably have an *Oh, wow!* moment of clarity, realization, and understanding.

Not What You Expected?

Sometimes the animal that appears to you is not what you might have expected. While you may love tigers or feel a strong connection to the wolf but you're constantly seeing salamanders, ants, or iguanas, then your energy animal messenger is the animal you keep seeing, not the one you like best. Don't ignore animals because you're certain they couldn't possibly be your energy animal. Spirit can appear in all shapes and forms with important messages. Pay close attention to the smallest details.

Dream Animals

Have you ever had an animal appear to you in a dream? If so, then you probably experienced your energy animal trying to get a message to you. That is, as long as you didn't eat pizza before bed and were having what I call *pizza dreams* that are nonsensical. It's easier for your energy animals to connect with you on the dream level, especially if you're ignoring all of their attempts to connect with you on the physical or spiritual planes. When your waking mind is at rest, the subconscious mind is available for visitation from your spirit guides, angels, and energy animals. When Spirit, regardless of the form, is trying to get a message to you and you're not listening, they often attempt to visit your dreams where you're more apt to give them your attention and listen to their messages. Since animals are strong communicators, if an energy animal is appearing to you regularly, then it's important that you research and really pay attention to determine the message it's trying to deliver because it most certainly has something important to say to you.

When you encounter energy animals in your dreams, it's important to notice if they're wild, domesticated, or mythical, what they're doing, if they're moving quickly or slowly, or if they are coming toward you or moving away from you (take note of the directions in which they're moving). Can you see vivid colors in the dream or is it dull and monotone? Is the animal in its natural habitat or does it seem out of place? Is the animal healthy and vibrant or does it look sick? Most importantly, you should take note of your reactions and interactions with the animal because these often give clues to their message. Try to notice what you were doing (or thinking) when the animal first appeared in the dream. This is often an important key to the animal's message even if it appears when you're awake. Also consider if the animal was acting normally as it would in the physical realm or was it doing something that is abnormal for the physical animal, for instance, talking to you. If so, can you remember what it said? When animals talk to you in dreams, their message is usually very clear because they'll just tell you what they want you to know. It's your job to remember what they said.

Another technique to use when you encounter animals in your dream is to ask them questions. Why are you in my dream? Why are you acting the way you're acting? What is your message for my life? You can ask them anything you want that will help you understand their message. Speaking with your energy animals in this manner is something you can also carry over into your waking life. Taking some quiet time conversing with the energy animals, while also connecting with their energy, can be very enlightening. Make a list of questions before you start, but don't worry if you don't get to them all. Sometimes the session will take on a life of its own and the questions may not pertain to the direction the flow of information takes.

If you're having a hard time connecting to a specific animal's frequency, then right before you're about to fall asleep, ask the energy animal to come to you in your dreams.

Sometimes purposefully trying to connect during dreams can be very beneficial if you're having difficulties in the physical realm.

For me, I know when I'm connecting to an energy animal during dreams because the dream takes on a different quality. It comes alive with vivid colors and a sense of clarity. I feel a connection to the animal, as if it's calling to me. It may be different for you, but you can usually find one central thing that happens or a certain feeling you get during the dream that will let you know that this is a connection to an energy animal. Pay close attention to all aspects of the dream and make an effort to communicate with your energy animal both during the dream and in your daily life. You can do this by physically visiting with the animal, through meditation, or simply thinking about the energy animal to uncover the message that it is trying to deliver to you. It will often come to you again during these times. You might also want to start a dream journal so you don't forget things that happened during the dream. Keep it beside your bed and write in it as soon as you wake up before the dream memories start to slip away.

How to Use This Book

This book is intended to be a guide to help you learn to recognize and connect with the frequency of energy animals so you can more closely identify with them, which will make it easier to receive the depth of their messages. In these pages, I'm explaining how I connect to animals and am giving you guided imagery that will help you to accomplish the same goal for yourself. That being said, you have to trust in yourself and your own intuition when it comes to the actual frequency connection. I can tell you what works for me and I can guide you, but you should also learn from your own experiences during your frequency exercises by speaking directly to the energy animals, trusting in your own intuition, being present in the moment, and accepting of the messages you receive. Only by doing this will you truly grow on your own spiritual path. I'm here to guide you, to lead the way, to get you to the point where you feel secure in knowing you are indeed connecting to the frequency of the energy animal and bonding with them emotionally and spiritually.

I have included several different sections under each animal, so let's briefly go over them before you get started.

Traits: These are characteristics of the animal that can help you understand why it may have appeared to you at this time in your life. By considering the animal's traits you can see how they apply to your situation and take action as needed. In part 3, I've also included a short version of the mythology of the animal if it's not well known.

Talents: These are the animal's abilities, things that they do well. When the animal appears to you, it is a reminder that you share these abilities and positive traits.

Challenges: These are the animal's qualities that can be challenging to it and to you when the animal is encountered.

Element(s): These are the elements of nature that represent the animal. In the elements chart in appendix B, the characteristics of each element are stated. These qualities hold true for the animals connected with the element(s).

Primary Color(s): These are the colors that represent the animal. Look at the color chart in appendix A to see the qualities that this color bestows on the animal. Some animals have various colors or are multicolored. Consider the color(s) of the animal you interacted with when analyzing the message.

Appearances: This section contains the reasons why the animal might appear and some of the things you should consider or do after receiving its message. In this section it is also very important that you listen to your own intuition and trust your own impressions when you encounter the animal. I'm guiding you but the animal is there with you for a reason and has specific messages that only you will understand at a soul level and how you should act on it. Don't be afraid to trust in the rightness of your own intuition.

Assists When: This section offers explanations as to how the animal can help you.

Frequency: This is a description of how I interpreted the animal's energy and what it felt like to me as I connected to it while writing this book. By sharing this with you, I hope it will help you connect with the animal, too. Your experience may be different from mine, but this gives you a reference point.

Imagine … : In this section, I give you a brief guided imagery that will help you connect your frequency to that of your energy animal. This is a prompt to get you started, so if your intuition takes over and goes in a different direction from what I'm saying, go with it and let your imagination run free. You'll be shown the animal's message as you're supposed to see it. A lot of this section (but not all) is set outside because that's where the animals live. If you've been staying inside try to spend some time outdoors. It will make connecting easier.

The layout of this book is set up as a reference tool. You don't have to read it from beginning to end (but you're welcome to if you'd like); instead you can quickly flip through the book to find the animal and read about it. This will help you connect to its frequency and understand the message it's trying to deliver when it appears to you or when you decide to seek it out. You can use this book to look up animals you've always felt drawn to, that you're afraid of, or that you are curious about, to see what messages they offer.

You can also use this book as a bibliomancy tool. For example, if you need assistance making a decision, ask that you are shown the energy animal that will be most beneficial to you in your specific situation. Then open the book at random. The animal that is featured on that page is the animal that will be relevant to your current situation. The message from that animal will be helpful to you as you make the decision for which you sought help. If you need a more in-depth answer, you can also use the book to do a mini reading. You'll open the book three times at random. The first time will show the past of the situation, the second the present of the situation, and the third the future outcome of the situation.

Do you need to find animals to help you but you don't know where to begin? You can use this book for that as well. Before beginning, ask that you are shown the three to five animals that are most important for your spiritual growth and enlightenment at this time in your life. Then move your thumb across the outside pages of the book (opposite of the spine) until you feel like you're supposed to stop. Open the book to that page and the energy animal that appears is one that will help you. Repeat this until you feel you've found all of the energy animals that are supposed to be assisting you at this time in your life. Then focus on getting to know them and connecting to their frequency.

Once you know how to get started, you can discover for yourself the sheer joy that the power of energy animals can bring into your life. They can guide you, heal you, bring you messages, teach you, and enable you to open your mind and soul to the universal energy that is within them and make it your own. You can ask them for help and guidance at any time that you're ready to receive their assistance. It may seem difficult at first, especially if you've never had a lot of contact with animals, but I assure you that if you try, you too will be able to benefit from the vast positivity of the animal kingdom and energy animals.

Part 1 contains mammals, birds, reptiles, and insects. There are many different species and all are wild and untamed. Part 2 describes domesticated animals, but that doesn't just mean the animal is a pet. It also contains farm animals and animals that were once wild but humans have tamed and who now depend on humans for their care.

Part 3 includes mythical and fantasy animals. I've included some of the mythology if the animal isn't well known. In a number of cases, the mythology is very complex and there isn't enough room in this book for all of the details. If you're intrigued, please research further to learn the complete mythology.

Using Frequency Connections to Receive Energy Animal Messages

Before we get into connecting your frequency with animal frequency, it's important to know that you are surrounded by energy, you are energy, and this also applies to animals. Everything in nature has a high vibration. Animals' vibrations are high because they don't worry about their existence or fret over silly things like we do. They live in the moment. Animals can worry when they think they're in danger, but that's not the same as obsessing over the date you're about to go on or your financial situation. Animals are happy to just be themselves with no worries bogging them down. They eat when they are hungry and rest when they're tired. There are no schedules to keep. They are accepting of whatever life throws their way and don't worry over things they can't change because they aren't judgmental.

You might have heard the expression *dumb animal*. Just because animals don't speak words like you and I do, doesn't mean that they don't communicate with one another or have feelings. In order to understand animal frequency, you also have to understand how animals think and how they can communicate with you. I'll explain this through the following example but communication applies to all animal species.

We own and breed Barock Pintos (pronounced Baroque) and Friesian horses. Each one of our horses is a unique individual with specific traits and personalities. Most of them are young, which puts the responsibility on me to make sure that they grow up to be well-adjusted adults. If you're in my barn, you'll hear the horses communicating with each other. They'll softly nicker, snort, or whinny in various levels of loudness in order to talk to one another. They also use body language to let each other (and me) know how they're feeling. This isn't the same as animal communication or animal frequency, but it is behavior that clues you in to their moods. You can tell if a horse is listening to you or is confused, irritated, or upset just by watching its ears and eyes. Mares with foals will give warnings to other horses to stay away from their babies, and it can be anything between a mean glare to an all out attack, depending on the reactions of the horse they're warning and the mood of Mama Mare. When I walk into the barn, they'll all whinny in greeting and it's usually very loud, which is an amazing thing to experience and always brings a smile to my face. I answer back by greeting each one in turn and rubbing their noses before starting my chores. When I work with horses, whether it's training them or handling them, I am constantly using both standard animal communication and animal frequency to connect with them. I'll create pictures of what I want them to do in my mind and send those pictures to them via the energy pathway between me and the horse I'm working with. Sending images while talking to the animal always makes my job easier because it's easier for them to understand what I'm asking of them. Quite often I'll receive images back from them in return. If you use this same technique when connecting to your energy animal, you'll find that the task is much easier to do and the connection can be made quicker than if you didn't send the pictures.

Feel the Animal's Frequency

Connecting to energy animals through animal frequency requires that you *feel* the animal's spirit and become one with its frequency. You will do this consciously, but there will be times when it's an unconscious act. At the soul level we all speak the same language, animals included. When working with animal frequency, it is important that you make a soul connection with the energy animal. You do this using telepathy and your energy to connect soul-to-soul.

Telepathy is a natural part of intuition used by all species to send and receive images, emotions, and thoughts over distances. You approach the process through feelings of compassion and love to reach out to the animal. Feeling empathy with the animal not only draws them to you but also allows you to feel their feelings, thoughts, and, most importantly, who they are. There's not one horse in my barn that is like another one. They're all different and these differences are what make them unique, just as you and I are unique. When you connect with animal frequency, then you are in tune with their needs and are showing them love and respect for their sacred gift, and it is truly a gift from the animal to be able to share their frequency. It is important that we honor them for this gift.

Understanding your own frequency and intuition go hand in hand when you're working with animal frequency. When you are in touch with your intuitive self, it's easier to be in touch with the animal world. With the telepathic communication between animals and intuitives, animals can warn us when we're going off of our spiritual path, remind us to be aware in certain circumstances, and give positive messages when we're moving along the right path.

It's important to trust in your intuition and gut feelings when you're working with animal frequency. You will not be working with your thinking mind but instead with your emotional and spiritual self. You'll use empathy, telepathy, and intuition to spiritually connect to the frequency of your energy animal. It's a feeling, not a logical thinking process. It's easy to do, so don't make this harder than it has to be by doubting your ability to connect your frequency to the frequency of animals. Doubt blocks you and should be set aside during animal frequency exercises. Just believe in yourself and trust that what you hear or see is indeed a message from your energy animal and you'll be successful.

Start by setting a positive intention and then focusing on the energy animal that you've selected. Open your mind to seeing pictures the animal may send to you or words you may hear or suddenly *know*. In order to really connect your frequency with that of the animal, you have to be very *in the moment* and in tune with the energy animal. That means if a sand crane walks up to you or a bluebird lands beside you (even if you set out to connect with butterflies) you should take the time to commune with that animal and try to connect your frequencies instead of immediately running off to look up what it means or keep searching for the butterfly. There will be time for comparison later, after the animal encounter has unfolded. It's more important to receive their messages in the moment than to go look up what someone else thinks the message is. While books like this one can guide you, nothing takes the place of listening to your own intuition and feelings during an energy animal experience. Energy animals can mean different things to different people based on each person's unique circumstances, beliefs, and where they are on their spiritual path.

The other part of an energy animal encounter is to be aware of what you were doing or thinking when the animal appeared to you. Were you worrying over a situation with a coworker or a family member? Or maybe you were feeling unsure of your path. When you're aligning frequencies, both the message of the animal and the reason for its appearance are important for helping you understand the message. Also consider what the animal was doing when you noticed it. Was it flying, walking, or staring at you?

When you're connected with your energy animal, you will feel many different things during the transfer of frequencies. You might feel a sense of peace or a calmness come over you, or you may hear a sizzle or static in the connection. Make sure you're aware of how the transfer of energy feels and also how it sounds. Did you feel like you were just zapped in the head when you paid attention to the energy animal and now you suddenly know something that you didn't know before? It can happen like that, or it can feel like a gentle breeze floating over you. Remain aware because all of these little things are part of the overall message.

Once you've learned how to connect your individual frequency with an animal's frequency, you'll notice that all animals are more aware of you. They can feel your love, your higher vibration, and that you are aware of them on a soul level. In my case, animals are very drawn to me, even when I'm not consciously doing anything to connect to them. If I go to a pet store, I usually end up petting dogs that *never go to anyone* but pulled their owner over to me. I've had lost dogs follow me home, and I've found their owner for them. The fact that animals are drawn to me doesn't go unnoticed by other people and is commented on quite a bit. I'm honored that animals put their trust in me. It is this way for many, many people in the world who also recognize animals as kindred spirits. If you're not already, you can be one of us if you open your heart and intuition to the animal kingdom.

Is Your Pet Your Energy Animal?

There are several schools of thought regarding animal totems and pets. Some believe animal totems can only be a wild animal. Others believe domesticated animals, including pets, aren't actually capable of being a totem because they have lost their true wild essence, which in turn lessens the connection to spirit when they became domesticated. I disagree with these schools of thought because I have experienced powerful energy from pets, past-life memories, and spiritual connections that were just as powerful as my experiences with wild animals. Granted, not every domesticated animal will connect with you on a spiritual level, nor will every wild animal, but when they do the energy is extremely powerful and the experience extraordinary. This is another reason I use the phrase *energy animals*. All animals are made of energy, whether domesticated or wild, and we connect with them through energy pathways.

Connecting with Your Pets

I also believe our pets can come back to us after they pass in order to continue to guide us within the physical realm or, if they choose not to reincarnate, they guide us from the spiritual realm. I've had it happen both ways. You will know when your pet is with you as a guide or an energy animal because you will feel a deeper connection to it and will sense it has a greater purpose in your life other than just being your pet. You'll be able to easily communicate telepathically and empathically with this animal. You may feel this animal loves you more than any other animal has ever loved you before. These pets don't come along often, but when they do you'll experience a deep knowing that this pet is connected with you on a spiritual level. They help you heal, inspire and uplift you, and make you want to be a better person. Their absolute acceptance and love for you will keep you grounded and let you know there is no greater spiritual truth than pure and unconditional love.

Start with an Animal Communication Session

To get started with an animal frequency session, you're going to begin with regular animal communication, which is the sharing of thoughts, emotions, and images between you and the animal. Animal communication is not reading body language or behavior. While that is very helpful in training animals, it's not what you're trying to achieve in animal communication. Think of it as learning another language. You're learning how to communicate like the animals since they can't form words like you do. The more you practice the better you'll get at it. Keep a journal so you don't forget your experiences or the animal's message.

You're going to use your own intuition and telepathy to send and receive thoughts, feelings, words, sounds, sensations, ideas, sudden knowing, and pictures to the animal. You'll know what you're receiving from the animal is accurate because your own clairvoyance will be absolutely sure that it is the truth. You don't have to be in the same room with the animal, you don't need a picture of it; you just need to sense its energy to connect with it.

Amp It Up with Animal Frequency

Next, you're going to amp the animal communication into the stratosphere of universal consciousness using animal frequency. Here's a hands-on exercise to get you started:

For this exercise you and your pet should be in the same physical space. Sit, stand, or do whatever feels comfortable to you. If you have a horse, you might want to lean against the stall wall; if you have a dog, you might want it in your lap while you're sitting in the recliner; if it's a big dog, it might be on the floor beside you. Do what feels the most comfortable for you. Let the animal wander if they'd like. Some will stay right with you, looking at you the entire time, others will move around. Some people like to touch the animal during the session and others prefer to remain a short distance away. Now, you're going to clear your mind of all extraneous thoughts. Forget your to-do list, forget about dinner, and let your mind focus solely on the animal you want to connect with. In the beginning you might find it easier to clear your mind if you take some slow deep breaths, but after you've been doing this awhile you'll be able to clear it in an instant. Now you can begin sending images, thoughts, and emotions to the animal. Ask questions or tell them something about yourself or how you feel about them. Make sure you're receptive to the images, thoughts, and emotions they send back as answers to your questions or responses to your comments. It's important to trust your intuition and not question the information you're receiving.

That is a basic exercise of how to do an animal communication session. Now let's take it further and amp it up with animal frequency. As you're exchanging information with the animal, feel your energy—your personal vibration, your frequency—building over your heart until it's swirling with positive intention. Slowly send your energy to the animal. Imagine it as colorful ribbons of pulsating energy leaving your heart and flowing toward the animal. Don't let it touch the animal but instead invite the animal to share its frequency with you. Soon you'll feel the animal's energy start to build, and then you'll feel it reaching out to you, until your energy and the energy of the animal touches. Now there is an explosion of information moving freely between the two of you. It's an unexplainable, intuitive knowing flowing on intense positive waves of energy as your frequencies merge together. You see what the animal has been through, feel what it feels, and it does the same with you through flashes of images, feelings, hopes, and dreams, and, most importantly, all of this is done willingly with feelings of love and trust. It's an intimate, personal, and soulful experience. When the session is almost over, thank the animal for sharing itself with you and pull your frequency back inside you.

Once you're accustomed to using animal frequency, you'll find that it becomes second nature and you can bypass the beginning animal communication part and skip right to the animal frequency connection.

Color and Elemental Meanings

Both color and elemental meanings are important considerations in animal frequency because they can give you additional information about the encounter with your energy animal. In the back of this book there is more in-depth information, including charts that define the meanings of many colors (appendix A) and the elements (appendix B).

This book is a tool—a reference manual you can refer back to as needed. Use what feels right to you and make it your own. If it doesn't seem to fit your exact circumstance, then take what fits and discard the rest. You own the ability to connect with animal frequency through your own unique frequency. It's all in your hands. Enjoy the journey.

Part 1
Wild
Animals

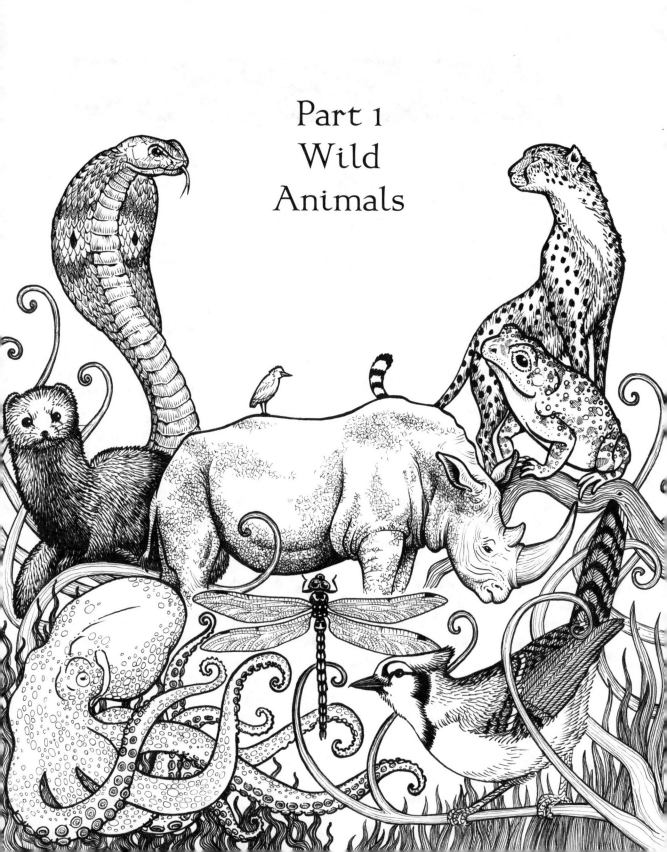

Aardvark

Traits: Aardvark symbolizes cautiousness and slow progression, digging for what's underneath, adaptability, and change. It is active at night, can cover long distances, and doesn't stay in one place too long, preferring to move on to new and unexplored areas. It possesses a cautious and timid nature but trusts its instincts, acute hearing, and sense of smell to signal danger. It has a very thick, tough skin, which saves it from predators. It can be feisty and aggressive when necessary but prefers a quiet life of solitude.

Talents: Adventurous, clairaudient, communicating intentions, discovery, efficient, excellent hearing, exceptional instincts when searching for truth, exploration, finding safe places, good planner, loves to travel, organization, peacefulness

Challenges: Becoming reclusive and antisocial, difficulty putting down roots in one place, fear of losing control, hiding away at home instead of going out, nervousness, overly focused on methods and procedures and not stepping outside of the box, overly timid and shy

Element(s): Earth

Primary Color(s): Brown, gray

Appearances: When aardvark appears, it is a sign to stop, look around, and make sure the people in your environment are really who and what they appear to be and aren't projecting one image but have different intentions. If you're embarking on a new adventure in your career or relationship, use caution and be certain of the steps you'll take instead of jumping in headfirst and asking questions later. Aardvark means you need to take some time for yourself in quiet solitude to aid in relaxation and for clarity of mind and spirit, which will enable you to see the truth of situations, reconnect to your core spiritual being, and gain amazing insights and realizations. You accomplish more after dark than during the day. You have thick skin, don't let the negativity of others get you down, are organized and methodical, and like to stay in control. Your hearing is excellent, and you probably have the gift of clairaudience. Aardvark warns to listen to not only what is being said but what is being insinuated.

Assists When: You're starting a new job or relationship and are unsure about it. Aardvark can help you find the truth in situations where you feel uncomfortable or suspect dishonesty. If you'd like to engage in more social activities, ask aardvark to assist. It will help you take the appropriate precautions as you step out of your comfort zone of solitude so you engage in wonderful experiences when interacting with others. If you're planning a move, it can help you find an interesting place to live. You tackle many subjects of interest, digging deeply to learn as much as possible. You never know when you'll need to pull from your huge knowledge bank. If you're overwhelmed, aardvark can help you get organized and add structure to your life.

Frequency: Aardvark's energy is calm and smooth, patient and kind. It feels like a ribbon of warm water that wraps around you, tugging you gently into the unknown. It sounds like a drop of rainwater dripping from the leaf of a tree.

Imagine...

You're in the forest, sitting in a clearing about thirty feet from an aardvark den with your legs crisscrossed in front of you. You know it's inside, waiting for just the right time to make an appearance. You project feelings of love and comfort toward the den to help the aardvark feel at ease when it sees you. Several minutes pass before you see its long nose cautiously emerging. It sits at the edge of its burrow, its eyes glued to you, as if it's peering into your very soul. You send positive thoughts that it is safe in your presence. Eventually, it bounds out of its den to stop directly in front of you. It sniffs your legs, moving up your body until it sniffs your face. Sensing you aren't a threat, it looks along the ground beside you for food. After a while, it moves deeper into the forest. Before it's out of sight, it looks back at you as if to say, *goodbye, it's been nice knowing you.*

Alligator (Crocodile)

Traits: Alligator symbolizes fearlessness, an exceptional sense of timing, agility, a fierce protectiveness, determination, and drawing power from the sun. It is representative of an ancient, prehistoric time when survival depended upon efficiency and resiliency. Alligator has a tough hide, which makes you hard to read but very authoritative. It slinks through water, concealing itself until it is ready to attack. This quality makes you successful in your chosen career because you instinctively know when to make a move. Alligator watches without being seen. It encourages you to do the same. It represents a highly intuitive, creative nature, one you may have been blocking or avoiding. It's time to embrace that part of you. Like the alligator, you are a timeless, wise being filled with the wonder of the universe.

Talents: Birth, brave, creativity, cunning, dependable, fearlessness, inconspicuous, indestructible, ingenuity, keen vision, power, protective, resilient, secretive, speed, stealth, strength, wisdom

Challenges: Aggressive, appearing callus, cruel, ferocious, fierce, guarded, intimidating, jumping to conclusions, overly sensitive to criticism, ruthless, too quick to pass judgment

Element(s): Earth, water

Primary Color(s): Green

Appearances: Alligator means you're fearless, have deep emotions, and appear indestructible. Alligator's appearance means to use your inner strength. Sometimes this means waiting until the time is right before taking action. If you move too soon, you could miss your goals. It means to reassess how you're interacting with others. Are you insensitive, cold, and uncaring? If so, alligator is a reality check to change your behavior. While you prefer to be a loner and you may want to show a strong presence or appear standoffish when it comes to business, alligator warns that this is not how to treat family and friends. Alligator helps you attract the right people into your life, helps you make deliberate decisions, and assesses the situation before striking. It warns against making decisions before gathering all available information. Once a decision is made, do not hesitate—act.

Assists When: Anytime you lack clarity or need a boost in your inner, physical, or emotional strength call on alligator. It assists when you're making decisions and aren't sure if you should wait or pounce. If your productivity is low and you feel unmotivated, alligator can give you the increased energy you need. Alligator can help you keep secrets, maintain your own high standard of ethics, and keep you grounded and emotionally stable. Alligator can also help when you need to keep your mouth shut or if you need to make use of strong jaws and sharp teeth. It can open your flow of creativity to help you come up with new projects, ideas, or inventions.

Frequency: Alligator's frequency sounds like one deep strum of a bass guitar. It feels steady, strong, and powerful but then, heard over the strum, is the pounding of drums. It begins slowly at first until it quickly becomes a swift stiletto and then suddenly stops and all you hear is the steady strum again.

See Also: Bunyip

Imagine...

You're on an airboat in the Everglades. As you meander through the brackish water, you see birds and other wildlife. Your attention is riveted on two small bulges protruding out of the water about thirty feet away. Eyes watch you, but there is no other movement. You feel tension in the air as the eyes slowly sink into the murky depths. Moments later, an alligator climbs out of the water, walking slowly on the shore of a small island. It turns and seems to stare right at you. It lies down and opens its mouth wide so you see its enormous teeth. It snaps its mouth shut and stares at you. You feel the energy of ancient knowledge, of survival and wisdom, flowing from the alligator toward you. In mutual respect, you send positive energy from your essence to it. You move the boat through the glades, but you're captivated by the energy that is now a part of you.

Ant

Traits: Ant is powerful even though it is tiny. It can move things up to fifty times its body weight. Ant symbolizes a sense of organized community, meticulously working together to reach a common goal. Ant is accepting of its position, dedicated, loyal, a hard worker, a good team player, relentless, and determined. An ant doesn't walk in straight lines. It tends to meander along a path, sometimes even backtracking, but always with a goal in mind. When in danger, an ant will bite or sting and groups of ants will swarm to attack. This is a reminder that there is safety in numbers. Ant communicates through pheromones, touch, and sound, which means to listen to your own senses as you go about your work. Ant means you're very adaptive and motivated, which ensures success. You take action and make decisions based on what you feel will be best for the group instead of what is best for you.

Talents: Dedicated, determined, discipline, good team player, hard worker, industrious, order, organized, patience, persistent, relentless, sense of community, structured, supportive, traditional

Challenges: Becoming too focused, forgetting the big picture, making things harder than they need to be, meandering instead of following a direct path to a goal, repetitiveness, rigid, working too much

Element(s): Earth

Primary Color(s): Black, red

Appearances: Ant is a sign to work harder to accomplish your goals or an indication that you need a break to rest and reorganize. Ant means you're an achiever with a team mentality who sees projects through to their completion. You're industrious, creative, and patient. You are one part of the whole and must trust in both your ability to get the job done and in the abilities of those you work with. You prefer structure and order to chaos. You tend to make sure any new venture has a solid foundation and is organized and structured to ensure its success. Ant teaches others in the colony through tandem running, so an ant's appearance means to look for someone in need of help. Ant means that if you've been isolating yourself, now is the time to get back in touch with others. If a queen ant appears to you, it means that you are either in the role of a leader or a parent or you are about to step into that role. Is there a project or a young person you can nurture into greatness with your knowledge, guidance, and instruction?

Assists When: You are trying to do everything alone instead of asking for help from others. Ask for help. Ant means to take charge of your life and, if needed, restructure and rebuild a new foundation during new starts, moves, and choices. Ant can lower your stress levels, help you alleviate frustration, and give you more patience. Ants are social, so their appearance means you should look at how you're relating to the people in your life.

Frequency: Ant frequency sounds like a faint scratching noise that you can barely hear because it's buried beneath the surface. If you listen closely, it is almost like static from a TV channel that's gone off the air. It prickles at your skin, a tiny scurry of energy moving over you.

Imagine...

You're leaning on the edge of a fence when you feel something on your arm. It's an ant and you immediately brush it off. Looking at the fence, you notice a line of ants moving along the top. They take a few steps, stop, go backward a bit, then continue forward. It's as if they're waiting for the ant behind them to catch up. When it does, it moves forward again. If it encounters other ants, they move out of each other's way. You feel a tickle on your hand and notice that another ant has climbed on you. This time, instead of knocking it away, you watch it walk across your hand. You concentrate on its energy and feel a sense of calmness. The ant climbs back down to the wood. It continues on with purpose, so you follow its progress. At the next post, it travels down the wood toward the ground. At the base of the post, you notice that there is a small ant hill. It disappears inside as other ants follow its lead.

Antelope (Pronghorn)

Traits: Antelope symbolizes a cautious, alert nature and the tendency to retreat at the slightest warning. Antelope relies on its heightened sense of awareness for any changes in its environment. When those changes occur, it reacts quickly and with the utmost speed. Like antelope, you think on your feet, tackling problems with ease and finding a resolution swiftly and efficiently. You are very intuitive and can detect the truth of a situation and take the appropriate action. Once antelope makes a decision, it sees it through to the end. If you start something, you see it to completion. Antelope also means new opportunities are presenting themselves to you at this time. Be very aware of what is going on around you and go after any opportunity you feel is right for you. Like antelope, you have an affinity for water and the forest. You may enjoy time at the beach, at the lake, or in the mountains. Antelope is graceful in its movement and is indicative of the graceful way you handle yourself.

Talents: Adaptable, attention to details, careful observer, clear communicator, confident, courage, poised, explorer, find adventures in everyday things, gentle nature, good judgment, graceful, inner strength, planning, strong survival skills, successful actions

Challenges: Argumentative, fear of failure, flightiness, ignoring truth, ignoring your intuitive abilities, running away, too defensive, untrusting

Element(s): Earth

Primary Color(s): Black, brown, red, white

Appearances: When antelope appears, it is a sign that you are going to have unexpected changes happening in the very near future. The changes will pop up quickly, so grab the opportunities when they present themselves so you don't lose them. Overall these will be positive and exciting, but you might run into someone who is negative or jealous. Antelope lives in a herd. If you've been avoiding people or are being a loner, try to find others with similar interests. Once you do, you'll make new friends and find even more opportunities to grow. Antelope warns against being out of balance. If you're feeling irritable, take some time to be alone and sort things out in your mind. When you're feeling normal again, head back to the herd. You often prefer being part of a group because it makes you feel safe, but every now and then you also need time to yourself to recharge.

Assists When: You're experiencing changes in your life, especially when they are unexpected and happening fast. Antelope can help you stay grounded during these times and help you grab new opportunities. If you're starting a new project, expanding upon current ideas, or making a career change, antelope can help you see the big picture and anything that might be hidden. Antelope helps to clarify mixed messages, whether they come from another person or within you. Antelope assists any time you need an energy boost or clarity of mind. It warns of danger, can help you stay on task, and urges you to be aware of your surroundings. It can help you unblock and develop your intuition, create abundance and prosperity, expand your consciousness, and assist in helping you understand your place within the universe.

Frequency: Antelope frequency feels like a warm breeze flittering over your skin. It pulses with the beat of your heart, rising to high-pitched heights in the face of danger. It sounds like a low groan followed by a chirp.

See Also: Deer, White Stag

Imagine…

In a large field, tall brown brush blows gently in the wind. A herd of antelope graze nearby. They sense your presence, alternately looking up with a quick glance between bites. You don't appear to present a threat but one or two freeze when they see you, not moving a muscle. You send positive energy to them, the calm and quiet part of yourself. Moments later they go back to grazing, some of the babies are leaping into the air, frolicking in the summer sun. You sit and watch their beauty and grace in spirit.

Armadillo

Traits: Armadillo symbolizes a tough, armored exterior that protects a sensitive and warm being inside. If threatened, armadillo rolls into a ball to protect its delicate belly. Armadillo moves at a slow, steady pace, will dig into the dirt to get out of the heat, loves water, and is a solitary creature that lives alone. It is adept at finding things in the ground, especially meals, and moves often in its search. Armadillo means to take the path less followed, to protect your inner self, and to dig deep to get to the truth of your soul.

Talents: Compassionate nature, courageous, determination, easygoing, empathic, exploration, intuitive, keeping secrets, kind, natural curiosity, peaceful, understanding, unearthing truth, works well alone

Challenges: Aloof, defensive, destructive, insensitive, overly sensitive, reclusive, secretive to the point of lying, skeptical, untrusting, withdrawn

Element(s): Earth

Primary Color(s): Brown

Appearances: Armadillo is a sign to protect your inner self from the negativity of others. Make sure those around you understand your life rules and stay outside of your personal space. If they cross over your boundaries, retreat within yourself to keep them at bay until you can unearth their true intentions. Armadillo reminds you to keep your mouth shut about things you don't want spread around the gossip mill. Armadillo warns if you tell too much, it could negatively impact you. Be specific and clear about what you expect from others and stay quiet about your own personal or work situations at this time. Keep your secrets secret. Armadillo means to connect with water to rejuvenate your intuition, sense of trust, and empathic abilities. Water cleanses and restores vitality and energy, can help you find the deeper meaning of events in your life or new areas of study. It can wash away frustration and replace it with a deep calm while giving you the benefits of cleansing on a spiritual level. Armadillo warns not to wear your heart on your sleeve but to keep a close hold on your feelings. You don't often reveal your true inner self to others, and when you do it is a gift.

Assists When: You are making decisions, meeting new people, or trying to get to the truth of a situation. You do things in your own time and tend to not feel pressure from others, even when they're forcing an issue. There's something to be said for taking things slow to make greater overall progress. Armadillo is helpful in protecting yourself from unwanted attention, especially if the person giving it is being negative toward you. Armadillo prefers quiet solitude and can help you maneuver out of the hectic environment to a peaceful place. If you're feeling stuck in life, armadillo can help you look deeper at your intentions and motivations to get you back on track and moving forward on your path.

Frequency: Armadillo's frequency feels far away, as if it is a light in the distance that beckons you toward it. It is solid and strong, yet light and airy. It sounds like the roar of a distant waterfall with the patter of raindrops mixed in.

Imagine...

You're working in your garden when you hear a scratching sound. You move closer to take a look and come upon an armadillo. You don't want to scare it, so you crouch down. It doesn't seem to be paying any attention to you, but you sense it knows you're there. It moves methodically through the garden, sniffing, digging, and moving its nose through the grass. As it gets closer, you hold very still. Then it starts to sniff your knee and leg. It looks up at you, so you very slowly move your hand down your leg so you can touch its rough, armored side. It allows your touch and you're surprised to find that it's not brick hard like you thought but feels like a thick layer of leather. Though you touch it, you don't feel its essence, so you imagine your energy leaving your fingertips. In return, you receive a feeling of compassion and love reaching out to you. It scurries away, leaving you in awe.

Badger

Traits: Badger symbolizes a fearless, persistent, and fierce nature. Badger is independent, self-reliant, and, while it prefers to be left alone, it doesn't hesitate in its actions if confronted. Badger isn't picky about food and will eat anything it finds. Some badgers especially love the sweet taste of honey. Badger is a social animal that lives in groups and communal dens. Because of its bone structure, it is impossible for a badger to dislocate its jaw, which makes its bite one of the most powerful in the world.

Talents: Confident, courageous, eager, focused, good communicator, independent, protective defender of others, sharp witted, stands up for self and beliefs, strategic, willing

Challenges: Aggressive, antisocial, holds grudges, inconsiderate of other's opinions, insensitive, off-putting, rough, sharp tongued, short-tempered

Element(s): Earth

Primary Color(s): Black, gray, white

Appearances: Badger means "to never give up." Decide what you want and go for it without delay, pursuing it until the goal is accomplished. Be persistent and fierce in your drive to obtain what you want. This isn't a time to be soft, complacent, or let others fight your battles for you. Be firm, direct, and strong while standing on your own two feet. Badger encourages you to fight for what you desire through courageous determination. You have excellent communication skills, so use your words; they hold great power. This not only applies to goals you've set for yourself but in defending those you believe in who may have been wronged and the ideals and principles you hold as your own truth. Be firm in your communication with others so there is no doubt of what you want. Better yet, ask for it! Badger warns against eating too much unhealthy food, especially sweets, and now is a good time to monitor your diet and exercise.

Assists When: You need to speak well in order to communicate your thoughts in a clear and concise manner. Because of badger's excellent communication skills, it can help you when you are working on any written assignment or work-related project. If you're trying to get your point across but it's just not happening, then ask badger to give you the words you need to connect with your audience. If you're in a situation where you have to stand up for yourself, badger can give you the strength and courage to speak your mind in your own defense. Badger's independence and somewhat lofty attitude can enable you to stop caring about what other people think of you. You live to the beat of your own drum and badger can help you see that you're as unique as it is. Be what you believe and believe in who you are.

Frequency: Badger's frequency is a deep tone that vibrates at a low pitch. It feels like you stepped into the rumble of thunder, which surrounds and moves through you. It is fierce and uncontrollable yet focused and direct.

Imagine...

You're driving your car when you come across a badger in the road. You slow down, but it doesn't move. Worried that it's been hit by another car, you get out and slowly approach. It spins and faces you, growling and snapping its jaws and then runs into the open field beside the road. You're cautious but concerned, so you follow it a little ways into the field. Now it's acting normally and runs toward you, hunkered low to the ground, growling, and on the attack. You back up and send it peaceful thoughts and positive energy of your concern for its well-being. It stops the attack, considers you, and begins to run away, stopping often to turn and look at you, sometimes running backward and stretching itself up into the air on its hind legs, which makes it appear larger than it is. You feel the low tonal energy rumbling toward you, but it makes no further attempt to attack. Once it's a good distance away, it runs and never looks back. You feel energized but on edge. Back in your car, you cast one more look in its direction but now it only appears as a tiny dot on the horizon.

Bat

Traits: Bat is the only mammal that can fly. It sees the world through sound and is able to navigate the sky using sonar. It makes a high-pitched call as it flies, which bounces off of the area around it, allowing bat to create pictures of its surroundings. Contrary to the saying "blind as a bat" all species of bats can see. Bat prefers to roost in groups. Some species prefer to have their own individual space (about six inches) within the group; other species pile upon one another for added closeness.

Talents: Constructive changes, creative, exceptional hearing, fearless, flexible, great navigator, intelligent, intuitive, meditative, navigate in the dark through the unknown, observant, often has prophetic dreams, open-minded, see what others miss, sensitive to vibrational energy, wise

Challenges: Fearful without reason, loner, naïve, overly sensitive, unaware

Element(s): Air

Primary Color(s): Black, brown

Appearances: Bat appears when transformation is necessary. This can be a physical or inner transformation or a move to a new location or career. There are changes coming, and you need to prepare yourself to handle them on all levels. If you prefer solitude to crowds, you might find yourself participating in group events or vice versa. Bat encourages group interaction instead of a solitary life. Release any fear, doubts, or hesitations that are holding you back from being a participant instead of an observer and step forward onto a different path. Watch, listen, and think before you react. Maintain your keen sense of observation because it will be an integral part in your development and progress on new ventures. All change means progress and how you handle it will make it a positive, exciting event or a negative one. Bat means you should embrace the positive qualities within yourself and look at the world from a different point of view.

Assists When: You are transitioning from one phase of your life to another or are experiencing major life changes or small changes in your day-to-day routines. It doesn't matter how big or small the change, bat can help you during the transition. If you're working on your own spirituality, bat can draw the information you need to you, help you understand it, and assist in your spiritual change. If you've been avoiding facing the truth about a situation in your life, bat can help you see it clearly. Bat can make you more aware and help you look at situations from a different point of view. Bat is helpful when you are trying to discover past lives, use your intuitive sonar detection skills to find out what is happening around you, and connect to your power to regenerate or reinvent yourself. Bat encourages you to let go of that which you do not need. Once it is released, new opportunities will come your way. This is all part of the transformation process.

Frequency: Bat's frequency sounds like the beating of a million wings in flight. It is a high-pitched squeal wrapped in the *thump, thump, thump* of wings moving through air. It is warm and soft but also prickly and rough. It is surrounded by the smooth feeling of stillness within the dark.

See Also: Jersey Devil

> ### Imagine…
> You're standing outside a cave at twilight waiting to watch the bats that live inside make their nightly pilgrimage for food. You're excited to see the flurry of activity as they fly into the coming night. Soon the bats start emerging, at first a few at a time, until there are hundreds exiting the cave. The beating of their wings fills the night air as does their high-pitched screams. You hear a thump on the ground beside you and turn to see a small baby bat that has landed on the ground. The behavior is odd, but you pick it up, holding it for a moment, and feel the power contained within its small body. You stroke its back with your fingers and then open your hands. It steadies itself and flies away, circling back and dipping down toward you before rejoining its family.

Bear

Traits: Bear symbolizes a fierce strength and a gentle nature that is often underestimated. There is agility and lightning speed tucked inside a body that looks as if it would be cumbersome and slow. Bear means being introspective, taking the time to carefully examine your thoughts, feelings, and ideas through soul-searching, to come to decisions without outside influences of other people's opinions. There is a need for time away from others to revive and reflect within. Bear is loyal to a fault, has a great deal of integrity, and has a protective nature especially for loved ones. A heightened sense of smell enables you to sniff out truth. Bear also enables you to see visions and have strong intuition. It encourages you to be your own advisor.

Talents: Agility, contentment, courage, introspection, intuitive, knowing when to back down and when to fight, loyalty, peacefulness, reflective, soul-searching, speed, strength, truth of the matter

Challenges: Becoming a loner, being a rogue, losing sight of your inner truth or the goals you want to reach, poor judgment, reclusiveness, rigidity, stubbornness

Element(s): Earth, water

Primary Color(s): Black, brown

Appearances: Bear often appears when you need to take time away for yourself so you can revive and find your center or balance. It can indicate a need for more rest, extra sleep, and downtime when you're frazzled by life. It can mean you'll need to protect someone, or reflect on a situation you're not sure about. There is a need to stick to your beliefs without compromise. Seeing bear means to look beyond a person's physical appearance to what's inside. Bear also appears when you have lost your way or when you need to reconnect with your inner self at a soul level. To really know your path, you must know your true self. Take quiet time just for you. Use this time to silently contemplate your mind, body, and spirit to move forward. You may need healing at this time, either physically, spiritually, or emotionally, so it's important to find balance and get plenty of rest. You're a survivor with plenty of new ideas and the assertiveness to bring those ideas to fruition. Don't hide but step out and take what is yours.

Assists When: You need a boost in your strength and energy or are having trouble making a decision. If you feel betrayed by someone, bear can help you understand not only your own feelings but reasons for the other person's actions. It offers guidance in self-discovery on the physical and spiritual planes. Bear assists when you're searching for an answer and can help you get to the truth of the matter.

Frequency: Bear's energy sounds like a deep rumbling, powerful and steady with the slightest bit of unpredictable shakiness. It feels soft, warm, and silky.

See Also: Panda

Imagine…

You feel its breath like a strong wind in your face as a black bear roars ferociously at you. Its large, sharp teeth are only inches from your face. It could easily shred you to pieces, but you're not afraid. You stand tall and wait. As its roar dies down, you look it in the eye. You feel the powerful strength and integrity within it. Energy radiates from its body, surrounding you in its deep, pulsating power. It settles down on its haunches to stare at you, and you reach out, tentatively touching the side of its snout. Bear's eyes close and it leans its head into your hand. You caress its face, feeling the love and gentle nature of its soul. You move your hands farther back to scratch its back, your fingers running through its dense, silky fur. Suddenly it rolls over to its back so you can scratch its stomach. You do and laugh at its playfulness. You take its paws in your hands and are amazed at the peaceful power within them. You send your energy to bear as its frequency fills you. It opens its eyes, sits up, and grasps you in a big hug. Setting you aside, it takes a long look at you and then walks away. You know without a doubt that it is now your protector, your champion.

Beaver (Muskrat)

Traits: Beaver has a gentle, hard-working nature and symbolizes the ability to take on an enormous project, put in long hours to see it to completion, and to create your dreams in reality. Beaver can build huge dams out of wood that can change the course of rivers and streams. It is an excellent architect and swimmer, and it can see the bigger picture, including the detailed steps needed to get to the end result. You can use these same traits to change the course of your life and bring your goals and dreams to fruition. Water is necessary for beaver's health, livelihood, and vitality. It is the same for you. Water can invigorate and energize you, so submerge yourself often. Beaver's fur is waterproof, which protects the animal and symbolically protects you from negative energy.

Talents: Alert, aware, cooperative, creative, diligent, does whatever is needed to complete a task, durable, flexible, focused, gets along well with everyone, great planner and builder, hard worker, independent, insightful, loyal, organized, protective, resourceful, team player, understanding, wise

Challenges: Loses track of everything else when focused on something, materialistic, obsessive, stubborn

Element(s): Earth, water

Primary Color(s): Black, brown

Appearances: Beaver means to be resourceful and work with intention. Utilize your time and energy in a way that you're not wasting either. Stay focused and don't wander off of your path. Avoid procrastination. Beaver means you're self-sufficient even though you prefer working with a group. You're loyal to family and friends and a bit wary of outsiders who want to be part of your inner circle (which is different from working with someone). You tend to protect those you love and hold them close, out of harm's way. Beaver means you're quick to volunteer to head up new projects or to take on additional work and often have several projects going at the same time. You're very creative, motivated, and aren't afraid of hard work. Beaver's appearance is a sign to move forward with your plans or start the project you've been thinking about. It also means you may forget to take time to relax. If so, participate in a water sport to help you connect to your inner self and restore your energy.

Assists When: You want to create your dreams in reality. If you've been thinking about starting a business ask beaver to help you. If you have to finish a job quickly, want to get out of situations where you feel trapped, resolve conflicts with others, clean up, declutter, or reorganize, beaver can guide you through all of these situations so you are successful. Beaver helps when you're overwhelmed and need quiet time to meditate and contemplate your path. If you want to change your life, consult beaver because it is one of the few animals that changes its environment to fit its needs.

Frequency: Beaver's frequency feels silky as it flows around you. It is filled with radiance. It sounds like the babble of a brook, the tinkling of water over rock.

Imagine...

You are standing on top of a hill above a creek, and you're amazed at the scene below. The entire area seems serene yet busy. In a large arc, all of the smaller trees have been cut down by beavers. They've placed them across the creek in what looks like a very haphazard manner to block the flow of water. In the pond area that's developed behind the dam, they've built a lodge that protrudes above the water. You see the beavers swimming through the water toward the lodge and then disappear inside. One large beaver swims over to the edge of the pond and peers up at you. You feel the power of its energy surging up the hill, wrapping around you. It is soft, like you imagine its fur feels. You feel its focused, wise energy deep inside as it gazes at you. After a while, you walk away with the feeling that you can do anything.

Bee

Traits: Bee symbolizes accomplishing impossible tasks if you only set your mind to it. Scientists had a difficult time understanding how a bee could fly. The sheer size of its body in relation to its wing size should have prohibited flight. But the bee, not knowing it wasn't supposed to fly, beats its wings at such an elevated speed that it is able to lift its weight. That's pretty spectacular! Bee also symbolizes fertility, productivity, and manifestation. Are you doing all you can to pursue your dreams and live a productive life?

Talents: Accurate, can handle many activities at once with ease, committed, dedicated, determined, diligent, focused, industrious, inspiring, mega energy, organized, self-sufficient, speed, successful, team player, tireless worker, works with dignity and grace

Challenges: Attacks quickly, being a workaholic, sharp tongue, taking on too much, touchy

Element(s): Air

Primary Color(s): Black, brown, gold, yellow

Appearances: Bee means you're too busy and need to rest or you need to stop resting and get busy if you've been procrastinating. You've been given more responsibility and must organize to ensure success. Bee means you can easily manage a group effort and inspire others to be more productive and reach their goals. You enjoy the sweetness of success. Don't eat too much sweetness though, or you could find yourself having problems with your teeth. You're often able to keep a busy environment organized and running smoothly. Bee warns against being too quick to temper or stinging too much. Bee means you should look for sweetness in your life and avoid aggravating situations. Bee is also a sign of hidden wisdom and to look for the wisdom within you. The queen bee represents birth and ruling over your domain. If you feel you're in a situation where you're not appreciated or are taken for granted, now is the time to create a new environment where you are important, appreciated, and can be the creative being that you are.

Assists When: You have a project or a situation where the outcome seems impossible to achieve. By connecting with bee, you will be able to accomplish these goals through hard work and diligent progress. Bee and the wax it creates can be a warning that you will be facing a negative or sticky situation and should use your own positive energy to overcome it with ease. Bee also helps when you're having a difficult time enjoying the fruits of your labor. If you go from project to project without feeling a sense of accomplishment at the end of each one, then you're taking on too much and need to give yourself time to enjoy the success you've earned.

Frequency: Bee's frequency is a monotone buzzing sound that is steady, strong, and calming. It feels hot yet cool, busy yet calm. It swirls and flies around you like a small whirlwind.

Imagine...

You're taking a walk in the park when you decide to take a shortcut through the trees. You're making quick time when you hear a loud buzzing noise over your head. Looking up at the tree, you notice a hole in the trunk that is surrounded by bees. While your first instinct is to run, you remain calm and watch as the bees enter and leave the hole to the hive. A couple of bees fly around you, but they don't land on you. They're more intent on returning to the hive. You feel a zinging sensation through you as they fly by, similar to a sting but without pain. Then one lands on your shirt. It moves its feet up and down, tasting the fabric. It walks and you feel its energy swirling into your chest, filling you with determination and elevating your frequency. It walks toward your bicep and then takes flight again. You breathe a sigh of relief that you didn't get stung and start to walk away from the hive with a feeling of energized purpose.

Beetle

Traits: Beetle symbolizes persistence and faith during changes in your life, especially ones that do not mesh with your beliefs. Just as beetle makes the most of what it's given to survive, you will find a way to compromise and obtain positive results. You learn from hard times and experience spiritual growth because you pay attention to the lessons being taught. Beetle evolves from a grub, which means transformation is an integral and continuing part of your life. Beetle has a hard outer shell that protects it from the environment. Dung beetles make meals from large animal poop, which is a sign that no matter what happens in your life, you can turn it into something useful.

Talents: Adaptability, clairvoyant, creativity, endurance, faith, finds use for everything and wastes nothing, high integrity, highly sensitive, instinctive, never gives up, protection, resourceful, spirituality, survival, transformation

Challenges: Aloof, doesn't allow others to get close, making things more complicated than they need to be, overprotective, overthinking, rigid, untrusting

Element(s): Earth

Primary Color(s): Black, blue, brown, green, red, orange, and multicolored patterns

Appearances: Beetle means changes are coming that will require you to transform in some way. It can show up during difficult times to lead you to a positive resolution. Beetle protects and energizes you, giving you the strength you need to see the situation through to the end. Beetle has often been thought of as an indication of the soul of man. When it appears to you, it means to take a look at your own spirituality. It is time to expand your knowledge and to experience growth within your spiritual self. Beetle means to keep things simple to make the most progress. You're practical, grounded, and methodical, but you can be introverted and prefer a solitary, contemplative life over one that is hectic and filled with an abundance of people. Beetle is seen as wise and sacred with a deep knowledge of spiritual ideals. It means to notice the small things in life to glean greater knowledge.

Assists When: You are trying to stay on track and finish a job. If you're responsible for the completion of a project, beetle can show you the most direct and resourceful way to get the task done. Beetle helps with spiritual growth, developing life principles, transformation, and manifestation. It is divine wisdom and finding knowledge from the small things in your life. Beetle helps you to keep moving in a straight line instead of zigzagging around and losing focus, even if the burden you're carrying is large. Beetle encourages you to keep your integrity and to be responsible for your actions.

Frequency: Beetle's frequency has a hollow sound. It is a little chilly and damp. Connecting to beetle's frequency feels a bit sticky, like glue stuck to your fingers, but it warms if you rub your fingers together. The closer you get to its energy, the warmer and more settled it feels.

Imagine...

It's late afternoon in early spring, and you're sitting in a chair under the shade of a maple tree, enjoying a glass of tea and watching the June bugs flying around. One of the beetles lands in your lap (almost in your glass of tea!). You like the little guys, so you let it crawl onto your finger, noticing the way its legs bend and move. It opens its hard shell and flutters its wings. You feel the warmth of its energy flowing toward you. Your mind is filled with thoughts of your own spirituality. You turn your hand so you can look at the beetle's face, and you feel the wisdom of the universe surrounding you. Absorbing it, you allow your own energy to merge with the profound feelings of almost overwhelming wisdom coming from the beetle, and you send it back toward it. Halfway between your chest and finger you sense many colors merging together as one. The beetle flutters its wings again and then flies away, leaving you with a feeling of awe and wonder at the energy exchange you just shared.

Black Panther

Traits: Black panther symbolizes a protective, courageous, and powerful guardian. It means darkness, death, and rebirth, and it connects to the astral realm. It symbolizes beauty and grace of movement. Black panther is a loner but will socialize with other loners. It symbolizes the feminine power of a mother and the dark moon. This enables you to eliminate fears (especially of the dark) and turn your life around if needed. Black panther is a quiet hunter who can freeze in position as it watches its prey. This is a sign to you that sometimes it is better to be still and quiet than to move forward in a rush.

Talents: Beauty, clairvoyant, courage, cunning, darkness of the moon, death, empathic, enlightened being, feminine power, grace, hunter, independent, intuitive, magical, power, precise, rebirth, secretive, silent, skillful, strength of being, strength of character, wise

Challenges: Becoming too involved in the dark areas of metaphysical ideas, calculating, ferocious, overly secretive, ruthless, unsociable

Element(s): Earth

Primary Color(s): Black

Appearances: When black panther appears, it is a sign that now is the time to reclaim any of your strength and power that you may have given to someone else or lost. You are at home in the darkness, are powerful, and can be aggressive when needed. You are an empathic intuitive who holds your natural abilities close. Black panther is a sign to embrace your fearlessness and to go after your prey, which may be a new job, a new home, or any other goal. You will begin a new chapter in your life if black panther is walking by your side. Black panther gives you strength of success. It symbolizes the need to listen more. You can uncover a lot of valuable information by paying close attention to what others are saying without getting so involved in the conversation that you give away your secrets.

Assists When: Black panther helps to heal wounds of the past and gives you the strength to learn from the past and move into the future. It can help you awaken to your clairvoyance, clairaudience, and empathic abilities. Black panther encourages you to listen to your inner voice and to act on your intuition. It can help you through hidden wisdom to keep your secrets. It will help you see upcoming opportunities. When you need to see minute details or the bigger picture of a situation, black panther can enlighten through positivity to enable you to see clearly. It awakens your passion and desire to succeed.

Frequency: Black panther feels like you've been wrapped inside a large, flowing piece of black silk fabric. The fabric wraps around you as if you were in a dark cocoon—warm, safe, and secure. Black panther will protect and guide you through the darkest of nights.

See Also: Cheetah, Cougar (Mountain Lion, Puma), Jaguar, Lion, Tiger

Imagine…

You're lost in the woods at night and feel as if you're being followed. Your breath sounds like panting—but wait—that's not you, is it? Holding still and holding your breath, you listen and hear nothing. From your peripheral vision you see the slightest movement, and then gold eyes are staring at you in the night. You watch as the eyes move closer, and then you feel sleek fur beneath your fingertips, the shape of the animal's shoulders and head. You realize that a black panther is standing beside you. It glances up at you and then starts to walk away. You hold on to the fur by its shoulder blades, feeling power rippling into you. Mile after mile you walk. The farther you go, the more connected to the black panther you feel. It is your protector, your guardian, your guide. As the first light of dawn breaks, you get your first real look at it. It's massive but filled with a special kind of energy, a universal knowing. There's a break in the trees and you step onto the road that leads back to town. You thank the black panther for its help. It sniffs and licks your hand, and then it disappears into the forest.

Blue Jay

Traits: Blue jay symbolizes how to use power most effectively. Blue jay is an assertive bird without fear, especially when it comes to protecting its young. It will hold off invaders to its territory and fight fiercely to keep predators away from its nest. Even when the odds are against blue jay, it never gives up or gives in. Blue jay symbolizes a connection to your higher self and universal knowledge of the spiritual realm.

Talents: Assertive, clear thinking, colorful, communication, courage, curious, determined, excellent speech capabilities, faithful, fearless, flashy, intelligence, mimic, protective of territory and offspring, vibrant

Challenges: Aggressive, can be a bully, dabbles in a lot of things without focusing on one, easily distracted, inconsiderate, overly talkative, procrastination, pushy, selfish, taking advantage of others, thoughtless

Element(s): Air

Primary Color(s): Black, blue, white

Appearances: When blue jay appears, you're getting ready to enter a time of growth on a mental or spiritual level. This growth will be long reaching and can ultimately change your life. It can clue you in to deceit by making you notice small things that you might have ignored. Blue jay can help push fear aside so you can see situations as they really are and face them without fear or doubt. It can put you on an even playing field with others who you may feel are smarter or more cunning than you are. Blue jay helps you see yourself equal to others and will help you resolve any conflicts and see the truth behind other people's actions and the motivations that cause those actions. Blue jay also means that you have a wide array of knowledge about a large number of subject matters. It means to be more curious to uncover more information.

Assists When: You need to be more daring, need someone to leave you alone, or want to connect to the Divine. If someone is bothering you, blue jay can help chase them out of your area. Blue jay can help you be more aggressive in going after what you want if you tend to hold back and wait to be noticed. It will give you the right words if you need to stand up for yourself or your beliefs. If you're in a situation where you need to follow the lead of another, blue jay can help you mimic that person while still putting your own unique flair on what you're trying to achieve. If you've gotten too big for your britches, blue jay can make you more humble and modest. It can give you the confidence to create and live the life you want and not settle for the life others think you should have. The only person holding you back is yourself, and blue jay gives you the ability to soar above the others, protect your territory along the way, and reach new heights.

Frequency: Blue jay's aggressive frequency feels jagged and sharp, like tiny lightning bolts darting around you. Its sound is a high pitch with short squealing sounds mixed in. When it's calm, it feels soft and sounds like a song floating on the breeze.

Imagine...

You're going to get your mail and as you pass underneath a tree a bird suddenly swoops down toward you, screeching in protest. You duck down a bit and continue walking while keeping an eye on the blue jay. It lands in a tree, still protesting. On the way back, you slow down by the tree and look into its branches. You see a nest and know there are babies in it. This explains the bird's actions. You don't want to upset it again, so you walk farther away from the tree while sending pictures and thoughts of congratulations on its new family. As you near your house, the blue jay lands on a bush in front of you. Instead of the screeching warning, this time it sings a few notes, flutters its wings, and flies back to its nest. Happiness fills you as you go inside your home.

Boar

Traits: Boar symbolizes life without fear. Once you're able to overcome your fears, then life will flow in an easier and more positive rhythm for you. Boar goes after what it wants with a ferocious aggression, especially if it feels threatened. Boar's tusks grow throughout its lifetime, and it is continually rooting and foraging, which indicates that you will continue to grow, seek out, and learn new things during your lifetime. You'll continually expand your knowledge, spirituality, and other areas of interest. Boars are continually aware of their surroundings, even when it looks like they're not. They can react with lightning speed.

Talents: Aggressive, assertive, communicative, courageous, embraces self-discovery, faces challenges head on, fearless, ferocious, fighter, initiates transformations, makes the best out of difficult situations, protective, strength of character, using all of your senses, vocal

Challenges: Combative, confrontational, contrary, creates enemies, destructive, excessive anger, impatient, inconsiderate, procrastination, quick tempered, too aggressive

Element(s): Earth

Primary Color(s): Black, brown

Appearances: When boar appears, it means that you are on the path of personal growth. It holds the mysteries of the natural world, spiritual strength, and knowledge, and it brings quick resolutions. Boar means you can't be afraid to stand up for yourself, other people, or something you believe in. To do otherwise will inhibit your personal growth. Boar will help you learn from taking a stand and grow in knowledge. Boar encourages you not to hesitate or second-guess your intentions. Listen to your instincts and act accordingly. Follow your own rules, think outside of the box, and never let anyone tell you that it can't be done. Boar brings out your competitive side, and you're not afraid to take risks to win. If you're feeling down about yourself, boar can boost your self-esteem and confidence.

Assists When: Boar can help when you need to calm down or get your anger under control. It's very easy for you to go too far with your actions or words when you're filled with anger. While boar can be just as aggressive, it also knows when to stop and can help you in these situations. If you're facing a situation where you need to overcome fear, work through problems, or confront someone you've been avoiding, boar can help you handle this with ease. If you're feeling unorganized and out of sorts, boar can help you get back on track. Boar can help bring closure.

Frequency: Boar's frequency smells like the forest after a summer rain. It's damp and scented of rain, leaves, and earth. It has a musty yet fresh clean scent. It sounds like a rustling in the brush, quietly electric in its intensity.

See Also: Erymanthian Boar, Pig

Imagine...

You feel the sharp tip of a boar's tusk tap against your arm. It wants you to follow it. You walk along a creek, over large flat rocks. The wind is blowing into your face, and it feels as if a storm is coming. Boar moves into the forest. You follow until you reach a clearing. Inside the clearing are several boars. The one you've been traveling with leaves your side and goes to the others. They grunt and squeal, greeting each other in happiness. Looking around, you see moss and small brush surrounding the clearing. The trees are tall and slightly sway in the wind. A sense of peace fills you. You're content, calm, and suddenly understand that lately you have been too aggressive in your reactions to people. You let the feeling go and breathe in the warm air, letting all negativity leave you as you exhale. *Thank you,* you say to boar, but when you look at the clearing, it's empty.

Buffalo (Bison)

Traits: Buffalo symbolizes strength, endurance, and an unpredictable nature. It is an enormous animal with exceptional strength. It lives in herds and protects one another. This is a sign to you that it is okay to rely on others instead of being alone. Buffalo prefers not to waste energy. It gets what it wants when it wants or needs it and goes straight to the heart of the matter. It doesn't have to walk around a fallen tree to get to water in a pond, it can simply step over it. Buffalo is connected to the Divine, the mystical, and the unknown. It can show you the way if you follow in its footsteps.

Talents: Abundance, achievement, being nonjudgmental, caring, challenges, faith, finding the silver lining, fortitude, harmony, helping others, knows true sacrifice, love, plentiful, resourceful, reverence for life, trust, understanding, walks own path

Challenges: Dislikes change, insensitive, overconfident, possessive, prideful, unpredictable

Element(s): Earth

Primary Color(s): Black, brown

Appearances: When buffalo appears, it means that you need to reexamine your respect for nature. Are you connecting to the sacredness within yourself and of the earth? If not, it's time to get in tune with the abundance of the earth and your own spiritual nature. Look for new ways to understand the natural laws of the universe and make use of the resources available to you to expand your spiritual growth. Buffalo means to appreciate what you've been given. You may not always get what you want but you'll always have what you need. When a white buffalo appears to you, expect an exceptional transformation that will completely change your life for the better. White buffalo is considered the most sacred living animal and can bring forth miracles. It represents peacefulness and a sense of calmness that connects to your spirituality. Buffalo is a reminder to be respectful to yourself and your elders, family, and friends. Buffalo warns against losing your temper. Keep calm, relax, and look at the whole picture first.

Assists When: You're enriching your life through spiritual connections, changing jobs, or starting a new project, business, or any new endeavor. If you're experiencing life-altering changes, buffalo helps you get into survival mode and stay there until things settle down. Buffalo enables you to embrace your creativity, especially if you can make something using your hands. Buffalo is a sign that good things will come to you but sometimes you have to wait for them. If you try to force an issue, it will probably have the opposite effect than what you're trying to achieve. Buffalo lives in balance with nature and can help you find your way when you're feeling lost through increasing your strength, wisdom, and connection to the sacred.

Frequency: Buffalo's energy is calm, serene, and peaceful. It feels as if you've lit a candle and gotten lost gazing into the flame. It connects to the Divine, to universal knowledge. It has a lumbering sound, a heaviness with a light beat mixed in.

See Also: Yak

Imagine…

You're captivated by large brown eyes that seem to stare deep into your soul. Sharp horns and a wet nose are mere inches from your face. A large male buffalo sniffs at you. It touches its wet nose to yours and inhales deeply, capturing your scent. Satisfied, it sidles up toward you, placing you at its back. You hear *climb on* telepathically, so you grab the scruffy part of its fur and pull yourself up. Once you're settled, buffalo starts walking toward the wide open fields. Before you know it, it's running to catch up with a herd in the distance. You hang on tightly and feel the earth energy beneath its feet and the sun energy overhead. Buffalo slows and ahead you see a female buffalo giving birth. You climb down and sit on the ground and watch the miracle of life. You feel the love of family surrounding you as mother and father buffalo watch the newborn calf and are honored that they put their trust in you.

Butterfly

Traits: Butterfly has four wings that symbolize birth, growth, transformation, and death. These wings are covered with scales and hair, which give the butterfly its color. It uses its antennae to sense wind direction and for scents that will direct it toward food sources. If butterfly is missing an antenna, it will fly in circles. This means if you're feeling lost, butterfly can help you step out of repetitive actions and find your way back onto your path.

Talents: Beauty, camouflage, carefree, change, cheerful, curious, eloquence, entertaining, excitement, flexible, fun, gentle, grace, happiness, high hopes, intuitive, joy, lightness of being, optimistic, social, spiritual, strength, tenacity, tougher than you appear

Challenges: Being too serious, fickle, hiding instead of being seen, not giving situations the importance needed, overly casual, problems focusing, repetitive actions, superficial, unorganized

Element(s): Air

Primary Color(s): Butterfly is represented by all of the colors of the rainbow.

Appearances: When butterfly appears, it means you need to add more fun into your life. It can indicate that you're becoming more popular, meeting new people, and are embracing a lighter, more carefree attitude. Butterfly means it's time to embrace change, including changes to your way of thinking. It can help you become more spiritually minded. If you've been living a solitary life, come on out of your cocoon and show the world your beauty and light. Butterfly can mean it's time to add color to your life. If you've thought about taking up painting or another type of art, seeing butterfly means it's a good time to start a new artistic hobby. Butterfly represents letting go of the old and emerging from periods of transition as a new you.

Assists When: You are contemplating a major change in your life. Butterfly can guide you through the decision-making process and help you choose the right course of action. It can help you be more expressive with your emotions instead of keeping them locked inside the cocoon you've created to hold them. Butterfly gives more vitality and excitement. If you're considering changes to your appearance, ask butterfly to help. If you're having difficulties adjusting to changes occurring in your life, butterfly can give you the strength and tenacity to make it through with grace and to emerge from the change filled with joy, peace, lightness of being, and excitement for the future. Butterfly helps you be more sensitive to those around you and your environment. It can assist during times of personal and career growth. Butterfly lets you see the beauty in all things. If you tend to be a worrywart, butterfly can help you see that worrying isn't helpful and can assist you in releasing it to be stress free.

Frequency: Butterfly's energy is light and airy, mystical and powerful. It sounds like a tinkling bell and feels like a warm breeze tingling your skin and flowing through your hair.

Imagine…

It's early fall and you're out raking leaves in the backyard when you notice a monarch butterfly flitter by in all of its splendid glory. You watch for a moment then go back to your work. Then another one passes right by your shoulder. You stop again, and this time you look behind you. There are hundreds of monarch butterflies headed your way. You're awed by their beauty and the sheer number of them. Soon they're flying past and you're caught up in their mystical energy. You feel tingling all over and there seems to be a light breeze in the air. You let their high-level frequency move through you, and you imagine what it's like to be a monarch butterfly traveling with such a large group. After a while, they've all passed by, yet you still watch them, transfixed by the positivity you feel from then. Suddenly, a small monarch sits on your nose. It moves its wings a few times then flitters off behind the rest of the group. You laugh. Joy, love, and a deep peace resonate through you.

Catbird

Traits: Catbird symbolizes communication, language, and connections with others. Catbird's unique call sounds like a cat mewing. Most catbirds are gray and lay turquoise eggs, but there is also a multicolored species called the white-eared catbird that has green wings, a yellow chest with black spots, and white going over its ears. Its call sounds like a cat hissing. Catbirds can mimic other birds, frogs, and machines. They can also make more than one sound at a time, although they sing phrases only once. They also like to sing hidden from view inside a small tree or a bush.

Talents: Brilliance, can read people easily, changing perspectives, communication, contemplation, empathic, intuitive, mimics, mindfulness, observant

Challenges: Can't keep secrets, getting involved in other people's business when you should stay out of it, gossipy, lack of clarity, noisy, talking when you should be quiet

Element(s): Air

Primary Color(s): Gray

Appearances: When catbird appears, it is a sign that you are a great communicator. You are able to mimic the words of others yet make them your own. Catbird advises to listen closely and put what you've learned to use. Catbird warns that your words can be distorted by others, so think before you speak and make sure you use words that make your intentions and meanings easy to understand so there's no chance of misunderstandings. Catbird also warns that what you say may become public knowledge, so make sure you only tell secrets or personal information to close, trustworthy friends and family. If you don't want something to be known, don't say it to anyone. Catbird appears when you're going to be meeting new people. Listen closely to what they say and learn from them.

Assists When: Catbird assists when you need to be clear and concise in your communication, whether it's the written word or if you're speaking to someone. If you're stumbling over your words, ask catbird to help you speak with clarity. Catbird warns against bringing too much attention to yourself because it may be the kind of attention you don't want. Catbird can also help you deal with nosey people. It can give you the words to politely say it's none of your business without offending others. It is also a reminder that you shouldn't be putting your nose in where it doesn't belong either.

Frequency: When it's singing, catbird's energy is like a fast-paced snare drum or a drawn-out version of a cat's meow. When it's quiet, it's the peacefulness of a nearby stream. Light and airy, excitable and calm, catbird portrays harmony in opposites.

Imagine…

You're taking a morning walk when you hear the mournful cry of a cat. You stop to look around, but you don't see it anywhere. Concerned, you follow the sound to a small tree. You look up into the branches but only see a little gray bird sitting there studying you. It hops from one branch to another until it's only a few feet in front of you. Tentatively, you hold out your hand, palm down, and much to your surprise and delight, the bird jumps onto the back of your hand. You feel a calm peace wash over you. Then suddenly the bird opens its mouth, and a cat's meow comes out of it. You laugh softly and tell the bird, *thank you for helping me find the cat*, and then it flies away. You can't quite get the grin off of your face though, and it's there for most of the day.

Caterpillar (Inchworm)

Traits: Caterpillar symbolizes hidden potential, strong use of the senses, and the promise of a beautiful tomorrow. Caterpillar is a picky eater that will play with food to make sure it is delicious before using its strong jaws to bite into it. Caterpillar uses its antennae to sense its environment, which is a sign to use your own senses more, including your sixth sense. Caterpillar often blends into its environment, secretly hiding until the time is right to transform into the beautiful butterfly it is meant to be. This is a reminder to keep secrets until your plans are well established. Inchworm means to be make sure your path is clear in purpose, take accurate measurements, and smaller steps to get to your goals.

Talents: Cautious, creative, determined, endurance, forward movement, growth, hidden potential, intuitive, looking at the little things, lucky, meditative, metamorphosis, patience, precision, preparation, promises, renewal, spirituality, strength, transformations

Challenges: Impatient, overly secretive, perfectionist, reclusive, too picky, trying to rush ahead instead of taking it slow

Element(s): Earth

Primary Color(s): Brown, green

Appearances: When caterpillar appears, it is a reminder that everything in life happens in its own time, not the instant you want it. Live in the moment, moving at your own pace while taking time to smell the roses along the way. It means to keep what you're doing, planning, and creating under wraps until you're ready to reveal it in its magnificent completion. Revelations should not be discussed during the transformation process. Be one with the process and trust that what you are doing is necessary for growth and change. You do not need anyone else's opinions at this time. Trust in yourself. Caterpillar reminds you that in order to transform, you must release the old and embrace the new. Let go of what no longer serves you and embrace the new manifesting in your life. Inchworm's appearance means to slow down, you're moving too fast.

Assists When: Caterpillar appears when you need to look at the hidden potential inside of you, when you need to give yourself credit for a job well done, and when you need to boost your self-esteem. Look at yourself as a work in progress and be positive and upbeat about your future. Caterpillar means that you don't let other people get you down but instead listen to your own higher self and believe you can accomplish anything. Caterpillar helps keep you on track and brings positive change. It enables you to see those who want to block your success for who they really are and can bring their intentions to light. Caterpillar helps you keep your secrets secret and gives you energetic creativity. Inchworm helps when you need to be accurate and precise. It means to take small, slow steps and get it right the first time so there aren't any errors later.

Frequency: Caterpillar's energy sounds like middle C being held down on the piano keyboard. Inchworm's energy sounds like a stretched rubber band being plucked. Both feel like a warm hug.

Imagine…

After work, you walk out to the parking lot. You turn toward your car and see an inchworm suspended in midair. It's just floating and turning slowly. You reach out and let it land on the back of your hand. It scooches up then stretches out, scooches up and stretches out as it crawls up your arm. You take a detour to some nearby bushes and set the little inchworm on one of the leaves near a caterpillar. It starts its signature walk along the plant. As you watch, it occurs to you that the little inchworm will get wherever it's going in its own sweet time, and that seems like exactly what you should do today, too.

Catfish

Traits: Catfish symbolizes looking deep to find truth. People may not be what they seem or there is information hiding beneath the surface that you need. An adult catfish can be from one centimeter up to eight foot ten and 646 pounds, depending on the species. This wide range of growth is a sign that you have unlimited potential.

Talents: Able to sort through information and categorize it, adaptable, discriminating, emotional, excellent communication skills, go-getter, good judgment, hard worker, lives life to the fullest, sensitive, takes what is needed and discards the rest, understanding

Challenges: Clings to clutter, fear, hoarder, isolation, lazy, moves around too much from location to location, overly sensitive, procrastination, self-pity, underachiever, unmotivated

Element(s): Water

Primary Color(s): Gray

Appearances: When catfish appears, it means that someone is pretending to be someone or something that they're not. This can happen in social media settings or in your daily life. Catfish is a warning to keep your eyes and ears open for the truth and to use your intuition to uncover answers in order to protect yourself. It means to be choosey in the people with whom you're interacting. Don't follow along blindly but know all of the details. Be practical and aware. Catfish also means that while you don't waste your time or energy on unnecessary tasks, now is the time to really hunker down. You may be on a deadline or planning an event where details matter and time is of the essence. Catfish means you're an emotional person who can sometimes find slights when none were intended. If there are people who are pulling you down into the depths of their despair on a continuing basis, now might be the time to back away from them for a while. It's one thing to be a caring, supportive friend and another thing to have a negative friend trying to bring you into their darkness. Choose wisely.

Assists When: Catfish can help you navigate life when you're feeling down. It can help you find the goodness in the dark. Catfish has heightened senses and can help you increase the frequency of your own intuition. Clairvoyance may become more vivid, dreams prophetic, or you may suddenly develop a new ability when catfish is guiding you. Catfish often increases your empathic abilities because it is directly connected to emotions. If you're feeling stuck in the mud in your intuitive development or in any other area of your life, catfish can help you wiggle free and start making forward progression. It's time to stop struggling.

Frequency: Catfish's energy feels like you're floating on your back in the middle of a swimming pool, lake, or river on a hot summer's day. It's warm and soft and moves slowly around you.

Imagine...

You're fishing at a pond when you realize it's getting late and you should start thinking about packing up and heading home. Just then you feel a tug on your line. You start reeling in and see the flash of a tail break the water. When you get the fish to shore, you see that it's not a bass or brim like you've been catching all day but a big catfish. You carefully lift it from the water's edge, noticing the slickness of its skin and its long whiskers. You remove the hook from the edge of its mouth, and suddenly you're slammed by an intuitive vision. You see the answer to the problem you've been deliberating about all day. You look at the catfish in your hand, say *thank you, my friend,* and lower it into the water. It swims away, but you know it touched you deeply and gave you the answer you sought. You pack up your gear and head to your vehicle, feeling satisfied that everything is going to work out just fine.

Centipede (Millipede)

Traits: Centipede symbolizes movement. With its abundance of legs it can move quickly and indicates forward motion in life and the ability to do many things at once. As centipede matures into an adult, it grows more legs as needed. This means you are well equipped to handle new things by growing and adjusting to change. Centipede lives in damp, moist environments. You can find it underneath rocks, in decomposing leaves, and under logs. Some even live in the dark places in a house. Centipede grooms itself after eating and will clean each leg in a methodical order. Its bite is poisonous, and it doesn't like to be handled.

Talents: Active social life, athletic, balance, brings good luck, cleanliness, coordinated, doesn't hesitate, energetic, fast mover, ferocity, healing, high energy, sensitive to intuition and dreams, stability

Challenges: Does things too quickly without thinking first, gambling problems, obsessive about things being clean and in their proper place, preferring darkness to light in all things, reclusive

Element(s): Earth

Primary Color(s): Black, brown

Appearances: Centipede means taking care in what you say and the manner in which you say it to avoid misinterpretation. Its antennae symbolize a connection to all things intuitive. When centipede meets a mate, the two touch antennae and seem to have an intuitive connection. The appearance of centipede means that you're likely to meet someone in the near future with whom you'll have a close psychic or past-life connection. Centipede means you'll come into your own and achieve success later in life rather than earlier. Safety and security are important to you, and if centipede shows up, it means to check your safety measures to make sure everything is okay. For instance, check the batteries in your smoke detectors, be more vigilant about locking doors, and be more aware of your surroundings and carry pepper spray if you're walking alone.

Assists When: Centipede helps when you want to have more coordination, for example if you're learning to dance. If you feel disorganized, out of sorts, or at odds within yourself, centipede will help you feel grounded and find balance and harmony within. Centipede warns to get out of the spotlight and retreat to where you're most comfortable. You need this time to reevaluate and recharge, to plan, and to create. Once you have done these things, you can reemerge with a new message and greater goals. Centipede is believed to ward off bad luck and negativity, and many people will carry them in their pockets for this reason. If you'd like to do this but don't want to carry a real centipede, you can use a toy one if you spiritually cleanse it and give it a specific purpose, such as good luck, more energy, healing, quickness, or making more friends.

Frequency: Centipede energy scurries, moving very quickly and in a coordinated effort like its legs. It feels gritty and cool. It sounds like hundreds of high-pitched *pings* mixed together, as if you've spilled BBs onto the floor.

Imagine…

You're spending the afternoon exploring and feeling at one with nature's energy. You've wandered into a small city park filled with trees. You sit down underneath one and lean your back against the rough bark. Beside you there are a few rocks. You pick one up to examine it and underneath you see a small centipede. Putting down the rock, you pick up the centipede and put it on the back of your hand, curious as to what its movement will feel like. As it crawls up your arm, you connect to the energy of its many feet tickling your skin. You are careful in your handling of the centipede as you place it back in the dirt. It quickly crawls away, heading for the edge of the other rock where it buries itself under some leaves. You put the rock back in its place so you don't disturb the centipede's habitat.

Cheetah

Traits: Cheetah symbolizes speed, stealth, and strength. You may need all three in the near future and your life may feel like it is on fast-forward. This is a temporary situation and will slow down to a normal pace soon. Cheetah lives in closely bonded groups but also prefers time alone. They protect their offspring and other young in their group with a vengeance. They have excellent sight and can see things in the distance.

Talents: Aggressively pursues goals, courageous, directness, elusive, empathy, flexibility, focused, independent, intelligent, killer instincts, not intimidated, skill, speed, stealth, strength, tough love, vitality

Challenges: Aggressive, impatient, inconsiderate, loses interest quickly if not immediately successful, prefers instant gratification over long-term pursuits, ruthless

Element(s): Earth

Primary Color(s): Black, tan, white

Appearances: If cheetah appears, you need to respond to situations without hesitation. This isn't the time to plan but time to act. It means something you had on the back burner has become a top priority and you must deal with it now. Cheetah means to stay grounded as you move with top speed. You must remain focused and pursue your goal with intensity, stealth, and speed while using your instincts, intelligence, and courage to see it through to the end. Cheetah reminds you that once you've attacked a situation take the time to recharge and recover from the effort to bring you back to center and a place of balance. Cheetah can show up as a message that you need to become more active and get into better physical shape to avoid health issues. Cheetah will lead you down a direct path and won't let you stray. Cheetah warns that sometimes you must overcome a struggle in order to succeed. Have faith that your actions will lead to a successful conclusion.

Assists When: Cheetah helps you get things done quickly and efficiently. It helps you think fast, and it gives you the energy to get your body in high gear if needed. Cheetah helps with self-defense and overcoming challenges in business or in your daily life. It helps you become more assertive and fast-paced and gives a sense of urgency in meeting your goals. Cheetah helps you become flexible in your opinions, more open-minded and willing to quickly alter course to accommodate the changing needs of situations. If you're floundering from one thing to another without purpose or structure, cheetah can help you focus and discover your purpose. It can help you see where you can make improvements in your life and how to strategically go about implementing those changes to add joy and abundance to your days. Because cheetah has excellent eyesight, it can help you see the bigger picture instead of getting caught up on the details. Cheetah symbolizes an empathic nature and can help you get in touch with your feelings and connecting to the feelings of others.

Frequency: Cheetah's energy feels like you're standing in the middle of a whirlwind, and then, just as suddenly as it appeared, it's gone. It moves fast, feels strong, and is electrically charged. It heightens your energy and emotions, making you more aware as it wraps around you.

See Also: Black Panther, Cougar (Mountain Lion, Puma), Jaguar, Lion, Tiger

> ### *Imagine…*
> You're pinned against an extremely large tree trunk staring into a face full of ferocious bared teeth. A cheetah is mere feet from you, hissing and growling. It steps closer and you push your back harder against the tree. Suddenly it quiets and sits down in front of you, waiting. For what, you don't know. You try to slow the rapid beating of your heart and even your breathing, calming yourself. The energy radiating from the cheetah is neutral. It's trying to figure out why you're in its space. You send loving thoughts to it, explaining telepathically that you wanted to connect to its speed and strength to help you in your daily living. Moments later, it walks over, licks its rough tongue across the top of your hand, spins around, and runs away at lightning speed.

Chickadee

Traits: Chickadee symbolizes adaptability. This tiny bird can lower its metabolism in order to survive in frigid weather. It doesn't migrate and often makes friends with other small bird species. When foraging for food, it will often hang upside down. This is a very social animal with extreme curiosity and fearlessness. It is very interested in people and will often land in someone's hand. If you put out a bird feeder, chickadee will be the first to find it.

Talents: Ability to influence people, accepting, adaptable, agreeable, attracts people easily, brutally honest, can take care of yourself if challenged, cheerful, communication skills, curious, doesn't worry or let things get them down, easygoing, friendly, happiness, intelligent, interaction, joy, life of the party, motivated, nonjudgmental, popular, problem-solving, singing, social, vigilant

Challenges: Anxious, blunt, commitment anxiety, crying wolf, indiscriminate, inefficient, overly dependent on others, overly opinionated, tactless, too obsessed with being popular, underestimated by others

Element(s): Air

Primary Color(s): Black, gray, white

Appearances: Chickadee means that you need to be aware of the people around you. It can warn you when someone isn't being honest and reminds you to always tell the truth no matter how uncomfortable it might make you feel. Chickadee influences personal and business relationships and is a clear sign to communicate effectively, to be diplomatic, and to refrain from getting into a conflict. Chickadee means that now is the time to be open and excited about ideas, projects, proposals, and the people in your personal life. Now is not the time for secrets but time to open up to creativity and your true feelings. Chickadee's song is unique and once heard is easily remembered. It means you too can be as vocally expressive as chickadee and as hard to forget.

Assists When: If you're feeling down about yourself, if your self-esteem is low, or if you're being overly critical about what you've been able to accomplish in your life, chickadee can help you overcome all of these things and see the brightness within them. You are more than you think, and chickadee can help you be more accepting of yourself, flaws and all. If you're having a hard time fitting into a new environment or making friends, chickadee can give you the courage to be more outgoing and increase your social circle. Is someone bothering you? Ask chickadee for help. This small bird will fiercely attack much larger birds if it feels threatened. It protects others in the flock and its young in the same manner. Chickadee is very intelligent. It can help you with studying, tests, decision-making, and oral presentations. Chickadee enhances your musical talents.

Frequency: Chickadee's energy sounds like its song. It is a light and airy chirp that seems to resonate in the wind. Its energy feels vibrant and alive, as if it's tickling and then bouncing off of you. It's a happy, joyous feeling of love.

> ### Imagine...
>
> You've decided to put some new bird feeders in your backyard. You're hanging them from tree limbs when a tiny black and white bird lands on the limb beside you. It's not afraid and is interested in what you're doing. You work alongside the chickadee until it flies down to grab a few bites of feed before the feeder is even tied off. When you're finished, you get off of the ladder to watch the chickadee eat. You hold out your hand toward it, and it flies over and lands in your palm. It watches you, tilting its head side to side, and then whistles *ti-ti-ti-der-der* as if to thank you for the food. Its song fills you with light and love, cheer and joy. You can't help but smile as you finish putting up the feeders with the little chickadee following you around. It's a good day.

Chipmunk (Ground Squirrel)

Traits: Chipmunk symbolizes confidence, certainty, and quick decisions. Chipmunk is a great planner and organizer and has winter food stored up in advance to ensure its survival. Chipmunk is a very social creature and represents happiness and fun. Chipmunk encourages you to get outside and investigate your surroundings. Take a walk or go exploring to see new things. It symbolizes protection, inflections, and clarity of speech.

Talents: Agile, busy, change, determined, discovery, efficient, friendly, gregarious, happy, not wasteful, playful, practical, pragmatic, resourceful, security, social, varied interests, wealth accumulation, wise investor

Challenges: Being high-strung, excessive talking, greedy, hoarder, indecisive, materialistic, nervousness, obsessed with making money or obtaining material possessions, possessive, workaholic

Element(s): Earth

Primary Color(s): Black, brown, red

Appearances: When chipmunk shows up, it's time to get busy storing up for winter. Don't waste time. You've much to do so you'd better get busy doing it! If you've been thinking about investing or increasing your material possessions, now is a good time to start. If you're considering new ways to make more money, start implementing them so you will see results soon. Chipmunk means to stay balanced between work and your social life. If you overdo either one, you'll be out of balance and may be ill-adjusted. Chipmunk advises to pay particular attention to how people are speaking. Listen for the inflections in their voice, how it rises and falls, and whether they're speaking in soft or loud tones. This will tell you a lot about how they're feeling.

Assists When: Chipmunk assists when you're being overly talkative. Sometimes it's better to let others take the lead in a discussion instead of you doing all of the talking. If you're working on a group project, get ideas from everyone to make it successful. This will help you be more productive. Chipmunk also means to wait before telling secrets that aren't ready to be revealed. If you're unsure what someone is talking about, or if they're saying one thing but mean (or feel) another, chipmunk can help clarify their intentions. Chipmunk has a great sense of timing and can help if you're on a deadline or need to be precise. Chipmunk also helps when you need to increase your monetary value. It can show you all of the niches that could turn into a successful enterprise. Are you letting fear hold you back from having fun in life? Chipmunk can help you let go of that fear. You may not be jumping off of bridges on bungee cords, but you will find more fun and happiness in your life if you ask chipmunk to come along.

Frequency: Chipmunk's energy is somewhat spastic, is in high gear, and moves with quick, jerky motions. It feels scattered, as if you're looking around all the time, searching and seeking. Its tone is a high-pitched chirp. It feels like the joy associated with playing.

Imagine…

There is a plinking noise against your window, so you go outside to investigate. It's just a small branch rubbing against the window, so you fold it up into the other branches to temporarily stop the noise. A motion near another tree catches your eye, and you see a tiny head poking up out of the ground. Suddenly the movement explodes across the yard as a tiny chipmunk runs out of its den. It scurries across the yard toward you. It runs up and jumps onto your shoe, puts its paws on your pants, and looks up at you, then takes off across the yard again and disappears into its burrow. You wait for a few moments, but it doesn't come back out, so you go inside and grab your hat. Chipmunk has encouraged you to take a walk. The air is fresh, the sun is bright, and all is well in your world.

Clam

Traits: Clam symbolizes that it's imperative for you keep quiet at this time. Clam is known for quickly closing its shell if it feels threatened. It is a sign to retreat, stay quiet, and wait to see what is going to happen. Now is not the time for taking action but for waiting. Clam protects its delicate body within a hard, impenetrable shell. You too have this same type of shell at your disposal any time you need to quickly protect yourself.

Talents: Appreciative of self and others, caring, gentle, giving, good judgment, intuitive, kind, knows the value of silence, looks for answers within self, patient, quiet, reserved, resourceful, sensitive, tenderhearted

Challenges: Defensive, fears of theft, finding balance, not acting on your dreams, overly shy, paranoia, procrastinating, reclusive, secretive, wasting your talents

Element(s): Water

Primary Color(s): Gray, yellow

Appearances: Clam means to keep quiet until you've been able to judge exactly what's going on. If you're unsure of a situation, let it happen as it will happen. Sometimes it's better not to get involved, especially if you don't have something constructive to add or if your involvement will be misconstrued by others. Clam lets you know that silence is golden at this time. Don't let others know what you're up to and be careful. If you've got the next great idea, don't share it. Instead protect it. That said, don't go overboard either. Clam means you're an amazing person with incredible talents, but you don't let the world see your true self. You're much more comfortable hiding your talents and abilities within your shell so others don't make fun of you or steal your phenomenal ideas. Clam means that sometimes you have to open up in order to shine. It's difficult for you to trust, but when you do, it's done wholeheartedly.

Assists When: Clam helps when you're in a situation where you don't know what to do. If you're feeling out of sorts, it can help you get back into the rhythm of your life through mind, body, and spirit. Clam can help you build inner strength and tap into strong emotions. Even though it retreats into its shell when it's threatened, clam can help you become more outgoing. You have a lot of plans and positive intentions about the things you want to accomplish, but you sometimes don't follow through. Clam can motivate and inspire you to let go of some of your secrets and enjoy the company of others. Clam teaches you when it's better to be more closed off from others and when you should open yourself up more. It's a matter of personal empowerment and balance, which clam has perfected.

Frequency: Clam's energy feels solid and strong, unforgiving and unmoving, yet inside it is soft and sensitive. It sounds like the rhythm of the tide.

> ### *Imagine…*
>
> You're visiting a pet store and are looking at the aquariums. In one of them there is a clam sitting on the top of the substrate. Intrigued, you watch as it reaches out its muscular foot to touch the floor area around its shell. Soon, using its impressive strength, it tilts its shell with the slightly opened side pointing down. It digs with its foot, pulling itself down into the substrate until it has completely disappeared. You glance at your watch and realize that you've been observing the clam for an hour, waiting to see what would happen.

Cockroach

Traits: Cockroach symbolizes cleaning away the old to make way for the new. Cockroach has been around for millions of years, and its adaptability is nothing less than phenomenal. It has tremendous survival skills in changing environments and unsavory conditions. Cockroach prefers to live under the cover of darkness and out of the light. This means you can navigate in any conditions using the resources available to you. You intuitively know when danger is nearby and to get out of the way.

Talents: Adaptable, healthy, longevity, quick reactions, readiness, resourcefulness, self-reliance, survival skills, tenacious, thankfulness

Challenges: Antisocial, easily influenced by peer pressure, fearful, living in filthy conditions, prefers to hide rather than face situations, reclusive, ungrateful

Element(s): Earth

Primary Color(s): Brown

Appearances: When cockroach appears, it means that you may soon encounter a change in your living conditions. You may experience an unexpected need to relocate, whether it's your own decision or a forced move. You'll face this change with ease because of your excellent survival skills and adaptability. You never give up on the things you want. It may take years to accomplish your goals but that's okay with you. You can weather any storm, bear any burden, and come out of trying times ahead of the game. You're very sensitive to the needs of others due to your empathic nature. Your preference is a quiet life without a lot of change or activity but when those things do come, you handle them with ease. If you notice you're depending on others too much or are feeling pressure from your peers, cockroach can help you learn to rely on yourself more and make your own decisions instead of falling in with the ways of a group. Cockroach's appearance means you need to take some alone time to let go of stress, rejuvenate, and do some spring cleaning both in your home and within your person.

Assists When: If you're feeling highly emotional, flighty, or like your head is in the clouds, cockroach can help you become more grounded and connected to the earth again. It can change your emotional distress into courageous determination. If you're in a hostile situation where all seems lost, where you're upset and out of sorts, ask cockroach to lend you its inner strength and adaptability. Cockroach is seen by many to be one of the nastiest bugs on the planet due to its ability to overpopulate an area in a short amount of time and because it prefers to live in filth. Yes, that's gross, but this type of lifestyle has provided the species with an enormous life span. Take a minute to be thankful for any negativity you have to deal with and know that while you might not like it, sometimes it's necessary for your progress, for your survival, and to learn lessons that will allow spiritual growth. Difficult situations will eventually pass, and soon you will once again be able to embrace the lightness of being.

Frequency: Cockroach energy is the hum of the earth's essence, low, strong, and pure. It is as old as time, solid in substance, and vibrates slowly and with unwavering steadiness.

Imagine…

You're traveling and are spending the night at a hotel. In the middle of the night you get up to get a drink of water from the kitchenette area. Flicking on the lights, you freeze when you see a large cockroach sitting on the counter as if it was waiting for you. It doesn't run as you'd expect but instead wiggles its antennae at you. You're not particularly fond of cockroaches, but this encounter seems strange. It should have run away as soon as you turned on the lights. Thinking about its energy and making a frequency connection, you ask if it has a message for you. Images flash in your mind's eye as you receive the message. You feel a slow vibration rumbling inside your chest. You look back at the cockroach, but it's gone. You go back to bed, but it's hard to fall back asleep as you go over the message's images in your mind.

Conch

Traits: Conch is a large sea snail that lives in the ocean. Conch shells are spiral inside and come to a point at both ends. People used them as trumpets to alert others of coming danger or as a call to gather together. Conch's shell often enables it to blend in with its environment, which represents security and defense. As such, conch is a symbol of family, security, and success.

Talents: Awakening, balance, call of the wild, camouflage, defense, emotions, empathy, enlightenment, focused, group gatherings, honesty, inspiration, music, security, spirituality, wisdom

Challenges: Blunt, boastful, overly emotional, prideful, tactless

Element(s): Water

Primary Color(s): Pink

Appearances: Conch means to speak the truth with power, conviction, and belief. You are a leader, and others look up to you for your wisdom and spiritual enlightenment. Sometimes people may not want to listen because it's easier to avoid the truth than face it, but your words are delivered in such a way that they will understand and benefit from them. Conch means you're not afraid to toot your own horn if it means helping another person. While you prefer living in your shell, you'll come out to inspire and teach others. Your strength is in your balance, wisdom, and ability to see within the spiritual realm and to share the knowledge you've gained. You're an inspiration to others and help them develop their own abilities and walk their own spiritual path. Conch means you have musical talent as a singer or in playing an instrument. The spirals within the conch's shell are an indication that you are able to pull deep within yourself, connect with your inner consciousness, and experience enlightenment. The best part of this is you're able to share your experiences with others in ways that will allow them to do the same thing for themselves.

Assists When: If your life feels turbulent, as if wave after wave of problems are crashing over you, conch can help calm the waters and show you the light shining through from above. It can help you speak your own truth, find your own voice, and remain calm during tumultuous times. Conch can guide you so you know when it's appropriate to speak of your accomplishments and when you should let others talk about what they've done. Sometimes listening to someone discuss their accomplishments gives them a feeling of respect and admiration that will empower them to do more with their lives. This doesn't mean that you have to sit and listen to a braggart for hours on end. There is a difference between the two and conch helps you see it. Conch symbolizes the awakening of the heart to love. It can assist you in affairs of the heart, relationships, and with family.

Frequency: Conch's energy moves slowly with a *slish* and a *slug*. It feels like warm water flowing around you with the gentle pull of the oceans current. It's soft and pliable yet strong and powerful.

Imagine…

You're scuba diving and are filled with a sense of oneness with the sea creatures and the water they live in. As you continue your exploration, you see an enormous conch shell moving slowly across the ocean floor. You swim down for a better look and see the fleshy body of the conch sticking out of its spiraled shell as it moves along. The shell is pointy and whitish tan. You know the inside is pink, but you can't see it because the animal is still living in its shell. You feel, more than hear, a musical tone around you as you watch the conch make its way. You're experiencing a moment of spiritual enlightenment as you realize this odd creature moves forward with conviction and belief in itself that it will reach its goals. You take a moment to think about your own life and how connecting with the power of the conch will help you when you return home. You leave the conch to continue on its way as you search for other cool animals along the reef.

Coral

Traits: Coral symbolizes a solid, structured foundation of support for life. Coral is a small invertebrate animal (its body is called a polyp) that lives in compact colonies that result in reefs—underwater ecosystems held together and protected by the calcium carbonate secreted by coral. It is commonly found in shallow, tropical water, but some species of coral are also found in deep, colder waters. Coral reefs are sensitive to changing water temperatures. Coral polyps are usually clear, the algae that lives within their structures is what gives coral its color.

Talents: Adaptable, awareness of life rhythms, balance, connecting to your inner self, creativity, generous, giving, nourishing, nurturing, patience, provides shelter, solid foundation, stability, structured, supports life, trusting others, trusting yourself

Challenges: Hovering over people, immobile, pushing your ideals onto others, rigid, self-sacrificing, untrusting

Element(s): Water

Primary Color(s): Every color imaginable!

Appearances: Coral appears when you need to share with others. It may be material goods, advice, or just a shoulder for someone else to cry on. You are a strong person mentally and emotionally, can weather the turbulence of another's emotions, and are a great listener. When you give advice, it is filled with the wisdom of the ages, even if you don't realize it. You innately know what to say to put someone at ease and to calm their storm. Coral means a younger person may look up to you as a role model, and you're willing to help them in any way you can. Coral urges you to embrace the artist within you. Creativity in all forms acts as a stress reliever. When coral appears, it is warning you to nourish yourself so you don't become weak. You often get so busy that you skip meals because you forget to eat. Being productive is also a sign of coral. New projects and opportunities are coming your way.

Assists When: Coral represents perfect timing, so if your timing feels off, ask coral to help you get back on track. You're a loving, nurturing person, but sometimes you can feel neglected or taken for granted. You built a solid foundation, so you don't need praise to know you're doing an excellent job. Coral helps you give value to your own accomplishments. Coral is constantly changing with the flow of the ocean, so expect changes to come your way soon. Flow with these changes instead of fighting against them for the best possible outcome. Coral symbolizes spiritual growth, emotional support, and practical understanding of spirituality and the human psyche. You intuitively know what steps to take in any given situation, so don't doubt yourself. Coral means to make a deeper connection with your own feelings. It encourages you to see beauty in every aspect of your life, to trust in universal guidance and accept the happiness and rewards that come to you.

Frequency: Coral energy is like a bright light shining down on you. It fills you with hope, love, courage, and strength. It is warm, is soothing, and feels like a natural glow within you.

> ### Imagine…
>
> The amazing colors of the coral reef dazzle you as the sun filters through the warm, clear waters of the ocean. As you snorkel through the water you look at the corals' shapes and colors connected side by side. Some look like small trees with branches while others are in the shape of rods, flat, or wavy. Some remind you of the human brain, others of multiarmed organisms or of a fungus that might grow outward from the trunk of a tree. The way they are grouped together reminds you of a bunch of small communities making up a whole underwater world, which is the reef. As you swim along, you often dive down to take a closer look before returning to the surface for air. The coral is intricate in its design and hosts a plethora of colors. The coral is a solid, nurturing foundation that supports many sea animals. It reminds you of the people in your life and the way you interact with them each day. They are unique and supportive like the coral.

Cougar (Mountain Lion, Puma)

Traits: Cougar symbolizes speed, strength, and knowing when to be aggressive and when to be gentle. Cougar can make giant leaps (over forty feet) and is a fast and powerful hunter. It helps you make the best use of your own power and avoid misusing it. It symbolizes a transformation is about to take place in your life. You will need to move quickly to claim the power presenting itself to you. Cougar prefers solitude and is a reminder to take time for yourself to stay in balance.

Talents: Agility, assertion, assertiveness, balance, courageous, cunning, decisiveness, doesn't hesitate, foresight, freedom from guilt, intention, leadership, loyal, powerful, responsible, self-confidence, speed, stealth, strength, takes advantage of opportunities, takes charge

Challenges: Aggression, belligerent, brutal, cruel, misuse of power, ruthless, territorial, unfeeling, violent

Element(s): Earth

Primary Color(s): Brown

Appearances: When cougar appears, it means to be very decisive right now. It's not a time to be wishy-washy. Make a decision and stick by it. Stay strong, don't procrastinate, and be clear in what must happen in the situation. Handle it with courage and determination. Have faith that you will achieve the desired results. Cougar lets you know that some people may not like your take-charge attitude and will criticize what you're doing. The best way to resolve this situation is to get that person more involved, give them more responsibility, and take their opinion to heart. They may feel like prey when they should feel like an accomplice. Cougar reminds you that others don't have to follow you if they don't want to. It's their choice, so don't insist. Cougar means to own up to and learn from your mistakes. Don't let others hold you back from taking on challenging situations. You know how to be in charge of your own life, so do what you need to do but don't hurt others along the way.

Assists When: Cougar can help you make decisions when you feel torn and unsure of what to do. It gives you strength and patience during hard times and helps you see how to handle yourself with grace. If you're doing too much, cougar can teach you balance. Cougar can boost your confidence if you have to head up a meeting or present any information in a public venue, or if you're just feeling down about yourself. If you need to take over in any situation, cougar gives you the strength and determination to turn the situation around so it is successful. Cougar can help you defend yourself from the attack of others who may disagree with your policies. Be strong but don't back down. Cougar reminds you that being a superb leader means you always speak the truth, believe in what you are doing, respect others, and have the courage to see things through to the end.

Frequency: Cougar energy ripples and leaps, yet moves steadily forward. It sounds like the soft padding of feet across the floor but can quickly rise in pitch and tone to a wild, monstrous scream. It is hot and pulses in waves.

See Also: Black Panther, Cheetah, Jaguar, Lion, Tiger

Imagine…

You're hiking up a steep mountain. The air is getting thinner, and you're starting to become winded. The path is in the open and you can see quite far ahead. This section is rocky and rough, making you pay attention to where you're stepping so you don't fall. Suddenly you hear a loud roar. Looking up, you see a mountain lion standing on the edge of a large rock formation about a half of a mile in the distance. You stop and stare. Again it calls out. Suddenly two cubs bound up toward the mountain lion. They bat at each other with their paws and pounce on their mother. She licks them and lies down to play with them for a moment. You're filled with the energy of their love for one another. The mother stands up, looks right at you, and then leads her cubs away. You decide you've had enough hiking for one day and head back down the mountain, leaving mother and babies to enjoy the rest of their day.

Coyote

Traits: Coyote symbolizes that there is truth behind pandemonium and illusion; you just have to seek it out. Coyote is a playful animal when it's interacting with other coyotes. It lives in close-knit family groups. Coyote is adaptable to changes in its environment. It is a very vocal communicator and the howl of a solitary coyote is distinctive. Coyote is often thought of as a trickster or a joker, but it is a survivor, as are you.

Talents: Adaptable, balance, clever, communication skills, complicated, cooperative, crafty, creative, cunning, enlightenment, foolish, instinctual, inventive, playful, resourceful, sense of humor, serious, trickery, trust, truth, wisdom

Challenges: Aggressive, can become reclusive and dark, deceptive, lazy, weakness

Element(s): Earth

Primary Color(s): Gray, red

Appearances: When coyote appears, it means you need to laugh more. If you're stressed out and taking everything too seriously, try to lighten up a bit. It also indicates trickery, a joker, and being able to laugh at your own mistakes. You don't like for people to get too close to you. If they do, you are cautious until you feel they are trustworthy. Yet, you don't put on airs with others. They either like you for yourself or they don't. Like the coyote, people may feel that you're hard to understand because you tend to see humor in difficult situations. Coyote enjoys games, loves practical jokes, and is a reminder that you should play more. It means you're clever and can often find easy ways to skirt around difficult situations. Life isn't a struggle unless you make it so. Coyote reminds you that you don't have to thrash your way through life but can move through it with stealth and cunning.

Assists When: Coyote means that there are lessons to be learned in everything that you do. If you look for those lessons and actually learn from them, then your life will be easier. If you're having a hard time finding humor in situations, look to coyote for assistance. Coyote can enhance your verbal skills so you speak effectively, are engaging, and add humor to what you say. If you're bored, stuck in a rut, or can't find motivation, take coyote's advice and do something fun that makes you happy. If you do something you enjoy, that oftentimes can shake you out of the rut you've been stuck in. If you're struggling, coyote can help you see a clear path to get out of difficulties. Coyote means to never think in absolute certainties. Coyote warns not to make a simple task overcomplicated. The way to accomplishment is often achieved by taking a simple path. Be flexible, adaptable, and make small adjustments when life doesn't go as expected. Coyote encourages you to look at the positive instead of the negative, to live fully in the moment, never take anything for granted, and appreciate the joy in your life.

Frequency: Coyote's energy sounds like its howl. It is a long, low tone that spikes to a higher pitch. It feels like a chill running through you, an increased awareness of the night, and a giggle that wants to burst forth from you.

See Also: Wolf

Imagine...

Night has fallen and it's cold outside. You've built a fire in the fireplace but need to bring in more wood. You go out to the woodshed by your back door and have picked up a couple of pieces when you hear a snarl behind you. Slowly you turn. Standing in front of you is a very large coyote. Its teeth are bared, and your breath hitches. You take a step away when suddenly the coyote leaps at you, knocking you to the ground. Flat on your back, the wood scattered, you look up into its eyes. It's panting now, drool dripping on your face. It lowers its head, touching its nose to yours, and then begins to lick you all over your face. You laugh, reach up, and rub its neck and shoulders. It climbs off of you and sits beside you. When you sit up, you rub its coarse fur for a few more moments, scratching along the top of its back. When you stand, the coyote licks your hand then runs away, back into the forest.

Crab (Crayfish, Lobster)

Traits: Crab symbolizes rejuvenation and transformation. It is able to regrow any lost appendages during its molting/shedding stage. Lobsters will even cut off their own appendage if they feel threatened. Crab symbolizes getting in touch with your deep emotions in order to find your way to enlightenment, rejuvenation, and transformation.

Talents: Abundance, coordination, discovery, holding, molting, nobility, protection, pure emotions, regeneration, rejuvenation, resolution, restraint, scavenging, sensuous movement, simplicity, strength, strong character, strong grip, temperance, transformation

Challenges: Aggressive, backpedaling, defensive, feels emotions too deeply which causes excessive stress, indecisive

Element(s): Water

Primary Color(s): Red

Appearances: When crab appears, it means you're about to experience rejuvenation, regeneration, and transformation. Just as the crab grows within its shell and then molts if off, prepare to enter a cycle of spiritual, mental, or physical cleansing that will result in a complete renewal in some area of your life. This is a time of emotional growth as well. You may connect deeply with your intuition and healing abilities and experience more emotional depth and understanding of yourself. Crab is a scavenger, which reminds you to analyze bits and pieces to come to a greater understanding of the whole. To crab, self-preservation is crucial. Make sure you're looking out for yourself at this time. If you're feeling unsafe, take a self-defense class, get a new alarm system in your house, or do anything you need to do in order to feel protected. You're in self-preservation mode, but you also have to be patient to see how developments occur. That said, crab also warns not to let fear rule you and keep you from experiencing fun and happiness in your life. You should be concerned with taking care of yourself and your family, but don't wall yourself behind locked doors just because you think something *might* happen to you. Allow yourself to experience something grand and amazing!

Assists When: Crab can help you feel more protected. Just as it has a hard, protective outer shell, it can lend this feeling to you. If you need to hold on to something, ask crab to help you with its strong claws. If you're feeling held back, then ask it to show you what is holding you back so you can let it go and free yourself. Sometimes you can purposefully hold yourself back from reaching your goals without realizing you're doing it. If you find yourself in a situation that's not good for you, lobster and crayfish give you their ability to move backward, out of the situation, at a quick rate of speed.

Frequency: Crab energy feels like you're standing in the ocean as the tide is going out. Water swirls around you, pulls you toward the ocean's depths but you stand firm. It sounds like a soft scratching sound with a *tink, tink, tink* chime mixed in.

Imagine...

You're down by the creek, goofing off, when you see a crayfish scooting backward along the bottom of the creek bed. Barefoot, you walk into the water and stop near the crayfish. Slowly you put your hand into the water, sneaking up behind it. Then you quickly snatch it, lifting it out of the water. You hold it in your hand as its antennae move to and fro and its little pinchers grab at your fingers. You're careful not to let it pinch you, as you stroke your finger down its back. You feel the hardness of its exoskeleton and the softness of the uropods at the end of its tail. Its legs are wiggling across your palm as it tries to move backward. You place it back into the water and then release it. This time when it moves backward, it quickly hides behind a rock.

Cricket

Traits: Cricket symbolizes incredible good luck. With its long legs and enlarged thighs, cricket has tremendous jumping power. It's a common myth that cricket chirps by rubbing its legs together. The sound is made by the wings. At the base of the front wing is a ridged vein and the upper part is hardened, the papery parts inside will amplify the sound. To chirp, the cricket raises its front wings and rubs the hardened upper part across the ridged vein. Some crickets have hind wings that are used for flight, but most species are flightless.

Talents: Always on the go, communication, contentment, enhanced intuition, happy, expert timing, initiative, intelligence, introspection, many varied interests, musically inclined, power in your own voice, protection, quantum leaps, song, spiritual energy, vibrations

Challenges: Bothered by minor things that don't phase most people, have a hard time staying in one place, overly independent

Element(s): Earth

Primary Color(s): Black, gray, green

Appearances: When cricket appears, it means that you are incredibly lucky. Everything seems to always go your way, and you're always in the right place at the right time. Cricket also means you are aligning to higher vibrational energy on a regular basis and use your inner song to enhance your energy. Cricket means that you're coming into your own, aligning with your inner self, and making great progress in understanding your spiritual path. Embrace your intuition because you're more accurate than you realize. Make sure you're grounded and balanced when doing intuitive work. Believe in yourself and the impressions you're receiving. Cricket means singing even in the darkest of times. Cricket's song can bring you out of darkness and into the light. Cricket also means that now is the time to let go of any emotional baggage weighing you down. Release the past to embrace the future. Crickets are thought to mean you're going to have some type of financial windfall. It's considered bad luck to kill or put outside a cricket that chirps inside a house.

Assists When: Cricket is a symbol of protection. It watches out for you as you jump from one project or area of interest to another. Cricket can help you know when it's time to leave a situation, when to sing in a big, strong voice, and when to be introspective. If you're trying to improve your communication skills, call on cricket to lend its voice. It encourages you to speak with authority and in a commanding voice. Cricket lives by vibration, so if you're working on increasing your own personal frequency, invite cricket to stay by your side as you grow. Self-expression is an important part of your personal and spiritual growth, so don't be afraid to embrace new ideals and voice your own ideas about any projects you're working on. You're very busy, just like cricket, who can help you recognize when you need to slow down just a little bit to catch your breath. Then off you go again.

Frequency: Cricket's energy is bright and clear. It is the light of thousands of stars sparkling in the night sky. Its energy feels alive with hope, vibrancy, and joy. Warm, high-pitched, and musical, cricket's chirp will calm and relax you.

Imagine…

The chirping song of a cricket has you getting up out of your chair to look for it. You follow the sound toward your back door, and there you see a rather large cricket happily chirping away. That's when you realize that your back door isn't closed all of the way. You head toward it, but the cricket jumps ahead of you and out the door. As you go to shut the door, you hear an orchestra outside. You step out into the cool night air to listen, closing the door behind you. The night is alive with cricket's chirping song. You let its music wash over you, filling you with a relaxed sense of peace. When the music quiets down some, you thank the cricket for letting you know that your door was open and head back inside.

Deer

Traits: Deer symbolizes a gentle nature, sensitivity, unclear direction, and sacrifice. There is beauty and wonder in this nimble creature. Deer connects to the purpose of your soul. This is a time of awakening, of realizing your true self and the path you must take in this lifetime. Deer inspires you to be aware, focused, and observant. Its large eyes remind you that the eyes really are the windows to the soul. Look inside to see the wonder that is you.

Talents: Beauty, calmness, compassionate, delicate, empathic, gentle, graceful, gratitude, humble, intuitive, nurturing, peacefulness, senses danger quickly, sensitive, serenity, swift, tactful

Challenges: Fearful, inconsistent, nervous, overly sensitive, reclusive, shy, timid

Element(s): Earth

Primary Color(s): Brown, white

Appearances: Deer means you prefer a simple life filled with quiet and peace. You get overly stressed in hectic environments. Having to work in an overly competitive, hectic workplace can make you want to just run away and find a different type of work altogether. You'd rather stay in the background and out of the spotlight but your beauty, gracefulness, and compassionate nature pulls you to the forefront time and time again. Deer alerts you to danger, aggressive people, or negative situations, and it advises you to distance yourself from them. When deer crosses your path, it is a sign that you need to re-evaluate your feelings. Are you trusting your gut instincts like you should or are you ignoring them? Are you being overly sensitive, holding grudges, being judgmental, or too fearful? Now is the time to make changes if you're doing any of these things. Let deer show you a calm, peaceful path where you can turn any negatives into positives. Deer means there are opportunities coming your way and this time, instead of saying no like you usually do, say yes. Step out of your comfort zone to enjoy a phenomenal experience. Take time to truly live.

Assists When: Deer can help when you need to take action with focused movements, speed, and determination. If you've run into a roadblock, deer can inspire and motivate by showing you beauty and joy. You have an affinity for the outdoors. Travel and adventure appeal to you. Deer can help you enjoy these things on a deeper level. It can show you the greener pastures and help you to find the gifts within you. If you're having trouble with stress or are a worrywart, deer can help you find calmness and peace. If you tend to make mountains out of molehills, deer can help you keep things simple. Deer is a reminder that recognizing and living the simple truth in your soul is the purpose of your being. In this purpose you must be strong and true. Live, love, and laugh with humble gratitude for all that is.

Frequency: Deer's energy is powerful, still, and strong. It feels like bands that ground you to the earth, yet they can spring free at any second, sending you airborne as you leap from place to place. It sounds like silence, vast in its enormity.

See Also: Jackalope, White Stag

Imagine…

It's dusk, and you're driving home from work when a deer wanders out into the road a ways in front of you. It pauses in the road. You stop, turning on your hazard lights, and wait for the deer to move across the road. Instead it walks toward your car, caught up in the brightness of your headlights. You turn on the low beams and wait. The deer doesn't move, just stands there watching you. Suddenly it leaps across the road. You start moving forward when you notice movement off to the side, so you stop again. In wonder you watch as deer after deer leap across the road. Their beauty and grace fill you with a sense of awe. You count eight in all. Just when you think the coast is clear, you see a massive buck walking majestically toward the road. You can't believe the power and strength radiating from its noble presence. It looks toward you and then walks across the road, disappearing into the woods on the other side.

Dolphin (Porpoise)

Traits: Dolphin symbolizes curiosity, mindfulness, meditation, and enlightenment. Dolphin can play by holding itself upright and scooting across the water, but it can also dive into the depths of the ocean. Dolphin shows you both the fun and depth of any situation. It encourages you to look for meaning in all you do because, by considering all aspects, you will become enlightened. Dolphin symbolizes freedom, balance, and harmony in all things. It is a very intelligent creature that knows how to enjoy life to the fullest.

Talents: Compassionate, emphatic, excellent communicator, excitable, graceful, happiness, intelligent, intuitive, musical, playful, social, telepathic

Challenges: Gullible, lazy, never taking things seriously, talkative

Element(s): Water

Primary Color(s): Gray, white

Appearances: Dolphin shows up when you need to lighten up and find the fun in your life. It appears when it's time for you to begin a quest to understand your own spiritual being and to find enlightenment. You're on a path and dolphin encourages you to look at every little thing along the way. Don't leave any stone unturned and crash through every wave until you can settle within yourself to be more mindful and calm. It means to pay special attention to your intuition. If you get an impression, don't blow it off as your wild imagination, instead, take it for what it is and own it. You're getting it for a reason, so don't dismiss it. Dolphin encourages you to be careful of the people around you. Are you hanging out with a good crowd or are you going to get into trouble with them? If you need to make changes, now is the time to do it. Dolphin means to get creative. Start a project, fill it with your feelings and emotions, unleashing the creativity within you and then display it for all to see. Dolphin helps you recover from emotional wounds by tapping into your healing abilities. Connect to your joy, your inner truth, and be empowered.

Assists When: You're bored and have nothing to do. Dolphin can help you find the fun in anything, even if you're doing chores. Dolphin encourages meditation or quiet time to think so you can find harmony and balance while connecting to your inner wisdom. If you're thinking about the past too much, let dolphin bring you back into the present to find meaning in the here and now instead of dwelling on the past. Dolphin can resolve conflicts you're having at work or in your personal life by helping you see all aspects of the situation through a calm perspective. It reminds you to breathe instead of drowning yourself. If your social life is nonexistent, dolphin can help you reconnect to your circle of friends. It encourages you to think, feel, and be smart about your choices so you can live in balance. Intelligence is boosted when dolphin is around, so it can help you do well in school or in situations when you need to make smart decisions.

Frequency: Dolphin's energy is smooth as silk. It feels like a light, silky fabric is wrapping around you in the breeze. It is warm as the ocean and bright with light. It is high pitched and echoes within your soul as it touches the deepest part of your core essence. It surges through you, gently rocking your body with its positive ebb and flow.

Imagine…

It's a beautiful summer day, so you decide to take your boat out. You're cruising across the ocean when you see a dolphin jump out of the water. It jumps again, racing along with the boat but now it is accompanied by what must be a hundred friends. You slow a bit and you enjoy the show as they leap into the air, disappear, and then leap again. You look over the side and can see them in the water, swimming fast, twisting and turning as they speed along. The boat is surrounded by dolphins. You feel their delight and can't help but laugh out loud as their happiness washes over you. Just as suddenly as they appeared, they turn away, still jumping for joy but moving away from the boat and out into the open water. It's an experience you'll never forget.

Dove

Traits: Dove symbolizes peace, love, and devotion. The white dove symbolizes purity, surrender, and hope. Doves mate for life and both parents work together to build the nest and raise the young. Both parents also provide crop milk to the baby birds. Unlike birds of prey, dove doesn't attack other birds. Its diet consists of seeds and nuts. Doves are found all around the earth.

Talents: Calmness, devotion, family, friendly, gentle, harmony, innocence, joyful, longevity, loving, optimistic, peaceful, prophetic, purity, quick learner, sacredness, soul connection, spiritual

Challenges: Emotionally out of balance, gullible, martyr, naïveté, too trusting, unfocused

Element(s): Air, earth

Primary Color(s): Gray, white, and a wide variety of other colors

Appearances: Dove is a reminder to be peaceful and calm. If you've been out of sorts, fighting with someone else, or just on edge, dove can help you find balance and calm down. It is a sign to embrace those you love. Make sure they know how you feel about them. If you've been taking someone for granted, show your love and appreciation to them in a grand way. Let them know how you feel. Dove also means to make amends with anyone you've been arguing with or haven't spoken to in a long time due to a misunderstanding. Be the bigger person, the peacemaker, and let go of the past hurts so you can lift the weight of the situation from your shoulders. Dove encourages you to eat healthy foods and to cleanse, both physically and spiritually. Dove means to be hopeful for the best positive solution to any problem you encounter. You are the epitome of love and positivity. All will be made right within your world if you embrace dove's messages.

Assists When: Dove often shows up when you're feeling like all is lost, if a loved one has passed away, or if you've ended a relationship. It means you should take a minute, really look at and give respect to the situation, and then let your emotions move deeply within you. Give your love to those you've lost and know that some part of them will always be with you. Face your own future with optimism and hope. It's difficult to let people go, but there comes a time when it has to be done. When this time comes in your life, even if it's not a death but a breakup (which can feel like a death), let the peacefulness in your soul guide your actions so you can move forward in harmony and with joyful intent. Dove is a sign of new beginnings and can help you with yours. Dove also means that you may feel as if you don't get the same amount of love and devotion in return for the abundance of it you give out. Know that all is well, you're just better at showing how you feel than other people. Look at the little things they do and say to understand how much you mean to them.

Frequency: Dove's energy feels like a cool breeze in the middle of a scorching hot day. It immediately refreshes you. It is a low mournful sound in the fog of an early autumn morning. It vibrates with high intensity like a million clicking sounds blurred into one. It is calm, peaceful, and filled with the energy of love.

Imagine…

You are visiting an aviary filled with many different types of birds. You sit down on a bench and are enjoying the sounds of the different calls, songs, and the flutter of wings. A white dove flies down from the top of a tree and lands on the bench beside you. It sings a few notes of a song and steps closer. You reach out your hand just to see what will happen. The bird moves around your hand but hops up on your knee, observing you as much as you're observing it. You're filled with strong feelings of love and peace. The bird sits with you for a while, and you tentatively reach out to touch its wings. It hops over to your other knee but still doesn't fly away. As you think of what this dove's message is to you, a slight wind picks up and you feel a sense of calmness settle over you. Moments later, the dove flies away but you're forever touched by its message of hope.

Dragonfly (Damselfly)

Traits: Dragonfly and damselfly symbolize lightness of being, change, and adaptability. Damselfly is lighter in build than dragonfly and tends to fold its wings close to its body when resting, whereas dragonfly keeps its wings out at rest. Damselfly has a weaker, fluttery flight pattern instead of the strong flight of dragonfly. Both insects are predators. For several years, they live as nymphs in freshwater before emerging from the water during their last molt to become the winged adult.

Talents: Adaptability, beautiful, change, colorful, emotional, exciting, illusion, intelligent, intuitive, iridescent, mysterious, passionate, quiet strength, showy, transformation, versatility

Challenges: Emotional imbalance, erratic, flighty, inconsistent, irrational, overly aggressive, unpredictable behavior

Element(s): Air, water

Primary Color(s): Blue, green, red, yellow

Appearances: When dragonfly or damselfly appears, it is a sign to tap into your intellect and emotions. You can seem unpredictable at times, but this is what gives you an edge in competition. You're a game changer—a passionate person wrapped in a beautiful iridescent package. People often don't see past your beauty to the depth within and that's when you're able to surpass their expectations. Dragonfly means to show off your abilities and strive for success in every aspect of your life. Dragonfly means you need to add lightness to your life. Don't get bogged down in the heaviness of the world but be the light, airy being that shines in a multitude of colors. To be light means to be free and to be free means to be connected to the wisdom of the universe. Find joy and happiness in the world around you. See the goodness and light within others and encourage them to do the same. Dragonfly means to find balance, harmony, and meaning. Life can feel like an illusion but you can make your own brilliance shine into reality.

Assists When: Dragonfly helps you make a good impression. If you're managing an event that needs to be theatrical and magnificent, call on dragonfly's power of illusion.

If you're trying to achieve a goal, dragonfly encourages you to use your impressive intelligence and your accurate intuition to get there in record time. Passion comes naturally to the dragonfly, but sometimes you have a hard time showing it to others. Instead of bottling it up inside, let dragonfly set it free. Once it's soaring through the sky, the beauty and mystery within will give you the power to transform. Dragonfly also helps when you're going through a personal or spiritual transformation. Becoming enlightened is a key element of dragonfly. It encourages you to find that which will help you grow into a higher place along your spiritual path.

Frequency: Dragonfly's energy flitters and flutters. It moves quickly and stops often only to take flight again. It is powerful and engaging and feels like a bubble is about to burst inside of you. It fills you with strength, purity, and the knowledge that you can do anything you set out to do. It sounds like a faint, high-pitched buzz.

Imagine…

You're working outside, tending to your yard, when a green dragonfly lands on your arm. You consider the beauty of its wings, its slim body, and big eyes. It stays put for a minute then takes off again. A while later, another one lands on the end of your rake. You're filled with delight but don't dare move so you can observe it. You feel excited that they've chosen to connect with you and now find yourself looking for them. Later, while driving to the store, you're at a stoplight and feel as if you're being watched. You look out of the driver's side window and see a baby red dragonfly sitting on the glass peering in at you. You smile broadly and say, *Hi, little guy!* Just as the light changes color it flies away. You feel a lightness within your soul and a deep connection with dragonfly energy.

Eagle

Traits: Eagle symbolizes it's time to fly high and to lead with vision and precision. This exceptionally large predator is a symbol of freedom, justice, and independence. A bald eagle can see small prey from two miles away and can dive after that prey at rates of up to two hundred miles per hour. Eagle can show you how to use your innate power and speed to accomplish the goals you've set for yourself. Eagle symbolizes liberation from being held back. It encourages you to fly high.

Talents: Constructive, determination, excellent vision, freedom, independence, long-range views, majestic, natural leader, noble, perfect timing, power, precise actions, sees the big picture, speed, spirituality

Challenges: Aggressive, controlling, opportunist, predator, ruthless, self-centered, short-tempered

Element(s): Air, water

Primary Color(s): Brown, white, yellow

Appearances: When eagle appears, it means that you are not limited in any way, so do not let anything hold you back. You are a free spirit who needs to take time to connect with your own spiritual nature. There is vision, focus, and power within you. Now is the time to let it fly free into the world. You see the bigger picture and the long-term goals and strive with determination to control your path and meet each opportunity with action and skill. When eagle shows up, it means you are protected or you are going to be protective of someone. This could be physical or emotional protection or simply a compassionate shoulder. You command authority wherever you go and can present an imposing presence for those who don't know you. For those who do, they know you are an inspiration and a guardian and have a deep sense of community pride. You are a natural leader that others respect and follow. Eagle is a reminder that your keen insight will be needed in the near future.

Assists When: You are stuck in a rut of the mundane. Eagle pushes you out of the nest of complacency while giving you the inspiration to achieve your goals. Eagle energizes, gives you an expanded view of situations so you can see what direction you should take, and encourages you to soar to great heights. If you've been too concerned with making money or other materialistic ideals, eagle can help you look to the spiritual and the Divine for inspiration. Eagle shows up during times of change, challenge, or struggles to help you see the light at the end of the tunnel and take advantage of opportunities coming your way. Eagle keeps you focused instead of wasting time and energy on things that aren't important. Eagle is a reminder that you can do too much for others; sometimes it's better to help them learn to stand on their own two feet instead of holding them up.

Frequency: Eagle's energy is powerful and strong. It beats in a steady, quickly pounding rhythm, pushing through the air and creating a swirling flow in its wake. It sounds like the rolling beat of a bass drum.

See Also: Griffin, Hippogriff

Imagine …

The wind is blowing strong as if a storm is approaching. You're walking along a path at the edge of a lake, getting your exercise before the rain sets in. Looking up, you see a bald eagle circling over the lake. You watch its majestic flight. You feel the first drops of rain, so you hurry along. Up ahead there is a bench and sitting on the back of it is the eagle. It's facing the lake, its body proud and strong. You slow down, the rain forgotten as you take in the majestic sight. The eagle turns its head and stares at you. You're overcome with a sense of powerful independence. You feel protected and safe even though an enormous bird of prey is mere feet away, watching your every move. The wind gusts down, pushing against you as the eagle looks away, stretches its wings, and takes off, flying high up above the lake. You watch it fly higher and higher until it's out of sight. You realize that it's raining hard now and you're completely soaked, but it doesn't bother you. Joyful with the encounter, you sprint around the lake and back home.

Earthworm

Traits: Earthworm symbolizes that little things mean a lot. Earthworm may be small, but it can reshape the soil. Earthworm doesn't have lungs, so it breathes through its skin. Its whole body is its digestive system, it's 90 percent water, and it lives underground. It takes its nourishment from the earth and gives nourishment back in the form of potassium and nitrogen into the soil. Earthworm is the earth's gardener, cleansing and nurturing to inspire new growth and renewal.

Talents: A deep thinker, cleansing, compassion, completing one task before beginning a new one, detail-orientated, examination, gardening, growth, hopeful, intense emotions, persistent, revitalization, sensitive to vibration, sincerity, unassuming

Challenges: Coldness, hiding in the dark, inhibitions, lack of aspiration, reclusive, uncaring, vulnerable, withdrawn

Element(s): Earth

Primary Color(s): Brown, red

Appearances: When earthworm appears, it means that you have to take time to look at the little things in your life. Scrutinize and absorb the minute details—turn them over and work them out as if you were tending a garden. Only in working through a situation can you bring it to a successful resolution. Cultivating and tending your life with love, joy, and happiness allows for new growth. You may feel that the efforts you're making are small and inconsequential, but your actions will reshape your environment. Earthworm means you need to dig deep and move slowly and methodically in order to make substantial, lasting progress. You are persistent in your attention to detail. A natural caretaker, you find joy in helping other people and animals, and you often fight for causes that will positively impact the environment. Earthworm encourages you to clean house both physically and emotionally, letting go of anything clogging up your system. Earthworm warns against people who may try to take advantage of you, so be wary of anyone who suddenly has a keen interest in you and what you're doing.

Assists When: If you're looking for meaning in any situation or need to understand your own feelings, earthworm helps you look deep within to find the answers you seek. Earthworm helps you be more patient with those around you. If you're studying a new topic, it can encourage you to dig deeply into the subject matter. It can keep you focused and on track, help you to see the details, and make you more sensitive to your own frequency and the frequency of others. Earthworm is tireless in its work and can give you an energy boost when you need one. It is a reminder that sometimes you have to get dirty to bring about new growth. Earthworm can assist you when you're working with other animals because it gives you patience, the ability to see the smallest changes in demeanor, and the empathic ability to connect with them.

Frequency: Earthworm's energy is cool and slick. It feels like a heavy silence wrapped around you, but it's not suffocating. It is like a warm blanket on a cold winter's day. Earthworm sounds like a low rattling that resonates through you.

Imagine...

You're making a flower bed, so you're digging in the soil, prepping it for the plants you've bought to put there. You're excited about this project because you can't wait to see them bloom in vibrant colors. As you dig, you're thinking about things going on in your life when you notice a large earthworm moving along the top of the dirt. You pick it up, and it wiggles around in your hand. Since you're already in a contemplative mood, you consider this small creature. It feels cool to the touch, sort of rubbery and slick. Then it seems to curl into your palm, settling down as you hold it. You feel its energy resonating up your arm. It is vulnerable lying in your hand and you are inspired to protect it. You move over to a bush close by your flower bed and dig a little hole. Placing the earthworm inside, you lightly cover the hole with dirt so the earthworm doesn't dry out. You're happy that you took a moment to notice the little things in life.

Eel

Traits: Eel symbolizes transformation, mystery, disguise, and hiding. Eel is excellent at using camouflage to protect itself from predators. Eel is fast and swims by moving its body side to side. The electric eel can deliver a six-hundred-volt shock to stun its prey. Eel tends to have poor eyesight and relies on its radarlike ability to seek out food. During the day, it burrows into the mud and rests until it's ready to hunt again.

Talents: Attractiveness, engaging relationships, flexible, intimacy, nocturnal, observation, sensuality, vitality

Challenges: Elusive, guarded, overly cautious, reclusive, slippery

Element(s): Water

Primary Color(s): Brown. Moray eels come in a wide variety of colors and patterns.

Appearances: When eel appears, it means you are in hiding or need to take a step back into the shadows to regroup. You are about to embark on a journey. This may be traveling in the physical world or a spiritual journey of the soul. Either of these voyages will result in a dramatic transformation within you on an emotional or spiritual level. You are filled with energy. Some may even call you electrifying. People are attracted to you because of your positive energy. You adapt to new situations easily, have an inner defense mechanism that you supercharge when you feel threatened, and are able to slip away unnoticed if you so choose. Eel prefers hunting at night. If you're looking for a new opportunity—whether a new relationship, career choice, or business venture—you're most likely to encounter it after dark. Eel reminds you to rest instead of burning the candle at both ends.

Assists When: You need to observe a situation without being part of it. Eel can help you dig out of the mud of circumstances that wears on your energy and make the changes needed to leave it behind. It encourages you to keep quiet, slip away, and think instead of being too vocal. Eel can give an electric charge to your love life. It can help you find new relationships and add spark to old ones. Eel lives deep within the water. It can help you develop a deeper understanding of yourself and those around you. Others may not realize you are a deep thinker or the depth of your knowledge until you begin to open up to them. Eel warns that you can appear aloof, standoffish, and too guarded. Sometimes you have to let your barriers down in order to get to know others better and to build relationships. You tend to prefer escaping instead of standing up for yourself, but if you're forced to fight you shock your opponents with your fierceness.

Frequency: Eel's energy is a soft, undulating, whisper of movement floating around you. It is strong and solid and emits great power through electrical surges. It sounds like a sharp, high-pitched, loud blast that retreats to silence before surging again.

Imagine…

You're scuba diving in the ocean along a coral reef when you notice a large overhanging piece of coral. Underneath you see a giant moray eel swimming along the edge. Its body is undulating side to side as it moves forward. You swim alongside, a safe distance away, because this is the first large eel you've seen. Its coloring is extraordinary—black with yellow spots all over it. The eel swims toward you and opens its mouth. That's when you see its razor sharp, needlelike teeth. You wait, trying not to move, so that it swims away. You know that eels can't see very well, so you don't want to give it any reason to bite at you. It quickly loses interest and swims in the other direction. You're thrilled with your first eel sighting.

Elephant

Traits: Elephant symbolizes inner strength, a wide range of emotions, and the physical ability to overcome obstacles. Elephant lives in a herd led by the oldest female. It is loyal to the other members of the herd, especially newborns, and all take part in teaching, loving, and nurturing the young. Each one would risk its life to protect another family member. Elephant has an incredible memory and even if separated for years, it will still remember another elephant it has previously known. Elephant grieves and can shed tears, just like we do.

Talents: Commitment, communication, confidence, connected to ancient wisdom, deep emotions, gentleness, inner strength, intelligence, joyful, keen senses, longevity, loving nature, loyal, patient, physical strength, social, telepathic, tough exterior, trusting

Challenges: Jealous, overly sensitive, rage, revengeful, stubborn

Element(s): Earth, water

Primary Color(s): Gray

Appearances: When elephant appears, it means you need to be more communicative and committed to your personal relationships. Take the time to really listen to what others are saying. What feelings hide beneath their words? Be gentle in nature, intelligent in your choices, and willing to be deeply dedicated to the person. Once you truly listen, you will develop a deep understanding of one another. Don't assume the people you care about know how you feel. Tell them, show them, and value their presence in your life. Elephant means to push obstacles out of the way; don't let anything hold you back from what you want to achieve. Elephant tends to only look forward, which is a sign not to have a narrow focus but instead look all around you and be aware of your environment. Elephant gives you its determination—nothing can stop you from achieving your desires. You push past obstacles that stop others in their tracks.

Assists When: Elephant connects with ancient wisdom, which can help you advance your spiritual growth. If you're venturing down a path of spiritual enlightenment, elephant is the perfect animal to guide you. Elephant's physical strength can help push obstacles out of your way, and its inner strength can see you through difficult times.

Elephant helps when you need to be silent in your approach. It's a heavy animal, but it walks with graceful movements and little noise. If you're unsure about sharing your emotions or how to express yourself, elephant can show you the right way to move forward. If you've taken to a new source of study, elephant can help you understand and remember the information through its high intelligence. Elephant encourages you to dig up memories from your past, look at them with an impartial viewpoint, and then release them. Holding on to some memories can hold you back from future growth. Take time to enjoy water activities; it is essential to your survival.

Frequency: Elephant's energy is wise and peaceful. It feels as if you're standing on the edge of a cliff, looking out across vast tundra, secure in the knowledge that all is as it should be. It feels like the joy of an unexpected hug—warm, tight, and filled with love. It sounds like elephant's trumpeting, a short, high-pitched call to come home.

Imagine...

You take a trip to a safari park where all types of wild animals native to Africa live in a natural, open environment. As you drive through the park, you see the animals off to the sides. You see several large elephants walking toward the road. You stop and wait for them to cross. There are mothers with babies, who seem to be dancing as they try to keep up, swinging their trunks side to side and shaking their heads as they hurry along. Then, an extremely large elephant brings up the rear. It walks up to your car and looks in the window. You don't know what to expect, but you are also in awe at how close you are to this wild creature. You place your palm flat against the window. The elephant touches the glass opposite of your hand with the tip of its trunk, then turns and lumbers away.

Firefly (Lightning Bug)

Traits: Firefly symbolizes light in the darkness and the mystery and magic of life. At twilight, these winged beetles produce bioluminescence to attract prey or mates. This light can be yellow, green, or pale red. Even firefly larvae emit light and are known as glowworms. Firefly is nocturnal, preferring night to daylight. Firefly doesn't eat a lot, which means to take only what you need. Don't be wasteful.

Talents: Aspirations, attraction, awakening, cheerful, clarity, creative, efficient, encouraging, energetic, guiding light, happiness, hopeful, illumination, insightful, inspiration, joy, majestic, noble, optimistic, patience, shines light on new ideas, unassuming

Challenges: Burns self out due to overwork, flighty, idealistic

Element(s): Air, earth

Primary Color(s): Black, orange, yellow

Appearances: Firefly gives you hope when all seems dark. It lights your way as you travel life's pathways. Firefly means that while you may seem plain in the daytime, when you glow, you radiate your inner light for all to see. If one were to look closely at you, they would see this light in your eyes, but not everyone will take the time. Your inner beauty is a wondrous sight to behold. Your kind and caring nature can light the way for anyone who is lost or in need of guidance. For this reason, you're often the shoulder someone cries on and are the first to give a hug even if the person says they're fine. You see deeply and can tell they're going through something and need a hug. Firefly profoundly speaks to our spirit, the essence inside our bodies, inviting it to attract the light of other similarly minded people. Firefly's light doesn't contain heat, which is a sign to take life at a regular pace instead of going too fast and burning out too soon. Firefly encourages you to live a simple life.

Assists When: You need self-illumination to see your core being as you truly are in spirit. Firefly means to light your inner fire, to be passionate in reaching your goals. Firefly helps you find the freedom within your core essence and allows you to let your spirit fly free upon the night. Firefly can lead the way when you're lost or following blindly along the wrong path. Its blinking light will grab your attention and draw you away from negativity and into the lightness of being. Firefly shows you that anything is possible if you only believe. Strong belief can enable you to manifest your deepest desires. Firefly can lead the way. It can bring you back to memories of the innocence of your childhood, allowing you to remember who you are and to become all that you're meant to be.

Frequency: Firefly's energy is bright and clear. It has a gentle pull as it draws you toward the knowledge deep within you. It flickers and glows, blinking with the wisdom of the universe. It sounds like the gentle strum of harp strings with the accompaniment of tinkling bells.

Imagine...

Night is falling, and you're sitting out on your porch enjoying the summer evening. A tiny spark of yellow light flashes in the yard. Moments later another spark happens. In a few minutes it seems as if your yard is twinkling with the light of the firefly. Remembering your childhood when you'd catch the insects and put them in a jar with holes on top, you wander out into your yard and catch one by cupping your hands around it. Peering into the space between your thumbs, you watch the firefly crawling around, blinking its light. You feel nostalgic about your youth. As you watch the firefly, you feel as if you're connecting to something much bigger than yourself. The essence of purity seems to be contained within that little blinking light. You think of yourself as a spiritual being and how your light shines into the world for all to see. You're like the firefly, bold and free. You open your hands. It crawls to the tip of your finger and then flies away.

Flamingo

Traits: Flamingo symbolizes social interaction, teamwork, and emotional understanding. An adult flamingo can grow four to five feet tall, which is a sign for you to reach for greater heights. Its pink color comes from the beta-carotene in the plankton and crustaceans it eats. That's why some may be very dark pink and others nearly white. Flamingo urges you to add seafood and vegetables rich in beta-carotene to your diet. The feathers under its wings are black, which means you keep any darkness and negativity you're going through hidden from view.

Talents: Balanced, beauty, charming, colorful, congenial, discernment, family oriented, graceful, leadership, lots of friends, organized, responsible, social, teamwork

Challenges: Dependent on others, hard to please, vanity

Element(s): Air, earth, water

Primary Color(s): Black, pink, white

Appearances: When flamingo appears, it is a sign for you to either become part of a team or a group with similar interests or participate in more social events. If you're too social, retreat for some alone time and steer clear of hectic events, especially if you're overreacting or becoming stressed out when in the company of others. Flamingo is often connected with psychometry. Your intuitive *knowing* from touching objects is an integral part of your life. If you're out of balance, this ability can be affected and your impressions may not be as clear. When flamingo eats, it dips its head upside down and scoops up a mouthful of mud and water. Its mouth is designed to siphon out the food. This is a sign that you should siphon out the important things in your life and discard any muck that is holding you down. Flamingo often sleeps or stands with one leg tucked up close to its body. Scientists believe it does this to conserve body heat due to the coldness of the water. This is a sign to conserve your energy and rest when you're fatigued instead of pushing yourself too hard.

Assists When: Flamingo helps you find balance. If you've been juggling a lot of things at once, flamingo suggests letting some of those things go so you can regain your sense of equilibrium. It's difficult to move forward when you're overwhelmed and out of balance. Flamingo means you need to delegate more instead of trying to do everything yourself. You're a great organizer but often take too much of a role instead of assigning duties. Find the balance so the job gets done without anyone, including you, being overloaded with work. When two flamingos touch beaks, their necks create a heart shape. This indicates that you do everything in life whole-heartedly and love with great depth. Flamingo can help you find relationships with another person who has those same qualities.

Frequency: Flamingo's energy vibrates from a low chirping sound to a high-pitched squawk. It moves quickly, rising and falling, pitching and undulating. It is invigorating and hot, and it feels like sparks dancing around you.

Imagine…

You're wandering around a zoo when you come across a large, shallow lagoon. It's filled with plant life, and along the edge, standing in the water and on some rocks, are lots of pink flamingos. Some are standing on one leg, their heads tucked beneath a wing, taking a nap. Others are holding their bills underneath the water, stirring up mud from the bottom. Their bills are moving rapidly, filtering the food from the mud. You lean on the railing to watch and from this position you see a small baby flamingo. It has gray down feathers and is sticking its beak into the water. Every time it does, it makes a squeaking sound. You notice the varying shades of pink within the group. All at once there is a bunch of squawking and you see two males acting aggressively toward each other. The air seems to vibrate with their energy but after a minute or two of disagreement, they move apart and go their separate ways. The disagreement is settled without grudges. This is a reminder to let go of grudges in your own life. You silently say *thank you* to the flamingos for the lesson and move on to the next exhibit.

Fly

Traits: Fly symbolizes change, growth, and persistence in reaching goals. Fly populations increase rapidly with the female laying up to five hundred eggs at a time. This is an indication that you're productive and can have great accomplishments in a short amount of time. Fly prefers disgusting meals and loves garbage and manure. This is a sign to keep your environment clean. Fly uses its antennae to smell and can fly up to forty-five miles per hour. This symbolizes your acute senses and ability to move quickly when necessary.

Talents: Abundance, adaptability, change, determination, excellent eyesight, flourishes in harsh circumstances, intuition, prosperity, resourceful, strong willpower, transformation

Challenges: Annoying, bigotry, intolerance, pestering, unfairness, unhygienic

Element(s): Air

Primary Color(s): Black

Appearances: When fly appears, it means you are letting small things irritate you. Instead of focusing on those little things, look at the bigger picture from a different perspective to see clearly. Fly means change is coming, and it will happen in an abrupt manner. You may be caught unaware, but your survival skills and ability to make quick decisions and take action will allow you to overcome any negativity to prosper. Fly never gives up. It keeps going after its goals regardless of how much of a pest it's making of itself. You have this same quality, so if you realize that you're annoying others, quickly change your course of action to ensure success without making enemies along the way.

Assists When: You need to look at a situation from a new perspective. Fly has two eyes, but within each eye there are more than four thousand smaller eyes. Can you imagine having more than eight thousand ways to look at a situation? The incredible eyesight of fly can help you see situations from multiple points of view all at the same time. This can give you great insight into people, projects, and situations where you need to see a broad range of possibilities. Fly can also help you see value in things that others consider trash.

You just might find treasure, so take the time to really look before passing judgment. If you've been looking down on yourself or if your self-esteem has taken a blow recently, fly encourages you to have a positive point of view instead of being negative about yourself. You have true value and must see it within yourself even if others don't appreciate the greatness in you.

Frequency: Fly energy moves very quickly, zooming to and fro, in a buzz of activity. It feels like you stepped into an electric current that zips and zings against your body, touching then vanishing in an instant. It feels alive and energizing, transforming you with positive charges. It sounds like fast-falling sleet bouncing off of a tin roof.

Imagine…

You're working at your computer when you hear a buzzing right near your ear. You swat at it and jerk your head away looking for the culprit. You see a house fly zipping around your work area. You really don't like to find a fly inside so you roll up a piece of paper to swat it. You get up to look around but can't find it. Giving up, you go back to your desk, sit down, and start to place your fingers on the keyboard. Sitting on the letter *I* is the fly. You think it's very strange that the fly is sitting on the letter *I*. Could there be a message it wants to deliver? You find your center and open your intuition to the fly. The first thing you hear is, *I want to go outside.* You send a message back, *Go to the door and I'll let you out.* The fly doesn't move, but you go to the door and wait. Moments later the fly is buzzing around you again, so you open the door and it flies outside. You settle down to work, glad that you looked at the situation from a different perspective.

Fox

Traits: Fox symbolizes family. It tends to live in small family groups, but some, like the arctic fox, tend to live solitary lives. Fox has a relatively small body but a very bushy tail, which makes it appear larger than it is. It also has partially retractable claws. Fox will crouch down and then leap up to pounce on its prey. The gray fox is one of two canine species that can climb trees. These qualities allow you to surprise opponents with your cunning. Fox prefers to avoid a fight, but it will defend itself if necessary. In business, fox can help you gather info and pounce quickly and with sharp precision.

Talents: Adaptable, balance, beauty, clever, cunning, excellent hearing, graceful, intuitive, keen observer, makes quick decisions, master of camouflage, often goes unnoticed, sly, strategic, sure-footed, swift, wise

Challenges: Dishonest, superficial, trickster

Element(s): Earth

Primary Color(s): Black, gray, red, silver, white

Appearances: When fox shows up, it means to spend more time with your family. Participate in family outings and activities and just quiet time with one another. Fox has incredible eyesight, which is a sign to watch what people do more than listening to what they say. Actions speak louder than words, and at this time you'll glean useful information through sight instead of sound. Fox means you should stay in the background unnoticed. Fox warns to be wary of people who don't have your best interest at heart. Are they being sly and cunning? Trying to trick you? Fox means to be alert to these qualities within yourself but to also look for them in others. They can be very revealing of the individual's true intent. You're a great problem solver, can intuit the intentions in others, and are unafraid to take risks.

Assists When: You want to stay out of sight and observe the activities of those around you. If you're traveling as a family, fox is a great animal to ask along to help keep you safe. If you find yourself in any kind of predicament that you need to get out of, fox's ability to slip away will aid you. Fox can help you restore order to a chaotic situation or, if necessary, allows you to outwit your opponents by confusing a situation so you can get out of it quickly. Fox is associated with moving between worlds and can help you see and hear Spirit. Fox's tail is used to help it balance as it's looking for prey. You can use this ability to help you gain balance in your life. Fox encourages you to be flexible. Look at all possibilities before making a decision. Fox means you are a smooth talker, easily communicating with others while hiding your true intention. This makes you a great detective, able to uncover information by making someone feel at ease and comfortable talking with you.

Frequency: Fox's energy beats to a slow and steady rhythm. It is interlaced with loud, high-pitched tones that sound like a scream. It is cool and crisp, and makes you feel like you just stepped into a dark, cold forest late at night.

Imagine...

Enjoying your vacation in the mountains, you decide to sit outside and read for a while. It's late in the afternoon, nearly evening. You lie down on the lounge chair and are soon involved in the story. You hear a noise that sounds like someone is walking through the bushes on the side of the house. You look up, and sitting in front of the plants is a red fox. Its features appear somewhat dainty, so you think it must be a female. You put the book on the table and sit up so you can get a better view. It still doesn't move, so you stand and slowly walk toward it. You stop about five feet away. It still watches you, as if it's waiting for something. So you softly whisper, *Hi there. I'm happy you could visit with me today. You're very beautiful.* The fox seems to smile, then leaps straight up in the air, startling you. It runs around you twice then bolts off into the woods. You just stand there awhile, absorbing what just happened, grateful for fox's gift.

Frog (Toad)

Traits: Frog symbolizes change, adaptability, and survival. Frog's front legs tuck close underneath its body. Its back legs are strong and powerful, enabling it to jump out of danger or to catch prey. This means you should keep important thoughts close to you. Don't blab your intentions to the world. If you feel threatened, get out of the way. Frog's skin protects it and is used for respiration. It is filled with glands that produce nasty tasting or toxic liquids to protect itself. This means that in stressful situations, breathe deeply and use your words to protect yourself from others.

Talents: Abundance, adaptable, change, clear communication, deep emotions, empathy, flexible, intuition, new beginnings, peaceful, practical, renewal, resourceful, sensitive, transformation

Challenges: Feelings hurt easily, inconsistent, jumps from one thing to another, overly emotional, overly shy, reclusive, too sensitive, unimaginative

Element(s): Earth, water

Primary Color(s): Brown, green

Appearances: When frog appears, it is a sign that you need to focus on one thing and do it well. Frog has a tendency to jump from one project to another. It warns that now is not the time for being unfocused, but instead you need to concentrate on the most important situation in your life and give it all of your attention. You may feel the need to walk away but don't. It's time to be serious, hold your ground, speak your mind, and let your emotions out. This is a time of cleansing, of transformation, and of future growth. Relationships can be restored at this time. New opportunities can be locked down. Don't let things slip away from you because you're not giving it the attention it deserves. Frog means you have a knack for giving great advice because you really listen to someone's problem before speaking. You tend to have close and meaningful relationships with others. You'll do anything for your family or close friends. You're the friend who is reliable, dependable, and who will always show up when called. You love with abandon and with your whole heart. There's no middle road with you. If you don't like something, you don't like it. You don't pretend or hide your feelings.

Assists When: You need to release negative emotions and doubt. If you're stuck in old ways of doing things, frog can help you see the benefit of putting new methods and procedures into place. Frog can help you create new beginnings for yourself. It encourages you to leap forward, leaving the past behind to embrace the future. Some things are out of your control. Frog enables you to see that you've done as much as possible in the situation and lets you know when it's time to move forward and away from it. Frog will help you adapt to any changes coming your way. It can help you dive into projects or jump out of the way. When speaking, frog helps you to move past an awkward, croaking attempt and be able to speak with a loud, bold, commanding presence. Frog helps you recognize new opportunities so you can jump on them to enhance your life.

Frequency: Frog's energy sounds like the splash of a stone skipping over a pond. It varies in intensity, jumping to and fro. It is cold, tingles, and feels like you've stuck your hand in a jar of jelly.

Imagine…

It's a hot summer day and you've got to clean around the shed. You start to go inside when a green tree frog jumps and lands on your shirt. Your first impulse is to knock it off, so you do. Startled, your heart is pounding, but you look for the frog on the ground. You find it in the grass, and, using your gloved hands, pick it up and take it to a tree behind the shed. Before you let it go, you feel its energy connecting with your own. You feel tingly all over and innately know that light must replace dark thoughts and feelings within you. You thank the frog for its message and let it climb onto the tree, noticing its wet, slick skin. It walks higher and sits on a small branch. Once you know it's safe, you get back to work.

Giraffe

Traits: Giraffe symbolizes making new connections, keeping your head up, and trusting your intuition. Giraffe's most prominent feature is its long neck, which allows it to see farther in the distance and to reach leaves in the treetops. This means you can foresee events before they happen and have the farsightedness to see outcomes when making plans. Giraffes live in groups, but they aren't tightly bonded as a family unit. This quality means you have an ever-changing flow of friends and acquaintances around you. Giraffes hum to each other at night, so you may need some background noise to help you sleep.

Talents: Balance, beauty, clever, communication, cooperative, discernment, elegance, farsightedness, foresight, friendly, gentle, graceful, holds self to a higher standard, intelligence, intuitive, mysterious, patience, perceptive, protective, resourceful, sees between realms, strong relationships, visionary

Challenges: Head in the clouds, impractical, naïveté

Element(s): Earth

Primary Color(s): Brown, white, yellow

Appearances: Giraffe appears when you're experiencing trying times. Your broad perspective allows you to see more than most. You look for the positive in every situation, are graceful, tactful, and patient that it will work out. You're not bothered by small things. You hold yourself to a higher standard, going the extra mile to help others or to accomplish your goals. You tend to have a pleasant personality and are tenacious when striving to reach new heights. People notice your inner and outer beauty. You tend to stand out in a crowd with your elegant grace of being. Giraffe means to listen to your intuition. You're a leader with a high level of awareness. Giraffe gives you a long-range plan by increasing your vision. You easily communicate with those around you with gentility and patience. Giraffe keeps you on your toes, always looking and planning for the future. You'll stick your neck out to help a friend or when you feel someone is suffering from injustice.

Assists When: You strive to reach greater heights of success. Giraffe's farsightedness means to connect with your intuition. Giraffe is particularly associated with clairvoyance. Giraffe helps you stay the course, remaining on your chosen path. When you deviate from this path, focus can be lost and it may seem as if your world has turned upside down. Giraffe can gently guide you back to where you should be. Giraffe can help you regain your composure, patience, and gentle nature if you've become frustrated, irritable, or are losing your temper frequently. In the wild, giraffe only needs thirty minutes of sleep a day. It rarely lies down and usually sleeps standing up due to predator threat. When it does lie down to sleep, it curls its neck over its back and will only sleep five minutes at a time. This means you need to get rest when you can, especially if you're working on a time-consuming project.

Frequency: Giraffe's energy is calm and peaceful. It sounds like a low hum reverberating on the wind. It feels warm to the touch, solid, and firm but tingles your fingertips with its power.

Imagine...

While visiting the local zoo, you make a point to seek out the giraffes. They're one of your favorite animals, and you like to spend time at their zoo habitat because you enjoy feeding them. When you get to the top viewing area, there isn't anyone else there and you see a mother giraffe and its baby on the far side of the field. You've purchased some lettuce leaves to feed them so you wait, but they don't seem to notice you. You decide to call out to them, and when you do, they look over, then come running. You feed them the lettuce and watch as they wrap their black tongues around the leaves then chew in a side-to-side circular motion. While you feed them, you scratch behind their ears and rub their necks and manes. You feel content and joyful in their elegant presence. All of your worries seem to melt away, and you're filled with a sense of your inner strength.

Gopher (Groundhog, Woodchuck)

Traits: Groundhog symbolizes digging in, looking deeply, and not accepting things as they seem on a superficial level. Groundhog knows there's more going on than it sees and it doesn't stop until it's gotten to the bottom of the matter—the truth, the essence. Groundhog's curved spine gives it incredible flexibility that increases its agility. This means that if you've been a couch potato, get up and move. It also means you shouldn't be rigid in situations. Have an open mind. Groundhog lives under the ground in burrows that can be five feet deep and thirty-five feet wide. This means you need to live in a roomy, open space as well so you do not feel confined.

Talents: Clairvoyance, cooperation, creative, digs deeply, expressive, friendly, predictions, social, team player

Challenges: Controlling, destructive, lack of discernment, negative, vicious

Element(s): Earth

Primary Color(s): Brown, gray

Appearances: When groundhog shows up, it means that it's time to get moving, be more ambitious, and really labor to achieve your goals. Sometimes getting what you want requires hard work. Groundhog moves more than seven hundred pounds of dirt to create its burrow, so to achieve results you'll need to be diligent, stay focused, and not give up. Once the goal is accomplished, you can rest and enjoy the fruits of your labor. Groundhog urges you to keep things clean. When your living environment is clean, energy flows better and there are fewer blockages around you. Groundhog is an indication that you need to take responsibility for the things you do (or don't do), the choices you make (especially if they affect someone else), and the things that you say. You are accountable for yourself, so don't play the blame game and put fault on others. Groundhog means you're drawn to spirituality, metaphysical topics, dream analysis, and developing your intuitive abilities. You enjoy studying new material on these topics, which in turn helps your own spiritual growth.

Assists When: You need to be prepared for upcoming events but don't know where to start. Groundhog can help you get organized, create a plan of action, and carry out that plan. It also helps you to stock up on items you may need in an emergency. If you feel like you're missing something on your list, ask groundhog to help you finalize it. Groundhog likes quiet, so if you're in a loud, noisy place and want to get away, it can help you seek out the silence in the midst of chaos. Moving? Ask groundhog to go along with you to find the perfect new home. Its sense of location is excellent. Its other senses are superb as well. Groundhog is sensitive to vibrations around it, which can help you recognize your own frequency, how to connect to it, and how to elevate it. Groundhog can help you understand your dreams.

Frequency: Groundhog energy sounds like a shrill chattering with a whistling, rising and falling pitch. It is an instant alertness, a warning to look around and make sure danger isn't at your door. It feels like you're on edge, constantly looking around until you reach safety, where it changes to a laid back feeling of contentment.

Imagine…

You decide to have a picnic outside, so you take your lunch and a blanket and sit under a tree. After you finish eating, you stretch out on the ground, enjoying the warm breeze. Suddenly you hear a shriek and look over toward the sound. You see a groundhog with its paws on the ground, but you can only see part of its body. You realize it must be coming out of its burrow and you must have startled it as much as its call startled you. Sitting up, you watch to see what it will do. It considers you for a moment then climbs out of the hole and wanders around, keeping an eye on you. A little while later it shrieks at you again and then disappears back into its burrow. You keep watching where it disappeared, and then you see its head peek up again to look at you. It disappears and peeks at you several more times, so you gather up your belongings and go back inside.

Grasshopper

Traits: Grasshopper symbolizes being a unique individual. There are eleven thousand species of grasshoppers, and each has its own individual song. The males sing to the females to attract their mate. This is a sign to you that there are many different ways to achieve the same goal, so find your own unique way of doing things. Grasshopper can jump twenty times the length of its body. This means you can't let your size hold you back from making great strides in your life. Grasshoppers are small but they eat sixteen times their weight every day. This is a warning to watch your diet so you don't overeat or to make sure you're consuming enough to maintain your health.

Talents: Individuality, ingenious, instinctive, intuitive, quick progress, uniqueness

Challenges: Destructive, lacks direction, unorganized, unstable

Element(s): Air, earth

Primary Color(s): Brown, green, orange, yellow

Appearances: Grasshopper appears when you're about to experience a dramatic positive change in your life. It urges you to leap at opportunities because they may have *once in a lifetime* potential. Trust your judgment and instincts to make great leaps forward. Your natural rhythm and pacing is on point. When needed, grasshopper uses its wings to fly toward quick progress. You can soar by trusting your decisions instead of second guessing. You're willing to go off the beaten path and to find uniqueness hidden in unconventionality. This is the part of your character that will open new doors to wondrous possibilities. Right now you have so many doors and windows opening all around you that you're unsure which way to jump. Take a moment to look around, trust your feelings, and take that leap. You'll be happy you did.

Assists When: You're stuck and need a new, unique approach. This can be a project at work or you might just be redecorating your home. Whatever the situation, grasshopper helps you see unique ways to approach it. You may feel like you're taking the long way around to accomplish your goals, but grasshopper doesn't move in a straight line so you don't need to force the situation into a rigid path. Leave frustration behind, enjoy the scenery as you consider it from all angles, and know that the end result will be amazing. If you're having trouble trusting your decisions and instinctual nature, grasshopper can reinforce that you're moving in the right direction. If you're not, it can get you back on track. Grasshopper warns you to jump out of the way if you feel frustration or danger or if a situation has gotten too gnarly to deal with. Leave it behind for the moment and approach again from a different direction. Unless it's dangerous, then leave it behind for good.

Frequency: Grasshopper energy sounds like a slight whirring noise right behind your head. When you turn to look, it moves with you, always out of sight. Its tone is a steady rhythm with some fluctuations in pitch. It feels like the wind at your back, pushing you forward into unknown territory.

> ### Imagine…
>
> You're outside when you notice there are grasshoppers everywhere. You wonder where they all came from since you hadn't seen this many out in a while. You catch one and let it crawl on your fingers. Its legs feel prickly against your skin. You rub your finger along its back, and it lifts its wings as if it's going to jump or fly away but it doesn't. Its dark eyes seem to reflect your image back at you like a mirror. You feel a charge in the air around you, positive and uplifting. Holding your hand out, you invite the grasshopper to fly away, but it turns around in your hand to look at you and then starts to walk up your arm. It's not afraid and makes quick progress up to your elbow. Now it tickles, so you pick it up and put it on a nearby leaf. You consider how it investigates new situations and think that maybe you should do the same.

Grouse

Traits: Grouse symbolizes an elaborate, attention-grabbing display of action. Whether this is dancing, making sure you're seen and heard at work, or preening to garner the attention of the opposite sex, grouse will help you get *all* of the attention you seek. Sage grouse's mating display is very copious, with its spiked tail feathers, inflatable air sacs in its chest, a mane of white feathers, and a unique circular dance. When sage grouse inflates then deflates its air sacs, a loud popping noise is made, which also attracts mates. Grouse has feathered nostrils and legs, and in the winter its toes even grow feathers or small scales that help protect its feet from the cold and snow.

Talents: Beauty, excellent dancer, graceful, manifesting, rhythm, sensitive to vibration, showy

Challenges: Complainer, cranky, greed, often irritable, out of sorts, power hungry, repetitive and ritualistic behavior, too over the top

Element(s): Earth

Primary Color(s): Black, brown, red, white

Appearances: When grouse appears, it means you need to take time to dance. Lose yourself in the music, letting your body move freely to its rhythm. This will allow you to connect to your true essence. Allow your mind to be free, without worry or stress, and be at one with the sound around you. Grouse means everything has its place in your life and when things get out of place, you might freak out just a little bit. Stay calm and put everything back where it goes. You're deeply attuned to patterns, rituals, and your own specific way of doing things. Just remember the world isn't going to end if things don't go according to plan one day. Grouse warns against being too rigid instead of going with the flow. When you're out of sorts, grouse can help you return to center, preen, and get back into the majestic flow of your dance.

Assists When: You need to look your best for an event, increase your positive rhythm, or de-stress by loosening up through movement. Grouse helps you to manifest by showing you how to use movement, intention, and performance to attract what you want to come into your life. Try creating your own dance or hand movements to add power to your intention during manifestation exercises. This increases the flow of energy to you. This also allows you to reach higher levels of consciousness and enables faster paced spiritual growth. Your understanding of the spiritual realms has enhanced tenfold. What was once unclear and out of reach is now readily available to you. Grouse teaches harmony and to enjoy the natural rhythm of life instead of trying to force movement along your path. When you quit pushing and start dancing, you lighten your energy and allow yourself to become one with the universal flow. Grouse is a great stress reliever, can give you energy, and enhances your ability to trust others.

Frequency: Grouse's energy is very busy. It sounds like clicking, popping, cooing, and scratching all rolled into one big cloud of positivity. This cloud surrounds you, warms you, and lifts you up. If feels like a hug from a long-lost friend.

> ### *Imagine...*
> You're driving in the wide open spaces, flat land for as far as you can see, when you come upon a rest stop. You decide to take a few minutes to stretch your legs. You grab a drink from the vending machine and walk around. There's a field to the back of the parking lot, so you walk over that way. Out in the open there is a male grouse courting a female. His feathers are puffed out, his tail feathers raised as he struts his stuff in front of the female. She is ignoring him, so he comes closer and inflates his air sacs, but she doesn't even look at him when they make a loud popping sound. He moves around in front of her, lifting his wings, showing off his plumage and inflating his air sacs again. This time she does look up, but the show continues. You think about the rhythm of its dance and realize you have a little spring in your step as you walk back to the car.

Hare

Traits: Hare symbolizes independence, survival, and speed. It is a sign of abundance, fertility, and good fortune. While they may look similar, hare is a completely different genus than rabbit. Hare is born with its eyes wide open, is fully furred, has black markings on its ears, and is able to take care of itself within an hour of being born. It is also bigger with longer ears, front legs that are longer and thinner, more muscular back legs, and larger feet. Hare runs at speeds of up to thirty-seven body lengths per second. That's faster than a cheetah. Hare's diet is different as well. It prefers hard bark, twigs, and shoots instead of grass. Hare can even change its color to white during winter to allow it to blend in with the snow.

Talents: Abundance, ambitious, artistic, creative, diligent, fearless, fertility, flexible, good luck, independent, quick thinking, solitary, speed, stands up for self, strength, survival, transformation, virtuous

Challenges: Deception, delusion, fraud, greedy, impersonation, jokester, nasty attitude, not social, selfish, skittish, spooky, trickery, trust issues, unreliable

Element(s): Earth

Primary Color(s): Brown, gray

Appearances: When hare appears, it means you are different than you appear. You have a stronger core essence than others give you credit for. While you prefer to handle disagreements with finesse, you'll fight hard if necessary to get your point across and to defend others or your territory. This is often a surprise to those around you because they *didn't know you had it in you* to react in such a take-charge manner. You're sensitive, independent, and tend to prefer solitude to group activities. Hare urges you to take quick action when opportunities arise. Don't overlook the obvious because you want to see something different from what the situation really is. See the truth in the matter, then make a deliberate, intelligent decision.

Assists When: You need to take charge and act quickly. Did you know a female hare will punch a male hare in the face if she isn't interested when he's making the moves on her? This is a sign that you have to stand up for yourself, your morals, and your ideals instead of following along with the crowd. That doesn't mean to go out and punch someone but to be strong in your beliefs and don't let others sway you when they disagree. Speed is important to you right now. There are situations coming your way where you're going to have to think fast and take quick actions to be successful. Don't overthink what you're doing. Trust that your instincts and intuition are leading you in the right direction. Hare warns to be wary of who you trust, especially in new endeavors. Hare warns that just as hare is completely different from rabbit, someone near you is not what they seem.

Frequency: Hare's energy is a high-pitched, shrill, long tone that drops off suddenly to silence then after a few moments begins again, repeating the sound. It feels hurried, jumpy, and like you just felt a small electrical shock.

See Also: Jackalope, Rabbit

Imagine...

You're out for a jog on a path that moves out of the park toward an open field. You run up a slight incline and then you see a hare near the edge of the path. When it sees you, it turns and runs alongside you. So, you decide to race. You pour on the power, moving faster and faster, but the hare has you beat hands down. Out of breath, you slow down and then stop, putting your hands on your knees, bending to catch your breath. You didn't realize you had that kind of speed in you. Then again, you've never tried to race a hare before either. Smiling, you look up and, sitting there in the middle of the path, is the hare. You just laugh and say, *Okay! You won! I can't race again.* As if it understands, the hare hops away, out of sight.

Hawk

Traits: Hawk symbolizes seizing the moment, finding prey, and hunting it down. This helps you tremendously in business. Hawk's eyesight allows it to see the visible, ultraviolet, polarized light, and even magnetic fields. This allows you to see opportunities with clear vision while you hunt for the path that will lead to the most success and allow you to take the lead position at the right time. Hawk's vision and its ability to soar to great heights connect it to the spiritual realm, for which it is a messenger. This means you too are connected in the same way. You may receive visions, have prophetic dreams, or be able to communicate with the animal kingdom. Whatever your intuitive talents, hawk boosts them.

Talents: Creative, fearless, insightful, inspiration, intuition, leader, messenger, spirituality, visionary, wisdom

Challenges: Overly focused, predatory, ruthless

Element(s): Air

Primary Color(s): Brown

Appearances: When hawk appears, it means you're taking the lead, you have a vision of something you want to achieve, or you're embarking on a spiritual quest for enlightenment and personal growth. Hawk means you can reach great heights as you accept new opportunities. Hawk connects you to the higher realms, where you can interact with spirit guides, angels, and the masters. Your clear vision lets you see accurately into the Akashic Records. This spiritual quest is a life changer and once you've opened to Spirit, you see existence from a different perspective. Hawk's ability to soar in the open sky symbolizes you soaring in your new knowledge. Hawk encourages you to maintain focus in your life. Don't get distracted by trivial things. Continue to reach for the stars, aim high, and fly swiftly to reach your goals.

Assists When: You need to get something done in a hurry. Hawk helps you when you need to complete a task quickly. It can help you dive in and make short order of finishing the work. When you need to be flexible but are having a hard time bending, hawk can help you loosen up. Hawk can help you navigate any twists or turns life throws at you by swooping you out of the way. Hawk also helps you face challenges head on by plunging into it and grabbing hold with sharpness and strength. If you feel stuck when trying to meet your goals, hawk reminds you to visualize what you want to draw it to you. It keeps you focused and helps you keep an eye on the people and events around you. Often you perceive what others don't, so use this vision to help you succeed in life.

Frequency: Hawk's energy sounds like a strong, fast *swoosh* through the wind. It feels tight, focused, and strong. It pushes at your back, forcing you forward and upward as you reach new heights. It feels like a pull on your wrists, encouraging you to follow.

See Also: Cetan

Imagine…

You're at the barn mucking out paddocks when you feel like you're being watched. You look up, and sitting about ten feet away from you on the top of a post is a hawk. It's steadily watching you, so you take a moment to acknowledge its presence and then get back to work. Occasionally you look up to see that the hawk hasn't moved but is just observing. When you've finished that area, you leave and move on to the next. The hawk follows and lands nearby on a tree branch. Now you realize this hawk is really trying to get your attention, so you stop what you're doing and stare at it, sending telepathic messages requesting that it shares its message. Hawk says, *The time to begin is now. The path is clear, you must simply step forward.* As you process what you heard, the hawk flies away.

Hippopotamus

Traits: Hippopotamus symbolizes intuition, set patterns, knowing what is underneath, and protecting oneself. Hippo spends most of its time in water with only its eyes and nostrils exposed so it can see and breathe. Its skin is thin, and the water protects it from the sun. This means that while you may love water sports, days at the beach, or simply being outdoors, make sure you protect your skin from the sun and drink plenty of water so you don't get dehydrated. Hippo is one of the most aggressive animals on the planet, which is a warning to you to keep your temper in check.

Talents: Agility, creative, emotional depth, endurance, graceful, healing, imaginative, intuition, keen observation, longevity, powerful, practical, protection, stable, tenacity, wise

Challenges: Aggression, controlling, power hungry

Element(s): Earth, water

Primary Color(s): Black, gray, pink (hippo's milk is pink)

Appearances: When hippopotamus shows up, it means you need to act on your intuition. Don't overanalyze it or question if what you're receiving is correct. Simply trust that the universe and your guides are giving you the information you need. Hippo means you tend to be grounded and don't get caught up in hype. You like to create patterns of behavior and stick to those patterns. Hippo's appearance means now is not the time to stray from your path. You may feel drawn to distraction but push that feeling aside and focus on what you're doing, where you're going, and your ultimate goal. Hippo lets you see what's underneath the waters. If you're searching for answers, take a better look at what's hidden. That's where the truth will be found. Hippo means you can easily find balance between your physical being and spiritual being. Abundance surrounds you.

Assists When: You need stability in your life. Hippo can help you analyze situations and find the balance in all things. If you're starting a new project, hippo can help you stay focused on your path without distraction. If you doubt your purpose, hippo will show you how to connect to your core spiritual self and lead the life you were meant to lead. Hippo urges you to explore your own spirituality instead of blindly accepting what the masses preach. Your soul knows; you just need to listen. Hippo warns against becoming too aggressive, controlling, or letting the feeling of power overtake you. When you allow these things, you are stepping away from positivity and into negativity. Don't let frustration turn to rage. Maintain control of your temper. If you need an outlet for your less-than-positive emotions, turn to something creative. Build something, paint something, write something. Just don't let that something turn into nothing because you let anger fuel a fire that engulfed it, cindering it to ash. Dream big, live big, and you will accomplish anything you desire.

Frequency: Hippopotamus's energy is a low, deep resonance that vibrates through the earth into your feet. It rumbles, shakes you, and grounds you. It is the low groan of a tree bending in the wind, the patter of rain on water. It chills you, making you shiver in awareness.

Imagine…

During your visit to the safari park, you drive by a large lake. In the water you notice the top of a hippo's head, its eyes and nose protruding just above the water's surface. Several feet away, you notice another hippo moving closer to the first one. Suddenly the water erupts in huge splashes of water, big open mouths, and huge teeth as the two hippos go at each other. Their mouths are wide open, and they face each other nose-to-nose and jaw-to-jaw, each waiting to bite. You can hear the grunting and snorting through the closed windows of your vehicle. Their power radiates from the lake, and you're filled with a knowing that, like the hippo, you must make sure you're stable in your position of power, strong in your show of strength, and that you listen to your intuition. This lasts for almost ten minutes before they both instinctively move away from one another.

Hummingbird

Traits: Hummingbird symbolizes lightness of being. It means enjoying life to the fullest, drinking in its sweet nectar. It is holding those close to you closer, loving with abandon, and being present in your life. Hummingbird is the smallest bird species, with some only measuring two and one forth inches. They can't walk or hop like other birds but can scoot sideways on a branch. They can also fly backward, don't have a sense of smell, and lick nectar instead of sucking it up. They do everything fast. Their hearts beat twelve hundred times per minute; they can lick ten to fifteen times per second and digest their food in twenty minutes. Some fly five hundred miles nonstop when migrating. Hummingbird is considered one of the most aggressive bird species, regardless of its tiny size. It will attack other birds, including hawks, if they enter their territory.

Talents: Adaptable, connection to spirit, creative, enjoys sweetness of life, enthusiastic, loving, intuitive, optimistic, resilient, self-confident, swift

Challenges: Aggressive, egotistical, extravagance, unpredictable

Element(s): Air

Primary Color(s): Blue, gray, green, red, but can be any color

Appearances: When hummingbird shows up, it means to stand up for yourself and don't let others intimidate you. It encourages you to embrace your lightness of being. Hummingbird gives you speed, and you often do things quickly. Sometimes you have to slow down like hummingbird, too. It will hang upside down from a limb and appear dead or asleep. To you, this means that while you move quickly, you can't wear yourself down. Make sure you take time to recharge before taking flight again. Hummingbird can fly both forward and backward, and it can hover, which means you go with the flow, adapt quickly to changes, and take the time to stop, look, and listen. Hummingbird encourages you to embrace the playfulness inside you. Take time to just goof off, do nothing, and relax. It's essential to your well-being to find a balance between going a hundred miles an hour and sleeping. Sometimes you just need to slow down without actually stopping.

Assists When: You need to be more optimistic, playful, or joyful. If you're in the doldrums, let hummingbird lift you up to a place of happiness. If you feel like you're burning the candle at both ends, hummingbird can show you how to slow down and manage the workload without completely shutting down or feeling overly stressed. Hummingbird can help you be more present in your life so you enjoy each moment and appreciate the sweetness in the world's simple pleasures. Embracing hummingbird's lightness will attract love, joy, and happiness to you. Hummingbird's efficiency will help you develop new skills and fine-tune old ones. It can lighten a bad mood, turn a frown into a smile, and shine light through the rain. It can help you heal even when you think your heart will never be the same again. It might not be, but change is a lesson everyone learns.

Frequency: Hummingbird's energy is a mid-toned buzz that pitches up and down and back again. High chirping sounds are dispersed throughout the humming. Its energy is hot, fast moving, and feels like a shudder running through you.

Imagine...

You've set up a hummingbird feeder in your backyard. One day you decide to see if they'll drink the mixture from your hand. You fill a small red cup with the nectar and sit in a chair close to the feeder. You send out positive energy to the birds, inviting them to drink the nectar from your cup. After a while, one of the hummingbirds notices the cup in your hand and flies closer to investigate, its wings buzzing with their fast movement. It drinks from the cup, filling you with delight. After it drinks a bit, it trusts you enough to sit on your hand while it drinks. You're amazed at how light it is, at the scratchiness of its tiny feet, and the beauty of its iridescent wings. When it has drank its fill, it flies away.

Jaguar

Traits: Jaguar symbolizes moving without fear through the unknown. Jaguar prefers a solitary life. It has a large territory that usually includes the territory of several females. It protects both the territory and the females from other males. Like most big cats, jaguar hunts on the ground, but it will also jump into the water or climb a tree and leap down upon its prey. Jaguar's unique spotted markings resemble roses and are called rosettes.

Talents: Assertive, authoritative, beauty, bravery, charisma, empowerment, good communicator, graceful, independent, intuition, stealth, strength

Challenges: Aggressive, antisocial, calculating, manipulative, stubborn

Element(s): Earth, water

Primary Color(s): Black, brown, white, yellow

Appearances: When jaguar appears, it means to move forward with stealth and use your intuition and good communication skills. This isn't a time for indecision. Instead, set your goal; use your authority and strong willpower to steadily move toward accomplishing what you've set out to do. Your beauty, skill, and independent strength of character will help you make positive forward progression. You're secure, self-confident, and have high self-esteem. You're not afraid to go after what you want. You tend to take situations and people at face value instead of always looking for a hidden agenda. When you need to look deeper into a situation or are having a hard time trusting someone, use your intuition to guide you. Jaguar encourages you to reclaim your inner power through fine-tuning your intuitive abilities and soul empowerment. Jaguar's beauty is good camouflage for its intense inner fierceness. People may not realize the strength, cunning, and stealth you carry inside. You may use your beauty to help you achieve your goals, but you'll fight for what you want or need.

Assists When: You have to face your fears. Jaguar isn't afraid of the dark or going into unknown territory. Its bravery can help guide you away from the source of your fear and let you see it in a different light so you'll no longer be afraid. Jaguar helps when you want to surprise someone close to you. You are a natural leader but at times can feel overwhelmed with the amount of work you are required to do. Jaguar can help you see the right paths to take if you're caught at a crossroad. It can teach you how to regain your balance and forward momentum if you're feeling unsure or off-kilter. Jaguar urges you to get in the best physical shape you can be. Strength, stamina, and powerful movements are important now. If you're not in the best physical shape, start working out, running, or doing some activity to strengthen your muscles and increase your flexibility.

Frequency: Jaguar's energy feels like you're taking large, lightly placed steps as you walk. It glides within you, powerful and strong. It is focused, intense, and gripping. Its sound is deep, raspy, and rolls over a low, rumbling pitch.

See Also: Black Panther, Cheetah, Cougar (Mountain Lion, Puma), Lion, Tiger

---

Imagine…

Stalking around you, its spotted rosettes rippling across heavy muscles, a jaguar holds you in its sights. You marvel at its beauty, its fierce presence. You feel a pang of nervousness when it stops in front of you, scrunches its nose, and growls low and deep, like a rolling rumble. It steps closer and pushes its head against your leg, making you take a step back. It pushes you again, but this time you don't move. Instead you think, *Don't push me,* and send it a mental image of it stepping back a few steps. When it does, you tell it *thank you.* It stalks around you again, so close that its tail rubs along your legs. The next thing you know the jaguar is rubbing up against your legs like a house cat. You tentatively touch its fur with just the tips of your fingers. It's coarser than you expected but soft and thick. After a couple of minutes of this interaction, the jaguar walks away, glancing back at you once before moving out of your sight.

Jellyfish

Traits: Jellyfish symbolizes to stop trying to force things in your life and instead go with the flow, analyze your emotions, and whether you're moving forward with purpose or drifting on the waves. Jellyfish can emit light through bioluminescent organs, which means for you to shine your light just as brightly. Jellyfish has two stages in its life cycle. The first is the polyp and the second the mobile medusa phase. There is one species of jellyfish that is called immortal because it has the ability to revert from the mobile medusa phase back to the polyp stage during times of stress. This is an indication of rebirth; going back to the beginning and starting over again. Jellyfish can clone themselves, creating two new organisms if they're cut in half, or, if injured, they can produce hundreds of offspring during the cloning process.

Talents: Calm, certainty, cheerful, comforting, confident, contentment, easygoing, flexible, going with the flow, happiness, honest, independent, joy, nonresistant, peaceful, pleasant, sureness, trusting, unconcern

Challenges: Dependent, drifting aimlessly, lazy, naïveté, sluggish, tactless, unfocused

Element(s): Water

Primary Color(s): Blue, red, yellow, and all other colors

Appearances: When jellyfish appears, it is a sign to begin again. Get back to the basics and find your balance. You're very adaptable, but if you make things complicated, you can slow your own progress. Jellyfish means to let things happen in their own time, don't try to force your will on situations. You're open and honest but sometimes come across as too blunt or appear tactless, even if it's unintentional. Your words can sting and cause undue upset if not spoken with finesse. Be sensitive in your approach to obtain positive results. Jellyfish means to trust your inner self. You are connected to universal wisdom. Jellyfish warns that it is easy for you to get dehydrated. When working or enjoying being outside, make sure you stay hydrated by drinking plenty of water.

Assists When: You're stressed out, aggravated, impatient, or feeling on edge. Jellyfish can help you relax, give you patience, and take away some of the tension of your emotions. Jellyfish brings harmony and peaceful feelings if you'll listen to its message. It means to have faith in yourself during trying times. Everything will work out, especially if you're transparent in your feelings about the matter. Jellyfish relies on the ocean currents and waves to help it along or will pulsate its bell (the rounded top part) to move forward. This means you may need to rely on the help of others to get where you're going, but you also have the inner strength to get there on your own if you choose. You are easygoing but also independent so it might be hard for you to accept help. Acceptance is an integral part of jellyfish. It doesn't question but accepts what is going on around it. You too are unafraid to accept what is and handle difficult situations with ease and fluidity. You are a loving individual with deep emotions. Jellyfish means things are looking up in your life.

Frequency: Jellyfish energy is soft, fluid, and warm. It moves slowly, with repetition. It sounds hollow with a slight echo.

Imagine...

While visiting a public aquarium, you turn a corner and gasp in awe. In front of you is a very large window with the water behind it filled with hundreds of bright orange jellyfish with long tentacles. You stand in front of the window, mesmerized by their hypnotic movements through the water. Some appear to be floating, while the bells on others pulsate to propel them through the water. You notice the tentacles flow directly behind the jellyfish when it's moving forward and float around it when it stops. It is emitting light as it moves along. You can't help but think that the jellyfish is like your spiritual being. Your light shines as you go about your daily activities. It's not something you consciously think about but is an intricate part of you.

Kangaroo

Traits: Kangaroo symbolizes a solid foundation, positive energy, and forward motion. Red kangaroo is the largest marsupial. It is between five and six feet tall, weighs up to two hundred pounds, can run forty miles per hour, and can jump ten feet high and twenty-five feet in distance. The smallest kangaroo is a tiny dwarf wallaby called *Dorcopsulus* that was discovered in 2010 in the forests of New Guinea and only weighs between 360 and 680 grams. This small wallaby is active during the day while most kangaroos are active at night. Kangaroos can't move backward. What this means to you is that it doesn't matter if you're big or small in stature or if you're more active during the day or night, as long as your sense of self is built on a positive, strong, solid foundation, you will be able to grow in forward motion by leaps and bounds without looking back.

Talents: Balance, courage, escaping, faith, forward motion, speed, stamina

Challenges: Aggression, easily distracted, restless, unfocused, unpredictable

Element(s): Earth

Primary Color(s): Gray, red

Appearances: Kangaroo means to leap over problems, stay grounded, and move on. Don't look back or regret the steps you've taken. You have a deep connection to the earth, a stable foundation on which you stand (both personally and spiritually), just as kangaroo's foundation is its large feet. If you've lost belief in yourself, kangaroo reminds you to reassess to recognize your truth. If others make you feel bad about yourself due to their actions (or trying to blame their actions on you), try not to take it personally or take steps to distance yourself from them. Know who you are at your core, a truly unique and wonderful being of spirit, and believe in yourself. Kangaroo encourages you to stay close to the ones you love most during times of difficulty. They offer a support system that will enable you to be the best you can be. Kangaroo also means your life may be jumping in a different direction soon so stay focused on what's going on around you. As you reach for your goals, this isn't the time to battle obstacles head on. Just go around, or over, them.

Assists When: You need forward momentum. If you've gotten stuck in past situations or are letting negativity get you down, kangaroo encourages you to leap forward into positivity. It can also give you confidence in any situation where you feel unsure or where you've taken on too much responsibility. Kangaroo encourages you to stay on your path. There might be twists and turns along the way, but if you stay the course, you will achieve great things. When you're afraid to start a new venture or make a change in your life because it takes you out of your comfort zone, even if you know it's the right thing to do, kangaroo can help you overcome the fear and move forward. Kangaroo is a social animal and can help you come out of your shell. It also enjoys its solitude. If you've been overly active in your social life, kangaroo can help you slow down and find some alone time.

Frequency: Kangaroo's energy bounds with positivity, it's hot and feels like you've stepped into a lava lamp. It moves around you, but you never know which way it's going. It sounds like a *blurp, blurp, blurp, zing*! It's filled with joy.

See Also: Jersey Devil

Imagine...

The day is hot, the sun bright, and the wind brisk as you're hiking in Australia. As you approach a forested area, you notice kangaroos grazing along the edge of the trees. You alter your route to go around them. You enter the trees and sigh in appreciation of the shade. You stop for a moment, take off your backpack, and get out your thermos of water. Sitting on a nearby rock, you take a short break. You get up and turn to leave and are face-to-face with a large male kangaroo. It reaches out and lays a hand on your shoulder. The light of its soul shines through its eyes, and you feel as if you've been touched by an angel. It nods, then bounds away and, taking a deep breath, you continue on your way feeling lighter and more connected to universal energy.

Ladybug (Asian Lady Beetle)

Traits: Ladybug symbolizes luck, fortune, happiness, and protection. Ladybug's life cycle is one to three years depending on the species. Ladybug means to live life to the fullest every single day. Ladybugs lay both fertile and infertile eggs so that the ones that hatch will have the infertile ones to eat. This means you shouldn't be wasteful. Ladybugs also gather in the thousands to share body warmth when it's time to hibernate. Warmth is also why they'll come into people's homes in the winter. This means you should reconnect with friends you haven't seen in a while, be social, and make sure you stay warm when it's cold outside.

Talents: Abundance, balance, devoted, easygoing, enlightenment, faith, family oriented, happiness, high morals, innocence, joy, lucky, past lives, practical, protection, rebirth, regeneration, renewal, shielded, social values, spiritual idealism, spirituality, transformation, trusting, wishes fulfilled

Challenges: Delicate, flighty, overly sensitive

Element(s): Air

Primary Color(s): Black, orange, pink, red, yellow

Appearances: When ladybug appears, it means you're about to have a fortunate change in your life. Ladybug reminds you that you're protected from the negativity of the world, shielded by your own positive defensive shell. Ladybug warns not to stay hidden in that shell but to come out to ascend to new heights. It's easy for ladybug to stay inside where it's safe, but to open its wings, allowing itself to be vulnerable, is when the greatest accomplishments are made. Ladybug reminds you that sometimes you have to expose your inner self in order to fly. Ladybug is connected to spirituality and the development of your internal core essence. Your spiritual values are strong, so you need to take time each day for meditation, even if it's five minutes to reconnect to your spirituality.

Assists When: You've been deliberating over a choice. Ladybug helps you see the direction to take. If you want to bring more abundance into your life, ask ladybug for assistance. Ladybug can help you on your path to enlightenment. It can push away any illusions you may have and show you the truth of spirit. It can help you let go of fears and anxiety and replace those negative qualities with a trusting calmness and the faith that everything will work out as it should. Ladybug is a symbol of innocence and love. If you've become frustrated and disappointed with your life or the world, ladybug can help you find the purity in it again so you return to love. Ladybug warns against trying to force your will. The universe works in its own time, which is often out of alignment with the speed in which we'd like things to happen. Ladybug reminds you to stop pushing so hard and let things happen as they are meant to be.

Frequency: Ladybug's energy is light and airy, playful and filled with delight. It feels like getting caught in a quick summer rain shower. Refreshing, cleansing, and warm. It sounds like the tinkle of wind chimes drifting over the breeze.

Imagine…

The invasion has begun. Your home seems to be filled with ladybugs as the temperatures drop and winter approaches. You know ladybugs are considered good luck charms and that they like to spend winters inside a warm house but you're not too keen on living with them for the winter regardless of how much you like them. You enjoy letting them crawl on your fingers and watching their movements and flight when they leave your hand. You humanely remove as many as you can by vacuuming them up into a pair of panty hose and releasing them in the woods, hoping that they'll group together behind some tree bark. You turn the hose inside out and let the ladybugs crawl off and onto the tree. When you return home, you realize that you've missed a few. The sight of them fills you with warmth and a sense of spiritual renewal. You decide they can stay unless their numbers dramatically increase again, and then you'll have to make another trip to the tree.

Lion

Traits: Lion symbolizes courage, leadership, and loyalty. Now is the time for you to roar, strut your stuff, and let the world see your grandeur. It is ferociously protective, likes being the center of attention, and uses its strength when needed. Lion also symbolizes difficulty controlling your emotions. It warns to maintain inner strength to find emotional balance. Lion is a social animal that prefers to avoid any type of conflict. If provoked, or if it feels threatened, it will viciously fight to protect itself, its family, and its territory. This applies to you as well.

Talents: Authority, balance, courage, dignity, dominion, fierce, honorable, justice, leader, loyalty, power, royalty, self-confidence, social, strength, wisdom

Challenges: Controlling, lazy, prideful, quick-tempered, relentless, self-centered

Element(s): Earth

Primary Color(s): Brown

Appearances: Lion appears when you're about to step into a leadership role. It means you need to be more visible and in the spotlight and you need to take a dominate role in the situation. Lead, don't follow. Delegate, don't do all of the work yourself. It is your dominion, so protect your territory, and make sure all of your bases are covered. Lion also means to learn from the lioness. In the pride, the lioness is responsible for raising the family. She hunts for, protects, and socializes her cubs. By looking at how the lioness multitasks, you can learn how to bring harmony to your work environment by teaching those you're responsible for how to work in the most productive manner. If a lioness comes to you, it is to show you how to gain balance between work and your home life. Lion also means you're not being as productive as possible. You may be lying around or goofing off instead of doing the work you need to do.

Assists When: You need to increase your personal power. Stress can diminish your self-confidence and lower your self-esteem. Lion can help you relax and recharge by releasing nervous tension, aggression, and anger. It can give you the courage and assertiveness to face problems head-on instead of moving around them. Lion also warns you when a situation is getting out of hand or is threatening your personal and emotional strength. Maintain control, your dignity, and your pride when you're facing challenging situations. Lion can help you deal with the negative emotions of others. It gives you a noble, positive attitude that enables you to look at the reasons behind the other person's actions, evaluate them, and then make positive decisions on what action to take. Lion means you shouldn't respond on impulse, but take time to stalk and analyze the situation before making your move.

Frequency: Lion's energy sounds like a long, low rumble. It is a roar that reverberates deep within your chest, rumbling to your extremities. It is strong and pure. It makes you feel larger than you are and feelings of power surge through you. You stand taller, walk prouder, and feel you can conquer any obstacle.

See Also: Black Panther, Cheetah, Chimera, Cougar (Mountain Lion, Puma), Griffin, Jaguar, Nemean Lion, Shisa, Tiger

> ### Imagine...
>
> The roar of the lion resonates throughout the zoo. You feel it rumble through you and you're not even close to the lion enclosure yet. Heading toward the sound, you feel entranced by the majestic nobility of the lion's roar. You catch your first sight of the elegant beast around a bend. It is patrolling, watching over its pride of lionesses. It roars again, the sound is loud and strong. This time one of the lionesses answers the call. You notice that the reply came from a different direction. Looking over, you see a mother lioness with three cubs following her. She only comes part way into the open and looks up at the male lion. The energetic connection between the two is strong. It feels like arcs of lightning zinging between them. She gives him a soft roar before returning with her cubs to the safety of the brush. Satisfied, the lion lies down on the rock and goes to sleep.

Lizard (Gecko)

Traits: Lizard symbolizes detachment. In the wild, lizard will detach its tail if its life feels threatened. The tail will continue to move, which confuses predators, while the lizard escapes. In time, the lizard will regrow its tail, but it might be smaller and a different color. Most lizards also regenerate and replace their teeth throughout their lives. When water is scarce, lizard conserves it internally by excreting salt through their skin, which leaves a white residue. Some species can also squirt blood up to four feet out of their eyes when threatened by predators. Some don't have legs. This means that you too can let go of things that you don't absolutely need in order to survive, even if you think you can't live without them. You can.

Talents: Adaptation, connection between realms, detachment, dreams, faces fear, goes with the flow, heart connections, inner power, objectivity, quickness, reflexive, regeneration, spontaneous

Challenges: Deceptive, egotistical, introversion, overly shrewd

Element(s): Earth

Primary Color(s): Brown, green, also multicolored

Appearances: When lizard appears, it means to look for your hidden gifts. Seek your inner visions through meditation or ask that you are shown information while dreaming. By considering your dreams and aspirations, you can bring the most positive ones to light and you can see what is holding you back. Your gifts of rejuvenation will help you through difficult times. Lizards are cold blooded and enjoy time in the sun. They grow during their entire lifetimes and will shed their skin when they need to grow more. This means that you too absorb the warmth around you and grow throughout your life. You are continually learning and experiencing both personal and spiritual growth. You listen to your heart, aren't ruled by ego, and can regenerate when needed. Of the more than 5,600 species, the only one with vocal cords is the gecko, which means you communicate well through body language. Lizard means you have to connect to your imagination, for that is where your dreams live. If your forward motion is slow, imagine what you want and go for it to get back on pace.

Assists When: You are having a recurring dream or vision that you need to decipher. Lizard is connected to dreams and visions, moves between realms, and can help you discover the true meaning of what you're seeing. It does this by helping you connect with the stillness inside of you, so that you can see the significance of the images, or hear an explanation of what they mean. While others might consider you lethargic, you're simply easygoing and are always very aware of everything happening around you. You often use this to your advantage because people relax and feel comfortable in your presence. Quite often they reveal important information without even realizing they're doing it.

Frequency: Lizard's energy moves quickly then stops, only to begin again. It feels cool to the touch but is bursting with possibility. It sounds like wet fingers against glass or a high-pitched light chirping.

See Also: Basilisk, Iguana

Imagine...

You decide to get out of the house and commune with nature. You walk until you come to an old barn. It has an overhang and underneath is dirt. Sitting down, leaning your back against the wood and clay structure, you contemplate the issues that affected your mood and try to find a resolution. You look around. There are lots of lizards nearby all in different stages of growth. You catch one and it freezes in your hand. You rub its rough skin, feeling as if you're caught between realms, suspended and unmoving. You consider the spiritual being that you are deep inside and the spirit of the lizard. Your energy connects and you feel coolness move through you, stabilizing and steadying your vibration. When you set it back on the ground, you feel better, more sure of yourself and the direction you must take. Your mood has brightened, your spirits lifted, thanks to the detached calmness of lizard.

Loon

Traits: Loon symbolizes looking into the depths for the truth. Unlike most birds, loon has solid bones, which adds weight and gives it the ability to dive to greater depths. It takes loon quite a bit of distance on a lake (one hundred to six hundred feet) to gain the momentum needed to obtain flight due to the heaviness of their body (needed for diving) and their short wingspan. Once airborne, they can fly long distances, but they have to flap their wings the entire time. This means you don't give up, even if it takes a while to get a project off the ground, and once it's flying, it can go the distance.

Talents: Connection to the universal higher consciousness, deep feelings, dreaming, hidden depths, imagination, intuition, longevity, personal undertaking for metaphysical information and inner power, wish fulfillment

Challenges: Detached, imagining the worst, impractical, reclusive, too sensitive, unfriendly, unrealistic

Element(s): Earth, water

Primary Color(s): Black, white

Appearances: When loon appears, it means you need to look within. Are you being overly sensitive, hiding out from others, or letting your imagination run wild? Loon can help you bring all of these situations back into balance. While loon prefers solitude, it isn't a completely solitary creature. It does enjoy being around others, as do you. Loon is connected to the spiritual world and moving between the physical and spiritual realms. This means you need to embrace your intuitive abilities. You may have been fighting them for a while; maybe even wishing they'd go away. They're part of you and always will be. So instead of fighting them, embrace them. Life will start to flow easier when you do. It's also time to begin work on your spiritual growth. Explore new concepts to see if there is more out there that makes sense to you. When you're ready to learn, the lessons will appear and loon can show them to you.

Assists When: You need to communicate in a distinctive manner. Loon has four calls. One sounds like maniacal laughter, another like a wail, one like a hoot, and the last like a yodel. That's a wide range of uniqueness! Loon shows you how to speak in interesting ways to get your point across. Loons are named for their clumsiness on land. Their legs are set so far back on their body they have a very difficult time walking. If you're feeling clumsy, ask loon to guide you back into the water to regain your balance. If you need to look especially beautiful or handsome for an event ask loon to help you get ready. They spend most of their days preening and oiling their feathers to maintain buoyancy and waterproofing. Loon can also help you bring your hopes and dreams to fruition.

Frequency: Loon's energy is light and buoyant. It has a smacking, flapping sound. It feels like a strong pull upward, lifting you to the sky.

Imagine…

While on a bike ride, you arrive at a lake and see a group of loons swimming around, dipping underneath the water and resurfacing. You walk to the water's edge to get a closer look. The loons ignore you as they continue their search for food. You see a mother loon with her chicks over near the edge of the lake. You decide to take a few minutes to meditate with these interesting birds. You ask them to share any messages they may have for you. During the meditation, you feel as if you're being drawn into hidden depths of knowledge. You have a strong desire to learn more about the Akashic Records and to develop your own spiritual interests and become more enlightened. As you open your eyes, you notice one of the chicks has wandered away from its mother and is now sitting on top of your shoe. You didn't even feel it get on there. You take this as a sign—a symbol of renewal, consciousness, and rebirth. Picking up the chick, you take it close to its mother and watch as it joins its brothers and sisters. You get back on your bike and continue the trip, but now you have an intense desire to research the Akashic Records and other metaphysical topics.

Lynx (Bobcat)

Traits: Lynx symbolizes possession of ancient knowledge, mysteries of the universe, infinite wisdom, and truth of being, and is the guardian of secrets. Lynx fur is thick with dark spots and changes colors with the seasons. Its ears are white with black tuffs of fur that enhance its hearing. It isn't a fast runner, so its favorite form of attack is the ambush. It will wait quietly, unseen, until it can surprise its prey, then it attacks. This means you obtain knowledge from your exceptional hearing, and when someone is threatening, you don't jump into a fight, you wait until you can win with the element of surprise. Lynx is nocturnal, very vocal, and cautious.

Talents: Excellent hearing, independent, intense observer, intuitive, invisibility, sharp vision, silent, solitary, vocal

Challenges: Ambush, isolation, loneliness, secretive, unsociable

Element(s): Earth

Primary Color(s): Brown, gray, white

Appearances: When lynx appears, it means that you must be careful not to disclose secrets others have confided to you and that you intuitively know the secrets others hide. You might know their fears, things they've done, or deceptions they've made to themselves and others. Lynx means you are the keeper of secrets; thus, you should never tell what you know. You have the inner strength to remain silent in all situations. You are at a high spiritual vibration, in tune with your core essence, and, above all, are honorable and wise. People, including strangers, feel at ease with you and trust you due to your inner light and often tell you things they'd never tell anyone else. At times, people may also feel awkward in your presence because they intuitively know that you see them as they really are at a soul level. They unconsciously sense that you know their secrets, and they're right. You tend to speak your mind, but you're also cautious around people. You do your best work at night.

Assists When: You feel the need to pursue metaphysical subjects. You're independent, like solitude, and have a strong desire to deepen your universal knowledge. Studies come natural to you. Knowledge is powerful. You tend to keep your inner strength at its maximum because you never know when you'll need it. If you're not sure about someone's intentions or if you have a gut feeling that they're being deceptive or are trying to take advantage of you or someone else, lynx can help you see the truth within them. Lynx shows you how to really listen. When you're unsure of how to proceed in a situation, lynx helps you remain silent and access your hidden wisdom to find a solution. It can enable you to be more independent and a better observer, and can enhance your intuition.

Frequency: Lynx energy is light, bright, and colorful. It harnesses the positivity of the Divine. It sounds like a chorus singing *ah* repeatedly in various pitches and in perfect harmony. It feels like a warm shudder running through your body, filled with positivity.

Imagine…

You're camping and wake up in the middle of the night but can't pinpoint what woke you. Lying still, you realize something is breathing on you. You turn on the flashlight that you keep in your sleeping bag with you. The pale illumination reveals a small lynx standing beside your bed. It has one paw up on the side as if it was going to crawl in. Frightened, you scoot back up against the far side of the cot near the tent wall. The lynx takes this movement as an invitation and crawls onto the bed, lying down beside you. This is when you realize that this is a baby and it must be missing its littermates who help keep it warm at night. You rub its side, urging it to sleep, but it stays awake, watching you. The next thing you know it's morning. The lynx is gone, and you wonder if you imagined the whole encounter. Then you see the stray hairs all over your sleeping bag and know the lynx was real.

Meerkat (Mongoose)

Traits: Meerkat symbolizes the support of family and friends, having the courage to defend, and having the ability to dig quickly and deeply for answers. Meerkat is a very social animal that lives in large family groups consisting of an alpha pair and all of their offspring. They have an established hierarchy within the colony. Meerkat has a long, thin tail that it uses for balancing when standing upright. As a group, there are often sentinels that watch for predators. When one is spotted, meerkat sounds the alarm with a bark and everyone runs and hides. This means you have a strong sense of family, are well balanced and very watchful, and will take cover to protect yourself if necessary.

Talents: Awareness, charming, confident, courage, curiosity, emotional connections, immunity, joy, keen observation, nurturing, playfulness, protective

Challenges: Aggressive, devious to advance social status, overly impulsive, turn on those close to you

Element(s): Earth

Primary Color(s): Brown, white

Appearances: When meerkat appears, it means that you have to watch out for danger and those who don't have your best interest at heart. Meerkat has built up its immunity to venoms, which allows them to eat scorpions, snakes, and other poisonous animals without fearing illness or death. Meerkat urges you to shore up your defenses against those who may mean you harm. Meerkat doesn't have fat stores, so it must eat daily in order to survive. This is a reminder that you shouldn't skip meals and to take your bodily nourishment seriously. If you need to slim down, develop muscle, or just get back into a healthier way of living, meerkat can help you achieve this goal. Meerkat also reminds you to be aware of your position in life. If you want to achieve higher ranks or elevate your status, meerkat can teach you how to climb the ladder of success. You are a natural leader with strong social skills and can handle many tasks at once. You work well in a group environment and enjoy management. You crave adventure and have a vivid imagination.

Assists When: You need to expand your vision. If you've been close-minded and avoiding situations, take the time to look farther into the distance, open your mind to what might be out there, and face the unknown. You are stronger than you think and can sense danger before it gets to you, giving you the ability to take appropriate action to get out of harm's way. If you're overworked or frustrated, meerkat can show you how to delegate, slow down, and relax. It's essential to your overall well-being, so try not to push yourself past the point of exhaustion. Meerkat draws heat into its body through a small patch of black skin sparsely covered with hair on its belly when it stands up and faces the sun each morning. Meerkat's lesson is to enjoy the sunrise and absorb its heat and energy. It's a wonderful way to start your day.

Frequency: Meerkat energy sounds like chattering laughter with a low, raspy pitch. It is bright and joyous and fills you with happiness. It is hot and moves quickly.

Imagine…

You've taken up photography and have the opportunity to go to Africa and photograph wildlife there. It's an opportunity you can't turn down. Soon you find yourself in the heart of Africa, in a section where the meerkat lives. You switch out your camera's battery pack to a fully charged one and immerse yourself among these surprisingly friendly little creatures. As you sit among them, they become very interested in you and what you're doing. They come up to investigate you, climb in your lap, run up your back, and sit on your shoulder. You lie down to get a shot of some babies. Now you have meerkats climbing all over you. You scratch the babies on the back, which they seem to love. You feel like you've been initiated and accepted into their extended family. Soon the day comes to an end and you'd prefer to stay longer so you could interact with the meerkats, but you know danger lurks at night and the meerkats will be safely tucked away underground until morning light.

Monkey

Traits: Monkey symbolizes understanding, compassion, and enjoying life. It is family oriented and protective of its young. This means you too have unlimited empathy and patience and use humor when caring for or teaching those younger than you. Monkey is intelligent and a fast learner that enjoys sharing its knowledge with others. This means you need intellectual stimulation to keep your busy mind occupied. Monkeys bite, which is a warning to watch your actions and the things you say so they don't come back to bite you in the future.

Talents: Clever, creative, curiosity, dexterity, enjoys challenges, honor, imaginative, ingenuity, innovative, instinctive, intelligent, loving, lucky, mischievous, mobility, playful, problem solver, protective, quick learner, resourceful, sense of community, shares knowledge, social, swiftness, understanding

Challenges: Aggression, distancing yourself from others, easily annoyed, hostile, lazy, overly reactive, serious, temperamental, too talkative, unpredictable

Element(s): Air, earth

Primary Color(s): Black, brown

Appearances: Monkey appears when you need to figure something out. Monkey enjoys a good puzzle, and its insightfulness can help you get to the root of problems. It means to take action instead of sitting back and waiting for something to happen. Monkey urges you to play and have fun. If you enjoy tricking or pulling practical jokes on people, monkey warns to be careful in your actions. Not everyone enjoys being the brunt of such jokes and may react in anger or a manner you're not expecting. What you mean in good fun they may not take as such. Monkey encourages you to be resourceful. You can find a solution if you try instead of waiting to be told how to do something. You're very flexible and nimble. You can swiftly move from one situation to another without an interruption in your focus. Grooming is an integral part of monkey's daily life. This means you may need to pay more attention to your appearance.

Assists When: You need nurturing or the companionship of family and friends, or they need support from you. Monkey encourages you to play more and not take life so seriously. Monkey warns against swinging from place to place without focus. Your swift movements will be more productive if you know where you're going and the reason you're heading there. Think before you act. Monkey can help you get over shyness and be a better communicator. If you need to step into a leadership role, monkey lends you its sense of humor, intelligence, and creativity to enable you to take the lead while ensuring those following you are enjoying the task at hand. Monkey's tail gives it control when it's high in the trees. You can also maintain control over all aspects of your life by listening to monkey's messages and connecting with your sense of self.

Frequency: Monkey energy is jagged and sharp but with a hint of a warm hug. It moves at odd angles, swiftly and with ease. It feels like ice, instantly waking you to everything around you. It sounds like a train speeding down the tracks.

See Also: Orangutan, Squirrel Monkey

Imagine…

You're visiting your local zoo and are at the window of a monkey exhibit. Some monkeys are in the trees, others on the ground, and still others huddled in a group grooming one another. One of the big males runs toward the window, actually crashing against it right in front of you. And you don't even flinch. Your lack of response causes the monkey to bang on the window. It is so obvious in its attempts to interact with you that you hold your hand up to the glass and knock twice. The monkey mimics your actions and knocks twice, too. Now it's a game. You knock three times and the monkey does, too. Four times, same thing. So you decide to change it up a bit. You do soft raps and two hard wraps. The monkey repeats your actions. You press your palm flat against the window and say *thank you.* When the monkey presses its hand against yours, you feel your eyes tear up.

Moose

Traits: Moose symbolizes blending in and not attracting attention to yourself. Moose prefers to go unnoticed and likes to be left alone. You tend to have the same qualities, and, like moose, people often underestimate your strength. Moose has huge antlers, which are indicative of great spirituality. At one with itself and nature, moose is deeply connected to the earth. You are grounded as well. Moose warns that you need to camouflage yourself at this time. Stay out of the forefront and in the background. Your time to step to the forefront will happen in due time.

Talents: Camouflage, dignity, gentleness, heightened senses, intelligent, intuition, mental prowess, observant, self-reliant, shy, spiritual power, strength

Challenges: Awkward, contradictory, lumbering, reclusive, unpredictable, unsocial

Element(s): Earth, water

Primary Color(s): Black, brown, gray (in winter)

Appearances: Moose appears when you're embracing your own self-expression. Moose has a unique set of antlers that sets it apart from other animals. This means that you need to search inside to find the qualities that set you apart from other people. Moose enjoys the waters of a marshland. Take time to enjoy a stream, sit by a lake, or take a warm bath to reestablish your water connection. Moose is very inconsistent and warns of you being the same. Moose wanders so you never know when it will show up, which makes it unreliable. If you find that you're consistently late to work or events, or you often have to cancel plans, then you're out of balance and need to refocus. This type of behavior reflects badly on you in the eyes of others, and while you don't care what other people think, this can be harmful to your reputation in the long run. Think ahead, not in the moment. Moose holds the knowledge of the ancients within its being. This knowledge is also within you, and moose can help you access it.

Assists When: You need to keep a low profile or disappear into the background. Moose can pull you away from the spotlight to give you time to regroup. You avoid forcing your way in any situation. You're not a bully, but your inner strength, motivation, and determination in reaching your goals can make you appear that way. If this happens, moose can help you step back, evaluate, and move forward with a different approach that feels less threatening to others. Your power is great and can be intimidating to those that don't understand you. You are unexpectedly quick moving and others often have a hard time keeping up with you. During uncertain times, moose can give you direction. It has excellent depth perception and can see below the surface. Look to moose to gain clarity. You are a figure of enormous authority, even if you don't always see it. People look up to you, want your advice, and honor your wisdom. Make sure you are setting a good example.

Frequency: Moose's energy sounds like heavy, muffled steps. It feels like a strong wind swirling around you. It is powerful, heavy, and strong, grounding you to the earth while lifting you up to infinite possibilities.

Imagine...

Your feet crunch through the snow as you head back to the ski lodge for the night. You look back over your shoulder and see a large moose standing on a rise behind you. The moon is behind it, casting it in a glowing light. Its huge antlers give it an air of dignity and strength. It's not moving, just looking out across the snow. The scene is beautiful, so you pull out your cell phone to capture the shot. As you watch, another smaller moose walks up behind the first one. They walk forward together, their large bodies moving with an unexpected elegance. Suddenly they both stop and look in your direction. You feel the energy of their spirit flowing toward you, swirling around you, heightening your senses, connecting you to their confident self-reliance. You feel stronger and more grounded just being in their presence. Moments pass before they turn away and walk down the rise and out of sight.

Mouse

Traits: Mouse symbolizes scrutiny, discovery, wisdom, and sensitivity. Mouse has a quiet, nervous nature, is a dependable worker, and prefers sticking with routine. Within its burrow, it has the equivalent of a kitchen, bathroom, and bedroom in separate areas. It keeps its home clean and organized. Everything has its place. You are like mouse in this regard. Your home might not be spotless but you always know where to find everything. Mouse makes facial expressions to communicate its mood to other mice. Scientists believe mice are able to empathize with one another and the feelings of others can affect their own mood. They are very vocal and their sounds are often outside of our range of hearing. If threatened, mouse will play dead until the danger is gone. A group of mice is referred to as a mischief, which they often get into!

Talents: Adaptable, balance, clever, detail oriented, exploration, fertility, intelligence, meticulous, mischief, plays dead, quiet, unobtrusive

Challenges: Timid, nervous, hoarding, possessive

Element(s): Earth

Primary Color(s): Black, brown, gray, silver, white

Appearances: When mouse appears, it's a sign to tone down the excitement in your life, pay attention to details, and stop wasting energy. You're approaching an upcoming change that needs to be handled with delicacy and finesse. Mouse loves exploration but stays close to home. It will only travel twenty feet from its nest and tends to stick to the same paths. This means that sometimes you have to force yourself out of your comfort zone to have adventures and experience new areas. Mouse is very fertile; it begins breeding at two months of age, can have a litter of up to twelve babies every three weeks, and gets pregnant again forty-eight hours after delivery. This is a sign that your endeavors will be very fertile and productive at this time. If mouse appears, look for new projects or businesses to start.

Assists When: You need to be organized and pay attention to details. Mouse can help you see important things you may be missing, scrutinize the specifics, and let go of whatever isn't needed. It can also help you see the big picture when you become so focused on the details that you forget the ultimate plan. Mouse has scales on its tail to help it climb. You tend to have a knack for business. It can assist you as you climb the ladder of corporate or entrepreneurial success. Mouse helps you take a hard look at your communication skills. If you're staying quiet instead of giving input, spreading gossip or rumors, or being forceful with your opinions, mouse can help you regain balance and replace negativity with positivity.

Frequency: Mouse energy scurries, scratches, and bites. It feels itchy, like you have something on you that you need to brush off. It sounds like a raspy squeak overlaid with a high-pitched squeal.

Imagine…

You're sitting on the floor sorting through the boxes scattered around you when you see a movement out of the corner of your eye. Sitting next to the wall is a tiny mouse. You wonder how it got inside and try to think of the best way to catch and release it. You get up and grab one of the boxes and the broom. You send telepathic messages and images to the mouse of him running into the box and you taking it outside to let him go. Moving very slowly, you put the box on the floor in front of him and the broom behind him. It looks up at you then runs directly into the box. *Huh,* you think to yourself as you pick up the box, *that was almost too easy*. You take the mouse outside and far from your house and place the box on its side on the ground. The little mouse runs out, looks at you, then stands up on its back feet and makes some squeaking sounds (as if to say thank you) before running away. Gathering your box, you head back inside to finish up the sorting.

Narwhal

Traits: Narwhal is a medium-sized Arctic whale known as the unicorn of the sea. It is rarely seen, but it is a very social animal that swims in pods. It has two teeth located in the upper jaw. After the males turn a year old, the left tooth starts to grow outward, spiraling to the left as it grows to form a tusk, which can grow to ten feet. It is used in courtship, to poke holes in the ice, to show dominance, and to amplify sonar pulses that the narwhal emits, but it is not used in hunting. In medieval times, narwhal tusks that were found on shore were thought to be from unicorns and given to royalty as such.

Talents: Achiever, analytical, beauty, calm, carefree, connection to the Divine, creative, deep feelings, hidden truths, dreamer, emotional healing, excellent memory, at ease in difficult situations, fights for beliefs, freedom, imagination, intelligent, knowing, lots of ideas, magical, mysterious, observant, passionate, planner, rational, resilient, romantic, rules own domain, sees the wonder in everything, sensitive to injustice, strong desire to succeed, unique, works better alone

Challenges: Easily frustrated, impulsive, moody, rebel, reclusive, too intense, unpredictable, wanderer

Element(s): Water

Primary Color(s): Blue-gray at birth, blue-black as juveniles, mottled-gray as adults, all white when elderly

Appearances: When narwhal appears, it means you need to find balance in your life. You're creative, have an overabundance of ideas, and have the drive to see them to fruition. Your brain never seems to slow down, even in your sleep. Finding balance is important right now. Without balance, you can burn out or get sick because you're wearing yourself out. Narwhal helps you to quiet your mind and make specific plans to ensure success with clear focus while getting the rest you need. Narwhal means you are always trying to understand yourself. You're interested in a wide range of subject matter, research, and applying the things you learn for self-analysis. Narwhal helps you find purpose in all that you do. You go the extra mile with passion and purpose to learn your own lessons in life and to help others learn their lessons. You may move from job to job or relationship to relationship often, but when you finally settle down, it is with the knowledge that you learned something from every experience.

Assists When: You need to complete a project fast. Narwhal gives you the drive, focus, and intensity to get the job done. Narwhal warns against becoming so focused that you push aside people who are willing and able to help you, causing both inner conflict and frustration for you and hurt feelings on the other person's part. Narwhal means you can be slow to mature and move from chaotic situations and relationships in your youth to more balanced, grounded, and accepting circumstances and relationships as you age. Narwhal urges you to be more romantic, mysterious, and magical. It can help you heal a broken heart. Narwhal can eliminate negative emotions, dive deeply to see below the surface, and be true to your soul's nature. Narwhal warns against living in a fantasy world, becoming too reclusive, and never accepting help from others.

Frequency: Narwhal energy moves in a slow, easy, undulating motion. It is cold, smooth, and fluid. It sounds like a squeaky door or a slow croaking frog.

See Also: Dolphin (Porpoise), Unicorn, Whale

Imagine…

In your dream, you're standing on a mound of ice, looking out over the Arctic Ocean. In the distance, you see narwhal tusks rising out of the water. You feel drawn to the water, to the narwhals, and you dive into the frigid water, but you're not cold. You swim to the pod of narwhals and they welcome you into their group, taking great care not to touch you with their tusks. Running your hand over their backs, you feel a sense of great knowledge—universal truths and a connection to the Divine pass through you, filling you with warmth, compassion, and acceptance. You wake from your dream feeling at peace, loved, and one with all there is.

Octopus (Squid)

Traits: Octopus symbolizes staying out of sight, keeping quiet about your plans, and making changes according to your circumstances. Octopus has three hearts. One circulates blood to the organs and the other two circulate blood past the gills to the rest of the body. Octopus prefers to crawl because when it swims, the heart supplying blood to the organs stops beating. Octopus is connected to ancient knowledge because it has been in existence for about three hundred million years. Each octopus has a unique personality, can solve problems, and remembers the solution, and takes things apart just for the enjoyment of it. After mating, the male octopus dies. After the female's eggs hatch, the female dies. This symbolizes that to be reborn, part of you must die. In the octopus's case it is a physical death, but in yours it can be a major, life-altering change in the spiritual, emotional, or personal part of you.

Talents: Adaptability, ancient knowledge, artistic, changes color, emotionally grounded, flexible, graceful, imagination, insightful, intuitive, invisibility, versatile

Challenges: Clingy, controlling, defensive, idealistic, inconsistent, possessive, slippery

Element(s): Water

Primary Color(s): It changes to any color it needs to be depending on the environment.

Appearances: When octopus appears, it means to take cover and blend into your surroundings because a threat is near. Octopus ink acts as a cover so it can get away and hide when threatened. Octopus ink is extremely harmful. It can attack the predator's senses of smell and taste and can blind it. If octopus gets caught in its own ink, it can die. This means you have to be cautious when instigating an attack on someone because you might just get caught up in your own darkness if there are lies hidden underneath. The mimic octopus can also camouflage itself by changing colors to match its surroundings. It does this so well it isn't even noticed by predators. Octopus appears when something is holding you back from forward motion. It can allow you to see what is restraining you, whether it's a relationship, job, or your own fears. Once you let go, you'll be able to float freely through an ocean of opportunity and select a new, exciting prospect that allows personal or spiritual growth.

Assists When: You need to do several things at once. Octopus has two thirds of its neurons in its arms, so the arms can be taking something apart while the brain is planning its next move. If you're juggling lots of different tasks, octopus can help you handle them with ease. When you encounter obstacles, octopus encourages you to just glide right over them and wiggle free from predicaments or uncomfortable situations. Octopus can help you reach out and grab what you want. It helps you reach goals through steady forward motion. When life feels murky or unclear, octopus reminds you to use your sixth sense to bring things to light. You can see clearly, even in darkness, if you use your intuitive abilities.

Frequency: Octopus energy is fluid. It can feel cool or warm. It sounds muted, thick, and a little bit hollow. It feels as if you're floating on your back in a pool and then let yourself slowly sink underwater.

See Also: Kraken

Imagine...

As you wander around the public aquarium, you arrive at a window with low light. You peer inside and wonder if it's an empty exhibit because there doesn't appear to be any marine life inside. Then it looks as if the floor ripples. You look closer and notice an octopus lying toward the back near some large rocks. It lifts a tentacle as if it's greeting you and you see the white suction cups on the underside. You take a seat on the bench in front of the window and watch for a while. You feel its energy as a fluid heartbeat surrounding you, embracing you. It makes you feel grounded and safe. You think about your spirituality and about universal and ancient knowledge. You decide that now is the time to get back in touch with your inner self. When you leave the exhibit, it is with a sense of purpose.

Opossum

Traits: Opossum symbolizes the strategic use of deception for protection. If threatened, opossum will play dead until the predator loses interest, then it runs to safety. Opossum is nocturnal, preferring darkness to cover its movements. It is secretive and mysterious, uses trickery to fool others into believing false information, and is calculating in its approach to life. It means to use your intellectual and intuitive abilities to get yourself out of sticky situations. If you need to temporarily put on a mask of falseness, do so to save yourself.

Talents: Clever, deception for protection, diverse, dramatic, element of surprise, guidance, pretending, recovery, resourceful, sensibility, strategic, strength, talented, wisdom

Challenges: Dirtiness, overly deceptive, pretense, putrid smell, trickery

Element(s): Earth

Primary Color(s): Gray, white

Appearances: When opossum appears, it means to check your appearance. Not only how you look, but how others perceive your personality, moral code, and character traits. While you aren't particularly concerned about impressing others, knowing their opinions can help you see areas where you can make improvements if you choose to create changes. Opossum means a strong love of family and devotion to those in your close circle of friends. Its pouch symbolizes nurturing, the closeness of loved ones, and hidden resources. This means you tend to always have something up your sleeve, a hidden surprise that can help you out of a jam. Opossum isn't easily intimidated by others higher up in the chain of command. It often has backup plans to ensure its success. Opossum has natural acting ability. This serves you well when you don't want others to see your true feelings or if you're going through a personal trauma that you want to hide from the world.

Assists When: You need a strategy. Opossum is creative and intelligent. It means you can plan a course of action, set that action into motion, and then go after your end goal with the strength of being needed to claim your success. If you're having difficulty coping with a situation that is out of your control, opossum urges you to look at it through a focused lens to see it as it truly is and not as you want it to be. You see people as they are, faults and all, even if they're hiding behind a disguise (as you may do as well) and you are accepting of their nature. You are physically in good shape and enjoy working out or sports. Nighttime activities attract you. You enjoy having fun and getting a little crazy sometimes, even hanging upside down! If opossum chooses to fight back when threatened, it is ferocious and violent in its attack. With razor-sharp teeth it can do a great deal of damage. It warns that your words can cut to the bone, so don't say things you'll regret later. Opossum also encourages you to live and love with fierce abandon.

Frequency: Opossum energy smells like stinky, rotten meat. It is strong and rancid, making your eyes burn. Yet, if you get past the smell, it is full of nurturing, love, and wisdom. It feels like a stinging salt spray into your eyes, sand biting into your skin, and wind whipping around you. It sounds like silence, darkness, and solitude.

Imagine…

It's late and you've just gotten home from a long day at work. As you walk toward your front porch and get out your keys, your thoughts are interrupted by a scratchy-sounding hiss and growl. You look up to see an opossum sitting in front of your door. You stop walking and wait for it to move out of the way. It complains at you for a while longer, so you decide to leave it alone and walk around the side of the house and go in the back door. A while later you look out of the window beside the front door. The opossum is still there, and now you realize why it was so upset earlier. There are three baby opossums walking around beside the mama opossum. After a while, they disappear under her stomach and the mama opossum leaves your porch.

Orangutan

Traits: Orangutan symbolizes manifestation, creation, longevity, family, and the bond between mother and child. Orangutan's life span is thirty-five to forty years in the wild or fifty to sixty years in captivity. Mothers take care of their young longer than any other animal. Babies nurse until they're six years old. Males stay with their mother for several more years, but females stay into their teens and only leave when ready to have a baby. Females only have babies every eight years. This means to take a look at your relationship with your mom, or remember her if she's passed on. Think about the things she taught you as a child and how you relate to one another.

Talents: Creativity, gentleness, honorable, independent, intelligent, logical, longevity, manifesting, movement, nurturing, problem solver, solitude, survivalist, travel, wisdom, wit

Challenges: Letting go, unsociable

Element(s): Air, earth (rarely)

Primary Color(s): Brown, red

Appearances: When orangutan appears, it is a sign that your life may feel like it's spinning out of control. Orangutan means you must pay attention to what's going wrong and take charge again to set things right. Orangutan doesn't give up. It has a high level of intelligence and can use tools and solve problems. Orangutan lends you these qualities to fix what's going wrong in your life. Orangutan also means to look upward, raise yourself to higher elevations both in your personal life and in your spiritual outlook. You can reach great heights once you start climbing. Orangutan lives in the tops of trees and rarely goes to the ground. Everything they need to survive is in the treetops. Males, because of their large size, will visit the earth more often than females, who usually never leave the safety of their treetop homes. This is a sign that you have everything you need within you already. You just have to access your core spiritual self to see the true essence of your being. Your soul is your home and you are at peace there. Get to know your higher self better. Orangutan means you need some time alone. Solitude is enlightening.

Assists When: You need to climb to great heights or hold on to something in your life. Orangutan uses both its hands and feet to grip objects and to climb from limb to limb. It can help you reach your goals quickly and efficiently. Orangutan can lend a hand when you're being creative. It can give you new project ideas or show you how to put color and form together to create a work of art. It also helps when you're trying to manifest your desires into your life. If you're unsure about someone's intention, orangutan encourages you to find the truth by watching their body language and facial expressions. They may be making all kinds of noise, but their movements and face will tell the truth of the matter. You are intuitive, gentle, and nurturing, especially with children. You spend extra time to make sure they grasp new ideas and understand what you're teaching.

Frequency: Orangutan energy is like a grumbling sound rumbling around in your throat. It spikes to a high mid-toned pitch with a kissy sound at the end. It clatters and clucks as it reverberates around you. It feels like small gravel that you're rolling between the palms of your hand but soft like a big fuzzy pillow.

See Also: Monkey, Squirrel Monkey

Imagine ...

You're at the zoo where the orangutan exhibit is located. You sit down on a bench to watch a mother and baby, who is nursing. The baby keeps looking at you, and then it climbs out of its mother's lap and gets as close to you as it can. You look at the mother, who is quietly watching you. You feel a bit of wariness from the mother, but also a sense of trust. After a while, the baby crawls back into its mother's lap and falls asleep.

Owl

Traits: Owl symbolizes wisdom, adaptability, and resourcefulness. Owl can turn its head 270 degrees due to the fourteen vertebrae in its neck, which makes up for the fact that its eyes are immobile. When owl turns its head, its blood supply is cut off to the brain, but it has the ability to pool blood for use by the brain when the neck turns. Owls have binocular vision that gives them great depth perception. This means that while you tend to focus straight ahead, you don't ignore what's happening around you. In fact, you see more deeply than others, are quick to understand situations, and store resources for future use.

Talents: Accuracy, exceptional hearing, intelligence, intuitive knowledge, silent movement, wisdom

Challenges: Detachment, secretive, standoffish, superiority

Element(s): Air

Primary Color(s): Black, brown, white

Appearances: When owl appears, it means you should pay attention to everything around you. Not only what you can see, but what you hear and what you intuitively know or feel. There are great important changes coming your way and you need to be aware and prepared to accept them. This is a time to be silent and observe. Anything hidden will be revealed at this time. Owl means you can see the truth behind the disguise, the intention behind the actions, the unexplained within reality. In many traditions, owl is the messenger of death. This doesn't mean a physical death but is symbolic of a major life disruption, transition, or other change. Maybe you're getting married, or having a child, or moving to a new country. This symbolic death is often very positive. Owl is also connected to the wisdom of the ages. It seeks knowledge through its keen observation skills. You too glean your knowledge by observing, reading, and absorbing everything you can to give you that same wisdom. You are insightful and tend to know just the right thing to say to open someone's eyes to other possibilities. When owl appears, it often means something big is about to happen to you. Be prepared!

Assists When: You need to see someone as they truly are or get to the bottom of something. Owl urges you to look at every situation from all angles to see the truth hidden inside. You are very intelligent, crave knowledge of all kinds, and also learn through observation. Owl can help you study better, retain information longer, and recall what you know when you need it. Since owl is nocturnal, you may frequently pull all-nighters when studying, or you may get so wrapped up in what you're reading that you don't even realize the time. If you're feeling lost or surrounded by darkness, owl reminds you that you see perfectly in such conditions so keep moving silently forward as it guides you into the light.

Frequency: Owl's energy is a heavy silence filling the air. It moves with fast precision, slicing through the darkness. It feels like an intense, unseen weight pressing down on the top of your head but then is quickly released, making you feel as if you're flying.

See Also: Owlman

Imagine…

You're having a difficult time falling asleep when you hear the hoot of an owl outside. You get out of bed and peer out of the window to see if you can see it. You see a shadow in the tree, but you're not sure if that's the owl or just a weird-looking branch. Giving up, you go back to bed and listen. Its hoots between periods of heavy silence relax you. You think about the wisdom of the owl, imagine it sitting in the tree outside, looking all around. You imagine its feathers, soft yet coarse, as the wind blows them around. As you listen to its distinctive call, you find that you're feeling drowsy. You open your eyes and the morning sun is shining into your room. You feel rested and refreshed.

Oyster

Traits: Oyster symbolizes connecting to your inner essence, balance, and peace. Oysters can make pearls (and it's a specialty of the pearl oyster, not the food oyster) when bits of debris get stuck in the oyster's mantle. It secretes multiple layers of a substance called nacre (the same substance it uses to create its shell) to cover the irritant and a pearl is formed. This means that the things that bother you, like a grain of sand bothers the oyster, can be turned into something beautiful.

Talents: Creativity, discernment, intuition, resourcefulness, wisdom

Challenges: Defensive, emotional imbalance, overly sensitive

Element(s): Water

Primary Color(s): Gray, white

Appearances: When oyster appears, it means you might have to shut down and retreat into your shell to protect yourself. You need to keep quiet, filter out the good from the bad, or put a lid on your emotions until the threat has moved on. Oyster can retain toxins within their body, so it's important for you to make sure you're eating healthy and drinking plenty of fluids at this time. It's also important to let go of any negativity that comes your way instead of letting it affect you. Like the oyster, you're sensitive to your environment. Take a look around. Is there anything you can change to make your work or living area more positive, energetic, or calming? Rearranging your furniture can change the flow of energy if it feels blocked.

Assists When: You are facing difficulties in your life and need to find a place of balance. If you're in a hectic environment, oyster can help you find some peace with the chaos where you can connect to your own spirituality and inner self. There are treasures buried within you. Once you find and acknowledge them, life flows easily, with purpose, and you'll feel more balanced. Oysters are difficult to open, and this teaches you that no outside force can change who you truly are on the inside. You don't have to give in to peer pressure but can simply be yourself. It allows you to see what once was hidden. With oyster as a guide, you'll always see the best in bad situations and learn from the experience. You're the eye in the middle of the hurricane, calm and filled with light even though dark storm clouds rage around you. Struggles become victories with oyster's assistance. You have the strength within to handle anything that comes your way. Oyster can help you find harmony in mind, body, and spirit.

Frequency: Oyster's energy is calm and quiet, smooth yet jagged. It feels cool and fresh. It sounds like a long gurgle underwater.

> ### *Imagine...*
>
> You've discovered an oyster bed and are examining the clumped together shells, which are hard and irregular in shape. As you walk around the edge of the bed, you peer down into the shallow water and watch the oysters. Most have their shells slightly opened. You reach down and touch one with your finger and it snaps shut. The shell is rough, craggy, and feels a little slick to the touch. You can easily pick up the oyster, examine it, and put it back into the water. You walk along, feeling at one with the quiet calmness surrounding the bed. The energy feels pristine here. You sit down on the edge of the embankment and commune with the oyster energy, thinking about how such a small creature can make such beautiful pearls and how the exterior doesn't come close to reflecting the beauty that can be found within.

Panda

Traits: Panda symbolizes solitude, emotional balance, and overall harmony. Panda may look cute and cuddly on the outside, but it is strong and determined inside. Panda lives alone except during breeding season. It spends most of its day eating and sleeping. It doesn't play much. Panda has a sensitive digestive system and eats lots of bamboo, shoots, and other plants. This means you need to watch your diet at this time. If you've been eating lots of meats, cut back on those and add more vegetables and fruit for cleansing. Even though panda doesn't play often, it means you must have a little fun now and again.

Talents: Adaptability, calmness, determination, emotional strength, fortune, gentle strength, good luck, modesty, nurturing, peacefulness, personal growth, positive outlook, sensitivity, spirituality, tranquility, willpower

Challenges: Aloofness, fertility problems, overly sensitive, strict boundaries, too emotional

Element(s): Air, earth, water

Primary Color(s): Black, red, white

Appearances: When panda shows up, it means to slow down. You're moving at too fast of a pace and need to take more time to achieve your goals. If you try to force things to happen quickly, you may not get the desired outcome. It might take a little longer to accomplish your task, but the results will be exactly what you want and need. Panda doesn't hurry through life; instead it enjoys itself along the way. This means you also have to take time to enjoy life, especially if you've been pushing yourself really hard for a long time. Stop, breathe, and relax with panda. You tend to keep your distance at group events or keep others at arm's length. There is fear that if you let others get too close, then you might get hurt. If you've been hurt emotionally in the past don't let that experience hold you back from living life to the fullest. Panda means it's okay to have boundaries, just know when you're extending them so far that you're pushing people away and adjust them accordingly.

Assists When: You're going through a time of emotional upheaval. Panda is highly sensitive and enjoys peace and quiet. It can also get emotionally stressed out if it's too noisy or chaotic. It moves slowly and likes it when everyone else does, too. Panda can help you get your emotions back under control by teaching you to climb to greater heights to get out of the fray. It may lead you on a walk in the woods, or even encourage you to climb a tree and sit for a spell. Let your mind wander. Think about why your emotions are a mess and how you can get them back in line. Is there anything you can do? If so, then be determined to take a course of action and follow it through. If your emotional upset is due to another's actions or situation and there's nothing you can do, then you must find acceptance within yourself. You can't change people; they will only change when they are guided to do so from within. Panda's colors are balanced and indicate the steadiness you can find within yourself.

Frequency: Panda's energy is slow, steady, and strong. It sounds like faint scratches against wood, a loud chewing noise, and a faraway gong all happening at once. It feels fresh, bright, and breezy.

See Also: Bear

Imagine…

You find yourself in a bamboo forest. As you walk along, you come across a black and white panda sitting comfortably on the ground between the branches snacking on a plant. It glances over at you and keeps on eating. You decide to take a seat on a large boulder nearby and observe the beautiful being. After a while, it gets up and walks toward you. As it gets close, it stops to sniff the air, then it walks past you and heads toward a medium-sized tree. It climbs up the tree until it gets to a couple of branches close together. There it turns around and sits on the branches to watch you. Speaking softly, you talk to the panda, but soon you realize you're talking to yourself because the panda has fallen asleep. Smiling, you continue your journey, feeling as if you've just told a bedtime story.

Parrot (McCaw)

Traits: Parrot symbolizes alertness, mimicry, communication, and prophecy. Parrot is a very social bird that communicates through very loud screeches and squawks. Only a parrot kept as a pet can mimic; this bird in the wild doesn't do that. Parrot also doesn't have vocal cords, so it is mimicking by blowing air out of its trachea. Parrots are zygodactyls, which means their first and fourth toes point backward and the second and third point forward. This helps them grasp and climb. This means that sometimes you have to move in two directions or take a step backward as you're moving forward. Stay original and unique instead of mimicking others. Otherwise you might come across as if you're full of hot air.

Talents: Bonding, colorful, communicative, déjà vu, diplomacy, guidance, highly intelligent, hope, impressionist, interactive, joy, mystical, promise, prophecy, renewal, thinks before speaks, wisdom

Challenges: Arrogant, disruptive, mockery, overly talkative, reactive, trickster

Element(s): Air

Primary Color(s): Blue, green, red, yellow

Appearances: When parrot appears, it means to take center stage and stand out in the crowd. Now is your time to shine in everything you do. It also means someone needs your help and understanding. You may be asked to be a mediator between people having a disagreement. Your inner light shines brightly, your personality sparkles, and your smile is infectious. These qualities draw others to you. They value your opinion, want your advice, or simply enjoy being in your presence because you make them smile. You are filled with joy and share it with everyone you meet. Parrot encourages you to take flight and go after your dreams. They are within your reach; all you have to do is go get them. Parrot is diplomatic and urges you to be tactful. Avoid spreading gossip or hearsay. There are times to talk and times to keep quiet. Be aware and make sure you're not speaking when you should be listening. Parrot also means to listen to yourself. You're great at giving advice to others, but do you listen and take your own advice? Sometimes the only advice you need is your own.

Assists When: You need an immediate witty response. Have you ever left a conversation and thought, *I should have said…?* Parrot will give you those power words when you need them. If you need to add more color to your life, to your home, or to yourself, parrot can guide you to choose colors that will enhance and emphasize specific areas. When you need to make a good first impression or if you're planning an event that you want to be exceptional and extraordinary, parrot will take to wing and help you make it phenomenal. If you're learning a new language or working on better communication skills, parrot can aid in your studies. It can help you become more positive in your speech and more aware of the effect your words, and the way you deliver them, have on others.

Frequency: Parrot energy is a high-pitched squeal that makes you shudder. It runs through you like fingernails on a chalkboard. It thrums at odd intervals between squeals.

See Also: Cockatiel (Cockatoo, Parakeet), Lory (Rainbow)

Imagine…

While shopping you visit a store, and in the front near the register there is a big cage with a parrot inside. The beautiful green parrot is walking side to side on its wooden perch raising its wings and squawking. It snaps its beak a few times and then eats a few seeds out of its bowl. You watch how it maneuvers its tongue against its wings as it grooms its feathers. It notices you and walks closer to the edge of the cage and says, *Hello.* You say hello back and smile when it rocks back and forth as if dancing, then moves its neck up and down and its head side to side. It seems to be performing just for you. It whistles a little tune then turns around, spreads its wings wide, and flaps them a few times. An upbeat song starts to play on the store's music track and the bird really starts dancing along. You wander off into the store but keep an eye on the friendly, happy parrot.

Peacock

Traits: Peacock symbolizes astral projection, lucid dreaming, waking dreams, purpose, and movement between realms. Peacock is a very flashy and showy bird with a massive, six-foot-long tail (called a train) that is shed after every mating season. The species are actually named peafowl. The male is known as peacock, the females are peahens, and babies are peachicks. The large birds are able to fly short distances. The design on its train resembles eyes, which means you have great insight, are intuitive and often clairvoyant, and have tremendous vision and insight.

Talents: Beauty, colorful, determination, endurance, fashion, flashy, glamorous, grace, patience, self-discipline, showy, style, vibrant, vivid

Challenges: Arrogant, fake, haughty, vain

Element(s): Earth

Primary Color(s): Blue, green, white

Appearances: Peacock is connected to the spiritual realms. When it shows up, it means you need to delve into learning and understanding more about spirituality, intuition, dreaming, astral projection, transformation, and approaching life from a place of joy and love. As you grow in these areas, your inner light will become brighter and, like the peacock, you will shine in all of your beautiful inner glory. Peacock is a determined bird, which means you should never give up on any quest you've set out on. You might even have to strut your stuff to get what you want. When it comes to love, peacock makes a copulatory call when it mates. To attract more peahens, peacock fakes the call to make the hens think he's getting busy more often than he really is. That's a pretty creative way to woo the girls. When peacock appears, it means you're being a bit too vain. Turn down the vanity and turn up the modesty to get back in balance.

Assists When: You need any type of help. Peacock's call sounds like it is saying *Help! Help! Help!* While it may sound like it's asking for your help, instead it symbolically means help is right here if you need it, just ask peacock for assistance. When you're feeling gloomy or sad, peacock can revitalize your self-esteem. It will boost you up and get you moving forward in positivity. When you're feeling down, you're not down for long because the brilliance of peacock's showmanship will ignite a flame of color within you that gets you going. Peacock also means protection from any negativity you may encounter, luckiness in life, popularity, and being the center of attention. Through it all, remember to remain true to yourself and your ideals so that when you shed your beauty, as the peacock sheds its tail, you're still beautiful on the inside.

Frequency: Peacock energy is the steady beat of a bass drum, the steady gradual increase of the rolling strum of a harp. It stands tall, struts, and preens in its elegance. It feels like a hot fire flaming your passion.

Imagine…

While visiting a park outside the city, you notice a blue bird with gray and white wings and a long train behind it. There are a few of them together wandering around pecking at the ground. The peahens only have the iridescent colors around their necks and a brownish gray body. You take out your cell phone, setting it to video just in case it decides to put on a show. You're not disappointed. The large male walks over to a peahen and lifts its tail and spreads the feathers out in an arch all around it, dropping its wings down low. It prances, shaking its wings and waving the long feathers of its train back and forth. The peahen notices but walks away. The peacock follows, elevating its courtship efforts to gain the peahen's attention. It turns around, showing her all of its brilliant feathers. When she resumes eating and wanders farther away, it drops the train back to the ground, lifts its wing feathers back on top of the train, and begins pecking the ground for food.

Penguin

Traits: Penguin symbolizes the ability to move between realms, hidden knowledge, and opening to new levels of awareness. Penguin easily moves from water to land. Its unique coloring is primarily for camouflage when in the water. From above, the darkness of its back blends into the color of the sea, from below the white belly and bright surface of the ocean seem to merge, making them difficult to see from both directions. Penguin survived the extinction of the dinosaurs. Scientists found ancestral fossils that are sixty million years old. All penguins are black and white except for one tiny species, which is blue. Let your uniqueness shine too.

Talents: Adaptability, astral projection, balance, camouflage, confident, determination, disciplined, fasting, focused, good manners, grace, intuitive, lucid dreaming, nurturing, orderly, parenthood, patience, politeness, purpose, sacrifice, waking dreams

Challenges: Abandonment, coldness, conflicted, overly serious, poor eyesight, rudeness, territorial, unmoving viewpoints

Element(s): Earth, water

Primary Color(s): Black, blue, white

Appearances: When penguin appears, it means to develop your spirituality. Analyze what you've learned, practice using your abilities, and look for more topics of interest. You're not finished with your spiritual growth, so keep exploring. Meditation and dreaming are two areas where penguin can show you hidden knowledge and open your eyes to new information, enabling you to become more spirituality aware. Penguin is nurturing. This means you care for the young and teach them how to be responsible, independent adults. Penguin doesn't have natural ground predators, so it's not afraid of humans and will approach with interest. This means you aren't a fearful person and have an insatiable curiosity, which can get you into trouble if you're not careful. Penguin is a flightless bird, which means you're grounded, balanced, secure in yourself, and can dive to tremendous depths to uncover any knowledge you seek. Penguin urges you to investigate new thoughts and ideals.

Assists When: You need to work with a team. Penguins congregate in large groups, especially during mating season. They can assist you with managing projects, people, and seeing an endeavor through to a successful completion. When you need to get dressed up for an important formal function, penguin can help you select the right attire and give you the confidence needed to mingle and mix with others at the event. Penguin means you are charismatic, influential, and well-spoken. Penguin can help you deal with the effects of any transitions. Penguin doesn't lose its feathers slowly, instead it molts, dropping all of its feathers at one time, leaving it naked and forced to stay on land for several weeks until the feathers grow back. This means that even if you feel you've been stripped of everything, the situation is temporary and life will return to normal, you just can't give up hope.

Frequency: Penguin energy is choppy yet fluid, sharp yet silent. It moves with a quiet strength, pushing, pulling, and lifting you on its currents. It is cold yet streaked with warmth as if you're standing a distance from a fire in winter and feel both elements at the same time.

> ### *Imagine...*
>
> At the zoo, they have an Antarctic exhibit that features penguins. You observe the flightless birds standing on rocks among snow and ice that is near the edge of a water tank. They shake their tails, waddle around, and play with each other by touching beaks. Some lie down and slide along the snowy ice by pushing with their wings and back legs. Some dive down into the water then come back up and swim along the surface. You walk down to the lower viewing area to watch them swim. They're sleek and fast in their movement, which is in strong contrast to their slow waddle on shore. Using its wings as propellers, one of the penguins swims up to the window to look at you for a moment before quickly turning and speeding away.

Porcupine

Traits: Porcupine symbolizes buoyancy, cleverness, strength, and a sense of awe. Porcupine is born with its quills, which are soft and harden a few hours after birth. The anatomical structure of the quill allows porcupine to float. It can't throw its quills, but they release easily from porcupine's body. When a predator gets too close, porcupine pushes against the attacker, the quills stick into the skin, and the attacker runs away. They have barbs on the end that make the quill dig deeper into the flesh.

Talents: Cheerful, childlike wonder, clever, curiosity, fearless, good-natured, helpful, inner power, innocence, joy, monogamous, sharp wit, trusting, unique defenses, vitality

Challenges: Bristly, hurtful, overly defensive, overly sensitive, prickly, sarcastic, spiky

Element(s): Earth

Primary Color(s): Black, brown, white

Appearances: When porcupine appears, it is a warning to stay alert for some type of attack coming your way. This could be in the form of a disgruntled coworker, family member, or even from a business. Porcupine also means to venture out and see the world. If you've been staying at home, porcupine urges you to get out and about. Porcupine usually lives alone or in groups of around six. This means that you work best in small groups. Have you lost your childlike innocence, your sense of awe and wonder? Porcupine can help you get it back when you've become disillusioned with people or the world. Today's world is so hectic and stressful that it's easy to get caught up in the negative and forget to see the beauty of our environment or the love of family and friends because we simply overlook them or take them for granted. Think about how a child is awed at the simplest magic trick when something disappears (behind your back) or when they see something they've never seen before (like rain). Can you see the wonder and magic in life again? Sure you can. Let porcupine lead the way.

Assists When: Someone is giving you a hard time and you need help getting away from them. It can also help if you are being too defensive or not defensive enough. Porcupine knows there's a thin line between protecting yourself and being overly paranoid that everyone is out to get you. It can teach you how to find that line and slightly lift your quills in warning when necessary instead of going into full-blown attack mode. Porcupine only eats plants. This is a reminder to review the way you've been eating recently. Are you eating too much meat? If so, increase your intake of vegetables. Your system needs them right now. Porcupine can also help you find time in your schedule to go exploring, take a nature walk, or even visit a petting zoo. You need some time in nature or around animals to regroup and get back to the center of your soul essence. With centering comes balance, with balance comes forward motion and growth.

Frequency: Porcupine's energy feels like floating down a lazy river on an inner tube. It sounds like it's saying *ah, ah, ah* and has adorable sounding pitches, squeals, and grunts. It can also feel sharp and prickly with a high-pitched warning scream echoing around you.

See Also: Hedgehog

Imagine...

You're camping and are just finishing up your dinner when a porcupine wanders into your campsite. When it sees you, and the ear of corn in your hand, it tentatively walks up to where you're sitting. You decide that this little guy must really be hungry if it's brave enough to approach you. Carefully you hold the ear of corn out toward it. You're very aware of the damage those quills can do so you take care not to make it feel threatened in any way. It stands on its hind legs, reaches out, and takes the corn cob you're offering. Then it hunkers down and gets to eating. It likes corn! You watch, softly chuckling at the soft, squeaky sounds of pleasure it makes while enjoying the food. When it is finished, it looks to you for more, so you hand it another ear. Once it's done with that one, it wanders back into the woods.

Raccoon

Traits: Raccoon symbolizes resourcefulness, intelligence, and communication. Raccoon is a nocturnal animal that lives in communities of four to five adults. It will eat a wide range of food and often go through human trash to find something delicious. It washes its food in water before eating it, but if it doesn't have access to water, it'll rub the food against its fur to clean it. Raccoon has great communication skills. It uses more than two hundred different sounds and about fifteen different calls when interacting with other raccoons.

Talents: Adaptability, cleanliness, clever, curious, dexterity, friendly, gentle, ingenious, intelligent, methodical, neat, organized, resourceful, stealth

Challenges: Fussiness, nuisance, overreacts, sneaky, snooping

Element(s): Earth, water

Primary Color(s): Black, gray

Appearances: When raccoon appears, it means you need to do something constructive with your hands. Draw, paint, or pick up a new hobby where you build something out of wood, metal, or clay. Maybe you like sewing, knitting, making albums, or beadwork. Any kind of hands-on activity will work. Raccoon is a friendly animal but can react ferociously if threatened. This same quality applies to you. You're outgoing, friendly, and will do anything for anyone, but if someone talks about you behind your back or threatens you in any way, watch out. Your reaction is usually quick, unexpected, and your words will rip through someone. You don't back down from a fight and will attack first if necessary. Raccoon warns not to lose your mind like that. Try to control the reaction and take measured, calculated steps. You'll still get what you want through controlled fierceness without coming across as crazy. Raccoon warns that it would be easy for you to become obsessed with washing your hands or food so make sure you're staying in balance.

Assists When: You need to succeed in an undertaking. Raccoon is ingenious and can figure out original and unique ways to accomplish tasks. It easily adapts to changes while finding clever resolutions to problems. Raccoon assists when you need to hide.

When you don't want someone to know your true intentions or if there is something about yourself that you don't want known, raccoon can help you stay behind a mask of secrecy. Raccoon can also be very talkative, so if you need to speak to a group or write a presentation it can give you interesting and fun ways to say things to engage your audience or reader. If you've let clutter build up at your home or in your work space, now is the time to clear it out and get organized. Raccoon enjoys an orderly existence and can help you clean up and reorganize. If you've been acting out of character, raccoon can help you remove whatever's bothering you so you can get back to your normal self.

Frequency: Raccoon energy sounds like a chattering, whistling grunt with a few screams mixed in. It hisses, snarls, and growls. It feels spooky, as if you have to keep looking over your shoulder to see what's behind you. It has positive energy, not negative, and soon wraps you in its affectionate glow.

Imagine…

You're sitting in your yard drawing the sunset with colored pencils. When you finish, you put away your supplies. When you remove the drawing from the easel and place it in a bag, you notice a small raccoon standing a short distance away. You keep an eye on it as you store the easel. You sit in your chair as it comes closer. Its energy feels like it's lost and sad. When it puts its front paws on your pants legs, you realize it's a baby and instinctively reach down to pick it up. You hold it in your lap, rubbing down its back as it snuggles close to you. You scratch softly behind its ears for a while. Then it moves and wants to get down, so you gently set it back on the ground. It walks away into the night.

Raven (Crow)

Traits: Raven symbolizes speaking up for yourself, learning new skills, and studying metaphysical topics. Raven's intelligence makes learning fun, and you'll retain the knowledge faster. Raven means there is a situation coming your way where you'll need to voice your feelings instead of holding your tongue. Raven uses its beak to point things out to other ravens and will hold things to get other bird's attention. Raven is sneaky and will steal food from other animals by working in teams. One leads the other animal away while the other raven takes its food.

Talents: Articulate, brings light, change in consciousness, comfort, communicative, courage, creation, fearless, honor, intelligent, introspection, keen observer, loyal, messenger, playful, protective, rebirth, renewal, sentry, social, transformation, vigilant, visionary

Challenges: Aggression, argumentative, overly critical, pessimistic, suspicious

Element(s): Air

Primary Color(s): Black

Appearances: Raven means to be aware of the meanings of dreams and visions. While raven has often been thought to be a dark messenger that foretells death, seeing raven can be a warning instead of meaning death. There may be someone who doesn't have your best interest at heart, or who might betray you or try to deceive you in some way. If raven appears, keep these things in mind, watch what you say, and stay alert to any changes in people's actions or words. Raven shows empathy for other ravens, remembers other ravens that it likes, and greets them in a friendly manner. It reacts negatively to enemies and is suspicious of ravens it doesn't know. This means people like you because you're understanding and empathize with their situations. You are friendly with everyone except those you don't like (you ignore them). When you meet new people, you're not as open as you are with your friends, but you treat them in a friendly, if guarded, manner. Once you get to know them, they receive your happy, friendly nature in abundance.

Assists When: You need to play more. Raven loves a fresh fallen snow and will find a slope and roll down it. Raven means that even though life is serious, full of mystery, and always on the go, you have to find time to play and enjoy yourself. Raven has often been referred to as the "keeper of secrets," which means that right now you've got a secret you must keep either for yourself or for someone else, and it's a doozy. You might be very tempted to tell this secret but don't. Keep it safe and secure inside you. Raven can mimic human speech better than a parrot. This means that if you need to learn to do something well, find someone who can teach you and mimic what they do. Learn from the mistakes of others so you don't make the same ones. Raven is metaphysical and symbolizes reaching through the darkness to find and resolve your inner conflicts, then letting your light shine bright. It's healing oneself from within.

Frequency: Raven energy is slick, oily, and warm. It feels like you're immersed in darkness but there is no fear. It sounds like an ambient deep space storm swirling all around you, whipping you from place to place as you uncover the mysteries of the universe.

Imagine…

Loud, raspy, guttural *cawing* sounds fill the air around you. Looking up, you see the sky is filled with a flock of black ravens. They land all around you. One of the birds flies down from a tree to land two feet in front of you. It walks in a circular motion, flaps its wings, and caws. Then it flies back to the tree. You know that action just meant something, but you don't know what it is. So you sit on the ground where the raven stood, close your eyes, and ask raven to show you its message. A scene moves through your mind, depicting a solution to a situation you're involved in, showing you moving forward from it in grace and light. You see yourself growing spiritually and undertaking a new task. When you open your eyes, the area is empty of birds. They've silently flown away.

Rhinoceros

Traits: Rhinoceros symbolizes strength, protection, insight, and ancient wisdom. Rhinoceros is more than sixty million years old. It is one of the largest animals on the earth. Most rhinos live a solitary life with the exception of the white rhino, which prefers to live in family groups. Rhino's horn, which indicates insightfulness and intuition, is made up of compacted keratin (not bone), isn't connected to its skull, and will grow back in about three years if cut off. Rhino also symbolizes uncovering hidden knowledge, communing with the inner self, and recalling past life memories.

Talents: Achievement, awareness, confident, craves social interaction, determined, discrimination, heightened senses, inner wisdom, insightful, intuition, likes to be the center of attention, lucky, never backs down from a challenge, resourceful, self-guidance, self-reliance, sensitivity, solitary, strong

Challenges: Aggressive, aloofness, braggart, difficulties relaxing, doesn't compromise, doesn't connect with others easily, impetuousness, intimidating, risk taker, untrusting

Element(s): Earth, water

Primary Color(s): Gray

Appearances: When rhinoceros appears, it means to slow down and be patient. A female rhino is pregnant for fifteen to sixteen months. This reminds you that some things in life can't be rushed. You simply have to wait until developments unfold. Trying to push or rush a situation will only have adverse effects. Rhino can't see well but instead relies on its heightened sense of smell and hearing to alert it to danger, trigger memories of where they're at, and to find watering holes. This means it's important not to rely only on what you see (because appearances can be deceiving) but to instead rely on all of your senses. Rhino's skin is very thick for added protection, but it is also incredibly sensitive to sunburn and bug bites so it frequently rolls in mud to keep a coating over its skin to shield it. This is a sign to connect with earth frequency. It can help you rejuvenate physically, renew your inner self, and heal emotionally.

Assists When: You need to return to center, remain calm, learn from your higher self, and find balance in your life. Rhino can help you know yourself better, not only as you are in the human experience but as you are in spirit. Rhino urges you to be true to yourself without letting peer pressure or other outside influences sway you from your path. You are powerful, centered, grounded, and secure in the awareness of your own spirit and universal energy. If you're distracted, worried, out of sorts, or feel like you're sinking into the mud, ask rhino to guide you back to solid ground with its sure-footed strength. It can also help you become thick-skinned so you're no longer upset by other people's actions or words. You see them as they are and maintain harmony within yourself instead of reacting to their drama.

Frequency: Rhinoceros energy sounds like a thundering, pounding, deep bass reverberation that moves in a four-beat tone. It is mist rising from the ground. You feel it weaving around you, mixing with your breath. It is ancient awareness that circles, waiting for you to reach out and touch it.

Imagine…

You wake from a dream to find yourself lying on the ground with something licking your face. You look over to see a huge horn right beside your head. You look past it right into the eyes of a huge rhinoceros. Immediately you panic but don't move a muscle, except your heart, which is now beating triple time. The rhino keeps licking you all over. When it moves toward your feet, you try to stand but are unsteady. You can't figure out what's wrong with your legs. They just don't seem to be working right. You look to the rhino for help and it lifts you up with its horn, helping you stand. Once you feel steady you take a few steps and then look back at it. That's when you see your side and realize that you are a baby rhino. Startled, you bolt upright in bed. The rhino came to you in a dream.

Salamander

Traits: Salamander symbolizes rejuvenation, bouncing back from hardships, and intuitive awareness. Some salamanders don't have gills or lungs, so they breathe through the skin. It can also grow back its tail and legs if they're somehow removed. This means you can renew yourself if you've experienced injuries or loss. You just have to look deep within and use your own resources, internal healing power, and intuitive nature to rebound from difficulties.

Talents: Adaptability, aware, balance, change, dreams, emotional stability, energy, enlightenment, growth, intuition, motion, psychic abilities, resilience, resourceful, secrets, self-renewal, spirituality, transformation, transitions, visions

Challenges: Drawn to darkness, inconsistent, indifferent, overly emotional, poisonous, slimy personality, unreliable

Element(s): Earth, water

Primary Color(s): Black, gray, green, orange, pink, red, yellow, and many other colors and color combinations

Appearances: When salamander appears, it means change is coming. This will probably be some type of major change in your life that will create new opportunities and forward motion. But it will usually result in the loss of something prior to seeing the opportunity. It's the door closing before the window opens. It's letting go of something holding you back so a new opportunity can come your way. There's only so much room available for the things you can do on the physical realm. When your cup starts overflowing, either you have to make a conscious decision to let something go to free up time and energy so new things will come to you, or the universe will do it for you. Everything always happens for a reason, even if you don't know the reason at the time. Salamander can guide you through all of the highs and lows as you travel the path of transformation.

Assists When: You need to make adjustments in your life. If you've experienced a major change or loss or if your life has been turned upside down, salamander can help you stay focused, calm, and in control during these stressful times. It can keep you on your path and intent on positive forward motion, instead of letting you wander around in hopelessness, not knowing which way to turn. Salamander can give you direction and help you recover from any setbacks you have experienced. Salamander warns of change, so if you see it and the change hasn't happened yet, just remain aware and let it develop as it will. Don't force it or overreact to it but go with the flow to ensure you'll recover from it in record time. Salamander can also help in times that aren't a crisis. If you're feeling bored or need a new project to keep you busy, salamander can point you in the right direction. Salamander also has an important role in helping with your spiritual transformation and growth. It can help you become more enlightened by showing you the topics of information that will be most useful to you at this point in time.

Frequency: Salamander energy feels like a cool mist on a hot day. It is damp, moist, and sticky. It sounds like *whish, boing, rullluump, bing, ticker, ticker, ticker* and moves in a quickly undulating, side-to-side motion.

Imagine…

You're moving some medium-sized rocks to form a display around your porch to improve the landscaping. You pick up one of the rocks and several black-and-yellow spotted salamanders are sitting in the crevice beside another rock. You set the rock down and quickly catch the salamanders. You take them over to another part of your property and place them on the ground near the bottom of a tree where there are some other rocks that you're not planning to move. They crawl between the rocks and disappear. Feeling that you've done a good deed for them, you go back to work on your landscaping project.

Salmon

Traits: Salmon symbolizes home, rebirth, and a positive attitude. Salmon is born in freshwater. Most migrate to the ocean and travel up to 3,500 miles to return to their freshwater spawning grounds. They don't eat when migrating upstream but instead obtain energy from their stored belly fat. They lay between 2,500 and 7,000 eggs. Fifty percent will die after spawning, but those that don't can spawn two or three more times. This means to experience rebirth you have to return to your roots. Your positive attitude will allow you to see what is important to your personal or spiritual growth at this time. You may need to let go of something that's holding you back or reconnect to something you've forgotten.

Talents: Agility, ancient wisdom, confident, courage, creative, flexibility, generous, gives good advice, humble, insightfulness, overcoming obstacles, passionate, regeneration, spiritual knowledge, strength, tenderhearted, tolerant, tough, understanding divine messages

Challenges: Combative, controlling, egotistical, inflexible, overly intense, reckless, risk-taker, stubborn, thrill seeker

Element(s): Water

Primary Color(s): Pinkish orange

Appearances: Salmon means you're about to go on a grand adventure. Pack your bags and let salmon lead the way. Salmon shows distant travels to faraway lands, but it always returns home to recharge before heading out again. Salmon means that during this journey, whether it's spiritual or personal, you'll discover divine meaning, purpose, and joy in your life. You're destined to see the universal picture, not just the big one. There is purpose in everything and you're shown how all parts are interconnected. You're very energetic and often forget to eat because you become immersed in your discoveries or the work you're doing. Salmon gives you determination, confidence, agility, and the ability to understand and share divine messages, spiritual knowledge, and ancient wisdom. Your insightfulness will be important in helping others understand their own purpose and path.

Assists When: You need to be more adventurous or daring. Salmon can help you jump over obstacles to get to your goals. It gives you the ambition and drive to overcome what others may think are impossible hurdles. To you, they're just things you have to conquer to reach your final destination. If you're considering starting something new but find yourself hesitating because you know it's going to be a hard path to follow that will require lots of time and energy, salmon can show you the rewards at the end of the path. Home and family are important to you. Salmon can show you how to keep things moving fluidly and gives the words of wisdom and guidance needed to keep the home fires burning strongly for your family.

Frequency: Salmon's energy is arching, long, and deep. It moves with smoothness and grace. It sounds like *whoosh, zing, plop* followed by a deep snappy muted rumble.

Imagine…

You've always wanted to see the salmon migration in person, so this year you make reservations at a hotel along one of the rivers where migration occurs. You sit out on the rocks by the river and watch as hundreds of salmon battle impossible odds to swim upstream, jumping up small waterfalls to get back to their spawning grounds. You're filled with a sense of purpose as you watch the large fish propelling themselves through the air then disappearing in the water at the top of the fall. Some don't make it on the first try, but they don't give up. They jump and jump and jump until they make it. Their courage is unfailing, their determination unparalleled. For three days you watch, and for three days you feel the connection to their divine nature. You return home filled with a sense of purpose and confident in your own abilities to succeed.

Scorpion

Traits: Scorpion symbolizes control, inner strength, and good defenses. It also symbolizes high sex drive, beauty, and jealousy. Scorpion's elevated sense of vibration alerts it to environmental changes. It then uses its sense of smell to seek out food and to find good hiding spots because it has poor eyesight even though it has six to twelve eyes. It is sensitive to light, so it is nocturnal. It can also tell the difference between light and dark. This means that you're sensitive to your surroundings and use your intuition to sense energy changes in people and places. You're attuned to your own sexuality, see the beauty in everyone, and use your sense of control and inner strength to protect yourself and avoid being jealous.

Talents: Bold, clarity, control, defenses, energetic, focus, healing, inner strength, mysticism, passion, perception, protection, psychometry, reflection of negativity back to the sender, resilience, secretive, seduction, sex appeal, solitary life, stealth, survival, transformation, transition, vitality

Challenges: Aggressive, bad eyesight, defensiveness, jealous, rebellious, retaliation, skeptical, treachery, vindictive, vulnerability

Element(s): Earth

Primary Color(s): Black, brown, green, red

Appearances: Scorpion artifacts date back 430 million years, which connects them to ancient wisdom. When scorpion appears, it is a sign to start doing research on a topic that interests you to expand your knowledge. Scorpion can live up to a year without food or water and when it does eat, it only consumes a liquid diet. If scorpion appears when you're dieting, it's a sign not to give up. When threatened, scorpion is fast and deadly accurate when delivering its sting. You too are quick-witted and speak with words that can pierce deeply. If you're involved in an altercation, you tend to act first and ask questions later. Scorpion has an exoskeleton that protects it from the elements and predators. Scorpion reminds you to protect yourself from those who mean you harm, to follow your own beliefs and convictions, and to always ask for what you want because that's the easiest way to get it.

Assists When: You're entering into or looking for a new romantic relationship. Scorpion's highly sexual energy makes you appealing to others and you can easily attract a new mate. It warns of becoming jealous, resentful, or overly protective. You don't need to be controlling in love, as that sting will drive away the one you're interested in. Scorpion warns you to keep an eye out for danger or betrayal. Scorpion doesn't always jump into a fight right away, but when it takes aim its sting is on the mark. That said, scorpion warns against thinking there is danger at every turn and being overly skeptical about everything. When you do this, you're blocking the flow of energy in your life. Remain alert but don't become obsessed. You are passionate, outgoing, and an inspiration to others who often seek your advice. If negativity comes around, don't let it draw you into its darkness.

Frequency: Scorpion's energy sounds like the strum of a metal rod vibrating with a deep resonance until it fades away. It feels as if it's connected to the vibration of the earth. It vibrates into your feet, up your body, and through every cell. It's heavy, calming, and peaceful.

Imagine...

On a trip to Arizona you take a break from your meetings to sit in the shade of a tree beside some large rocks to eat your lunch. The air is crisp and cool, refreshing you from the stuffiness of the office. You examine the rocks more closely and notice a large scorpion watching you. When you notice it, the scorpion moves closer to you and snaps its pincers. You feel more than hear the words *take your time on the green.* You shake your head in disbelief. You're working on the green account and were instructed to rush it through against your better judgment. Knowing that you need to follow your instincts and scorpion's message, you return to work with a new mind-set.

Sea Horse (Sea Dragon)

Traits: Sea horse symbolizes placidity, gentle movements, slowing down, and enjoying life. It is the power of your subconscious, your higher self. It means you have a unique outlook, which may often be different from those around you. Sea horse has exceptional eyesight, with each eye functioning independently (one can look forward and one backward at the same time), which means you often see what's happening around you at many different levels. People may tell you one thing, but you can see deeper to the heart of the matter. Sea horse mates for life and meet each morning to do a pairing dance, which includes changing colors. This means that you're compatible and giving in relationships.

Talents: Awareness, beauty, camouflage, communion, contentment, friendliness, generosity, good luck, gracious, patience, perception, persistence, protection, sacrifice, sharing, strength, surprise

Challenges: Inflexible, isn't ambitious, lack of motivation, lazy, rigid, self-serving, stubborn

Element(s): Water

Primary Color(s): Blue, brown, green, orange, pink, purple, yellow, multicolored

Appearances: Listen closely when sea horse appears. It can be hard to hear, as if it's whispering to you in a soft voice from a great distance. But its words will be filled with important messages that will help you grow in your personal life or in spirit. Sea horse means to focus and not take anything in your life for granted. It means to let go of anger, fears, and negative emotions; be present; live in the moment; and share joy with those around you. It means someone around you may need your protection or for you to stand up for them in the near future. Sea horse is a reminder to never give up. Keep going for your goals with persistence, patience, and with gentle forward motion to reap the biggest rewards. Sea horse means to be happy with yourself. Sea horse urges you to stop, evaluate, and consider your inner goodness and your accomplishments. Stop being so hard on yourself. You're a beautiful being filled with light and ambiance. You don't have to change anything at this point in time. Just be yourself and find joy, happiness, and contentment within. There will be time for change later, but for right now just enjoy being you.

Assists When: You need to bring peacefulness and gentleness back to your nature. Sometimes when you get so involved in the stresses of life in this hectic world, you can become frustrated, stressed, and irritated at everything and everyone. Sea horse is a reminder to let go of all of those negative traits and to embrace the gentleness within you. Everyone has the ability to be gentle, peaceful, and kind, but you have to choose to embrace those qualities and to share them with others. When you need to let down your guard in order to become closer to someone or in your work environment, sea horse can help you do this without feeling vulnerable. If you feel as if you're bobbling around in life without focus or any true plan for your future, sea horse can help you anchor yourself and evaluate the path you should take. It can also help you see barriers you've created that aren't needed and can help you break them down and move them out of your way.

Frequency: Sea horse's energy sounds like the soft tinkling of a high-pitched bell ringing at a fast rate of speed. It feels warm, soothing, and calming. It undulates slowly and feels like it's floating in quiet waters.

Imagine…

You take a seat in a waiting room next to a large corner aquarium. Inside there are lots of brightly colored fish. You look at the floor and see a couple of small sea horses with their tails curled around the stems of the aquarium plants. Captivated, you watch as one uses its tail to maneuver through the stems. It releases the plant to swim around in the tank. The fin on its back looks like a blur of motion because it's moving so fast. The sea horse swims all around the tank then returns to the plant and anchors itself to the stem.

Seal (Sea Lion)

Traits: Seal symbolizes creativity, inspiration, sensitivity, and protection. Seal doesn't have any natural defenses, other than biting, so it lives in large groups, which offers the maximum protection from predators. It has a thick lining of blubber, which keeps it warm in the ocean's cold water and slick fur that makes it easier for it to swim. It can live for months in the ocean, even sleeping underwater. Seal comes ashore to mate, give birth, molt its fur, or escape sea predators. This means you often feel drawn to bodies of water, can undergo a complete transformation in your appearance if you so desire, and are creative in finding ways around situations.

Talents: Artistic, colorful personality, creativity, decisiveness, dreaming, endurance, faithfulness, good luck, happiness, imagination, inquisitiveness, intelligence, intuition, joy, listening to your inner voice, love, organization, spirituality, success, transformation

Challenges: Daydreaming, easily influenced, hardheaded, impractical, unrealistic

Element(s): Earth, water

Primary Color(s): Brown, gray

Appearances: When seal appears, it means that while you're agreeable and friendly most of the time, your words can have a bite if pushed. Because of your inner sensitivity, you may often regret any negative things you say and often take steps to make things right with the other person. Your personality is warm and caring, and you're an inspiration to others. You have a protective streak for those you feel close to, for children, for animals, and for those you feel are being wronged in some way. If seal appears, it means to immerse yourself in your creative talents. Can you compose a song, write a book, or create beautiful pieces of jewelry? How about painting? Your ability to create with color is a way to find calmness after a hectic day. You may even choose to pursue a career using your artistic talents. Seal will appear when you've forgotten to be appreciative and joyful. It will show you how to find and express the happiness inside yourself.

Assists When: You need to be alert to changes that require adaptability. Seal knows when to change environments for reasons of safety or practicality. By listening to seal's message, you will instinctively know when you need to make changes to ensure easy transitions. Seal assists when you've been having dreams that you're having trouble interpreting. It can help you see the symbolic meaning of your dreams and how to apply its meaning to your daily activities. Seal can also jump-start your creativity through inspiration. Seeing situations in a different light can give great insights and clever ways to implement what you're trying to achieve. If you're feeling uncomfortable in a group, seal can help you fit in and feel at ease. Seal helps you see your beauty both inside and out.

Frequency: Seal energy is bouncy, roly-poly, and playful. It is soft and warm like a hug. It sounds like a sharp, echoing bark, the splash of water, or a loud roar. Its energy moves swiftly at times and slowly at other times, which indicates whether you need to speed up or slow down.

Imagine...

You shiver as you walk into the seal enclosure for the dinner feeding carrying two large buckets of fish. The seal comes out of the water and wiggles close to you. Wearing gloves so you don't spread germs, you hand-feed the bucket of fish to it, using hand motions to make it wait, so it doesn't become too impatient for its food. You rub the top of its head then give it the last fish and the hand signal that means there's no more food. With its stomach full, the seal slips back into the water for a swim, waving its flipper at you as it disappears beneath the water.

Shark

Traits: Shark symbolizes determination, strength, and speed. Shark uses its massive tail to propel itself through the water. It is believed that sharks swim continuously from birth until death. It can move slowly or at fast speeds, some will even use their fins to walk across the ocean floor. Sharks are known to go into a feeding frenzy and will often bite one another in an attempt to get food. This means you are a go-getter who knows what you want and will go after it full speed ahead. You're not afraid of competition and know when to make a lightning-fast move or when to hang back and wait for the perfect opportunity.

Talents: Ambitious, ancient knowledge, authority, calculating, curious, defense, determination, efficiency, fierce competitor, focused, honing ability, innovative, instinctive, mysterious, never caught off guard, peaceful predator, perceptive, power, speed, strength, visionary

Challenges: Aloofness, devious, ferocious, frenzied, remorseless, resistant, ruthless, sharpness, unprincipled, workaholic

Element(s): Water

Primary Color(s): Gray, white

Appearances: When shark appears, it means that you need to look at your behavior. Are you acting in an unprincipled, devious, or ruthless way to get what you want? If so, shark's message is to take it easy, regroup, and scope out the situation using tact and skill. Shark also means to increase your activity level. If you're not getting enough exercise you can become agitated and frenzied, taking out your frustrations on others. Shark warns against becoming a workaholic and not taking time to swim just for fun. Shark communicates through body language. When it hunches its back, swims in a zigzag pattern, lowers its pectoral fins, or dives to the ocean floor and rubs its belly on the sand, it's a sure sign that it's not happy. What signs of agitation are you showing to others? Shark will swim in naturally slow patterns when it's happy and comfortable. This is a sign to slow down, leave the anxiousness behind, and regroup. Shark's powerful and sometimes ferocious nature is a warning that you need to remain alert for threats so you can protect yourself.

Assists When: You're stuck in an emotional rut and can't find your way. Shark can help you be dignified and elevate your self-esteem, so you can move easily between emotions. It can help you achieve goals, dreams, and aspirations that you may feel are beyond your capabilities by lending you its power, determination, and focus. If you're participating in any type of competitive event, shark's speed and strength will give you an advantage. Shark also aids by lending you its primal ancient knowledge and amazing homing ability. This will allow you to zero in on exactly what you want; you'll know why you desire it and the right path to obtain it quickly and efficiently. With shark around, you'll never be caught off guard. Shark warns against being too controlling and calculating. It also reminds you to take time for yourself; to always move in a forward motion instead of looking back at what could have been.

Frequency: Shark's energy is wet, slick, and sharp. It feels like a massive expanse of openness, as if you're sinking into oblivion. It sounds like a whip flicking and popping in the air, the crunch of gravel under a car's tires or the loud *thrump, thrump, thrump* of helicopter blades.

Imagine...

You're in a metal cage in the ocean with sharks swimming all around you. You're careful not to let your legs or arms slip through the bars as you watch these powerful beasts propel themselves through the water with tremendous speed. At times they get so close you could reach out and touch them, but instead of reaching out with your hand, you reach out with your intuition and energy. You connect with the fierce predatory nature, the unwavering sense of control, and the sharp honing ability. You don't relax until the dive is over, and even then you carry the energy of the shark with you.

Skunk

Traits: Skunk symbolizes gentle defense and avoiding conflicts. Skunk will spray predators with a horrifically overpowering scent that smells like sulfur, garlic, or onion.
Skunk would rather avoid conflicts, and its foul-smelling spray is very effective in
keeping predators at bay. This means that you too would rather avoid conflict. You're
gentle with your defensiveness, in the way you stand up for yourself, and don't slink
away from trouble, but you don't let people take advantage of you either. Skunk
doesn't waste its spray, as it takes over a week to build it back up, during which time
it's defenseless. Like skunk, you make sure you need to take action before reacting.

Talents: Adaptability, assurance, awareness, charismatic, confidence, courage, doing
things in your own time, effective, good judgment, innocence, introspective, modesty,
pacification, peaceful, protection, prudence, self-respect, sensuality, silent, waddling
away from danger (walk your talk), willpower

Challenges: Antisocial, arrogant, defensive, fear, repressed anger, suppressing negative
emotions, threatening others

Element(s): Earth

Primary Color(s): Black, white

Appearances: When skunk appears, it means to examine the way you're dealing with
others, stop taking yourself too seriously, and lighten up. You're a pacifist at heart, you
don't enjoy large crowds, and you'd rather avoid any type of conflict. This means you
have to make sure you're not coming across as defensive without reason, arrogant, or
reclusive. Skunk encourages you to be adventurous, curious, adaptable, inquisitive,
playful, and loving. You're not easily intimidated and are courageous but not aggressive. People often look up to you for these qualities. Skunk means to begin a new
adventure. Take a trip, start a new project, or become an authority on a new subject. Skunk encourages you to keep learning, investigating, and uncovering interesting
things in your life. Skunk shows up when you need to have a calm confidence but feel
like a nervous wreck. It will calm you and guide you through turmoil.

Assists When: You need to stop letting others intimidate or push you around. If you're involved in a situation where someone is taking advantage of you, it might be hard for you to take the first step to defend yourself because of your kind, loving, gentle, and shy nature. You enjoy peacefulness and often make the best of any situation. Right now you need to step out of your comfort zone and stand up for yourself. The defense you need to take may not even be through the spoken word. If you feel it's better to walk away from confrontation, it may be that you need to silently do something to protect your property or other possessions. Whatever the situation is, when you make your move it will achieve the desired results without causing you too much grief. Skunk also gives you the courage for confrontations, can help you elevate your self-esteem, help you find time to play and have fun, and to do no harm in your daily activities.

Frequency: Skunk energy is a swirling haze of scent. It burns your eyes and nose and absorbs into your skin. It is hot, strong, and pungent. If you look deeper into the haze, you'll see wondrous beauty, feel its softness and gentleness caressing you. It has a raspy grunting and cooing sound.

Imagine…

You're cooking out for a holiday gathering on an old outdoor brick stove. You've built up the fire and the iron has heated. You're almost ready to put the food on to cook when you realize you need a couple more pieces of wood. You walk around behind the stove to where the wood is stored and are suddenly face-to-face with a large skunk. It takes one look at you and turns to spray, but you yell, *Wait! I'm not going to hurt you,* and send calming thoughts to it. It doesn't move, but it doesn't spray either, so you slowly back away, continuing to link your energy to the skunk with positive peaceful energy. Moments later you see it waddle away.

Sloth

Traits: Sloth symbolizes slowing down, making steady progress, and never giving up on your dreams. Sloth is slow and clumsy in trees and on land but is a fantastic swimmer. It has long claws that help it climb from limb to limb, moving steadily through the trees where it spends the majority of its time. Sloth's fur is home to a plethora of other organisms, including beetles, moths, cockroaches, and fungi and algae, which will make sloth turn green. This means that while you may stumble in some areas of your life, you excel in others. You take your time, and, because of this, you meet some interesting people along the way who you often help on their own journey.

Talents: Aloneness, camouflage, clairvoyance, giving, protection, sets own pace, unique perspective, visionary

Challenges: Antisocial, bitter, foul, harsh, problems fitting in, reclusive

Element(s): Air, earth, water

Primary Color(s): Brown, gray, green (when algae is present)

Appearances: When sloth appears, it means you need to go at your own pace and take your time to accomplish your goals. You're very aware of others and the way they perceive you. They may think you'll be easy to take advantage of just because your natural pace is more laid back than their own. They'll be sadly mistaken to mess with you because you're quite capable of protecting yourself against threatening aggressors. Sloth has a very slow metabolism, so it eats very little and then only leaves, which aren't very nutritious. It only goes to the bathroom once a week, and sleeps between ten and eighteen hours a day. This means you need to pay attention to your eating habits and cleanliness. If you're skipping meals and feeling sluggish, make sure you get three meals a day to rev up your energy. If you're overeating, then go for a lighter cuisine in smaller amounts. If you've been skipping showers, jump in the water to get cleaned up like sloth does when it takes a swim.

Assists When: You need to tap into and hone your intuitive gifts. You tend to have clairvoyant visions, but sometimes you don't know how to interpret them. Sloth gives you clear vision so you can see the event unfold and the perception to understand the meanings behind what you see. If you feel as if you're on a speeding train and can't keep up with your own life, sloth can help you slow down the pace so it's easier to manage. Sloth enjoys hanging upside down, evening sleeping, and giving birth inverted. The three-toed sloth can turn its head almost 360 degrees and see all around itself. This means sloth can help you look at life or specific situations from a unique perspective. When you look from a different angle, you may be surprised at what is revealed. You may feel out of place, as if you really don't fit in, but your uncanny, intriguing nature is a reminder that you have a very special and unique reason for being. Sloth protects you and reminds you to look inside yourself when you're feeling out of place in the world. Your true purpose is there within you. Grasp it and rejoice in the extraordinary strength of spirit that is you.

Frequency: Sloth energy moves as if it's in slow motion. It feels as if you've been pulled up into space and are floating along, slowly making progress. It feels prickly and sounds like two metal rods being hit together inside a cave. The sound echoes and reverbs around you, grounding you yet raising your spirits.

Imagine…

The sloth exhibit at the local zoo is filled with both living trees and dead trunks lying on the ground with their branches still attached and sticking up in the air. You see several sloths both on the truck and hanging upside down in the trees. They are all different sizes and colors (one is even green from algae) and you also see a baby in the group. They move ever so slowly, but they don't stop moving forward until they get to where they wanted to go. The sloth pulls some leaves from a branch and slowly chews on its dinner. You then notice that its eyes are closed. It has fallen asleep eating.

Snake (Viper)

Traits: Snake symbolizes transformation, awakening of creative forces, and connection to higher consciousness. Snake has the ability to shed its skin, revealing fresh new flesh underneath. You too can transform like the snake by letting go of the old and welcoming in the new. When this happens, you are opening your inner self to allow the connection to higher levels of consciousness which will open the flow of creativity within you. This is a time of rebirth, of healing, rejuvenation, and spiritual awakening. Snake has a forked tongue, which means you must be on the lookout for lies and deception.

Talents: Assertive, changes, connection to magic, creativity, cunning, cycles of life, elusive, fertility, fluidity, guidance, healing, life force, patience, primal energy, rebirth, sexual prowess, spirituality, transformation, wisdom

Challenges: Aggressive, betrayal, coldhearted, deceit, deception, duplicity, lies, promiscuity, vindictive

Element(s): Air, earth, water

Primary Color(s): Black, green, orange, yellow, can come in any color or any combinations of colors

Appearances: When snake appears, it means you're coming into a time of extreme spiritual growth, a jump forward in your intuitive abilities, and you'll become more connected to the energy of the universe. You're like a sponge, absorbing so much knowledge that it seems overwhelming but also addicting. You will experience a surge in all areas of your life during this period of spiritual growth. Your intuition will become more accurate, dreams may become prophetic, and you'll *know* more than ever before. Anything you're working on as a hobby or in your work will flow with ease. You'll be offered new opportunities, you'll become more ambitious, and will experience a metamorphosis at every turn. Snake is your protector as you grow and change. Snake's eyes are always open and protected by an opaque scale, which means that during this phase of your life, you will see more than you ever expected to see. With this sight comes an internal understanding without explanation. You just know things without being told. You're alert to everything happening around you and are embracing the surge in spirituality that you're experiencing.

Assists When: You need to make changes in order to pursue your dreams. Snake can help you achieve your dreams and give you the vitality and fire needed to bring those dreams into fruition. Snake makes times of transition flow with ease. Snake can also help when you're trying to attune to your roles in life. How do others perceive you? What do they expect of you? Does this mesh with what you feel and want on an internal level for yourself? If it doesn't, then maybe it's time to shed any images that no longer fit with what you feel about yourself and explain to family and friends that their expectations need to change, too. It's difficult living on the physical plane of existence, even harder when you're trying to be everything to everyone and are forgetting about what you want to experience and accomplish in your life. Snake can help you through the emotions of opening another's eyes to your truths.

Frequency: Snake energy is slimy, thin, and twisting. It feels cool to the touch and wraps tightly around you, making you catch your breath. It forces you to open your eyes, gasping for air, so you may truly see. It sounds like tall blades of grass rubbing together.

See Also: Amphisbaena, Chimera, Jormungandr, Ladon

Imagine…

You walk out of your door and down your sidewalk when you see the back half of a black snake lying across the concrete. You smile and say, *Hi, Ellie!* You've seen her around since she was a tiny little snake and named her a few weeks ago. Her head and front half are hidden in the grass. You say hello, reach down, and rub your fingers across the top of her back. At your touch, her head raises from the grass, and she looks at you as you continue to stroke her soft skin. She allows your touch for a few more moments then slithers away into the grass.

Spider

Traits: Spider symbolizes creativity, patience, and resourcefulness. Spider weaves an intricate web and then patiently waits for its prey to get caught in the sticky fibers. Spider's web is a beautiful piece of art; its beauty belies its intention. This means you are a diligent worker who can create beautiful displays in any physical medium you prefer. Like spider, you are patient and enjoy the craftsmanship needed to be creative. You're also cunning and can have a dark side as you wait for unsuspecting prey. Spiders have eight legs and four sets of eyes but they are nearsighted. This means you have the ability to see more than you let on but can lose sight of long-term goals. You can move quickly and efficiently when needed, but you need time to remain quiet and still. You're able to multitask and often have many projects going on at one time.

Talents: Choices, craftsmanship, creativity, cunning, cycles, fate, feminine energy, intuitive, patience, protective, rebirth, receptivity, resourceful, shadow self

Challenges: Betrayal, death, deception

Element(s): Air, earth

Primary Color(s): Black, brown, yellow, plus every other color

Appearances: When spider appears, it means to begin a new creative project. Have you ever considered letting the creative things you like to make become your full-time job? Spider means receptivity, and if you were to start a new business that embraces your creative talents it would be successful. You'll have to work hard, because all success only comes with hard work, but if you follow through, success will be yours. Spider helps you get in tune with the flow of life around you. Spider has an intuitive knack for being at the right place at the right time. This enables you to achieve success in your business ventures. Spider warns not to get caught up in a web of lies. Listen closely and use your intuition to connect to the truth under the words. By being aware you can avoid problems. This also means not to create your own deceitful web by presenting yourself as more than you are or by making promises you can't keep. Be honest and truthful in all areas of your life to make the speediest progress to your ultimate goals. Lies, deceit, and misrepresentation will ultimately catch up with you, so move forward in truth and honesty.

Assists When: You need to get rid of toxic people in your life. Spider helps you see the poisonous ones clearly and gives you the strength of character to cut ties. Spider encourages you to spend time alone after letting go of someone in your life because you need this time to find your new center of balance without them. Spider will help you weave a new, shiny web that will reflect any changes you've made. Spider warns against becoming involved with poisonous people or substances, both of which can be addictive and hard to remove from your life once they've taken root. Your spirit needs to be free to explore all realms of creation. Don't burden yourself with anything that can hold you back.

Frequency: Spider energy feels like little, tiny pinpricks moving down your arm, sticky, scratchy, and rough. It is a clattering, squeaking, snapping sound with thumping noises mixed in.

Imagine…

You live on a large fenced lot with a gate you have to manually shut each night. One night as you're closing the gate, you feel a spider web across your face. You immediately jump back and pull the web off of you, running your hands over your hair to make sure the spider isn't sitting on your head. Then by the light of the moon you see the spider hanging from the remaining web attached to a tree limb. You pick up a small stick off of the ground beside the gate and wrap the web and spider around it. You gently place the stick and spider at the base of the tree. As you walk back into the house you think of a person that is giving you a difficult time. Just as you moved the spider out of the way, you think of a plan to move the toxic person safely out of the way, too.

Starfish

Traits: Starfish symbolizes hope, courage, and confidence. Starfish isn't a fish at all. It's more closely related to the sand dollar or sea urchin. There are more than two thousand species of starfish. Most have five arms but can have up to forty. It has hundreds of tube feet underneath the arms. Instead of blood, the starfish uses a water vascular system to pump seawater into its body and to the tube feet so they can extend them and hold prey. Muscles retract the feet when not in use. This means you are a master at finding unique ways of doing things to achieve your desired results. It also means you don't let opportunities pass you by; instead you reach out and grab them with both hands and hold on tight.

Talents: Beauty, empathy, experience, good luck, guidance, hope, inspiration, intuition, light, longevity, movement, observation, optimism, persistence, regeneration, spiritual truth, strength, uniqueness

Challenges: Controlling, defensive, emotionally needy, manipulative

Element(s): Water

Primary Color(s): Blue, orange, pink, purple, red, yellow, and many mixed colors and patterns

Appearances: When starfish appears, it means you are looking at life in black and white instead of seeing the colors around you. Starfish doesn't have a brain but has an eye spot at the end of each arm that looks like a red dot. With it, the starfish can see light and dark. This means you're only seeing life in black and white. You may be taking things too seriously when they're meant in fun. Surround yourself with people with colorful personalities. You have a lot of confidence that you will excel in whatever task you undertake. Starfish can pull apart a mollusk shell with its arms. Then, it eats backward. Its mouth is tiny, so it pushes its stomach out through its mouth, digests its dinner while it's still in the shell, and then pulls its stomach back inside. This is an ingenious way to partake of a larger food source. It's also a reminder not to overeat and to use your manners at the table. Starfish also reminds you not to be too controlling with people. It's your nature to pry things open, but sometimes you have to let others open up to you instead of forcing them to let you see inside. Use finesse when interacting with others.

Assists When: You need to start over. Starfish has the ability to regenerate a lost limb. When you need to begin again, starfish can guide you as you rebuild your life and replace anything you've lost. It will not be exactly the same, but it can be better than before. When dramatic changes happen there's always a reason behind it. Just like starfish, you may not see it well at the time, but it will make itself known one day. The top part of many starfish is tough, leathery, and has spines to protect it from predators. This same toughness protects you during transitions. Starfish can live up to thirty-five years, which speaks of learning through your life experiences. Starfish is connected to spiritual truth and can help you on your spiritual path. Like starfish, you are unique, inspiring, and beautiful.

Frequency: Starfish energy feels like tiny bubbles popping against your skin. It can be warm or cool. It sounds like *whoosh, gurgle, whoosh.*

Imagine…

While vacationing at the beach, you decide to take a stroll along the sand. The ocean water is warm, and you're about knee deep. You stop for a moment to look out over the vast expanse of the ocean when you feel something crawl over your foot. You pull your foot back and look down through the crystal clear water. There is a large orange starfish crawling very slowly along the sand under the water. You bend close to the water to get a better view and then reach down and pick him up. You feel the roughness of its upper body and the softness underneath. You walk a little deeper into the water and then place him back on the ocean floor. You follow him for a while as he makes his way farther out to sea. Once you're chest deep, you say goodbye, head back to the beach, and resume your walk.

Stick Insect

Traits: Stick insect symbolizes blending into your environment, being independently productive, and being tactically creative. Stick insect lives in bushes and trees and camouflages itself by imitating twigs blowing in the wind, by rocking back and forth. It can also change colors to match the leaves or bark around it. Stick insect reproduces by parthenogenesis, which means the female doesn't need a male to reproduce. It will always have female offspring unless there is a male involved. Then there's a fifty-fifty chance of a male hatching. They are also tactically creative in that if a predator grabs its leg, the stick insect will use a muscle to detach the leg and will regenerate it the next time it molts. It will also drop out of a tree and play dead when it lands by holding absolutely still, making it difficult for predators to find it.

Talents: Accepting, calm, focused, hiding in plain sight, keeping secrets, knows the power in stillness, open-minded, parthenogenesis, patience, regeneration, stealthy, strategic

Challenges: Stuck in the past, too trusting, weak defenses

Element(s): Earth

Primary Color(s): Black, brown, green

Appearances: Stick insect appears when you need to build up your defenses. It has a rather weak first line of defense. It doesn't bite but will use its sharp leg spines to inflict pain. Stick insect shows you the power in stillness. By staying still, watching, and waiting, you will know the course of action you should take. You are extraordinary and people respect the uniqueness within you. Stick insect warns to not live in the past, which can cause problems dealing with current situations. Let the past go to experience forward motion.

Assists When: You need to have the element of surprise on your side. Some stick insects have brightly colored wings. When predators get too close, stick insect will flash the wings in warning, which confuses predators. If you're trying to surprise someone, follow the lead of stick insect by doing the unexpected. Stick insect can also help you keep things hidden. When it lays its eggs, stick insect scatters them all along the forest floor, sticks them to leaves or bark, or puts them in the ground because predators like to eat them. This ensures all of the eggs aren't in one place, so some are sure to survive. They look like seeds, so meat-eating predators ignore them. Ant, in particular, likes the outer covering of the egg, so it takes the egg into its nest. After ant eats the outside, it puts the egg into its garbage pile, where the stick insect inside continues to incubate. Once hatched, it leaves the nest. This ensures that it stays safe from larger predators during incubation. Stick insect urges you to not keep all of your eggs in one basket. Scatter things around because you never know what will be picked up and nurtured until it grows to fruition. You have many great ideas. It's impressive how much you can accomplish in one day.

Frequency: Stick insect energy sounds like dry leaves crunching under your boots. It snaps and pops with a little high-pitched *zing*. It is a slightly muffled, fast, ticking sound.

Imagine…

You're leaning back against a tree, smelling the fresh cut grass, and enjoying a nice spring day. A small branch falls into your lap. You hear the shrill call of a bird and look up to see a hawk sitting on one of the branches. Picking up the stick, you are about to toss it when you notice it doesn't feel like a stick. You examine it and realize that this isn't a branch from the tree at all. It's a stick insect. You sit it on the back of your hand and watch as it rocks back and forth. You notice its tiny head, the wings and the joints connecting its legs to its body. It has the perfect camouflage for living in trees. You get up and take it to a nearby shrub. Placing it deep inside, you make sure it's hidden in a spot where the hawk can't get to it.

Stingray

Traits: Stingray symbolizes steadiness under pressure, persistent movement, and forward navigation. There are more than sixty species of stingray. Some live in shallow water, while others prefer to live deep in the sea; their bodies have adapted to dealing with greater water pressure. Stingray is usually in motion, although it can hide underneath a layer of sand on the ocean floor, camouflaging it, and surprising its prey. Stingray uses its side fins to swim forward, backward, and to steer. Some undulate their whole body when swimming and others appear to fly through the water because the side fins look like wings. If you're feeling overwhelmed by the pressures in your life, feel stagnant, and feel as if your life isn't moving in the direction you want, stingray can guide you forward. You might take a step back to get on track, but stingray is adept in both directions.

Talents: Awareness, balance, beauty, camouflage, cautious, cleansing, flexibility, fluidity, graceful, inner guidance, intuition, large presence, maneuverability, persistence, protection, restraint, rhythm, sensitivity, tenacity, understanding

Challenges: Defensive, overly sensitive, overreacts, sharp retorts, vindictive

Element(s): Water

Primary Color(s): Black, white

Appearances: When stingray appears, it means you're able to blend in. Regardless of the situation, you are able to hide in plain sight and often go unnoticed. This is fine with you because you can find out the scoop about things going on around you. Like the stingray, you are graceful and move with elegance. You have a refined presence, and people look up to you. You listen to your higher self and follow your inner guidance. You're very aware; not much gets by you. Stingray's sense of touch is heightened, which means you may have heightened intuition especially in psychometry or as an empath. This is a time to stay focused and keep distractions to a minimum. You need to hunker down and get things done instead of procrastinating and putting it off. You've worked hard to get where you are, so don't move backward when you still need to be moving forward unless the step back is absolutely necessary for forward progress. Soon you'll be able to lie down and rest, just not yet.

Assists When: You aren't sure what direction to take. Stingray can help you understand when you need to wait and when you need to propel yourself forward. Sometimes you can be overly cautious and too sensitive, and your sharp retorts can hurt others. Stingray can help you see when you're using your barb properly or when you are over-reacting. Stingray can clear out any emotional situations you may have been clinging to. With a wave of its mighty fins, it can help you release anything holding you back from being successful in life. If your home, office, or even your inner self is cluttered and in disarray, stingray can help you put everything back where it belongs. Stingray can also help you keep your emotions under wraps if you don't want others to know your feelings. Its guidance can keep you remain calm and go with the flow.

Frequency: Stingray's energy beats in a steady, methodical, slow rhythm. It feels slippery and cool yet thick and strong. It sounds like a medium-pitched metal tone echoing and reverberating with high-pitched *wah, wah, wah* sounds mixed in.

> ### Imagine…
>
> The stingray sweeps across the bottom of the ocean, its large fins beating in a slow rhythm. It is enormous, and you can't believe you're lucky enough to see such a large specimen. You're snorkeling along the top of the water, looking at all of the sea life below you. The stingray moves toward some rocks. You follow a safe distance behind. For a moment it goes out of your sight, but as you get around the rock structure you're awestruck. Now, there are five stingrays swimming together along the ocean floor. Their movements seem coordinated and smooth. You've never witnessed such a display, and it makes you feel happy inside.

Swan

Traits: Swan symbolizes love, fidelity, and romance. Swans mate for life, yet each remains a unique individual. It is very protective of its mate, nest, and offspring, and shows loving emotions to its mate by touching beaks to kiss, which results in their necks forming a heart shape. Cygnets (baby swans) can swim immediately after birth and have gray or brown feathers until the age of two, when they get their adult feathers during the yearly molting. This means that when you're in a relationship, you're 100 percent committed to your partner and family.

Talents: Awakening, balance, beauty, creativity, divination, dreaming, elegance, emotions, fidelity, fluidity, grace, intuition, love, partnerships, premonitions, purity, spiritual enlightenment, transformation, unions

Challenges: Aggression, easily overwhelmed, idealistic, overly protective, too sensitive

Element(s): Earth, water

Primary Color(s): Black, white

Appearances: When swan appears, it means there is a new relationship coming into your life. You will meet someone new at work, make a new friend, or start a new love relationship. Swan means to look at inner beauty, not just someone's outer appearance. When it comes to any relationship, you have an intuitive knowledge of the other person and understand their emotions and the way they think. This makes you an easy person to work with and a likely confidant. You're loyal, and once you're committed to someone, you're committed for life. Even if you go your separate ways, if that person ever comes to you for help in the future, you'll be there for them. Swan reminds you to express yourself with clarity, to take time out of every day for silence, and to always hum or whistle a little tune at some point during your day. This will give you a sense of balance and keep you connected with your inner self.

Assists When: You need to have faith, see the mysteries in life, and reconnect with your bliss. You may be going through some things right now, either in your work environment or within yourself. If you're confused or feel misguided, swan can lend you its clarity of purpose. Swan reminds you to see the mysterious wonders of the world.

Try to learn something new every day to keep that sense of wonder alive. Swan can also help with improving a relationship. This can be a love relationship or a platonic relationship. Swan can help you find the root of problems that have occurred and find solutions to resolve them to get the relationship back on track. Are you making someone feel bad because you don't trust them? Are you being jealous or too controlling? Are you making a coworker feel inadequate because you're being too aggressive with them? Take a good, hard look at all of the intricacies of your relationships to see if you're the one causing problems or if the other person has an issue that needs to be addressed. Make sure you're honest with yourself and don't blame the other person if the fault might belong to you.

Frequency: Swan energy sounds like a sheet flapping in the wind. It has a strong rhythm that pulses with power like the steady beat of your heart. It is fresh like a spring breeze, warm and cozy.

Imagine…

You're paddling a small boat on a pond when you hear the low-toned, short honking sound of swans. You pause in your paddling to look up at six white swans flying toward the pond. They glide lower then, with a quick beating of their wings, they put their feet forward and slide across the water a bit before settling down on the surface. You paddle slowly toward them until they're on both sides of your boat. One has its long neck arched back against its body as it swims while others are holding their necks upright. Two of the swans start to swim in a synchronized motion, rotating in small circles, perfectly mimicking each other in a mating dance. Their graceful energy flows around you, pulsating with fluidity and balance. You paddle the boat so you stay in the middle of them, enjoying feeling at one with this group of glorious birds.

Swordfish

Traits: Swordfish symbolizes adventure and independence. Swordfish is a large fish that can grow to nearly fifteen feet and weigh upward of 1,400 pounds. It is known for its long, swordlike bill. It instills a sense of swashbuckling action, risk-taking, and entitlement. Swordfish uses its unique bill when preying upon its meals and to eat. Its physical power and uniqueness makes it command attention. You also have the ability to grab the attention of others because of your unique appearance or skills.

Talents: Adventurous, ambition, high energy, independence, intelligence, luck, outgoing, positivity, power, self-confidence

Challenges: Arrogance, bullying, cutthroat, risk-taker, ruthless, tactless

Element(s): Water

Primary Color(s): Black, dark blue, silver

Appearances: When swordfish appears, it means to live life to its fullest. You're an energetic, proud, but sometimes eccentric person who has big ideas and dreams, and you aren't afraid to go out and grab them. You're highly intelligent, adventurous, and work extremely well under pressure. You have a positive and happy outlook on life and are able to infuse those feelings into others with your outgoing energy and bubbling personality. Swordfish can take giant leaps out of the water, which indicates that you are willing to expose your inner self to others in order to spread positivity in life. You have a lot going for you, things seem to always work in your favor, or you're at the right place at the right time. When things are always going good, it is easy to feel entitled to the great things you receive. Feelings of entitlement can change your personality because it is a negative trait. Swordfish warns against developing this trait because it will slow down your forward movement and change your path. When you feel entitled, something will occur somewhere down the road to show you that you're not.

Assists When: You need to win. Swordfish can help you fight through any obstacles in your path with ease. You don't pay attention to the viewpoints of others when you're actively progressing to your goal. You can have tunnel vision and not see the waves you're creating when others get in your path. While you like to create waves (you enjoy seeing the shock effect) and often find yourself in the midst of controversy, swordfish encourages you to look in all directions as you move forward so you don't create waves so large they will be difficult to overcome. If you're having a rare moment of weakness, swordfish will give you the power to swim with enduring strength. Swordfish also helps when you need to be more organized, are developing a strategic plan for a new big idea, or are putting together a new wardrobe that is sure to grab attention.

Frequency: Swordfish energy is fast-moving, direct, and focused. It sounds like a speed boat racing across the ocean. It is slick, wet, and cool to the touch yet it makes you feel prickly, its sharp points scratching as it surrounds you.

Imagine...

You're taking a vacation cruise. One day you decide to hang out on deck to see if there are any marine animals out and about. The ship passes by a few fishing vessels, but it doesn't look like they're catching anything. As the ship leaves them in its wake you see a large fish jumping out of the water. You grab your binoculars for a closer look. It jumps again, and now you can tell that it's a very large swordfish, its dark blue and silver colors flashing in the sunlight. Its body twists in flight and lands on its side. The massive power of the fish causes a huge splash. It jumps two more times, both times flying straight and true before disappearing beneath the surface. You wait and watch. It doesn't jump anymore, but you're still filled with excitement and joy.

Tiger

Traits: Tiger symbolizes strength, beauty, and uniqueness. Tiger is the largest and strongest of the big cats. Tiger's stripes are unique to the individual animal like a human's fingerprints are unique to each person. Its stripes are also patterned in its skin, so if you were to shave a tiger, it would still have stripes. This means you are a distinctive, one of a kind, beautiful individual with an incredible amount of strength and willpower.

Talents: Beauty, confidence, courage, determination, devotion, doesn't hesitate, energy, focus, immediate action, independence, intuition, perseverance, power, sensuality, silence, solitude, strategic, strength, unique, vitality, willpower

Challenges: Aggressive, antisocial, ferocious, moody, predator, ruthless, unpredictable

Element(s): Earth, water

Primary Color(s): Black, orange, white

Appearances: Tiger has round pupils, sees in color, and appears when you need to see the true colors of someone. This means you're able to see with more perception than most. You trust your instincts. You're a strong leader, exceptional business person, and often run your own company. While you don't have any problems delegating tasks, the ultimate control stays with you. When you see something you want, you go after it with all you've got. Tiger means that others see you as sexy and passionate. You're a big flirt and go out of your way to make others feel better about themselves, but you never lead someone on if you have no intention of following through. Tiger loves to swim, which means you're probably drawn to water activities. When tiger is happy and content, it doesn't purr but simply closes its eyes, which is a sign of vulnerability. Sometimes you might think you can't be happy and content because someone might take advantage of you. This is fearful thinking. Always remember that tiger is fearless, unpredictable, and passionate. If the competition thinks they've got you figured out, then they don't know the tiger in you very well.

Assists When: You need to make plans and carry them out. Tiger knows that in order to be successful you must prepare a strategy, be persistent, and be able to change course swiftly in order to meet hard-to-attain goals. Tiger gives you the courage to stay the path, the diligence to maneuver around obstacles, and the determination to achieve the desired results. If you're trying to become more attractive to a potential mate, tiger can rev up your sex appeal. If your confidence has taken a hit, ask tiger to help you regain it. If you're feeling caged in, your inner tiger is roaring to get out. Take time to get away from everyone and everything for a while. You need time to yourself if you're feeling trapped. It's the only way to make the feeling go away, regain balance, and feel at peace.

Frequency: Tiger energy sounds like a deep drumroll that builds with intensity. It is a heavy pant near your ear. It feels hot, feels sharp like barbed wire, and makes you feel as if you're just waiting to be startled. It is a deep roaring vibration constantly in the background.

See Also: Black Panther, Jaguar, Lion

Imagine…

The tiger's roar is deafening, as if it's standing right behind you. Turning, you see the black and orange striped cat sharpening its claws on a tree. The tiger leaves the tree and runs at you, then leaps onto a tree trunk beside you. The tiger lies down on the large log and licks its front paws, watching you all the while. Then it stands up and comes even closer. It puts its face close to yours, its gold eyes staring deep into your own. Suddenly you feel a sense of tranquility wash over you, replaced by a mesmerized appreciation for the spirit of this tiger. Then it licks you, its rough, wet tongue covering one side of your face. Satisfied, it turns away and disappears, leaving you in utter bewilderment.

Turtle

Traits: Turtle symbolizes the creative source within, the connection to earth energies, and harmonious flow. Just as turtle retreats into its shell, sometimes you need to do the same in order to think things through, plan, or create. Turtle's connection to earth means you are balanced, grounded, and in harmony with all that is around you. Turtle means you take a sure and steady route, you work hard, and you're willing to begin anew whenever necessary.

Talents: Creation, creativity, detail-oriented, determined, endurance, innocent, longevity, order, organization, patience, protection, self-reliance, strength

Challenges: Hiding in your shell, lack of imagination, overly emotional, overly sensitive, sluggish, unmotivated

Element(s): Earth, water

Primary Color(s): Brown, green

Appearances: When turtle appears, it means you're moving too fast. Slow it down and take a detour to enjoy the scenery, so you don't miss the little moments in life. Connect with the creativeness of your inner self and your core soul truths. Turtle reminds you that slow and steady wins the race. Turtle also teaches the importance of being balanced and grounded. If turtle is out of balance, it can tip over onto its back and can die if it doesn't flip back to its stomach. This means you need to always head in the right direction. If you get turned around, set yourself back on course as soon as possible. Turtle is persistent and determined. It doesn't give up and neither do you. Turtle is also connected to ancient wisdom, which means that deep within your shell, you know the answers you seek. In this lifetime, part of your path is to accept that which cannot be seen so you can do what must be done. For when the task is complete, you will receive the recognition you deserve. Success awaits; take your time getting there. Turtle also means it's time to trust in the knowledge within you, be particularly attentive of how you're navigating your life, and shelter those you love or who are important to you.

Assists When: You are engaged in a task that requires attention to details. Turtle can help you see the minute little things you may otherwise miss. It can give you patience to help you handle the fine points as well as the overall project. Turtle gives you patience to handle delays, the dedication to work hard, and fantastic ideas. Turtle urges you to make the best of fresh starts in life and shows you the universal power at work during these times of change. Turtle means to honor your emotions. It doesn't matter how you're feeling—happy, sad, lonely—own that emotion. Don't deny it. If you're mad, then you're mad. If you're mad and you say nothing's wrong, then not only are you lying to the other person but you're lying to yourself. Built up emotions will explode one day, and it's not pretty when they do. Let them out as you go through life and you'll never lose control.

Frequency: Turtle energy is calm and pure. It sounds like a deep rumbling reverberating all around you. It seems to pull you toward the earth, with its powerful intensity. It feels nippy but not cold, warm but not hot. Balanced and strong. It zings with electric humming noises bouncing around you.

See Also: Tortoise

Imagine…

You're driving to work when you see a turtle crossing the road. Traffic is light at the moment, but the turtle is in danger of getting hit by a car. You pull over to the side of the road and exit the car. You make sure there aren't any vehicles coming before running into the road and picking up the turtle. You hold it with both hands and carry it over to the side of the road and into an overgrown field where you set it down. Once the turtle starts moving, you make sure it's not going to turn back toward the road. It's moving quite fast now instead of the slow pace it had in the road. Soon it disappears into the field, so you return to your car and continue on your way.

Vulture (Buzzard)

Traits: Vulture symbolizes life cycles, renewal, and cleansing. Vulture is also symbolic of death because it eats dead animals in all stages of decomposition (called carrion) although it prefers fresh kills. The symbolic death is often representative of a change in status or finances, or ending a relationship, business venture, or bad habit and doesn't mean a physical death.

Talents: Balance, cleanliness, earnest, loyal, not easily influenced, patient, perception, protection, renewal, resourceful, sensory awareness, tolerant, unique, vision

Challenges: Indulgence, intolerant, lack of discrimination, messy, too serious

Element(s): Air, earth

Primary Color(s): Black, brown, gray, white

Appearances: When vulture appears, it means it's time to equalize things in your life. If you're giving too much attention to work and not enough time to your home life, or vice versa, it's time to balance the time spent between the two. If you're working in a group and everyone isn't being treated equally, then bring it upon yourself to make sure that they are. It's all about finding balance and treating others right. Vulture means to look past outward appearances in order to see the unique individual inside. There's a story that when the sun got too close to earth, vulture pushed it away using its head and mighty wings. The feathers were burned off of his head as he saved the world. This story means that someone can have great strength of character inside, and reasons for their outward appearance. If you don't take the time to know others, then you're missing out on the possibility of making a wonderful new friend. Vulture is an expert in cleanliness. When it appears, it means to remove all of the clutter from your home and work environment, let go of all the excess baggage in your personal life, and let go of any clutter in your mind that is causing you excessive stress. When you have done a thorough cleaning in all areas of your life, then you lighten the weight of your load and will be free to soar on the wind in happiness and joy. Vulture enables you to see the good in people and make the best out of a difficult situation, and it encourages you to always look for the silver lining.

Assists When: You need purity of mind, body, and spirit. Vulture is a very spiritually based animal, and it can help you gain insight into your own spiritual essence by showing you how to look within. If you're experiencing spiritual growth, rebirth, or expanding your abilities to encompass more of your intuitive nature, vulture will help increase your vision so you see clearly along your path. Vulture can help you overcome obstacles and lets you know there aren't any limits to your capabilities. It is a time of deep awakening within you, and you'll never be the same after this transformation. When there are unpleasant jobs that need to be completed and no one wants to do them, vulture can give you the drive to take it on and get it done in record time.

Frequency: Vulture energy is extremely hot, liquid, and flowing. It feels as if you stepped into a sauna (which is purifying). It sounds like the deep pluck of a cello.

Imagine...

You look out of your front door window to see several black vultures sitting on top of your neighbor's house. You feel a moment of concern and then remember that vultures signify a symbolic death in order to move forward. You think about a situation at work and what changes you can make to save an account. As you're thinking about this, the vultures fly off of the roof and land on the grass in front of your porch. They're just staring at you, making you feel a little unnerved. One of them walks up to your window and pecks on the glass. You study its bald head, black wrinkly skin, and thick feathers. It turns its head sideways and makes a sound like a low grunting. It turns, and they all fly away. You know you've just received a direct message that what you're planning is the right thing to do.

Weasel (Maarten, Mink)

Traits: Weasel symbolizes keeping secrets, fast action, and expressing joy. Weasel is one tough, bloodthirsty animal. It will viciously attack prey (the instinctual bloodlust is triggered by movement), and it often kills animals up to ten times its size. It kills more than it can eat, which it stores deep in its burrow to eat later. It often steals the burrows of its prey, usually mice. Weasel does a war dance when it corners its prey. Sometimes weasel does this dance just for fun. This means you too are a tough person who goes for what you want. You strike quickly and can confuse your opponents with seemingly arbitrary movements; you keep back information for later use and never give up on the goal. You don't tell secrets, and you express your emotions easily. You also dance just for the fun of it.

Talents: Adaptability, analytical, balance, clever, communication, detection, excellent hearing, fast metabolism, independent, ingenuity, inquisitive, insightfulness, intuition, keen sense of smell, maneuverability, mental agility, observation, playfulness, resourceful, silence, social, stealth, swift

Challenges: Aggressive, claustrophobic, fierce, hoarding, impractical, overly talkative, sly, spiteful, suspicious

Element(s): Earth, water

Primary Color(s): Brown, white

Appearances: Weasel means to stop, look, and listen. There is something going on that you're unaware of, and you need to be very observant to uncover the truth in case there is someone planning an attack. You also may be in a situation where you'll have to be on guard, so proceed with caution. Weasel means that if you need to speak up, you do so without hesitation and often take the lead. But there are times when you are so silent people forget you're there. This enables you to obtain information you may otherwise not have heard that will benefit your path to achieving your goal. You tend to like your solitude as much as weasel does. Weasel can also spray a nasty, stinking fluid like skunk does when it feels threatened, which means you also have tricks that will take your competition unawares.

Assists When: You're feeling trapped, suspicious, or as if you're being pushed to do something that you don't want to do. Weasel can help you maneuver out of the situation and turn it around to your advantage. Weasel knows its boundaries, and its territory doesn't overlap with another weasel. This helps you know when you're going too far in any situation. Weasel can help you pull back to a place of safety if you've overstepped your bounds. Weasel's instincts make it hoard food. This is a sign for you to watch your diet, don't overeat, and if you're cluttering up your environment with stuff, do a massive cleaning and give things away. When your area is clear, energy flow increases and life is easier. When you're unsure, weasel encourages you to trust your instincts and your intuition because what you're sensing is usually right on target.

Frequency: Weasel energy feels like an electric shock. It's quick, is sharp, and stings. It moves very fast and in every direction, as if you're standing in the midst of a bunch of ping-pong balls being dumped all around you. It sounds like violins playing in fast, sharp strokes that escalate to a climactic crescendo.

See Also: Ferret, Skunk

Imagine...

You've seen a weasel in a field near your house. You want some video of it, so you sit down in the grass about twenty-five yards away from its den. You get out your camera, adjust the settings, and wait. After a couple of hours, you're about to give up for the day when you see movement near the tree. You start filming. The weasel comes out of its burrow to look around. You think it's going to go back inside, but instead it starts jumping around, leaping into the air and twisting its body, darting from here to there. You look around for prey, but there aren't any other animals around. After a bit the weasel goes back into its burrow. You're pleased that you were able to capture the animal during play time.

Whale

Traits: Whale symbolizes the power of vibrational energy and connection to spirit. Whale can live a long time; the oldest discovered is thought to be 211 years old, but scientists believe whales can live even longer. Its longevity is linked to wisdom and ancient knowledge. Whale enjoys singing and will create new songs if they get bored with the old ones. Whale songs can become popular and spread from one group of whales to another. This is directly related to your own creative nature. You never know when something you create will become the next popular craze.

Talents: Agile, creativity, emotional depth, graceful, imagination, insight, intuition, longevity, movement, passionate, sensitivity, social, strong, swift

Challenges: Instability, reclusive, withdrawn

Element(s): Water

Primary Color(s): Black, blue, brown, gray, white

Appearances: When whale appears, it means you're going through a time of transformation and enlightenment. Your intuition, creativity, and innate knowledge are growing rapidly during this time. It can be a bit overwhelming. Whale means you'll remain balanced as you move through these positive changes with graceful fluidity. Thought-provoking ideas will come to you, making you search deeper for answers. It's time to learn and grow and to express what you're feeling in your new knowledge. This isn't a time for remaining quiet but is for open discussion, singing, and happiness. Whale encourages you to put your intuition to the test by actively using it. Through use, the accuracy will increase. This is important to you, especially if you've doubted your abilities. You tend to stay to yourself at times and you only let people see what you want them to see when it comes to your personal life. If someone makes it into your close circle of friends, then they will have access to you on a deep, intimate, soul level. Whale means you often say prophetic things without even realizing you're doing it. By becoming aware of whale's message of spiritual growth, you can learn to tap into your own intuitive nature and have a better understanding of what you're seeing and feeling. This will enable you to pass along intuitive messages in a more precise way.

Assists When: You need to be inspired. Whale is able to dive to great depths and soar above the ocean. This means you can look deep inside for inspiration and then rise to great heights. Whale can help you find the creative venue that is best for you on your life path. Do you enjoy music, writing, drawing, or painting? Or maybe you're great at motivating others, teaching classes, or helping others understand themselves better. All of these are ways you can embrace your creativity and share it with the world. If you're having family problems, whale encourages you to reach out with love to resolve issues quickly. Whales are very social animals, with deep family ties and friendships.

Frequency: Whale energy sounds like a rolling gurgle, a high-pitched squeak, and an echoing mid-pitched *ah, ah, ah* all rolled up into one sound. It feels like you're rocking back and forth or side to side, calm and at peace within yourself.

Imagine...

You book yourself on a whale-watching boat ride. When the day arrives, it's clear and sunny. The captain explains about whales as you cruise out to sea. As the boat moves slowly through the water, you watch for any signs of a whale. After a little while, a big humpback whale is sighted a short distance away. You can see the whale lazily rotating itself in the water. It moves back and forth, around and around, slow and steady, then lifts its head straight up in the water. Swimming a bit, it arcs its body over the top of the water and blows air out of its blowhole before submerging again. During the day, you see several more whales casually rising out of the water. The highlight of the day comes when a large fish jumps out of the water with a whale following. The whale jumps completely out of the water after the fish then submerges back into the ocean.

Wolf

Traits: Wolf symbolizes wildness, independence, a courageous nature, solitude, loyalty, a pack frame of mind and sense of community, a curious nature, and strong will. Wolf puts love of family before all else, and its survival instincts are keen. Social, affectionate, and always finding time for fun, wolf empowers you to embrace the calm wildness within yourself.

Talents: Affection, family, fun, independent, love, loyalty, playtime, quickness

Challenges: Bossy, dislikes change, overbearing, shy in some circumstances, too high expectations

Element(s): Earth, water

Primary Color(s): Black, brown, gray, red

Appearances: When wolf appears, positivity is coming your way in the form of new prospects. Make sure you trust in yourself and have a high sense of clarity and integrity so you can pursue the new opportunities when they show up. It's also time to take stock of family and your close relationships. Be sincere in your dealings with loved ones. If you're being aloof with family, then become more devoted. You tend to avoid confrontations whenever possible but will fight to defend those you love. It's time to let go of that which no longer serves you, both in your personal life, work environment, and spiritually. Now is not the time for competition. Instead you should try to get along with others to reach common goals and to learn new ideas. You are very passionate and have a defined sense of social order, but can be shy with others outside of your immediate circle. If you're feeling like a lone wolf, isolated from the rest of the pack, now is the time to let go of past grievances and clear up any misunderstandings in order to regain the closeness of the group.

Assists When: You need to move from the fringes of isolation back into the activity of life. When you're not sure which direction to go when making a decision, wolf can show you the way. Spiritually, wolf can help you get back on track in finding your life's purpose and in connecting with your soul essence. It can help you find balance between your responsibilities and your sense of freedom. It can assist you in resolving issues with family and friends by clearing up misunderstandings. Wolf can help you look at situations from a different point of view if you're having trouble understanding. Wolf appears when you need a guardian that will help you find your way. When you're not sure of where you stand in a situation, wolf will help you find your place in the hierarchy of the pack.

Frequency: Wolf's energy is like a shrill keening with an underlying pulse of bass. It moves slowly, steadily, with determination and unpredictability. It feels on edge, warm and strong.

See Also: Amarok, Coyote

Imagine...

You're standing high on a hill under the full moon. In the distance you see a lone wolf approaching. As it grows closer, you see the intelligence in its eyes. There is no fear, simply curiosity. It has been seeking you and is happy to have found you. You feel its frequency wrap around you as it circles you, then comes closer to sniff your hand, your leg, your foot. You're surrounded by the pulse of bass and the shrill keening, which is a little much for you. So you send your energy forward to soften the keening to a mellow hum. It steps back and then looks up at you. It feels the connection between the two of you, so it sits, looks up at the moon, and howls. You look at the moon and howl, too. When you look back at the wolf, it looks like it is smiling at you. It tilts its head to the side, considering you, and continues down the hill.

Woodpecker

Traits: Woodpecker symbolizes recognizing when opportunity is knocking. Woodpecker's signature drumming sound grabs the attention of anyone and anything close by. Since it doesn't make vocal sound, woodpecker drums to attract mates, communicate, and to find food. They can peck up to twenty times per second. Depending on the species, woodpecker's tongue can be up to four inches long and barbed, and it wraps around its skull when inside its mouth. This means you can make a lot of noise, get attention when it's needed, and are adept at finding things that are hiding deeply out of sight.

Talents: Attention to details, attentive, cadence, determination, discernment, energy connections, equilibrium, fortification, initiation, intuition, listening, messages, opportunity, percussion, progress, prophecy, rapping, signaling

Challenges: Compulsive, obsessive, repetitive, stubborn, urgency

Element(s): Air

Primary Color(s): Black, red, white, yellow

Appearances: When woodpecker appears, it is a sign to figure things out on your own, to look at what has you puzzled, and to find an imaginative and distinctive way to solve the issue. It's telling you that now is the time to take action, openly communicate with others, and pay attention to details. Woodpecker is a sign of prophecy, of something you have been sensing coming to fruition. Woodpecker uses its head when creating its drumming. This means you need to rely on your own expertise, knowledge, and perspective and apply what you know to the job at hand instead of asking for someone else's opinion. You intuitively know what needs to be done; you have unwavering determination and patience. You have an uncanny ability to come up with innovative and imaginative ways around obstacles. Woodpecker doesn't back away until it has completed its goal, and neither do you. You can be hardheaded when you're after something. Woodpecker warns not to become obsessed but to flow within your natural rhythm. Woodpecker also shows up when you're being repetitive, stuck in the same way of doing things over and over, and need to break free from it. Woodpecker will show you alternatives, different ways to accomplish the same task. It can show you how to follow a new and exciting path that is still your own.

Assists When: You need to rejuvenate a project that you thought was dead. If you've been working on something and couldn't seem to get it off the ground, woodpecker can help you breathe new life into it so it will flourish. Everything has its time and place. Right now it's time to look at the things you started but never finished. You've got great ideas; you just need to finish what you started. Now that you've had some time away from it, you can see it from a fresh point of view. A tweak here, a change there, and before you know it, you're on a roll again. Woodpecker also helps you return to your roots, connect with your core inner self, protect what is important to you, and listen to your instincts. Are you taking care of your body in the best possible way? Are you eating right? Spending time with loved ones? Time is fleeting. Make the most of every minute.

Frequency: Woodpecker energy is a rapid-fire movement that feels like fireworks going off around you. It sounds like *rat-a-tat-tat* on fast-forward. It is hot, balmy, and humid.

Imagine…

You're early for an appointment, so you wait in your car to pass the time before you go inside. You're parked beneath a tree, and a red-headed woodpecker lands on the tree trunk and starts pecking at the bark. It turns its head side to side as if it's trying to find the very best spot to peck before pounding its beak into the tree. You lower your window so you can hear the loud pecking sounds. It moves around the bark, disappearing out of sight, but you can still hear it pecking. It reappears on the opposite side of the tree, still pecking away. Minutes later you hear a car door slam, and the bird flies away. You look at the clock and realize you're going to be late, so you hurry inside.

Zebra

Traits: Zebra symbolizes balance, community, and individuality. Zebra lives in a large herd, yet each one is a unique individual with its own set of stripes and personality. Zebra's stripes are thought to break up about 70 percent of the sun's heat, which prevents overheating. The stripes also act as camouflage and keep insects at bay. Zebra sleeps standing up and only when it's in the safety of a large herd. It is a very fast runner and moves in a zigzag pattern to confuse predators. These qualities mean you're not afraid of working in large groups. You can blend in quite well or stand out as an individual when needed. You quickly outmaneuver the competition and keep pests at bay. You're a shrewd businessperson who exudes a calm confidence.

Talents: Adaptable, agile, alert, attentive, balance, blending in, clarity, community, durable, friendly, individuality, playful, power, protection, social, strength, sureness, unique

Challenges: Deception, hiding in plain sight, indecisive, seeing only in black and white, willful

Element(s): Earth

Primary Color(s): Black, white

Appearances: When zebra appears, it means you're looking at a situation as *all or nothing* when it's not that way. Try taking a different approach so you're not confining your progress because you're being inflexible in your thought patterns. Zebra shows you that situations are not always categorized in absolutes. You're going to encounter people and have experiences that aren't either good or bad, all or nothing, or right or wrong. Instead, they fall somewhere in between. Zebra urges you to see the gray areas between the lines, the part where the black and white blends together. Sometimes it is in this gray area where the most important discoveries are made. Zebra encourages you to find your light, the heat inside you that drives you forward. Zebra means you're a devoted family person who will fight when one of your own is wronged or hurt.

Assists When: You are required to work in a large group but need to maintain your individuality. Zebra can show you how to blend in yet stand out. If you need to hide or hide something, zebra can guide you to the right place, often in plain sight, where you, or the thing you're hiding, will be undetected. It can help you get up to speed quickly if you're taking over for someone, filling in, or helping out a friend. Zebra can help you find balance between your daily life and your spirituality. Sometimes you may feel your intuitive nature is making you stand out in the crowd when really all you want to do is blend in. Zebra can protect you from any perceived danger you feel because you're exposing a private part of yourself to others. You're very clairvoyant and may feel drawn to help people by using your abilities but are afraid of what the naysayers will say. Zebra urges you to follow your path and know that you are using your abilities in a positive, helpful way and you will influence and help many people. It may be hard stepping away from the herd, but when you do, you'll run wild and free.

Frequency: Zebra energy is loud and brash. Its sounds like symbols hitting together, a sharp bark or bray. It is warm and silky, and it feels like a strong wind blowing in your face.

See Also: Donkey, Horse, Mule

Imagine…

While traveling, you decide to stop off at an exotic petting zoo. You're drawn to three zebras. You buy some food, and the zebras allow you to pet their heads while eating out of your hand. Their hair is short and tight to their body but feels silky. You're intrigued by the difference in each of their stripes, which are unique to each one. The short mane feels stiff and coarse but still soft to the touch. You wander around the rest of the petting zoo but return to the zebras before leaving. It's hot and you're a little sweaty. You're surprised when the zebra starts to lick the salt of your sweat off of your arm. After you leave, you still have the zebra on your mind, considering its balance of color and friendly nature.

Part 2
Domesticated
Animals

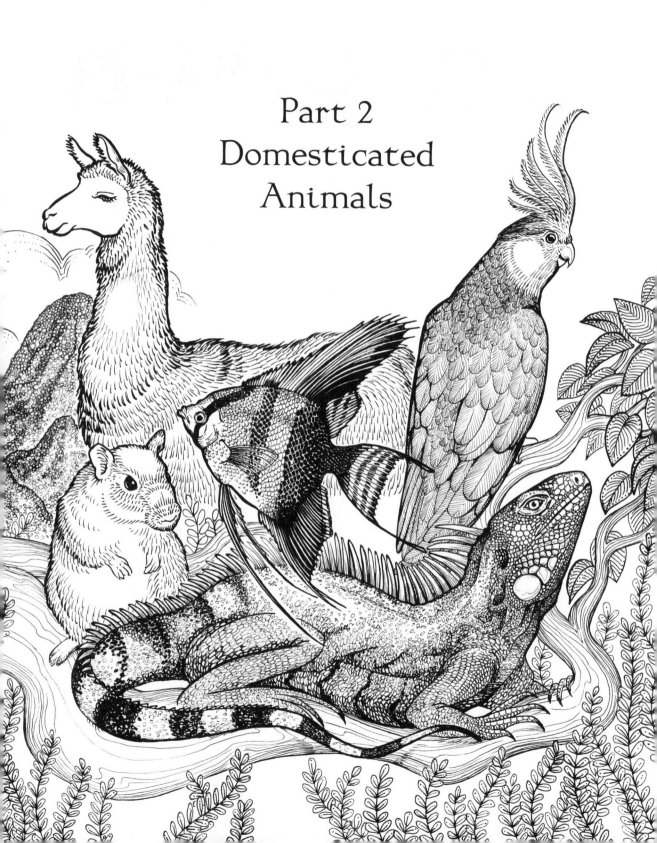

Angelfish

Traits: Angelfish symbolizes living up to your fullest potential, connection to the angelic realms, and transformation. Angelfish are triangular in shape, have flattened bodies, long fins, and a small mouth. Their triangular shape represents the cycles of birth, life, and death. Angelfish's vibrant colors in striking patterns indicate the brightness of hopes and dreams. It lives in warm, shallow water, which means you don't have to dig deep for the answers you seek. Everything you need is right in front of you; all you have to do is take a closer look.

Talents: Adaptability, assistance, awareness, beauty, colorful, connection to the angelic realms, defenses, emotions, empathy, enlightenment, flashy, hypnotic, independence, inquisitiveness, intuition, joy, lightness, navigation, pairs, potential, prophetic dreams, senses, transformation, vision

Challenges: Prone to parasites, shallow, unfocused

Element(s): Water

Primary Color(s): Black, blue, orange, red, silver, white, yellow, multicolored

Appearances: When angelfish appears, it means you are embarking on an adventure of spiritual growth. Angels surround you, guiding and assisting as you are awakened to your greater purpose. Angelfish means you will experience new intuitive abilities and the expansion of abilities you already use. If you are a lucid dreamer, you may discover that now your dreams are prophetic. If you're clairvoyant, you may also develop clairaudience. Angelfish offers you protection from negativity while lighting your path with purity. Angelfish means others may seek your guidance about spirituality or understanding their own gifts. You feel comfortable in your ability to guide and direct others. Angelfish is connected to emotions, so your empathic abilities will start to become clearer. In decision-making, angelfish can show you areas that need further investigation before you make a final decision. It allows you to see clearly in the darkest water. Angelfish offers assurance that whatever path you choose, it will be the right one for you at this time.

Assists When: You need to work one-on-one with someone. Angelfish often team up in pairs and can show you how to interact with another person to get a job done or accomplish a common goal. It also means you will be supportive of another during this time. If someone you know needs assistance, a shoulder to cry on, or simply to be guided in the right direction, angelfish gives you the dedication, lightness, and joy to guide them. Angelfish can also help you get yourself out of a funk if you're feeling blue. Its bright and flashy colors are delightful and radiant. Its colorful nature will elevate your self-esteem and make you feel more independent and strong while allowing you to adapt to whatever put you in the funky mood to start with. Angelfish teaches you to swim forward in bliss while transforming from within.

Frequency: Angelfish energy is light and buoyant. It feels as if you're floating on air, lifted high by an unseen force that slowly spins you around in lazy circles. It sounds like the tinkle of water over rocks in a stream.

> ## Imagine...
> You've decided to set up an aquarium in your home. You've put it all together and have the water inside. Now you just have to pick out your fish. At the store, you see several different types of angelfish and instinctively know this is the fish you want. You pick out several of the young fish, but the clerk tells you that as they get bigger you might have to separate them because they can become aggressive. You decide that's okay because you can always set up smaller individual tanks if needed. You get home and put the fish into the new tank following the instructions you were given. You feel a connection to the angelic realm while relaxing and watching their movement in the tank. Watching the angelfish helps you consider your own path in life and the actions you want to take to reach new levels of enlightenment.

Camel

Traits: Camel symbolizes reserving your energy, taking a journey, and being of service to others. Camel is used in the deserts to carry people and supplies long distances because of its ability to go without water. It is able to do this because it is the only mammal with oval-shaped red blood cells, which allows its blood to flow even if it is dehydrated. Its coat reflects the heat of the sun, it can close its nostrils to keep out wind and sand, and it has three eyelids—two have eyelashes and the third is a thin membrane it can see through while still protecting its eyes. Camel can eat anything when food is scarce, even thorny twigs, because it has thick skin on its mouth and its lips are split for easy grazing. The shape of camel's nostrils holds water vapor, which it can reabsorb. You share the qualities of being able to survive in any type of harsh conditions because you are resourceful and resilient.

Talents: Adaptability, carefree, conservation, determined, efficient, endurance, facing challenges, focused, giving, hardiness, humility, journeying, noble, pacing yourself, patient, protection, relaxed, resilient, resourcefulness, self-control, self-preservation, service, spirituality, stamina, strong, survival skills, transport, travel

Challenges: Lackadaisical, materialistic, retaliation, selfish, stubborn

Element(s): Earth

Primary Color(s): Brown

Appearances: When camel appears, it means to look within yourself for empowerment and clarity instead of seeking it from other people. You have everything you need to survive. Now is the time for you to be self-reliant and stand on your own. You are your own inspiration, cheerleader, and teacher. You carry your own burdens instead of sharing them with others. Camel means not to waste your energy on things that aren't completely necessary to your survival. Camel stores fat in its humps to use when it is without food or water. Camel means you're giving away too much of your time and energy to others instead of keeping it in reserve, or you're burning it up way too fast. Now is the time to step back and let others rely on themselves and to slow down your fast pace. Build up your reserves. You may need them sooner than you think.

Assists When: You need to be of service to others. You carry heavy burdens that don't belong to you with ease but often don't have support from others when you're going through your own trying situations. If you need to be more efficient, organized, and frugal, camel urges you to drink your fill of the things that will enable you to meet these goals. Camel replenishes its reserves by drinking up to forty gallons of water at a time because it doesn't know when it'll have access to it again. It's time for you to analyze your situation and boost your stores wherever possible so you can be self-sufficient. Camel helps you help others without draining yourself, open to your intuitive abilities, and remain balanced in any circumstance.

Frequency: Camel energy sounds like the *pflat, pflat, pflat* of a shoe being smacked on the floor. It moves steadily with a forward rocking motion. It feels hot and coarse.

Imagine...

You visit a camel safari facility where they offer farm tours and camel rides. You start with the farm tour and meet a baby camel first. It is friendly and loves to be petted. You offer it a bottle of milk, and it nurses noisily, bumping up against you and dribbling milk out of its mouth. When it's finished, it lets you pet it a bit more then it lies down in the stall. You move on to the adult camels. You're not sure if you're brave enough to ride one of these massive animals, but you're here and may not ever get the chance again. You look within for courage and then take an hour ride through lush green fields. The rocking motion of the camel has you adjusting your own movement so you're in sync with it—mind, body, and soul. You faced a challenge and overcame your fear, which was camel's message to you.

Canary

Traits: Canary symbolizes the power of song, speech, and creative expression. Canary is often kept as a pet because of its beautiful song and friendly attitude. Only the male birds sing. Canary enjoys a big, open, oversized cage with plenty of light so it can fly around inside and get exercise. This makes it happy, and when it's happy, it sings. When it sings, you're happy. This means you need to be aware of your voice right now, of tone and pitch. Make sure your living environment makes you happy, for without joy, your song is silenced.

Talents: Communication, compassion, elevated frequency, friendly, happiness, joy, kind, lightness of being, positivity, sensitive, singing talent, strength in the spoken word, understanding, vocal

Challenges: Delicate, indifferent, overly talkative, too sensitive

Element(s): Air

Primary Color(s): Green, red, yellow

Appearances: Canary means sound is important to you and a key connection to the spiritual realm. You may be called upon to speak, sing, or play a musical instrument. Your communication with others carries great power. People enjoy hearing what you have to say because your sound energy touches them on a deep level and brings light to their lives. Canary means to convey more joy and happiness in your life by recognizing the power of your own voice. You speak up for yourself and sing your own song instead of replicating the songs of others, which makes you a unique personality. You are filled with light and joy, and it's time to share your song with the world. Canary means you may help someone on their spiritual journey or teach them how to develop their intuitive abilities. Creative expression with sound is your strength. You may excel in sound healing and sound therapy to raise your consciousness and connect to spirit. While you're not usually one to sugarcoat your words, if it is needed canary can give you the ability to be kind instead of crass, influential instead of intimidating. Words are powerful, precise, and, if used as a weapon, can cut as deep as a knife. It is your responsibility, as a light being, to ensure your words are spoken clearly with precision to lift others up, encourage, and enlighten.

Assists When: You need to bring an energized light into your life. In the wild, canary only has yellow feathers. This is symbolic of the sun's energy and light. Canary urges you to get outside and experience the sun's brilliance and warmth, to get fresh air, and to exercise. If you are seeking enlightenment, healing, or spiritual awakening, canary will spread its wings and show you how to be free to fly to different dimensions. During troubling times or if you're feeling blue, canary can help you say what you really feel, and its song can lift your spirits and bring joy back into your life. It can help you feel the energy surrounding situations so you can remove any negativity or darkness surrounding you or that you're holding inside. With light there is dark, canary helps find balance between the two.

Frequency: Canary energy sounds like fast-moving, high-pitched chirps moving up and down the musical scale. The tone is clear and light; the pitch starts low, then goes high, then tapers to medium and can quickly run the musical scales. It feels like a brilliant light shining down on you, wrapping you in its glow and warming you with its heat.

Imagine...

You particularly like canaries and their beautiful song. One day when you stop by the pet store there are lots of new canaries. You reach into the cage and the birds fly to their perch and consider you, just like they always do. But then a bright yellow canary flies over and lands on your palm. You feel a connection to this bird, something that has never happened before. You know that this is your bird. So you whistle at it and the little bird answers back. Then an orange canary lands on your arm and sings at you, too. You leave the store with two new pets and a huge smile on your face.

Carp

Traits: Carp symbolizes travel, reproduction, and growth. Carp tends to grow to an enormous size. The largest ever caught was ninety-four pounds. Carp doesn't have a stomach, so its food is digested by the intestines. Because of this it is always eating (up to 40 percent of its body weight each day), which makes it grow quickly and avoid becoming prey but damages aquatic habitats. Female carp can lay up to a million eggs a year. It also travels through streams to lakes and is considered a pest fish due to its large numbers and the destruction it causes. Carp means you are in a time of growth, and whatever you pursue at this time will expand to massive proportions. Expect to travel as you pursue your endeavors.

Talents: Adaptable, bravery, endurance, good luck, hard worker, hardy, harmony, higher consciousness, longevity, presence, radiance, self-defense, spiritual connections, tenacious, versatile, willing

Challenges: Agitation, impartial, indecisive, moves around a lot, stirs up trouble, uncertain, vague

Element(s): Water

Primary Color(s): Brown, silver, yellow

Appearances: When carp appears, it means you need to make sure you're not muddying the waters, stirring up trouble, or being irritating to those around you. While your plans are taking off and you're moving into new territory, try to build friendships instead of making those who are already established feel threatened. Carp is considered the boniest creature on earth. It has a whopping 4,386 bones. This means your internal support system is strong, multilayered, and you often rely on your own intricate foundation instead of asking others for help. This can be off-putting to others when you're establishing yourself in a new venture, so make sure you handle yourself with finesse. Carp means you're always growing, you adapt well to any conditions you find yourself in, and, while you may be messy and unorganized at times, you do whatever you have to do to succeed. Hard work and getting dirty don't bother you one little bit.

Assists When: You need to fit in. If you're in a new situation or environment and are feeling out of place, carp can help you make friends and adapt. Carp also helps when you need to rise above something that is confining you. Carp is well known for jumping up to ten feet out of the water, often landing in boats, when it is startled by loud sounds like a boat's motor. It also jumps to adjust the amount of gas in its swim bladder (which helps it adjust its depth in the water). When it hits the water, the gas is expelled through the esophagus. This means it can help you adjust your buoyancy if you've gotten too deeply involved in a situation by helping you leap clear and distance yourself. Carp means you will be successful in life, continually experience personal and spiritual growth by being persistent in your pursuits, and able to reach a great depth of consciousness through intuition and spirituality. Heed its messages as you travel along your path.

Frequency: Carp energy feels murky and a little slimy. It is like sticking your hand into a bucket filled with slime when you're blindfolded. You have no idea what you're touching. Even with the ick factor, it feels strong, bold, and determined. It sounds like the slurping noise mud makes when you pull out your stuck foot.

> ### *Imagine…*
> You're on lunch break. The day is nice, so you go outside and sit at the picnic table overlooking the river. There is a small motor boat coming toward you. Suddenly the river looks like it erupts with movement. Large carp are jumping out of the water, plopping back to the surface with a loud smack. Their scales glitter in the sun. The boat slows as it moves by the fish and after a bit the jumping stops and the boater speeds back up. You feel the energy of the carp as a strong statement to settle down if you're in a situation that's disturbing you.

Cat

Traits: Cat symbolizes harmony, timing, and exploration of the unknown. Cat is very confident and curious. It isn't afraid to venture into strange territory to find what it seeks. Cat can rotate its ears 180 degrees and has keen hearing. Cat developed its meow to communicate with humans. It can make more than a hundred different sounds. While cat has exceptional eyesight, it can't see directly beneath its nose. Cat spends most of its day sleeping and grooming. This means that you're not afraid to go after what you want, even if it means going somewhere you've never been before. You have expert timing, hearing, and sight, but you can become so absorbed in yourself that you can't see what's right in front of you. You love adventure and seek thrills. Your appearance is important to you, and you go out of your way to make sure you look fantastic.

Talents: Adaptable, adventurous, attracts others, beauty, cleanliness, clever, communication, courageous, curious, dexterity, dignity, excellent timing, exploration of the unknown, graceful, healing, independent, intelligence, intuitive, lands on feet, magical, mysterious, patient, perceptive, selective, self-assured, self-reliant, social, watchful, wise

Challenges: Antisocial, easily bored, finicky, lazy, loner, restless, secretive, vanity

Element(s): Earth

Primary Color(s): Black, brown, gray, orange, white, various mixed colors and patterns

Appearances: When cat appears, it means you need to be patient, stay quiet, and just observe what is happening around you. Timing is important to cat. It will wait until just the right time to attack its prey or make a move. It doesn't expend energy until it's needed. This means to wait before taking action to ensure you're in the best possible position to obtain your goal. You're an excellent communicator who is independent and likes time alone but is also comfortable being part of a group. You enjoy being outside in the sun but usually work best at night. Cat means you need to be more flexible and harmonious in your relationships with others. Sometimes you can be too unpredictable, only heeding your own instincts without regard to others. While you'll always land on your feet, others around you may not, and will need your assistance to get back on track.

Assists When: You need to find what is hidden in the dark. Cats are mystical creatures that can see in the dark and will enlighten you on the path of self-discovery. Its curiosity helps you look at your spirituality, intuition, personal motivations, or emotions and discover ways you can grow. As you learn, you will accept what feels right and bypass what doesn't seem to fit. When you're ready, you'll circle back around and may find that what didn't fit before makes sense to you now. Cat is secretive and can help you keep things under wraps. It can help you get out of sticky situations by finding ingenious ways to slink around obstacles. Cat encourages you to get enough sleep, take care of your appearance, and, most importantly, find time to play.

Frequency: Cat energy is warm, cuddly, and sharp. It slinks around you. It feels soft and moves slowly, wrapping you in its magical mystery. It can sting, sharp and sudden, like a claw scraping against your skin. It sounds like a soft, low rumble vibrating all around you but can hiss and growl.

Imagine...

You've been out of town for a few days, and when you return to your house there is a white cat sitting by your front door. It's well groomed but doesn't have a collar and looks on the thin side. You don't have pets, so you try to shoo it away. That doesn't work because it gets up and starts rubbing around your legs, purring very loudly with happiness. You push it away as you enter the house, but before you can close the door, it streaks inside. You find it in the kitchen, sitting in front of the sink looking up at the cabinets. You make it some food and watch it eat. You post fliers everywhere looking for the owner. No one ever shows, so you name it and keep it as your guardian.

Cattle (Cow)

Traits: Cattle symbolize gentleness, patience, and tranquility. Cow is slow and methodical. It remains calm and doesn't get upset unless necessary. Cow also symbolizes a strong family unit and domestic ways. Cow is a social animal. Within the herd, cow bonds with some herd members and dislikes and avoids others. It is red-green colorblind, can hear lower and higher frequencies well, and doesn't bite grass. Instead it curls its tongue around it and breaks it off. This means you have a strong sense of duty to family and friends. You have a gentle disposition and are the one who remains calm in the middle of any dramatic situation. You have unique ways of doing things that others might not understand.

Talents: Abundance, alertness, calmness, compassionate, connection to past lives, destiny, fertility, generous, gentle, grounded, inner strength, insight, keen eyesight, kind, loving, motherhood, new beginnings, nourishment, nurturing, patient, possibilities, potential, protection, sacrifice, serenity, steadfast

Challenges: Becoming rogue, complacent, isolation, lazy, overprotective, puts others before self too much

Element(s): Earth

Primary Color(s): Black, brown, red, white, multiple patterns

Appearances: When cattle appear, it means you need to take it slow and easy, and enjoy life. You often tend to do too many things at one time, while putting the needs of others before yourself. Like cow, you can function without much sleep and still feel rested (cows only sleep about four hours a day). Cow has excellent panoramic vision and can see almost 360 degrees. It is very perceptive and alert. This means you need to look at everything around you, pay attention to details, and evaluate what is happening before taking action. Cow means you are steadfast and stand your ground even if a storm is brewing around you. Cow has a sixth sense about danger and knows where the best grazing lands are. Cow can lead you to understand your own innate intuitive abilities and lead you out of dangerous situations to a better place.

Assists When: You need to make sure you're taking care of your basic needs in order to help others. Cow eats up to forty pounds of food and drinks up to fifty gallons of water a day. If you're skipping meals or not drinking enough water, cow can help you be more aware of your daily nutritional needs and water intake so you don't get dehydrated and run down. Cow can teach you how to have stability in your life without being inflexible. It can show you how to move forward without wasting your energy while teaching others the importance of patience and persistence. Cow honors others and urges you to do the same. Cow has a connection to past lives and can help you connect to your previous incarnations.

Frequency: Cow energy is slow moving. It has a steady *blump, blump, blump* rhythm. It is warm and penetrating, and it feels like the sun on your skin after a storm cloud passes overhead.

Imagine...

One of your favorite parts of the state fair is visiting the livestock exhibits. Each year you patiently wait to see a calf being born, but you've never been able to see the whole miracle of birth take place. This year, you wander around petting the baby calves, touching their wet noses, and letting them lick your wrists. Their gentle nature soothes you, makes you feel grounded and calm. As you make your way around, you come to the birthing stall and there is a cow obviously in labor. Suddenly the cow is pushing hard. Could this be the year you see one being born? You wait in quiet anticipation. Then you see two feet emerge, and moments later the calf is pushed out. Soon the mother stands and starts to lick her baby. You're filled with awe and joy at the miracle of life you've just experienced.

Chameleon

Traits: Chameleon symbolizes change, blending in, and alertness. Chameleon is most known for its ability to change colors so it blends in with its surroundings, hiding in plain sight from predators. Scientists also believe they change color to communicate with other chameleons, or the color change happens because of the temperature or amount of light in the environment, or just because they're in the mood to be a different color. This means you pay particular attention to what is going on around you and can often follow more than one conversation at a time.

Talents: Adaptable, faces fears, insight, intuition, keen eyesight, precise timing, quick, reflexive, regenerative, sensitive, spontaneous, variation, wise

Challenges: Aggressive, detached, easily influenced, inconsistent, insincere, loner, overly introverted

Element(s): Air, earth

Primary Color(s): Black, blue, gold, green, orange, red, yellow, and many colors combined in many different patterns

Appearances: When chameleon appears, it means that there are things going on that you may not be aware of, so pay close attention and look around to discover what is lurking nearby. Chameleon is not deaf, but it doesn't hear very well. What it lacks in hearing it makes up for in eyesight. Each eye can move independently, can view 360 degrees, and can quickly focus and zoom in on objects. This means to rely on what you're seeing as truth more than what you hear. Chameleon can move slowly, creeping up unnoticed, and then strike out with its tongue at lightning speed to catch its prey. You need to move slowly and when the moment is right, strike quickly to achieve your goals. This is a time of change. You prefer being alone but may find yourself involved with a group. You'll intuitively know if you should blend in with the crowd or stand out and make your presence known. Chameleon warns against compromising your own beliefs or morals or letting other people's opinions influence you. You're steadfast, sensitive, and have precise timing. You're able to see a person's real intention. It's important for you to stay true to your own colors.

Assists When: You need to adapt to changes happening all around you. Chameleon stays grounded and balanced regardless of how much upheaval is going on around it. You have this same ability to stand in the middle of chaos yet see everything that is happening and quickly determine the best choices to make in order to bring order to the disarray. Your intuition drives you, so make sure you're listening to the messages you're given. Chameleon warns against becoming temperamental or moody. It's important to remember that while you can change your color, mood, or field of vision at will, it may take others a little longer to accomplish these things. Don't get short-tempered with them. Chameleon also helps when you have a big decision to make. It encourages you to look at all options, to see the bigger picture and to make sure you're well grounded in truth instead of hyped up on what-ifs. Chameleon can help you see the reality you're facing so you can make a wise and well thought out decision.

Frequency: Chameleon energy is cool, rubbery, and bumpy. It sounds like the low hum of a computer but has little spikes of energy that sound like the clink of a triangle. It tickles, moving over you like a cloud passing over the sun, leaving you refreshed and relaxed.

Imagine…

You're taking a walk when you notice a chameleon sitting on a tree limb. You find this a little strange and wonder if this is an escaped pet. You approach the animal and reach out your hand. To your amazement, it walks right onto your palm. Its colors are bright, its eyes are clear, and it appears to be very healthy. You take the chameleon with you, and it climbs onto your shirt sleeve, where it changes colors to blend in with the shirt. You hold your arm across your chest so it doesn't fall off. Once you get home, you put in it a box. Since the animal appeared to you, you feel you should keep it, so you learn all you can about chameleons.

Chicken

Traits: Chicken symbolizes fertility, nurturing, and communication. Hens cluck when they lay an egg and have specific sounds they use when caring for their young. Chickens are excellent communicators with more than thirty different calls, each with definitive meanings. Chickens mourn the loss of other chickens, even if it's a separation and not a death. They're adept at sensing danger and alarming the group of the threat. This means you're also able to sense when people are a threat to you, even if you have to scratch a little deeper to see their true intentions.

Talents: Alertness, balance, birth, boldness, creativity, determination, discovery, enthusiasm, fertility, generosity, growth, harmony, nourishment, optimism, patient, potential, pride, sacrifice, sexuality, social

Challenges: Fearful, ill-tempered, lack of motivation, nervousness, overprotective, too picky

Element(s): Earth

Primary Color(s): Black, brown, red, white

Appearances: When chicken appears, it means to look out for someone who may take advantage of your generous nature. Since you see the good in people, are very nurturing to others, and often put them first, especially family, you often don't see or even think about any type of manipulative or negative behavior until you're looking at a situation in hindsight. Chicken means to use your imagination and bring your creativity to life in whatever form you prefer. Maybe you enjoy crochet, knitting, or building birdhouses. Pick your medium and bring your ideas to fruition. Chicken is very intuitive, especially empathic, and is closely connected to the earth. When earth energy accumulates within chicken, it can become nervous and ill-tempered and have unpredictable behavior. This means to find some way to balance your own energy and find an outlet for it so that it doesn't build up and send you into an explosion of squawking. Chicken is a sign of new birth. While this can be a physical birth of a child, it is more often indicative of the birth of a new business, partnership, or other venture.

Assists When: You need to improve your memory. Chickens can remember more than a hundred different faces of people or other animals. If you're trying to improve your diet, especially if you're trying to cut back on salt, chicken can help. It can't taste sweets but can taste salt and often avoids it. Chicken's inability to taste sweets also means that you may be eating more sweets than you realize and should make an extra effort to monitor your sugar intake. Chickens also eat gravel to help crush up their food, which means you should up your fiber intake as well. Chicken means you're enthusiastic about life, have an insatiable curiosity, and are always learning new things. You often come up with unique ways to accomplish tasks. Chickens are very social, which means you tend to prefer group settings or events over spending time alone. You're able to maintain your individuality in a group environment instead of becoming lost in the crowd.

Frequency: Chicken energy is fast and sharp and moves from one direction to another very quickly. It feels hot, as if you picked up a potato right out of the oven, tossing it from one hand to the other. It sounds like the *tick, tick, tick* of a loud clock in a silent room.

See Also: Cockatrice

Imagine…

At the local farmer's market you take a tour of the chicken facility. You go to a large field with a big building in one corner. The chickens are free range and have the run of the entire acre sectioned off for them. When you enter the building, you realize it's a very large chicken coup. There are small boxes lining the walls where the hens go to lay their eggs, a huge feeding area, and many branches for the chickens to roost on at night. You pick up an empty egg carton and go around and pick up the eggs you want to buy. There are some hens still sitting on their eggs, and you reach underneath the hen to get them. Her feathers are soft, and the egg is still warm when you remove it from the nest.

Chinchilla

Traits: Chinchilla symbolizes growth, sensitivity, and compassion. Chinchilla's teeth grow continuously throughout its lifetime (up to twelve inches a year), so it must continually chew on things to keep its teeth worn down. It is a very sensitive and compassionate animal. The males do not harm the kits (babies) but will often watch them while the female eats. If one female can't produce milk, another female will nurse the babies for her. If people pick up a chinchilla, it doesn't bite because it enjoys being held. They are odorless and hypoallergenic.

Talents: Adventurous, analytical, communication, connection with the Divine, curiosity, excellent hearing, flow, good memory, growth, harmony, innocence, instincts, intuition, observation, rhythm, secrets, timing, warmth

Challenges: Holding grudges, loneliness if separated from the group, overly sensitive to heat and humidity, too analytical

Element(s): Earth

Primary Color(s): Gray, white

Appearances: When chinchilla appears, it means to keep your secrets close, to remain silent, and to give deep thought to the situations in your life. Chinchilla means to quietly observe those around you. You're very curious, and in watching you will discover many secrets that others hold close but reveal when they think no one is looking. Chinchilla is mysterious, intuitive, and reflects innocence yet maintains self-control. It is connected to the Divine and universal knowledge. This means you should retain your own mystery by not revealing all of your secrets. You are able to see someone's inner essence and know if they are deserving of your trust. Chinchilla urges you to embrace your intuitive divine nature to enhance your connection to ancient and universal knowledge so you will continually experience growth in your lifetime. Chinchilla takes dust baths to clean itself because its fur is so dense it has a hard time drying if it gets wet. This means you have to get dirty to find clarity. Take time to work outside. Chinchilla likes to sit in high places and look down at the world. This means to connect to your higher self in order to find ways you can grow on your spiritual path.

Assists When: You need to enhance your sense of timing to ensure forward motion. Chinchilla has perfect timing and can leap up to six feet in the air to move up a rocky terrain. This will help you understand when you need to leap ahead and when you need to stay still and quiet. If you're being too loud, aggressive, or egotistical, chinchilla can help you become softer, quieter, peaceful, and unselfish. If you've lost your sense of childlike innocence or the ability to see the joy in the smallest things, chinchilla can help you regain these qualities. If you're being too critical or overly analytical, chinchilla can show you how to listen to your instincts to find a resolution or to accept things as they are and enjoy life as it happens. Chinchilla will also help you improve your communication skills.

Frequency: Chinchilla energy is warm and fuzzy, and it feels like you wrapped yourself in a towel that you just took out of the dryer. It sounds like you stepped on a squeaky toy. It moves in flowing waves over you, lifting you into light and love.

Imagine…

You're sitting in a rocky area enjoying the scenery of the Andes Mountains. You see several gray, furry creatures meandering around the rocks. One jumps up on a rock beside you and another comes over and examines your shoes. You murmur soft, reassuring words to them, then reach down to touch one. Its fur is very soft, and it leans into your hand. It lets you pick it up. As it looks up at you with its big eyes, you feel a sense of awe and respect for this little animal. It wraps its front paws around your finger and lays its head against your hand. You pet it for a while and then place it back on the ground. It moves around, still exploring, then jumps up on a rock and disappears over the top. You stand up and look over the rock to see the chinchillas wandering away.

Cockatiel (Cockatoo, Parakeet)

Traits: Cockatiel symbolizes social interaction, loyalty, and devotion. Cockatiel is a social bird that needs interaction either with another bird or with its human. It is loyal and devoted to other members of its flock or, if there are no other birds around, to its owner. This means you need to be social and participate in activities where there are other people. Or you should have a best friend that you can do things with and talk to. You're loyal and devoted to those you care about and will go out of your way to help someone.

Talents: Caring, colorful personality, committed, communication, déjà vu, devoted, fruitfulness, guidance, happy, hopeful, intelligence, love, loyalty, mimicry, prophecy, supportive, trust, wisdom

Challenges: Flighty, gruff, long-winded, mockery, outspoken, overprotective, rash, trickster, wordiness

Element(s): Air

Primary Color(s): Gray, pink, white, yellow

Appearances: When cockatiel appears, it means you work well with others and are a clear communicator with a high level of intelligence. Cockatiel urges you to speak your feelings and thoughts instead of keeping them locked up inside. Cockatiel is a colorful bird, which means you often have a vibrant personality and enjoy bright, shiny things. Cockatiel likes to stay busy. It can get bored easily, so it's important to always have toys, perches, and swings so they'll have something to do. You can also become bored or distracted if you don't have things to keep your mind occupied. Flying is an important part of cockatiel's life. It needs time outside of its cage to fly around the house if you haven't clipped its wings. For you this means you need to soar. Go to the park and swing, go hang gliding, or climb a tree to get a feeling of height and the wind moving around you. If nothing else, go to the center of a flat rooftop and just stand there with your eyes closed and let the wind blow around you. Cockatiel is known for its exotic looks—its beautiful crest, sleek feathers, and colorful face. If cockatiel appears, it means to take more time with your appearance. Have you been letting yourself go?

Does your wardrobe need a makeover? Do you need a makeover? If so, cockatiel can help you make the changes you desire.

Assists When: You need to think before you speak, renew your dreams, or be more diplomatic. Cockatiel's beak and toenails grow throughout its life. It keeps them trimmed by chewing and walking on hard objects. If it doesn't, they become too sharp. Cockatiel warns against being too rash and gruff with your words. Make sure you're not mocking someone without realizing it and you're being tactful in your dealings with others. Cockatiel can help you get back on track in realizing the dreams and goals you've set for yourself. It can give you the spark needed to become more motivated, to take action, and to trust in your success. When cockatiel is alone for too long, it can become depressed and will start pulling out its feathers, banging its head on the cage wall, refusing to eat, and becoming angry. If you're feeling blue, cockatiel can help you get motivated to spend time with others and have fun instead of getting out of sorts. While it's good to have *some* alone time, cockatiel means you need to spend more time with others.

Frequency: Cockatiel's energy is busy and in constant motion. It flaps, jumps, and glides around you. It sounds like *click-click* pause *click-click,* and the pitch is hard and striking yet clear and ringing.

See Also: Lory (Rainbow), Parrot (McCaw)

Imagine…

You're at the pet store when a gray bird with a yellow head flies over and lands on your shoulder. The cockatiel steps down onto your arm, its nails feel blunt and firm, not scratchy as you'd expected. You touch its back with your hand and rub its feathers all the way down its tail. It moves against your hand, then, with a ruffle of its feathers, it flies to a top shelf to watch you. After a while, you've forgotten about the bird because you're shopping, until you hear a flurry of wings and it lands on top of your head.

Dog

Traits: Dog symbolizes loyalty, protection, and service. Dog will give its life for its owner without a moment's hesitation. You too are fiercely loyal and protective of those you love. You'll stick by them through thick and thin regardless of what they've done or the situations they find themselves in. Dog helps those in need by being a guide or a service animal. You're usually the first person to jump in to help in community emergency situations or if a friend, a coworker, or a family member is in need. Just as dog loves to run and play, you're able to lift the spirits of those around you with your sunny disposition and engaging smile.

Talents: Assistance, communication, cooperation, faithfulness, fidelity, friendship, guardian, happiness, intelligence, keen observer, loyalty, obedience, perception, protection, reliable, resourceful, service, trustworthy, unconditional acceptance, unconditional love

Challenges: Dependency on others, lack of discrimination, laziness

Element(s): Earth

Primary Color(s): Black, brown, white, yellow

Appearances: When dog appears, the first thing to do is consider the breed of dog and the unique characteristics of that breed. If it's a Chihuahua, it means your bark is louder than your bite; if it's a German shepherd, then you may need to be extra vigilant about protection. Dog means you have to remain faithful to yourself and what you want to accomplish in life, regardless of the distractions around you. When dog appears, it is a sign you should remain strong in your intention and have faith that everything will work out as it should. If you've been too hard or critical of yourself and others or are in attack mode, dog can help you see the positive over the negative and find your way back to your true loving and noble nature. Dog loves companionship and being with its people. It sees the good in everything and encourages you to do the same. Dog warns that you should always sniff out the people around you and the situations you're in to find the truth. If something smells off, even if you can't figure out what it is, listen to dog and pay close attention to discover what is hidden.

Assists When: You are feeling lost and don't know what direction to go in. Dog can guide you back onto your path. If you are feeling lonely, dog can help you find more companionship. Feeling wary, fearful, or intimidated? Dog gives you a sense of protection and the strength to handle the situation. Dog means to make sure you aren't cowering in fear or aggressively attacking just because someone else says you should do so. Dogs who act so out of character for the species have been abused or trained this way and are only seeking the approval and love of their owners. Remember to follow your own personal truths and values without letting others negatively influence you. Dog also helps you see when you've taken someone else's loyalty for granted and will open your eyes to who your true friends are when times get tough.

Frequency: Dog energy moves at a quick pace, flowing around you with speed and fast turns. It sounds like a spring going *boing-boing-oing-oing-oing*. It feels wet, warm, and tickly.

See Also: Shisa

> ### *Imagine...*
> You're working in your barn when a severe thunderstorm comes up. You see a little brown dog running up to the barn. It's obviously lost, so you try to call it into the barn, but a sudden loud clap of thunder and torrential rainfall has it running back out of your property and down the road. You send it pictures of being warm and dry in the barn and ask it to come back where it will be safe. You're standing in the center aisle watching the rain when you see the little dog running back to the barn. You crouch down and call it, and it comes over to you. You grab some towels and you wrap the little guy up. He's shivering and scared. You post his picture in some groups online. Soon you've found his owner, and he's back home safe and sound. You're so glad he trusted you enough to come back so you could help him get home.

Donkey

Traits: Donkey symbolizes the willingness to take on the responsibilities of others, a protective nature, and patience. Donkeys are very strong for their size and can carry 20 to 30 percent of their body weight. They are sure-footed and tend to analyze situations for potential danger. Donkey brays loudly to keep in contact with other members of the herd. They are protective and will fight off small predators like a fox, a coyote, or a wild dog, but they can only handle one predator at a time.

Talents: Determination, eagerness to work, endurance, gentle, intelligence, kind nature, patience, persistence, physical strength, protective, self-preservation, spiritual dedication, versatility, willingness

Challenges: Loud, noisy, obnoxious, stubbornness, takes on too many burdens of others

Element(s): Earth

Primary Color(s): Brown, gray, white

Appearances: When donkey appears, it is a sign of spiritual growth. It's time to embrace and grow your intuition, empathic abilities, and connection to the Divine. Donkey means you may be taking on too much in an effort to help others and sometimes you need to let them stand on their own two feet. Donkey warns to be alert in case someone is trying to take advantage of your helpful nature. You are analytical and tend to evaluate situations before taking action. You're cautious and want to make sure the route is safe before moving forward. Like donkey, if you decide a situation is dangerous or could have complications that will directly affect you, no one will change your mind regardless of how much they try to convince you otherwise. This isn't stubbornness, but a keen sense of self-preservation through both analytical skill and intuitive insight. When donkey moves forward, it does so in a slow, calculated manner. Donkey has a solid, stable character and is gentle and kind but can be fiercely protective. You share these qualities with donkey. People often don't expect to see aggressive or protective behavior from you because you're so willing to help other people and are gentle and kind. But if someone you love is in danger, you don't think twice about striking out in defense and loudly making your feelings known.

Assists When: You need to say no. You help so many people so often you can get overwhelmed with the burdens you carry. When you need to stop taking on so much and give back some of the burdens to their rightful owners, donkey will guide you along the right path so you can handle the situation with finesse. If you need a boost of motivation to finish something you've started or to move over an obstacle, donkey's endurance and determination will see you through. Donkey's strength, persistence, and patience can help you get through projects or jobs you really don't want to do but are necessary. It will lend you its willingness to help you until the task is completed. Donkey warns against being too brash, loud, or overly vocal. Sometimes a few words are all that is needed and other times silence is best.

Frequency: Donkey's energy is a solid four-beat *thump* that is steady and constant. Its sound is clear and strong. It feels like a firm hand on your shoulder, guiding you along the right path. It changes from warm to cold to warm again and at times can feel very hot and volatile.

See Also: Horse, Mule, Zebra

Imagine...

You're at a yard sale and see two small donkeys grazing who are free to a good home if you can catch them. Once you're close to the donkeys, you kneel down and call them. They walk toward you, so you send them pictures of you rubbing their necks and shoulders. Within minutes you're petting the darker one and stand up to scratch its back and rump, all the while talking to it. You ask the other one to come to you, but it's afraid. So you scoot closer and explain that its halter is on wrong. It's too tight, so you're just going to fix it. The donkey allows you to adjust it and lets you pet it on its shoulders and face. An hour later, you have the donkeys home in your own pasture.

Duck

Traits: Duck symbolizes home, family, and change. Duck is constantly moving about but tends to stay with its group or family unit. Duck has a strong nesting instinct, which symbolizes home and family, and it takes excellent care of its young. A mother duck will lead her young a half mile from the nest to find water for food and swimming. Duck's feathers are waterproofed with a waxy coating that will keep the down underneath dry even if the duck dives under the water. This means you are a strong family person, you often move about, and you protect your inner self by having a strong exterior. Nothing really ruffles your feathers, instead you let things roll off of your back like water rolls off of a duck.

Talents: Adaptable, balance, change, comforting, creativity, easygoing, even emotions, flexible, freedom, graceful, group activities, manages stress, mind/body/spirit balance, new opportunities, social, strong family ties

Challenges: Flies away from difficult situations, inconsistent, is a follower instead of a leader, succumbs to peer pressure

Element(s): Air, earth, water

Primary Color(s): Brown, green, red, white, yellow, mixture of many different colors and patterns

Appearances: When duck appears, it means you need to find a better way to handle your stress levels. When you're too uptight, on edge, and quick to anger, stress is usually the culprit. Duck can show you how to balance between water, earth, and air so you release the agitation, let go of worry, and find balance. Once back in balance you can connect to these three elements and duck energy to quickly get settled if you start feeling off-kilter. Duck is comfortable in all kinds of situations and can lend you its easygoing nature to help you feel at ease too. Ducks flock together, which means you know many people. That being said, though, you only have a few trusted friends who are close to you. If you find you're being too inflexible in any part of your life, duck can show you how to loosen up and be more flexible by looking at many different ways of doing things instead of sticking to your preferred methods. Duck can help you be emotionally strong and, when your emotions are high, see through them to find balance. Duck encourages you to live in the moment instead of dwelling on the past or worrying about the future.

Assists When: You need to get out of a sticky situation. Duck likes to take the easy way out and migrate to different waters if it feels threatened, but it can also help you face difficult situations or adjust to new people and places. Duck enables you to handle situations without getting upset about them. If you're starting a new project or business, duck can help your plans take flight and soar to success. Duck can also help you let go of emotions you've been holding inside, especially grudges, to feel carefree and relaxed. Like duck, you're not afraid of getting into a disagreement with someone, but once it's over, it's over and you move on instead of fretting about it.

Frequency: Duck energy is solid, light, and completely in balance. It sounds like an echo through the forest or the slow movement of your hand through water. It is cool, is refreshing, and fills you with happiness and joy.

Imagine…

You're in your yard cleaning out your car's interior. Suddenly, a duck flies into your car and lands on the passenger seat. It's not afraid of you and is walking around on the car seat, checking out the back and looking at you. Should you shoo it out? Or pick it up? The duck crawls into your lap and settles down like it would on a nest. This is such abnormal behavior that you think it has a higher meaning. Maybe this duck is your guide. As you think that, it looks up at you and quacks. *Okay.* You settle down, rub its back, and let the duck hang out for as long as it wants. You send positive thoughts to the duck and receive several telepathic messages from it. After a while, the duck climbs off of your lap and flies away. Messages delivered.

Ferret

Traits: Ferret symbolizes the fierce nature of a hunter and the wisdom of the universe. While ferret is quick to defend itself with a strong bite, it can also serve as your messenger for and connection to universal knowledge. Ferret is a great investigator that usually has a pleasant disposition unless it is hunting or if it feels threatened, and then it can deliver a nasty bite. This suits you well in business because you're a leader who can develop ingenious plans to beat the competition or to fight back if needed.

Talents: Alert, awareness, curious, drive, excitement, fearless, focused, growth, intelligence, intuitive, inventive, leader, motivated, opportunistic, optimistic, playful, popular, quickness, renewal, sensitivity, silent observation, stealth, strength

Challenges: Anxiety, exhaustion, ferocious, overly focused, secretive, thievery, too intense, tunnel vision, vicious, worrywart

Element(s): Earth

Primary Color(s): Black, brown, gray, white

Appearances: When ferret appears, it means to look for hidden meanings. This is a time for emotional and spiritual growth, to trust your instincts, and to delve into new and unexplored territory. Working through emotions can be difficult, but ferret gives you the intuitive insight to get to the root of problems as you lift layer upon layer of emotions away to get to the cause. You're highly motivated to make changes in your life at this time and ferret will push, pull, and snap at your heels to get you there, acting as your guardian along the way. Ferret also means you're coming into a time of financial growth. If you've been thinking about starting or expanding a business, this is a good time to move forward. The work you put in now will bring success and financial rewards. Ferret encourages you to trust your vision and sense of smell. When something looks and smells good, then go for it, but if it appears that all is not as it seems or smells off to you, then look closer for hidden agendas and steer clear. Ferret reminds you to remember to have a good sense of humor. Laughter and smiling will cheer up the dullest of moods and bring joy and happiness.

Assists When: You need to be more energized and outgoing. If you feel gloomy and down in the dumps or can't get motivated to move, ferret can push away those negative feelings, recharge you with positivity, and get you up and out the door. If you need to do any kind of research, ferret can help you find interesting details others don't usually uncover. Its ability to get into small spaces has you looking between the lines for hidden information. Ferret is independent, brave, and unafraid to be alone, so if you're going to be by yourself, ask ferret to guide you. It can show you when to be quiet, secretive, playful, focused, or aggressive. While you're always well prepared, ferret means to stock up on supplies and food now because they will be needed in the near future. It is essential for ferret to have a safe home that is its own. Take time now to add your unique flair to your home so you feel warm, cozy, and safe inside.

Frequency: Ferret energy feels electrified. It pulses, zings, and sizzles all around you. If it touches you, it feels like a spark, as if you walked across a carpet, touched something, and got a small shock. It moves fast, changes direction often, and keeps you aware and on your toes.

See Also: Weasel (Maarten, Mink)

Imagine…

You're cleaning a client's house when you feel something by your feet. You look down to see a gray ferret playing with the hem of your jeans. You reach down and rub the ferret's back, and it promptly rolls over and starts grabbing at your hand with its feet and mouth. You pick it up and return it to its cage. Later you find it running around on the bed. You catch it again, and take a moment to cuddle and rub it before returning it to the cage again. You notice it has a musky scent and feels a little oily. This time when you place it in its home, you add a twist tie to the door to keep it shut.

Gerbil

Traits: Gerbil symbolizes the little things, small comforts, and closeness of friends and family. Gerbil likes to dig and needs an environment where it can dig its own tunnels under a deep layer of dirt. Hamster environments don't work well for gerbil. It is curious of its surroundings and likes to explore. This means that while you feel most comfortable with the people you know, make time to allow others into your circle of friends, explore new possibilities, and don't close yourself off to new adventures.

Talents: Artistic, curious, developed sense of smell, digging into projects, family oriented, handy, hardy, high energy levels, social, very active mind

Challenges: Difficulty making friends, overly dependent on family, takes self too seriously

Element(s): Earth

Primary Color(s): Black, brown, gold, gray, silver, white, multicolored

Appearances: When gerbil appears, it means to connect to the things that make you feel the most comfortable and secure. You may feel drawn to being alone and spending time creating new projects, particularly crafts with intricate details. You pay attention to the small things in life that others may not notice. Gerbil is social but has no fear of exploring on its own. If you've become too much of a homebody, now is the time to get out of the house and do something. It doesn't matter what you choose to do. You may need to take time to dig into a new project or come up with a creative way to approach something you're already working on. Gerbil can show you how to dig in, tunnel around, and create something unique and intriguing. You may discover that others aren't as interested in your work as you believe they should be, or they don't take what you're attempting seriously, especially when it comes to artistry. Gerbil encourages you to continue on your path, write a book or a song, draw or paint something amazing, or audition for a play. Being artistic is part of you, and you excel at it. Be proud of your creations, pursue your dreams, and don't let anyone hold you back. Believe in yourself and you can do anything.

Assists When: You need to get closer to your friends and family. If you've experienced disagreements that have put distance between you, be the bigger person, release any negative emotions, and make an effort to repair the relationships. If you feel like you're stuck, gerbil's positive, determined nature can show you ways to start moving forward. You may have to take a different path to get unstuck, but that's part of the adventure. Experiencing new things, even at the risk of feeling uncomfortable, will help you grow as a person. You're good with your hands and are an intelligent visionary, so now is the time to spring into action. Get your hands dirty and dig in. You tend to take the road less traveled, preferring to do things your own way instead of following a crowd. Even if you're part of a group, you remain a unique individual who others look up to as a leader due to your engaging personality, ingenuity, and the amount of energy you put into everything you do.

Frequency: Gerbil energy is constantly moving in strong spirals around you. It is warm yet feels like it has little zings of static mixed in. It sounds like a torrential hard rain and smells like the outdoors after a spring shower.

See Also: Guinea Pig (Hamster)

Imagine…

You're feeding your pet gerbil when you notice it's just sitting there staring at you with sad eyes. You pick it up and hold it for a while, just spending time with it. You send it positive thoughts and ask it what's wrong. You feel a sense of loneliness. It's been a crazy week at work, and you haven't been spending as much time with your little guy as you normally would. You get your big shirt with the pocket and put it on, place your gerbil inside, and go about your day, reaching in to pet it often. Most times it's asleep in your pocket. At the end of the day, you put it back in its cage for the night and it looks up at you, radiating happiness.

Goat

Traits: Goat symbolizes bravery, trust, and reaching new heights. Goat is a curious, social animal, but it isn't afraid to go out on its own to explore. It enjoys climbing and will scale sides of mountains. Goat stays in contact with other goats through bleating. Goat has a rectangular eye shape and excellent vision. Goat symbolizes a connection with spirituality, especially intuition, and moving upward to a greater understanding of universal laws and consciousness.

Talents: Abundance, agility, ambition, balance, courageous, creativity, curious, determination, dignified, exploration, faithful, hardy, independence, intelligent, nurturing, peaceful, perfectionist, perseverance, pragmatic, quirky, respect, sacrifice, seeking new heights, self-reliant, shyness, social, spirituality, sturdy, sure-footed, understanding, vitality

Challenges: Aloofness, becoming too emotionally distant, self-indulgent, stubborn, sudden changes

Element(s): Earth

Primary Color(s): Black, brown, gray, red, white, mixture of colors and patterns

Appearances: When goat appears, it means that now is the time to take one step at a time, to be cautious and practical. Like goat, you are determined and don't let obstacles stand in your way. There are times when you can move forward very quickly, jumping to new heights and being a bit reckless in your pursuits. Now is not one of those times. Instead remain determined and fearless and access your inner strength to make calculated choices on your path. People may think you're being stubborn, but you're not. You're just making sure you will not falter in your success. You see the path clearly; don't let others steer you in the wrong direction. While you are open to listening to the advice of others, if the advice doesn't intuitively seem correct for the situation, then look to your higher self for alternative solutions. Goat means you will make great achievements because you don't give up when you set your mind toward a goal. Goat warns against overindulgent behavior, relying on others too much, or giving up too soon. The path to success can be a long one, but you're up for the journey.

Assists When: You need to get more physically coordinated or you need help coordinating projects at work. A goat's coordination is excellent, its balance is extraordinary, and it can climb steep mountains or trees with ease. Goat can show you how to find balance within your body by connecting to your inner spirit, or it can show you ways to handle multiple projects at work by jumping from one to the other at precisely the right time. Goat helps when you need to get in touch with your emotions. Goat doesn't have tear ducts, which means you tend to hold your emotions in check, bury them deep, and only let others see what you want them to see about you. There are times when you need to open yourself and make a conscious effort to examine your emotions. If you hold them in for too long, one day they'll come pouring out and you will not be able to control them. It's better to feel them now than to let them unexpectedly burst open.

Frequency: Goat energy is bumpy. It feels as if you're driving over a lot of ridges (washboard) in the road. It is hot and moves slow then fast, often having giant surges or jumps. It is loud and sounds like *bbbblllllaaaahhhhh,* with the tone and pitch moving up and down.

See Also: Chimera, Jersey Devil, Sea-Goat

Imagine...

You're out for an evening walk through your neighborhood when you suddenly come across a goat just standing in the middle of the dirt road. You recognize it as belonging to your neighbor. You slowly approach. It walks toward you and nuzzles your hand. You immediately feel a sense of relief from the goat. It doesn't know how to get back home. Luckily, it has on a halter, so you hold on to it and pet the goat's back and neck, telling it that you're going to take it home. You change your route, now with a walking partner, and take the goat back where it belongs. Before you leave, it licks you on the hand in thanks.

Goldfish (Koi)

Traits: Goldfish symbolizes transformation, growth, good fortune, and adaptability. Goldfish has long been a symbol of good luck in many cultures. It is connected to the spiritual realm, which means that growth and positive transformation is on your horizon. Goldfish doesn't have eyelids, so it can't close its eyes. It can live for a long time (the oldest known was forty-five years), prefers a bright environment, and can see ultraviolet and infrared light. When goldfish is kept in the dark, its color fades; when it's kept in a sunny environment, its colors become brilliant and bright. This means you have the ability to see much more than others, often through your intuition, and are positively affected by the light, both from the sun and from the inner light of other people.

Talents: Abundance, beauty, cheerful, connection to universal knowledge, good luck, harmony, insight, intuition, longevity, optimistic, perception, prosperity, savvy, serenity, strength, transformation

Challenges: Idealistic, naïveté, taking self too seriously

Element(s): Water

Primary Color(s): Gold, orange

Appearances: When goldfish appears, it means you're entering a time of luck and change. Everything you attempt will turn to gold, be positive, and bring prosperity your way. There are changes coming to you at this time but you will easily flow and adapt to them as they occur. Goldfish means to open your mind to new possibilities and opportunities. You are optimistic, interact well with others, and have a bright personality. These qualities draw influential people to you who have ideas that will cause you to start a new business or come up with a concept that will be highly marketable and prosperous. This is also time to keep quiet about any ideas, inventions, or projects. Goldfish will help you remain silent so you have time to create and manifest to bring them to fruition. Goldfish means to look for the enjoyment and fun in situations instead of taking yourself too seriously.

Assists When: You need to navigate the waters of life more effectively. Goldfish can show you how to go with the flow and attune to the currents around you. Goldfish does not have a stomach, so it needs to eat easily digestible foods often instead of one big meal. This means that you need to watch your diet and eat small, light meals more often instead of three square meals a day. If you're having trouble adapting to changes in your life, goldfish can help. It is able to survive in cold temperatures by lowering its metabolism. You too will survive by making changes to get you through until you adjust. Goldfish lives in calm, serene waters. This means to take time to experience the serenity around you. By doing so you'll experience a calmness of spirit and a connection to the Divine.

Frequency: Goldfish energy moves slowly but can also move quickly at times. It feels like thick, warm butter gliding over the back of your hand. It sounds like the quiet fall of snow.

Imagine…

You're waiting outside of your favorite restaurant to be called for seating. There is a very large koi pond in the landscaping at the front of the building. You wander over and watch the large goldfish and koi swimming around in the water. Their bright colors and fluid movement are mesmerizing. You find yourself wondering what it's like to be one of them. You notice that several of the golden fish seem to hang out together, swimming side by side from one area of the pond to another. There is one staying relatively still near the top of the water. It's looking at you so you reach down and touch its back with one finger. It allows your touch, so you stroke its back a few more times. When your table is ready, the goldfish quickly darts away as you stand up.

Goose

Traits: Goose symbolizes family, love, and affection. Goose is very kind and loving to other geese in its gaggle. If one gets hurt, another will stay behind with it until it can fly again. Only then will they return to the group. Geese mate for life, and if one of them dies, the other goose will live alone, not looking for a new mate. Both parents participate in the raising of their goslings, and they stay together as a family unit for up to a year when the gosling leaves to find its own mate and start its own family. A male goose will put itself in harm's way to protect its mate. This means family is important to you. Now is the time to surround yourself with those you love. Goose also represents fertility, so you, or someone close to you, may find out a new baby is on the way.

Talents: Ambitious, amicable, brave, communication, confident, determined, doesn't give up, driven, fertility, fidelity, flow, forward movement, guidance, happiness, helpful, imagination, inspiration, intent on success, joy, levelheaded, loyal, new beginnings, new ideas, patience, perseverance, protection, rejuvenation, reliable, resourceful, rest, social, stability, teamwork, wisdom

Challenges: Overly aggressive, rigid, self-doubt, self-involved, territorial, too focused

Element(s): Earth, water

Primary Color(s): Black, brown, gray, white

Appearances: When goose appears it means to analyze whether you should lead or follow. Goose is exceptionally good in both roles, as are you, and knows when each is appropriate. Goose is an excellent communicator with its loud, distinctive honk. Geese fly in a V formation, honk to keep the same speed, and change places to rest while flying. Goose means to rest so you can keep going. Once a year, goose molts and loses its tail feathers. During this time it stays in one place near water until the feathers grow back. Goose warns against getting so involved in the lives of others that you forget your own purpose and pursuits. While others may have good intentions by offering direction, ultimately you choose your own path, which leads to spiritual growth and enlightenment. Goose reminds you to remember your true self and life purpose.

Assists When: You need to make the best of a situation. Goose is wise, offers protection, and will lash out if it feels threatened. These qualities will help you feel comfortable if you're unsure about a situation you're involved in. It can help you find balance and guide you to areas where your energy is best utilized. This is especially true if you've been focusing on one area of your life and neglecting another. If you've been feeling stressful or experiencing drama, goose can guide you back to a place of harmony and peacefulness. Goose warns that others may try to take advantage of your kind, gentle, and loving nature. It urges you to stand up for yourself (and family) if you feel you're being manipulated and gives you the courage to do so. If you're traveling, goose can help you find the most direct path and exciting detours to take.

Frequency: Goose energy is a loud, unexpected blast of sound. It grabs your attention while its warmth encases you with feelings of love and peace. It moves in a smooth, flowing motion that engages your senses.

Imagine…

You've had a lot on your mind today so you stop by a small lake in the park near your house before going home from work. You find a bench and just sit there, looking out over the water, thinking. You see a couple of geese swimming along the water's edge. As you watch, they get out of the water and walk toward you. At first you feel a bit uneasy because geese are known to attack. You sit still, watching and waiting. They stop right in front of your feet, and to your utter amazement, one of them lays down and puts its head on your shoe. A calm sense of peace floods through you. Everything will be okay. Moments later, the goose stands up, looks at you for a moment, and then they both go back into the water and swim away.

Guinea Fowl

Traits: Guinea fowl symbolizes protection, warnings, and being grounded. Guinea fowl is a very loud bird that spends most of its time on the ground. Its connection to the earth will help you stay grounded in all aspects of your life. Its loud screeching acts as a warning system to other members of the flock, protecting them by alerting to possible danger. If you feel a need to stop what you're doing and move away from it for a while or if you feel the need to get out of your current situation, guinea fowl's message is to immediately listen to your intuition and move. Guinea fowl is excellent at pest control. It'll eat ticks, bees, grasshoppers, and any yard pests. This means that guinea fowl can help keep pesky situations and people at bay.

Talents: Freedom, grounded, independent, movement, protection, quickness, showmanship, spiritual guardian, warning, working in groups for the common good

Challenges: Doesn't form deep connections outside of its own flock, flighty, lack of physical strength, noisy, overly talkative, sounding false alarms

Element(s): Earth

Primary Color(s): Black, blue, gray, white

Appearances: When guinea fowl appears, it means working in groups. It is a very social bird that interacts in small groups. A guinea fowl can die from loneliness if separated from its flock or if kept as a solitary pet. Guinea fowl means to connect to your spiritual self, to listen to your intuition, and to voice your knowledge with confidence and authority. Guinea fowl typically mates for life, which means love and family are important to you. Its mating display is to chase each other and then circle around one another flapping their wings. Circles are sacred symbols in spiritual beliefs of many cultures. It is believed that universal power and spiritual strength move from the Divine to earth through circles and spirals. This means for you to spend time connecting to your own spirituality and determining what you believe to be your own universal truths. The helmeted guinea fowl has what looks like a spur protruding from the top of its head like a helmet. The crested guinea fowl has a tuff of black feathers on its head. This means you can still look good while protecting your head during risky activities by wearing a helmet. Don't succumb to peer pressure and not wear protective head gear whether you're riding a horse, motorcycle, skateboard, or bicycle. It's better to be safe now than to be sorry later.

Assists When: You need to defend yourself or run from a negative situation. Guinea fowl uses its powerful feet to protect itself by running away. When startled, it quickly flies a short distance and then glides back down to the ground in a different location. Guinea fowl also uses its beak to peck and its feet to kick and claw at its attacker. Guinea fowl means to use your feet to quickly run away from a situation, but if you're stuck and have to defend yourself, use whatever defensive means necessary to ensure that you win. This doesn't always mean a physical confrontation. It also applies to work-related or personal incidents where you find yourself being verbally attacked or accused of something where you must defend your decisions. Guinea fowl urges you to take quick action and manifest your heart's desires.

Frequency: Guinea fowl energy zings in fast-moving circles. It is annoyingly loud and sounds like *kurrr cha-cha-chee,* which reminds you of two pieces of wood rasping together or fingernails being run down a chalkboard. It feels prickly, spiky, and tough.

Imagine...

While at the farmer's market, you hear the most annoying, loud clacking sound. You follow the noise, and there are about twelve small gray birds with spots making a big racket. They notice you looking at them and run up to you, pecking at your sneakers and moving all around your feet. Their high energy lifts your spirits and makes you smile, even though the noise is grating. You turn to leave and they follow you for a while, then get distracted by something and run in the other direction. Your encounter with them makes you feel energized for the remainder of the day.

Guinea Pig (Hamster)

Traits: Guinea pig symbolizes spiritual growth, connecting with like-minded people, and welcoming new ideas. Guinea pig is a rodent (not a pig) and does not exist in the wild (although its ancestors did). Guinea pig enjoys social contact, loves being gently held, and even purrs like a cat. If it knows you're around, it will squeak at you to get your attention and some cuddle time. Guinea pig means to open your mind and heart to new thoughts and ideas of a spiritual nature. Socialize with others who are on the same path so you can learn from them and teach others along the way.

Talents: Affectionate, agility, communion, depth of character, developed sense of smell, family oriented, great memory, growth, hardy, healing, quickness, social, turns on a dime

Challenges: Fragile, not seeing what is right in front of you, sensitive to heat

Element(s): Earth

Primary Color(s): Black, brown, gray, red, white, multicolored

Appearances: When guinea pig appears, it means to watch your diet. It can't produce vitamin C and needs a supplement to make sure it's getting the required amount. Guinea pig can't sweat, so it prefers cooler, shady environments but not too cold, as it can also get chilled. It is a vegetarian that eats constantly. This means you need to watch your water intake and make sure you're not getting overheated during activities. Make sure you're not overeating. Even if you're eating a lot of small meals in a day, the calorie content can add up quickly if you're not keeping count. You may also need to supplement your diet with vitamins. Guinea pig's teeth grow throughout its lifetime and have to be constantly worn down. This means it's important that you find a way to stay active. Its toenails need to be regularly trimmed to prevent them from growing into its feet. Guinea pigs are avid groomers. This means you should take extra care of your appearance and practice good hygiene. They are also born with all of their fur, with their eyes open, and able to eat solid food. However, they can't see what's directly in front of them, which means they can't see what they're eating and is a warning not to overeat. You also have everything you need within you. By connecting to your spiritual self you will be able to excel in all that you set out to achieve.

Guinea pig warns to look at situations from all angles because sometimes you don't see what's right in front of you.

Assists When: You need rest but are on a tight schedule, which is cutting into your regular sleep time. Guinea pig takes lots of short naps instead of sleeping for long periods of time. If you do the same, you will be able to stay focused and feel refreshed even though you're not getting your normal amount of sleep. If you are being too solitary, now is the time to seek out groups where you can socialize, learn, and participate in activities. Guinea pig can help you find truth, especially the truth within you. It helps you see who you are on a spiritual level and invites spiritual growth and enlightenment. Now is the time to express yourself, to communicate with others and to simplify your life if you feel overwhelmed or that everything is too complicated.

Frequency: Guinea pig energy is soft, warm, and comforting. It sounds like a low rumbling hum, the flow of running water, and gives you a sense of calmness. It feels like a loving caress against your cheek.

See Also: Gerbil

Imagine...
You're throwing your trash into a dumpster when you hear scratching and squeaking coming from a large closed box on the ground. You slowly lift the lid, expecting a rat, but inside you find three small hamsters in a cage with food, toys, and supplies. You can't believe it and you surely can't leave them here with no water. You pick one up and it seems very friendly, so you take the box, and your new pets, back to your apartment.

Guppy

Traits: Guppy symbolizes fertility, beauty, and flow. Guppy matures quickly. By the time males reach two months and females reach three months old, they can breed. A female guppy can have up to two hundred fry (baby guppies) at a time. You can even see the eyes of the fry through the translucent skin of the mother prior to birth. They are often called million fish due to their reproductive capabilities. Guppy is known for its beautiful array of colors and large, flowing tail. Guppy's easy flow through water as it swims signifies the connection to universal consciousness.

Talents: Adaptability, awakening, beauty, creativity, fertility, flow, hidden truth, independence, potential, revelations, safety

Challenges: Hiding from life, irresponsible, population culling

Element(s): Water

Primary Color(s): Black, blue, brown, gray, green, gold, indigo, orange, pink, purple, red, silver, turquoise, white, yellow

Appearances: When guppy appears, it means you can easily adapt to any situation you find yourself in. If you're unsure how to handle yourself, guppy suggests hiding out of sight to watch what's going on and then make decisions on how to move forward. When a pregnant guppy and fry are tired, they retreat to the safety of the plants in the tank to hide away and rest, all the while keeping an eye on its environment. If their environment becomes overcrowded, guppy will eat its fry. Baby guppies should be moved to their own tanks soon after they're born to ensure their survival. This means you too may need a separation from family or those closest to you in order to rest or to make important decisions and to flourish. Guppy has been deliberately set free in a multitude of countries in order to fight the spread of malaria because they eat mosquito larvae. This means you are able to do many good deeds, but you have to let yourself be free to do them. Sometimes you hold yourself back instead of exploring the world. This is because you fear that you will not be successful. You may think *I can't do it,* but there's a saying that *can't never could do anything!* So let go of any negative feelings or doubt you may have about yourself, go out into the world and make an impression, leave your mark, make the world a better place. Because *can does it all!*

Assists When: You need to increase your financial portfolio or store supplies for a rainy day. The sheer volume of offspring that a guppy can have is phenomenal. Add to that the fact that guppy can get pregnant several times after one encounter with a male because they store sperm. This is a sign for you to stock up on supplies because you never know when you might need them but are unable to get them. Guppy can show you the best ways to increase your financial picture. Is there money hiding somewhere that you've overlooked? Or can you grow something two-hundredfold if you make one small change? If you're looking to buy something new that can generate income for you, now is a good time to take a look even if you don't take action at this time. Guppy urges you to connect to your inner essence, higher self, universal flow, and awaken to the development of your clair senses by getting in touch with the spiritual realm.

Frequency: Guppy energy is cool, smooth, and silky. If feels like a fine silk scarf flowing over your skin. It sounds like a light, high, even hum that moves up and down in pitch.

Imagine…

You've recently gotten a small fish tank and a couple of beautiful female guppies. One morning you discover a bunch of tiny little baby guppies in the tank with the girls. The little ones are all eyes. As they swim quickly around the tank you're filled with feelings of positivity and excitement. Later that day, you transfer the babies into their own tank. You're fascinated by the babies. Every day they seem to be a little bit bigger and start developing their own colorful scales. Soon they will have to be moved into individual tanks, so you consider calling the pet store to see if they'd be interested in buying them. Until then, you enjoy watching them grow into brightly beautiful creatures.

Hedgehog

Traits: Hedgehog symbolizes self-protection and curiosity. Hedgehog has between five thousand and seven thousand quills that it can raise and lower with its back muscles. If threatened, hedgehog will roll itself up into a ball, which makes the sharp quills on its back crisscross as added protection against predators. It is naturally curious and loves to explore and investigate its surroundings. Hedgehog is a solitary creature. It means you also tend to protect yourself from perceived threats but warns to make sure you're not just isolating yourself because of your own fear of being emotionally hurt. Hedgehog urges you to go exploring to satisfy your curious nature.

Talents: Curiosity, defensive, energy, fertility, inquisitive, intelligence, intuition, joy, protection, resourceful, understanding, unique, vitality, wisdom

Challenges: Misunderstandings, overly defensive, too protective

Element(s): Earth

Primary Color(s): Black, brown, gray, white

Appearances: When hedgehog appears, it means other people don't understand you or are asking too much of you. You're a very gifted person, you have a big heart and help out whenever you're needed, but people may think you're a little quirky because they don't get your sense of humor, your personality, or the path you've chosen to take. That's okay. Just because someone else doesn't understand you, that doesn't mean you have to be overly protective or keep to yourself and avoid others. You're closely connected to the energy of the earth and are at one with your intuition and spirituality. You often manifest what you need in your life and are open to receive what is coming to you. You have the ability to teach others how to connect to their own spirituality and understand their own unique gifts. You have the gift of sight, which is indicated by hedgehog's ability to see better in the dark than in daylight. You too can see through darkness to find the light and truth of situations. You also tend to have visions and prophetic dreams. Hedgehogs have poor eyesight and have to rely on their sense of smell and their hearing. This means you too must use all of your senses and abilities in life. Things will flow more smoothly and with much more clarity if you remain connected to your core essence.

Assists When: You need pest control. Hedgehog eats a wide variety of insects, snails, and earthworms as their main diet. This is helpful to gardeners who want a natural solution to pest control. This means they can help you deal with people who are annoying or being a pest toward you. Hedgehog is immune to snake venom and has no problem winning a fight with a snake. Hedgehog urges you to be aware of people who are shady, scheming, and manipulative, and to defend yourself against their negativity. If you discover people are often misunderstanding you, don't take it personally. If you feel like giving them an explanation, that's fine, but not always necessary. Everyone is on a different path in life, so you will come across people who don't understand you. Just take it in stride and move forward.

Frequency: Hedgehog energy is light and airy and moves in a slowly swirling pattern. It sounds like soft little grunts, snorts, and hisses. It is smooth but bristly, warm but chilly.

See Also: Porcupine

Imagine…

It's summertime, and you're enjoying a glass of tea while sitting on your porch. There's movement near one of the yard figurines, so you go investigate. You find a small hedgehog rooting in the grass. You watch it for a while then decide to approach it. You go near it and sit down. It doesn't seem to be afraid of you, so you hold out your hand. It sniffs at you then walks beside your leg. You reach over, touch its back, and notice the coarseness of its quills. It climbs over your legs and in that moment you decide this is its home for as long as it will stay. You bring a dish of water outside then head to the pet store for an outdoor house and food for it in the hopes that it will hang around your home.

Horse

Traits: Horse symbolizes loyalty, friendship, trust, and working together. Once horse sees you as part of its herd, it will trust you, too. It will work with you to achieve goals and give you its undying loyalty. Horse means to value the friends in your life, to be loyal and trusting to those who have earned it, and to work together to achieve common goals.

Talents: Alert, athleticism, awareness, beauty, bonding, communication, confidence, co-operation, empathy, endurance, faithfulness, fertility, forward movement, freedom, friendship, giving, grace, guardian, independence, loyal, mind/body/spirit connection, nobility, noble, overcoming obstacles, persuasive, power, regal, service, speed, stamina, strength, traveling, trust, vitality, warning, wildness, willingness, working together

Challenges: Fearful, hardheaded, inconsistent, overly attached, rebellious, restlessness, spooky, too independent

Element(s): Earth

Primary Color(s): Black, brown, gray, red, white, many other colors and patterns

Appearances: Horse appears when you are feeling confined, restless, and on edge. It means you need to run free, to work out the restlessness through exercise, and to feel the wind in your face. This will bring you back in balance, calm you, and help you work out solutions to any problems you are facing. Independence and freedom are important to you, but you are also willing, giving, and able to bond closely to those who treat you with love and respect. Horse means you're about to embark on a new journey. You may be traveling or the journey may be a spiritual one where you expand your consciousness of mind, body, and spirit. Horse means you have great power within you. You have unbelievable stamina and keep going until the job is done even if you're tired. You never give up on those you love or on your pursuit of your dreams. Horse means that sometimes you need to take a break from the weight you carry, to get back in touch with your own inner needs. When you're excited you go for your goals with gusto and can clear obstacles with ease. Horse warns to take things in stride instead of letting fear cause you to be spooked or rebellious.

Assists When: You need to accomplish a task with speed or precision and communicate information with confidence. People are drawn to your noble grace, beauty of spirit, and empathic nature because you make them feel confident and as if they can accomplish anything. Horse can help you awaken your inner power and make you aware of the needs of others. Horses intuitively know when their owners are feeling down and will nuzzle them so they feel better. Horse means to be aware of the feelings of those closest to you and warns against striking out because you're afraid or upset. Horse also warns against becoming too attached to one person and losing your sense of self. Horse assists when you're going through periods of spiritual growth by showing you how all life is interconnected.

Frequency: Horse energy feels like the wind blowing across your face as you're running free. It is warm and soft, calming and pure. It sounds like a soft nicker or the *clop-clop-clop-clop* of hooves against pavement. It smells like earth, hay, and a fresh spring rain.

See Also: Donkey, Hippogriff, Kelpie, Mule, Pegasus, Sleipnir, Unicorn, Zebra

---

Imagine...

You're in the barn. There's something unique about the mixture of smells; the horses, shavings, and hay. You walk over to your horse's stall and greet your mare, rubbing her nose through the rails. You go inside and hug her around her neck. You breathe deeply, inhaling her scent, feeling your heart connect with hers as she lowers her head on your back, and pulls you closer in a warm hug. You smile against her neck, feeling content and happy. You think about the beautiful being that she is; she takes your breath away with her movement, but this... this is what it's all about... the deep, unbreakable bond between kindred spirits.

Iguana

Traits: Iguana symbolizes acceptance, awareness, and self-confidence. Iguana understands the concept of being in the moment. It is never in a rush unless it is escaping a predator. Iguana's existence is simple and connected to the Divine. Iguana is aware of its environment, is excellent at camouflage, and is self-confident. There are no worries, just a relaxed simple existence for iguana because it knows everything it needs will come to it in time.

Talents: Accepting, appreciation, awareness, camouflage, centered, contemplation, content, cooperation, disguise, expectation, fast movement, self-confident, stoic

Challenges: Defensive, disguises true intentions, secretive, escapes when things get tough

Element(s): Air, earth, water

Primary Color(s): Blue, green, red, turquoise, white

Appearances: When iguana appears, it means to be more observant of your surroundings and to open to your senses by using your third eye. Iguana is constantly on the watch. It takes in every change in its environment, is acutely aware, and encourages you to look at the world through its eyes with a sense of curious wonder. Give everything you see your full attention and consideration. You will find that the world is awe inspiring. Iguana can show you your life's purpose and true nature. You only have to look within in the same way to find it. Iguana encourages you to let go of worries. Don't let life pass you by because you're obsessing over things. Iguana means to get outside and spend time basking in the sunlight. Feel the sun's warmth on your face and let it fill you, energize you, bring you closer to your spiritual self. Connect to your higher self, to find your own inner light, and move upward in regard to your own spirituality. You're embarking on a path of tremendous spiritual growth.

Assists When: You need to calm down and release stress. Iguana can show you how to slow down, return to center, appreciate your life to the fullest, and simply *be* within the stillness of the moment. If you're too involved in a hectic busy life, then you may be overlooking the small, yet important, things that will connect you to your spirituality. When was the last time you noticed the song of a bird or did nothing just to do nothing? Did you see the tiny blossoms on the ground or the puppy in the neighbor's yard that runs to greet you every time you go to your mailbox? When was the last time you truly enjoyed a good meal instead of just eating because you were hungry? Have you overlooked the little things happening all around you because you're too overwhelmed by the demands upon you? Notice the world around you to find calmness within yourself. Iguana can help you let go of the things holding you in stressful patterns so you can better appreciate your life. Iguana is an excellent swimmer. It can hold its breath for twenty-eight minutes, and some species can even inflate themselves so they can float if they're caught in a flood. It will scurry away very quickly if threatened. This means you are very adaptable and can handle any situation. Let iguana guide you back to yourself.

Frequency: Iguana energy is warm, bright, and colorful. It feels like you're lying on a warm stone in the mountains on a fresh, clear day. It moves slowly, scooting forward inch by inch but then suddenly zooms away. It sounds like water lapping at the edge of a lake.

See Also: Lizard (Gecko)

> ### Imagine...
> You're riding your bike when suddenly a huge, bright green iguana runs in front of you. Swerving, you miss it but circle back to take a look. It is sitting in the middle of the bike path, sunning itself. It is holding its face upward while standing up a bit on its front legs with the rest of its body touching the ground. You can't help but think that it looks like a small dinosaur. Suddenly it runs straight at you before disappearing back into the trees on the same side of the road that it ran out of before. You hear it scrambling away in the underbrush, so you return to your bike ride.

Llama (Alpaca)

Traits: Llama symbolizes climbing to great heights using endurance, strength, and sure-footedness. Llama doesn't have hooves; its feet have two toes with a thick, leathery pad on the underside. Llama is strong and can carry heavy loads for long distances but it is also stubborn. If the load is too heavy, it simply will not move until the weight is lessened to a comfortable amount. Llama means you are able to shoulder heavy responsibilities, are stable in your actions, and have the strength of heart to endure pressure while achieving great success.

Talents: Ambitious, carrying weight, clairaudience, determined, endurance, friendly, generosity, hardiness, responsible, service, strong sense of smell, sure-footed, vision

Challenges: Aggressive, control freak, inherited fear of dogs, coyotes, wolves, mountain lions, and other doglike animals, stubborn

Element(s): Earth

Primary Color(s): Black, brown, gray, white, variety of patterns

Appearances: When llama appears, it means you're carrying too much responsibility on your own shoulders. Llama urges you to take help whenever you can, delegate some responsibilities to others, and let go of your need for control to allow others to do things for you that you normally do for yourself. Llama is a very social animal that solves disputes by spitting. If you don't have time for social events or relaxing with family and friends due to your busy schedule, llama urges you to make changes before you get to the point where you can no longer move because the weight is so heavy. Don't turn into a control freak; instead, let go of some of the control to free up your burden. Llama means you have to take care of yourself before you can take care of others. Llama is also connected to the spiritual realm, especially clairaudience. Llama has exceptional hearing. This means you often hear messages from the spiritual and angelic realms. When llama appears, it means you can see your destination on the horizon. It's been a long and sometimes difficult journey, but the end is in sight. Llama means to take your time, move slowly but steadily, keep your balance, and make sure you know where your feet are at all times. Awareness and balance are keys to your success. Llama is also a sign of being too stubborn. Are you?

Assists When: You want to reach new spiritual heights through accessing the Akashic Records, universal consciousness, and ancient wisdom. Learning spiritual lessons can sometimes be very emotional. Llama can accompany you on this transformational journey to help you through the emotional breakthroughs, adjust the weight of the lessons learned, and find your balance again before moving forward to the next lesson. If you are working in a position where you are of service to others, or if you're having trouble getting along with someone, llama can help you find your balance in the relationship so you are back on even ground. Llama urges you to take time for yourself to visit the mountains. You are naturally drawn to the energy of that environment and will experience your greatest advancements along your spiritual path when you take time to commune with the oneness of being that exists within you.

Frequency: Llama energy sounds like *clump, zing, flleeeweeelll.* It moves in a plodding forward motion in a steady rhythm. It is cozy and warm and feels as if you're snuggled under a blanket in front of the fire on a cold winter's night.

> ### Imagine...
> It's the middle of the night, and you can't sleep. As you walk by your sliding glass doors you notice a llama looking in at you. After you blink a few times, you walk up to the door and peer outside. Sure enough, there's a llama standing there looking back at you. Still not believing what you're seeing, you turn on the patio light, crack the door a little, and reach out to touch it. Its fur is thick and plush, it feels warm, and is definitely real. After a while the llama disappears into the night.

Lory (Rainbow)

Traits: Rainbow lory (also known as rainbow lorikeet) symbolizes joyfulness, socializing, and play. Lory is a highly active bird that can get into trouble quickly because it has to investigate everything. It is a social bird that will bond with its human and gets very excited to be with him or her. Its personality is high energy due to the amount of nectar it eats, and it often acts like it's clowning around with its antics and chattiness. Lory encourages you to make friends, socialize often, and find the joy in life. When you're active like the lory, you're in forward motion that enables you to achieve your dreams.

Talents: Busy, chatty, clowning around, coaching, colorful, communication skills, curious, encouragement, entertaining, freedom, happy, high energy, intelligent, lively, personality, playfulness, sensitivity, transformation, vibrant

Challenges: Destructive, doesn't rest enough, easily frightened, easily stressed, mischievous, sweet tooth

Element(s): Air

Primary Color(s): Black, blue, green, orange, red, yellow

Appearances: When lory appears, it means to go after what you want instead of waiting for it to come to you. Lory is a very colorful bird. Lory urges you to find the vibrancy and joyful colors in your life. Lory can show you all of the possible outcomes to enable easier decision-making. Lory loves baths and sleeps flat on its back, so try the same position after a warm bath or shower if you're having trouble sleeping. Lory means to think things through. Lory is a highly intelligent bird that can figure things out, learn tricks, talk, and easily escape its cage unless it's locked. Lory urges you to use your own intelligence. You'll always be able to escape an uncomfortable or stressful situation if you have lory as a guide. Lory means to respect your own individuality. Embrace all of your unique quirks, your faults, and your gifts. By doing this you will be able to transform yourself and fly free in vibrant colors.

Assists When: You need to better understand and respect someone's point of view. Lory has excellent communication skills and will help you to look at both the positive and negative. When you look at what someone is saying from both sides of the spectrum, it will give you a clearer understanding of why they feel the way they do about a subject. Lory can help you understand every viewpoint in complex situations so that you can make clear and unbiased decisions while forming your own opinion. Because lory has a liquid diet of nectar, it is easy for their food to spoil. This means to be careful about leaving food sitting out too long or eating anything that's questionable. If any doubt, heed lory's warning and don't eat it. In the wild, lory will congregate around fruiting trees and if the nectar has fermented, the lory will get drunk. This is a sign to evaluate your lifestyle. Are you going to extremes in any area or consuming too much alcohol or sugar? If so, lory means to get yourself back into balance through moderation.

Frequency: Lory energy sounds like a high-pitched, shrill, rolling screech followed by a chattering clamor. It shoots around you, moving at ultrafast speed, zipping and zinging from here to there. It feels playful, happy, and innocent as it wraps you in its spinning heat.

See Also: Cockatiel (Cockatoo, Parakeet), Parrot (McCaw)

Imagine...

While visiting an exotic bird store, you walk past a cage with a beautiful multicolored bird that's labeled *Rainbow Lory*. As you walk by it says, *hey you,* and soon you're in a full-blown conversation with the bird. You're laughing and surprised as it answers your questions and asks you questions. You're leaning toward buying it, but it's such a big commitment, and you're just not sure it's the right decision. Every day over the next week you return to see the bird. One day you walk to the cage and it's not there. You immediately feel a sense of loss. The next day you return, and it's in its cage. You make your decision as a sense of relief washes over you. A short while later, you're leaving the store with your new lifetime companion.

Mule

Traits: Mule symbolizes independence, intelligence, and wisdom. Mule is the sterile offspring of a male donkey and a female horse. Mule is independent in nature, is extremely intelligent, and is wise. You can't use the same training process with a mule that you would with a horse. A horse is more tolerant and giving. For a mule, if the training doesn't make sense, then it will refuse to do the work. You have to train slowly and in a logical, sequential manner. This means you tend to approach situations in a slow, logical way. If things are confusing, you'll try to make sense of them, but if you can't, then you refuse to be involved.

Talents: Allowance, independent, intelligence, steady, wise

Challenges: Infertility, overly independent, stubborn

Element(s): Earth

Primary Color(s): Black, brown, red, white

Appearances: When mule appears, it means to trust in your own strengths, rely on your own wit and intelligence, and make sure you're capable of handling the things you take on. If you believe you've taken on too many projects and are feeling overwhelmed, let some of them go. If you're overloaded and overwhelmed, then there's no room for new things. Mule means you're a strong person with strength of character who prefers working alone. Mule reminds you that sometimes a very heavy load needs to be carried by more than one and it's okay to ask for help. Mule gets its intelligence from the donkey and its athleticism from the horse. This means it can handle heavy loads with ease, and it has a lot of common sense and a high sense of self-preservation. For you, this means that while you can do the work asked of you, if you feel unsafe or if it is illogical, then you have no problem refusing. When mule appears, it means to check yourself to see if you're being overly cautious simply because you don't want to be bothered to do the task at hand. Mule is also known as *long ears*, so make sure you're really listening to and understanding what others are saying to you. Use your keen sense of hearing to listen for insinuated meanings, things that are there in tone and pitch but are not voiced in words.

Assists When: You need to be steady and grounded or, if you need to, exit a situation quickly. Mule has a freeze reflex and a flight reflex, so if it is startled, it will freeze in place or bolt. Like mule, most of the time you're grounded and approach life with steady forward movement. Other times, you feel a pressing need to escape. Mule is a hardy animal that is more resistant to disease or parasites, has harder hooves, and can exist on less food than a horse. This means you too are tough and resilient and can accomplish much because your body is built to handle hard work. Mule can help you have better people connections. Mule has a natural affinity for humans, and when treated with kindness, patience, and understanding, it will trust you and do what you're asking of it. Mule reminds you to treat people as you would like to be treated; see them as unique spiritual beings with their own spiritual truths. Understand them in this manner and they will connect with you in the same way. When not seen in this way, people tend to rebel like mule.

Frequency: Mule energy feels like a pillar, straight and tall. It moves forward in a slow progressive way, methodical and steady. It sounds like a strong, slow, solid beat of a bass drum. It is low in pitch and evenly spaced apart *boom … boom … boom …* It feels warm and strong, as if you've been wrapped in a hug.

See Also: Donkey, Horse, Zebra

Imagine…

It's springtime in Virginia. You stop by the barn where you used to work and expect to see horses and cows but instead you find a lonely old mule. Having handled horses in the past, you halter the mule and put it in cross ties. Over the next hour you curry, brush, and pick out its feet. The mule tightens and wiggles its top lip in pleasure as you groom it. You're delighted that the mule shared this special time with you, so you smile at it and say, *you're spectacular.*

Pig

Traits: Pig symbolizes being social, cleanliness, and happiness. Pig invites you to be more social. It enjoys close physical contact, especially lying down together. Pigs form tight bonds with each other. It is peaceful and enjoys rooting around in the dirt. People think pig is dirty or unclean because it enjoys rolling around in the water or mud (it prefers water over mud), but pig is actually a clean animal that keeps its bathroom area very far away from its living and eating areas. Even piglets only a few hours old know to go potty in the bathroom area. Pig is a happy, affectionate creature that, if named, will come running when you call it. Pig means for you to make friends, enjoy life, and, if you've been messy or unhygienic, clean up your surroundings or yourself.

Talents: Congeniality, determination, fertility, finances, fortune, generosity, good luck, good-hearted, happiness, honest, intuition, law of attraction, manifesting, money, peacefulness, prosperity, quick changes of direction, swift action

Challenges: Complacency, dirtiness, greed, laziness, lust, overindulgence

Element(s): Earth, water

Primary Color(s): Black, red, white

Appearances: When pig appears, it means financial changes are coming soon. Pig is associated with money, luck, and the improvement of finances. This means you need to be aware that your personal financial picture is about to change and make sure it changes for the better. Pig is also associated with the law of attraction, which is when you manifest your desires through intuition, creative visualization, and positive thoughts. So, if you've been considering investments but are unsure about them, then your doubt is your intuition saying to wait. The changes pig brings can be either positive or negative, but when you're aware, you can avoid the negative most of the time. This also means that if you think of what you want in the wrong way you can also inadvertently bring negativity to you. So make sure your manifestation is always positive and precise. Pig means focus, determination, and change. When pig is focused on something, it is utterly focused, and you'd be hard-pressed to lure it away from what has its attention (like food). Pig and its determined nature ensure success.

Assists When: You need to find balance and take things in moderation. Pig is associated with overindulging and selfish behaviors. If you're eating too much or not sharing with others when you should be, then pig can help make you aware of these behaviors and enable you to do things differently so you can bring yourself back into balance. Pig can help you become more generous of your time and resources if you're always saving for a rainy day or hoarding supplies. Pig's ability to root out things in the earth can help you uncover truths and information you need. If you've been easily distracted lately, pig can help you regain focus and get organized so it's easier to stay on track.

Frequency: Pig energy feels warm and slick. It moves slowly in a thumping motion, up and down in short waves. It feels as if you're sinking into a bathtub filled with mud that relaxes and rejuvenates you. It sounds like *th-rump, th-rump, th-rump.*

See Also: Boar, Erymanthian Boar

Imagine…

As you're finishing your work day on the farm, you hear a loud squeal and turn to see a baby piglet running right at you. Without thinking, you bend down and scoop it up as it runs by. A little dog runs around the corner of a building yapping like it has lost its mind. You hold tightly to the out-of-breath piglet, nuzzling it against your neck, and keep telling it to calm down until it stops squealing. The little dog runs past and heads to the house, piglet forgotten. You put the piglet back in its pen and head home.

Pigeon

Traits: Pigeon symbolizes going home, messages, and family. Pigeons are known as the carriers of messages. Their homing instinct will always guide them back home, to their safe haven, even if they've traveled long distances. Because of this instinct, pigeon has been used throughout history to carry messages from one place to another. Pigeon is connected to love and family. Baby pigeons stay in the nest until they are two months old. At this age, they are still missing some of the adults' coloring and neck rings, but they are practically the size of an adult, which increases their chance of survival when they leave the nest. This means that now is the time for you to reconnect with your family if you're distanced from them, to go home to where you were raised to reconnect with your roots, or to just call to say hello.

Talents: Appreciation, belonging, community, divine connection, family, forgiveness, foundations, growth, heritage, home, intuition, love, security, spirituality

Challenges: Doesn't leave when asked but stays until ready to go, pest, separation from loved ones, traveling far from home

Element(s): Air

Primary Color(s): Gray, white

Appearances: When pigeon appears, it means to look upward to find your success. Pigeon can fly nearly straight up, which is a sign to look to your own spirituality in order to connect to the Divine. Pigeon means to access your inner intuition and universal flow to find your way safely home again. Pigeon can fly seven hundred miles in a day to get back home where it feels safe and secure. If you don't feel content or secure in your home, it's time to evaluate where you're living. Is it time to move or make other changes that will make you feel at ease when you walk through your front door? Pigeon means to look at your youth for answers, especially if you've been feeling restless and on edge, as if you're missing something in your life. It's not always easy to go home again but if you can, return to your roots in order to strengthen your foundation or explore your heritage. Pigeon urges you to be determined in your spiritual quest or in finding answers to any questions you have. Pigeon will not leave an area as long as it can find food. You can shoo it away, other birds can try to chase it away, but until it is ready to leave, pigeon will stay put. This is a great lesson in understanding how to stay the course to overcome obstacles in your path.

Assists When: You need a reminder that you're not alone in the world. Pigeon will guide you home to your family and close friends who have been there for you in your life. Pigeon can help you go back to the past to reconnect to your inner truth and purpose. Sometimes you need to go home to gain clarity and peace of mind or to remember what you have forgotten along the pathway of life. Pigeon reminds you to reconnect with your community and the support and camaraderie and sense of belonging you can find there. When it comes to communication, pigeon can help you make sure everyone is on the same page and no one is overlooked when important notifications are made.

Frequency: Pigeon energy sounds like a soft cooing, a *coo-coo-coo* repetition. It beats rapidly with a high pitch and medium tone. It is warm, breezy, and crisp.

Imagine...

It's a cold winter's day, and you're sitting on a bench at the park throwing food to the pigeons. The blustering wind whips around you, tugging at the scarf covering your head. The pigeons are sitting on the bench with you; some are even standing on your knees, waiting for a bit of food. You move them to the ground and give them some seeds. There's a small pigeon that keeps flying back to your lap, so you let it stay. You pet it as if it's a tame bird. Once you feel your cabin fever is gone, you return home. Sitting on the bush beside the front door is the small pigeon you'd been petting at the park. You rub its back, thank it for seeing you safely home, and wish it a good flight back to the flock. As you shut the door, you watch it fly away.

Praying Mantis

Traits: Praying mantis symbolizes spirituality, mindfulness, and inner wisdom. When praying mantis is waiting for prey, it holds its front legs in an upright position, which looks as if they're folded in prayer, thus its name. It holds perfectly still as it waits but then strikes out very quickly, grabbing the unsuspecting insect with the spines on its arm. This means for you to connect with your own spiritual nature to find your inner wisdom through stillness and quiet introspection. When you learn new information that feels as if it fits your path, quickly make it your own.

Talents: Awareness, balance, calm, connection to the Divine, creativity, empowerment, fast, healing, intuitive, meditation, mindful, patience, power, precision, purpose, reflection, silence, spiritual, stillness

Challenges: Isolation, loneliness, reclusiveness

Element(s): Earth

Primary Color(s): Brown, green

Appearances: When praying mantis appears, it means to embrace your creativity. When you're coming up with a new idea, the best way to achieve success is to find quiet moments when you can just think about what you want to do. Allow the flow of universal energy to bring concepts to you. When the right one comes along, it will feel right and you'll be able to give it power and positivity so it can grow into a productive project. Praying mantis also means to take time to just be. Commune with nature, soak in a hot bath, or listen to soothing music. When you push aside the noise of life and listen to your inner voice, that's when you'll get the best ideas and make the best discoveries about your own spirituality. Praying mantis means you need a little peace and quiet, so when you return to the hectic pace of life, you will have quick reflexes and it will be easier to follow your instincts. Praying mantis has excellent eyesight and can see something move up to sixty feet away and can turn its head 180 degrees. This means you need to not only pay attention to what's happening close to you but look in the near distance as well.

Assists When: You need to let your intuition guide you. Praying mantis can help you focus on your spirituality instead of being materialistic. This can lead to reduced stress levels, improved focus, and an overall connection of mind, body, and spirit. Praying mantis urges you to pay attention to visions, dreams, and intuitive impressions. Praying mantis can help you isolate yourself from situations that are draining your energy, keep quiet about things you don't want others to know, and connect to your higher self for rejuvenation of your spiritual purpose. When threatened, praying mantis will stand up on its hind legs, spread its front legs wide above its head, and spread its wings so its colors can be seen. If that doesn't scare off the predator, it will bite, pinch, and strike out with its front legs. This gives you confidence to stand tall and fight for the things you want.

Frequency: Praying mantis energy sounds like a sword slicing the air and the quick zap of electricity encased in silence. It moves slowly, deliberately, with a steady *tic-tic-tic* that is barely audible. If feels cool and tingles with anticipation.

> ### Imagine...
> You've just finished a short meditation to help you gain focus for the day. During the meditation, you kept seeing a large praying mantis telling you to find stillness in the moment. You're not exactly sure what that means, but you think about it as you grab your work gloves and head outside. You get a bag of mulch and start spreading it around the base of a tree but stop when you encounter a praying mantis the size of the one in your meditation. You sit and stare at it and suddenly you understand what finding stillness in the moment means. It's the calm, completeness you feel in this insect's presence. You feel as if you've tapped into universal frequency. Thanking it for the message, you gently hold your hand out, and it crawls into your palm. You move it out of the way and finish the mulching. When you look again, it is gone.

Rabbit

Traits: Rabbit symbolizes fertility, intuition, and physical agility. Rabbit is known for its reproduction rate. Beginning around six months of age, a female rabbit can have a litter of up to fourteen babies and can get pregnant again right after giving birth. Essentially it can have twelve litters a year. Rabbit is very intuitive and immediately acts on instincts. It is very agile and can jump about three yards at a time. This can get it into trouble because it reacts without thinking.

Talents: Abundance, adaptability, alert, artistic, clever, compassion, coordination, creativity, desire, elegance, emotions, family, fast thinking, fertility, foraging, gentle, gracious, growth, harmony, humility, intuition, joy, kindness, liveliness, luck, nurturing, observant, overcoming fear, quick reflexes, rebirth, self-reliant, sensitivity, shyness, speed, spontaneous, tenderness

Challenges: Anxious, impulsive, indecisive, lacks stimulation, reckless, restlessness, risk-taker, timid, unpredictable, worries too much

Element(s): Earth

Primary Color(s): Black, brown, gray, white

Appearances: When rabbit appears, it means you need to pay attention to what's happening around you so you can react quickly to the abundance of opportunities coming your way. Rabbit has 360-degree panoramic vision, which lets them see everything except one spot directly in front of their nose. This means not to miss something right in front of you. Rabbit is affectionate and has a gentle nature. If you've been distant or belligerent in your relationships because of past hurts, rabbit can show you how to regain the gentleness within your soul. Rabbit means you are focusing too much on the things you fear or that worry you. Let go of the fear because it is holding you back. Once you do, you'll find you're able to move forward in leaps and bounds. Rabbit encourages you to have fun in life. When feeling happy and playful, rabbit will twist its body and flick its feet while jumping high into the air. Its coordination and clever intellect help them get out of tight spots or difficult situations. Rabbit urges you to stay ready to act, react, and move when necessary to ensure your success.

Assists When: You need to dig deeper into a situation. Rabbit enjoys digging around in its environment to see what it can find and can show you how to locate tiny bits of information that will be helpful to you. Like rabbit, you have excellent reactions, are quick-witted, and rely on yourself to succeed. These qualities will help you out-wit others to quickly move past the competition. People may think you're lucky, but in truth you're relying on your intuition to guide you. Rabbit warns against getting bored and jumping from one thing to another without completing anything, especially if it is long term. If you're having conflicts in your job or with another person, rabbit can show you how to solve these with ease and without negative repercussions.

Frequency: Rabbit energy sounds like a low hum with thumping noises mixed in. It moves quickly, darting in different directions, almost as if it's bouncing off of the walls. It feels warm, cuddly, and affectionate.

See Also: Hare, Jackalope

Imagine…

Summer seems to bring the bunnies out in the early morning and evening. For the past several weeks, you've been trying to get one of the rabbits living in your yard to eat a carrot out of your hand. You go sit in your regular spot and wait. After a while, the rabbit comes out, following the carrot trail you've left. Soon it is within several feet of the carrot you're holding out. It slowly creeps forward, sniffing the air. Then it takes a bite of the carrot. You are overwhelmed with a powerful feeling of trust from the rabbit. It has overcome its most basic instinct to approach you and eat the food you offer. You telepathically send it picture messages of love and thanks. This connection has made your day. You feel more in tune with yourself and the world around you.

Sheep

Traits: Sheep symbolizes innocence and vulnerability. Sheep avoids conflict because it goes against its innocent nature. It will quickly leave any situation it feels is threatening. Sheep is vulnerable to attack because it is so docile. This means your innocence and purity enable you to see the good in people. But others, who may not have your best interest at heart, may try to take advantage of your compassion. Be aware. Sheep is born with a long tail that is usually docked shortly after birth. Sheep warns not to cut yourself short by always following the flock. Sometimes you may need to be the black sheep and do things your own way.

Talents: Beauty, compassion, considerate, docile, gentle, innocent, prosperity, social, spiritual development

Challenges: Awkward, dependency, following aimlessly, sheepish, unimaginative, vulnerability, weakness

Element(s): Earth

Primary Color(s): Black, brown, gray, red, silver, white

Appearances: When sheep appears, it means you will encounter a situation where you will have to obey the rules of tradition. You may be working on a project for which you have all of these great ideas, but the powers that be decide to stick with the way it has always been done. Don't take it personally if your ideas are shut down. You have a strong desire to fit into your groups and to have other people like you, so you conform to what is happening around you. Sheep warns against trying too hard to please someone else because you can lose your individuality. Sheep means you may need to attend a family gathering soon. If sheep appears, you are ready to commit to developing your intuition, understanding your spirituality, and taking care of your higher self. This will be a time of great self-discovery, a time of learning and exploring ideas that may seem foreign to you at first but are a touchstone to your soul. Seek guidance from those who have walked the path, but don't become part of the crowd, instead ask questions for yourself, take what feels right for your own spiritual growth, and leave the rest to consider again later.

Assists When: You need to recapture the happiness and innocence of your childhood. Sheep can show you how to get those feelings back again in order to look at life through different eyes. Sheep enjoys being with its flock and enjoying their camaraderie. Sheep reminds you to enjoy the simple things in life, like hanging out with your friends. It is a prey animal with a flight instinct, so if danger is detected, a sheep will run away as fast as it can. Sheep means you're about to go through a time of self-assessment and healing. If you've been feeling down, sheep can help you be more accepting, tolerant, and have feelings of compassion and understanding for yourself. This doesn't mean you get to have a pity party but instead means you see your positive and negative qualities and accept yourself as you are. You understand where you excel and what your limitations are, and you don't blame others for your faults. Sheep also enables you to see these qualities within others too and accept them with all of their gifts and flaws.

Frequency: Sheep energy moves slowly beside you in a steady, solid rhythm. It sounds like the sheep's call *baaa-baaa-baaa,* which lifts and falls in pitch. It feels warm, fuzzy, and soft.

Imagine...

You've just gotten a temporary job working at a petting zoo. You've been assigned to take care of the sheep. One ewe in particular looks very fat, but you're told she just needs to be sheared. You notice she isn't eating when you feed her one afternoon. Your intuition kicks, in so you stay after you clock out and watch her. A few hours pass and then, just as you'd suspected, she goes into labor. She delivers two healthy girls. Once mother and babies have bonded, you sit inside their stall and get to know the lambs. They are friendly and super soft, with little rough tongues that lick at your hands. Two unexpected little miracles.

Siamese Fighting Fish (Betta Fish)

Traits: Betta fish symbolizes aggression and nurturing. The betta fish is an aggressive fish that will violently fight to the death with other betta fish to defend its territory and for food. But when it comes to spawning, the male betta fish is the primary caretaker and runs the female away from the nest once she lays the eggs. If there isn't a female around, a male betta fish will still hang out in the comfort of a nest.

Talents: Adaptability, boundaries, clairaudience, clairvoyance, creativity, dreams, independence, mystery, protection, solitude, spirituality, understanding, visions, warrior strength

Challenges: Aggression, confrontational, egotistical, ferocity, violent

Element(s): Water

Primary Color(s): Black, blue, brown, gold, green, indigo, orange, pink, purple, red, silver, turquoise, white, yellow

Appearances: When betta fish appears, it means you're undergoing a spiritual awakening and will have more contact with the spiritual realms. Now is the time to let go of any aggressive feelings you may have, to understand why you're having them, and to find the root cause of those feelings. Learn as much as you can through books and articles about spirituality, intuition, and any other similar topic to which you feel a connection. Expect to experience a greater connection with the spiritual realm, including guides, angels, and master teachers. You may have more prophetic dreams and visions, or you may be able to better understand any intuitive impressions you receive. Betta fish means you easily adapt to changes in your life, are independent, and are filled with positive potential. Once you tap into your inner truth, you will go far and achieve much success. Betta fish can help you spend time alone to analyze and understand your own ego and the root cause of any confrontational or negative feelings. Are there issues you've avoided confronting in your life? If you addressed them, would you be able to move forward, leaving them in the past? The answers to these types of questions will help you find your own inner truth and sort out any emotional obstacles you may be experiencing.

Assists When: You need to attract attention to yourself and make a good impression. Are you going for a new job interview or on a first date? Betta fish can help you command attention and hold it. Male betta fish will twist its body, fan out its fins, and flare its gills to get a female's attention. Betta fish's strength of character, which is often compared to that of a warrior, helps you keep someone's attention once you've gotten it. That's when you can wow them with your captivating personality, creativity, and desire to succeed in life. Betta fish needs a small space that is its own where it can hide out and feel safe. This means you too need your own little nook in your home where you can be alone. Maybe you enjoy a good book in the library or tinkering with engines in the garage. This is an important part of your inner balance, so make sure to find your own little space to do something you enjoy.

Frequency: Betta fish energy feels like streaks of light passing by you so quickly you can barely see them. It feels hot, steamy, and as if it's about to explode. It sounds like car tires screeching as someone slams on the brakes.

> ### Imagine…
> You visit a large store that sells aquariums. In one of the displays there is a very large blue fish with beautiful fins and long, flowing tail. The sign says *Betta Fish—Not for Sale.* As you watch, the fish disappears to the upper corner of the tank near some bubbles, then swims around the very large aquarium. You are captivated by its beauty. It swims back and forth, stopping at times to face you. Its aquarium is filled with places it can hide and little structures it can swim through. It swims close to you then swims through a hoop and comes back around. You decide this fish is intelligent and intuitive.

Silkworm (Silk Moth)

Traits: Silkworm symbolizes moving from the darkness to the light, transformation, and intuition. Silkworm goes through several phases to transform into the silk moth. In the larvae stage, the silkworm is ravenous and eats mulberry leaves constantly. It will shed its skin four times before creating a cocoon made of raw silk from its salivary glands. From this cocoon, the adult silk moth emerges. Silk is harvested at the cocoon stage for commercial uses.

Talents: Allure, attraction, concealment, determination, dreaming, faith, finding light in the dark, healing abilities, inner knowing, intuition, movement, otherworldliness, power of suggestion, psychic awareness, secret knowledge, subtlety, transformation, vulnerability

Challenges: Disguise, hiding, shadows

Element(s): Air, earth

Primary Color(s): White

Appearances: When silkworm appears, it means you're being healed from the inside out. You may not even be aware of the changes happening within you, but you are growing and developing, transforming into a beautiful being filled with intuition, faith, and the uncanny ability to find the light in the darkest of nights. When you realize the changes you've made, it will come as a surprise, but you will feel as if you're one with the secret knowledge of the universe. Silkworm means you will attract like-minded individuals to your calm serenity. You may begin to experience deeper intuitive impressions, powerful dreams, and strong psychic abilities. Silkworm reminds you that difficult situations always pass in time, and it is up to you to see the beauty in the outcome. Silkworm works in silence and then awakens as a beautiful new being. You are doing the same right now. Let silkworm guide you to the light. Silkworm can lay three to four hundred eggs at a time. This indicates that anything you attempt right now will be fertile and successful. Silkworm warns against hiding from your own emotions. Don't hide your feelings away but instead deal with them in the now. How you handle the moments of your life will always affect your personal and spiritual growth. Deal with emotions now to avoid a meltdown later. Silkworm reminds you to do for yourself instead of letting others take care of your needs. When you give someone else complete power and control over your care, you could ultimately lose the ability to care for yourself.

Assists When: You need to be more creative. Silkworm means you have the capability of seeing situations from your own unique perspective. You can come up with innovative solutions to problems that others may not see. Silkworm can help you find the silver lining in every situation. Where others may see only darkness and negativity, you always see light and positivity. You listen closely to what is being said and are able to intuit the secret knowledge hidden within words and emotions. When you're experiencing complications, you remain calm, focused, and determined. You have faith things will work out as they should, so you continue moving forward with hope and joy. Silkworm can help you feel more confident if your self-esteem is low. It will show you the positive qualities that make you so popular and endearing to others, which you may have forgotten. While you don't like to toot your own horn, there are times when you have to recognize your strengths and the positive impact you make on others so you can move forward on your path.

Frequency: Silkworm energy sounds like soft, delicate, faraway chewing noises. It feels cool, supple, and silky. It spins around you at a slow pace, wrapping you in the warmth of a cocoon, where you will grow and transform into the beautiful essence of your soul.

> ### Imagine…
> You're leaving class one night and pass a moth sitting on a bush. You've never seen one like it before, so you quickly look it up on your phone. You discover that it is a silk moth, so you take a picture of it. After a few minutes, the silk moth starts to vibrate, warming up its flight muscles. Then it takes off, flying up into the sky and out of sight.

Society Finch

Traits: Society finch symbolizes good times with friends and family. This is a time of celebration, fun, and happiness. Society finch joyfully flies in an up and down bouncy motion instead of flying in a straight line as it enjoys the freedom of flight. Society finch is a very social bird that likes the company of others. This means you are able to find joy in the ups and downs of life.

Talents: Cheerfulness, colorful, creativity, diverse, freedom, grateful, happiness, high energy personality, journey, joyful, lively, optimistic, positivity, quick-witted, resourceful, simplicity, upbeat personality, variety, zealous

Challenges: Fanatical, lack of focus, overly enthusiastic, too chatty, unsystematic

Element(s): Air

Primary Color(s): Black, brown, gray, red, white

Appearances: When society finch appears, it means there will be more opportunities for livelihood, mingling, and social events. Your life may become quite busy, and your social calendar will fill up with events for you to attend. Society finch is a songbird, which means to sing your own unique song while enjoying the changes and activity around you. Society finch amplifies the positives in your life, allowing you to leave any negative situations in the past. Society finch changes your outlook to one of positivity, happiness, and joy. Life is a journey, and society finch implores you to live it with passion and vitality. It can help you navigate the twists and turns of your life as if it's an adventure instead of looking at them as obstacles. Society finch means not to waste time on negative situations or people. It can help you find balance in situations and in dealing with people who are always procrastinating or complaining. Your joyful attitude can rub off on them, allowing them to change their point of view. Society finch is like a smile. When someone smiles at you, their happiness rubs off and you want to smile back. Life is too short to dwell on things you can't change, unconstructive behavior, or living in a rut. Lift your wings and fly with enthusiasm. If you're in a career where you have to promote your work, make public speaking appearances, or attend social events, society finch can give you the presence and courage to put yourself out there for all to see. You are positive in your outlook, and people see you as a leader in your field. You encourage interaction from others and enjoy vibrant discussions.

Assists When: You need to appreciate what you have instead of coveting what you don't have. Society finch makes the best use of the things at their disposal and will create a nest just about anywhere. It would be just as happy in a cardboard box as it would in the expensive nest you bought for it. This means material things aren't a driving force in your life. You're happy with the simple things and make the most of what you have. You live in the moment, appreciating all of the gifts you've been given. If your energy levels have been low, society finch can help you elevate them so you begin each day in good spirits and with a song in your heart. Society finch can help you with communication. It enables you to speak clearly and to use words that will make a positive impact on the lives of the people around you.

Frequency: Society finch energy zips and zings around you in a brightly colored stream of ribbons. It feels buoyant and bouncy, as if you're jumping on a trampoline, spinning and flipping in the air. It sounds like the *ping-ping* of a coin dropped on a glass table, clear in tone and high in pitch.

Imagine…

At the pet store, you want to pick out a society finch, but you can't decide which one you want as your new pet. The little birds are jumping around so fast you barely see them move. Then you notice a brown and white one clinging to the cage, watching you. You point it out to the salesperson helping you. The salesperson catches it, you pet it for a few minutes, and then you decide to buy it. You're thankful you noticed the little bird's energy reaching out to you.

Squirrel Monkey

Traits: Squirrel monkey symbolizes balance, working in a group, and leaping over obstacles. Squirrel monkey doesn't have a prehensile tail, which means it can't use its tail to hang from branches or hold objects; instead it uses it for balance. Squirrel monkey is a social animal that lives in groups of twelve to a hundred individuals. It can usually leap over eight feet but has been known to leap up to twenty feet. This means you work well in a group atmosphere, are able to balance work and your home life, and overcome obstacles with ease.

Talents: Acrobatics, cleverness, communication, community, curiosity, emotions, feelings, games, gentleness, imaginative, ingenuity, intelligent, loving, mischievous, playful, protective, resourceful, speed, understanding

Challenges: Easily bored, overly chatty, reactive, unpredictable

Element(s): Air, earth

Primary Color(s): Black, brown, gray, green (olive), red, yellow

Appearances: When squirrel monkey appears, it means to connect to your senses in a deeper, more intuitive way. Instead of just looking, see with your clairvoyance. Instead of just hearing, listen with clairaudience. Squirrel monkey means you have the ability to travel between worlds. It lives between earth and sky in the middle part of the tops of trees. Because of its small size, it rarely goes to the treetops or down to earth. This means you also have the ability to travel between worlds and are a medium that can connect with those who have passed to the other side. Squirrel monkey reminds you to keep balance between these realms. It's easy to get drawn into communication with the other side so much that you ignore the human existence you're living in. Squirrel monkey uses its tail and feet to keep it stabilized and balanced on the branches of trees. It urges you to maintain this same balance when you're moving between worlds. Squirrel monkey urges you to look at all situations from multiple points of view before making decisions about the situation. Squirrel monkey agilely moves from tree to tree by twisting, turning, hanging, and jumping. It is quite acrobatic, and it's this constant changing motion that gives it the ability to see all sides of a situation. When it arrives at its destination, it will sit and look around, seeing everything before deciding to stay put or continue on. This is the same lesson for you. Look at and see everything before you decide anything. Change your perspective to get a clearer vision of what's happening around you.

Assists When: You need to keep quiet. Squirrel monkey makes very little noise even though it moves through the forest canopy at fast speeds. When a warning call is given, the females and youth get very still and quiet while the males check things out. If you're studying a new topic, squirrel monkey can help you remember the material. It has one of the largest brains compared to its body size and is the cleverest. If you're unsure where you're headed in your life, if you feel lost or stuck in the past, squirrel monkey can show you how to move forward and the best future route to take. It encourages you to never give up, stay focused on your destination, and move with graceful ease until you get where you want to go.

Frequency: Squirrel monkey energy sounds like a *chirp, purr, squeak, shriek, click* all intermingled together. It leaps and swings around you and feels coarse and scratchy as it brushes against your skin.

See Also: Monkey, Orangutan

Imagine...
You're visiting a zoo and come to a walk-through squirrel monkey exhibit. You've never seen one in the flesh and can't believe how small they are. Suddenly a little one jumps onto your arm and presses its face against your cheek. You're utterly amazed. You lift it off of your arm and hold it in your hands for a moment before placing it back on a tree limb. You thank it for the special gift of physically connecting with you before moving to the next exhibit.

Sugar Glider

Traits: Sugar glider is a marsupial that symbolizes flying high, leaping without fear, knowing where you're going and how you're going to get there. Sugar glider lives with a sense of purpose. It has focused energy. It must know exactly where it's going to land before it leaps. You share this same sense of purpose in your life. You know where you're going and what you need to do to achieve the results you want. Sugar glider urges you to apply this same focus to any decisions you are about to make. Look at all of the possibilities and where you'll end up before you take that leap. You soar with focused determination, which will make you successful.

Talents: Affectionate, bonding, comfort, flight, focused, high energy, physically soaring, trust, wisdom

Challenges: Acceptance issues, hostility, impatience, sugar addiction

Element(s): Air, earth

Primary Color(s): Brown, white

Appearances: When sugar glider appears, it means to look at how you're interacting with people. A male sugar glider marks the members of its group with his scent. If any others try to become part of the group, he will violently chase them away. Sometimes you will experience personal and spiritual growth by meeting and interacting with new people. Sugar glider warns against being cliquish. Sugar glider sleeps all day and is up at night. It does this to protect itself from predators. You may also do your best work at night, so consider nighttime careers. The sugar glider is a marsupial gliding opossum that keeps its young in its pouch. This means you have all you need within you. The creative ideas you come up with will grow into successful ventures if you nurture them. When you take note of the little things and apply them to your ideas, you will come up with phenomenal inventions or new ways of doing things. You're very much an inventor at heart. You feel energized by the creative process. It doesn't matter what you're making—art, books, or buildings—you're able to create unique and interesting projects.

Assists When: You want to bond with others in more meaningful ways. If your relationships are lacking feelings of closeness, sugar glider can show you how to deepen your interactions to develop the intimacy you desire. While this could be sexual in nature, it applies to platonic relationships as well. Oftentimes relationships lack the trust needed for extreme closeness. Sugar glider can teach you how to trust others but most importantly how to trust yourself. If you aren't connected to your own inner truth and believe in that truth, then how can you expect others to trust you or open up to you? Starting within yourself, overcome any insecurities you may feel or fears that need facing. Are you blocking others from getting too close to you because you see comfort as weakness? You're already strong. Giving or receiving comforting words or gestures is a sign of inner strength, not weakness. You'll be amazed with the changes you'll experience in your relationships as you make changes within yourself.

Frequency: Sugar glider energy feels like you're sliding along ice with slick shoes on, moving with fluidity and grace. It is a raspy barking sound that quickly moves up and down in pitch and tone. It feels cozy, warm, and cuddly.

Imagine...

At the pet store, you're interacting with three sugar gliders, trying to decide which one you want to buy. As they crawl over your lap, you hold them close together, looking at each of them. One starts to climb up your shirt, so you put it back in your lap. It does it again, so you let it go. It climbs to the top of your head and sits there, playing with your hair. You take it down and put it back in your lap, but it heads up to your shoulder this time and puts its hands on your cheek, trying to see your face. The other two are content to hang out in your lap. Then it crawls up to your shoulder and cuddles beside your neck. The little climber is yours.

Tortoise

Traits: Tortoise symbolizes home, family, and simple abundance. Tortoise doesn't need a lot to survive, and most of what it needs it carries around with it. Tortoise's home is its body. Its shell is an exoskeleton. It can retreat inside and close up tight any time it feels threatened. A tortoise's spine and ribs are fused to its shell, which is made up of bone and keratin. When danger threatens, tortoise pulls its legs and head inside. The head will either be in a vertical S shape or folded to the side. This means you can easily retreat back home when you feel threatened. There you can regroup until you're ready to face the world again.

Talents: Abundance, deeply connected to the earth, determination, endurance, graceful, grounded, harmony, inner wisdom, longevity, observant, pacing, patience, progress, resourceful, secure, self-protection, sensible, simplicity, steady, travel

Challenges: Insensitive, slow movement, uninspired

Element(s): Earth, water

Primary Color(s): Black, brown, yellow

Appearances: When tortoise appears, it means to slow down. If you've been going at a fast pace for a while, now is the time to stop and really look at what is happening around you. Pay attention to both the big events and the small details. When you're constantly on the go, you often overlook things you really should see and be aware of. Tortoise means to slow down your own pace so you don't burn out. Tortoise has a long life (the longest living one known to date was 225 years old), so it lives it simply and to the fullest. It gets enough sleep (up to sixteen hours a day) and takes its time as it moves from place to place. It can live alone or in a herd of other tortoises. Because of its connection to the earth, tortoise is grounded and in balance. Tortoise means to use your resources wisely, not wastefully, and to make the most of the things you have. Tortoise is patient, persistent, and easygoing. It doesn't have drama in its life and can help you eliminate the things that make you feel overwhelmed or stressed, or that cause you worry. On the other hand, if you've been moving in slow motion, are unmotivated, or feel you don't have purpose, tortoise can help you move a little faster, pick up the pace a bit, set goals, and move forward at a steady rate to accomplish them.

Assists When: You need lasting progress. When you're pursuing a long-term goal, tortoise can help you find the best path to take to reach it. By taking small, steady steps and building on a solid foundation, you can pace yourself to accomplish your task. If the task at hand seems complicated, tortoise can help you break it down into smaller pieces so you can see how it all fits together. If you need to do investigative work to find more information about a subject, tortoise can help you dig deeply to find what you need. When it's hot, tortoise will dig a burrow in the dirt and bury down into it to cool off. This is also a sign for you to keep your cool in hot (or volatile) situations.

Frequency: Tortoise energy sounds like a deep, low, grating noise. It feels hard, cool, and rough. It moves slowly yet steadily beside you, bumping against you in an evenly paced rhythm.

See Also: Turtle

Imagine...

You're visiting a local zoo that has a Galápagos giant tortoise exhibit. You learn the history and care of these giant tortoises. You observe them moving slowly around the pen, nibbling on leaves or approaching the caregiver for a treat. The tortoise stretches its neck nearly straight up to reach vegetation or to see what's in the handler's hand. Its skin is rough and scaly yet moves smoothly near the shell when the tortoise walks. One comes close to where you're standing, stretches out its neck to see if you have a carrot or other treat, then continues on. It moves very well for a 150-year-old animal. You think of how the world has changed since it was born.

Turkey

Traits: Turkey symbolizes sacrifice, abundance, and prosperity. Turkey is connected to sacrificing oneself to ensure the prosperity of harvesting and the abundance of nature. To you this means that through hard work and personal sacrifice you will harvest the fruit of your labor. Turkey reminds you to remember the importance of connecting to the energy of earth and to have respect for and to honor the land.

Talents: Abundance, awareness, blessings, community, connection to earth, cooperation, fertility, generosity, harvest, higher purpose, practicality, pride, prosperity, renewal, sacrifice, satisfaction, sharing, spirit, understanding, virility

Challenges: Aggressive, arrogant, overconfident, vanity

Element(s): Earth

Primary Color(s): Black, brown, white, and red and blue on its neck

Appearances: When turkey appears, it means you're about to reap rewards of some kind. This may be a raise in your wage at work, the successful completion of a project that is praised by others, or achieving a goal you are trying to attain. Turkey isn't only about receiving monetary wealth for the good things you do but to receive both intellectual and spiritual rewards. Turkey is connected to the earth and the gifts received from the harvest. If you enjoy gardening, turkey ensures you'll have a plentiful harvest of food. If you own a business, you are coming into a time when you'll see an increase in sales. Turkey means you give from the heart and go out of your way to help others. Turkey is connected to the spiritual realm and the knowledge that all life is connected and sacred. You give and work with others not out of a sense of what you'll receive in return but because you feel it is the right thing for you to do on your spiritual path. Turkey also means to honor yourself and the gifts you receive from others whether it is emotional support or assistance with your own spiritual awakening. Spiritually, turkey means you have risen above indulging in doing things for yourself and have moved into a higher frequency where you acknowledge and strive toward universal oneness. At this level, turkey gives you feelings of contentment and satisfaction as you live in harmony with all that is.

Assists When: You need to enhance your feelings of community and want to manifest abundance in your life. In the winter, turkeys group into flocks of males and females. When breeding season comes, they mix together again. This sense of community can help you work in small and large groups. Turkey doesn't mate for life. In fact, it is very promiscuous. Turkey urges you to look at your sexual behavior. If you want to improve upon your self-defense, ask turkey to guide you. If it feels threatened, a turkey will chase you or fly at you (even if you're not really a threat) and attack with the spurs on the back of its feet and peck with its beak. This means any type of self-defense using your feet and hands for protection will be beneficial to you. It also means your attitude with others may be too defensive and needs adjusting. Turkey is connected to the third eye and can help you see life with a sense of integrity, high morals, and self-respect.

Frequency: Turkey energy moves slowly, almost like it's stalking, but then moves quickly without warning. It slinks around you, hot and intense. It can also feel cool, relaxed, and distant. It sounds like a flurry of feathers shaking in a quick stiletto.

Imagine...

You're on a rescue mission to save some animals for the local shelter. You go into a barn on a property and are surprised to find several turkeys inside. It takes you a while, but you round them up and cage them so you can take them to the shelter. There's only one left, and it's a young turkey that is freaking out in the corner of a stall. You quietly go inside and explain that you're only trying to help it find a new place to live where it will have plenty of food. It takes about twenty minutes of making a frequency connection, but the juvenile finally calms down enough that you can pick it up.

Yak

Traits: Yak symbolizes survival, pacing, and longevity. Yak lives in elevations between 9,800 and 18,000 feet in the Himalayan Mountains of Tibet and surrounding regions. To survive the cold temperatures, yak has a thick, shaggy coat with a matted undercoat; a thick layer of subcutaneous fat; larger lungs and heart, which enable it to transport more oxygen through its blood; and almost no sweat glands. It has difficulties at lower elevations, and if the temperature is above fifty-nine degrees Fahrenheit, it can suffer from heat exhaustion. Yaks can live up to twenty-five years. When moving around, they walk slowly and at a steady pace.

Talents: Connection to ancient wisdom, dedication, dependable, determination, forward motion, hard work, healing, higher purpose, longevity, routines, steadiness, steady pace, stillness, survival

Challenges: Change, lack of emotional control, numbness, self-doubt, stubborn, unwilling to compromise

Element(s): Earth

Primary Color(s): Black, brown, gray, red, white

Appearances: When yak appears, it means to get in touch with your spiritual essence and your higher self, and to understand and connect with your life purpose. Yak is closely tied to ancient wisdom and universal knowledge. This is a sign you too should learn from the past. Yak urges you to familiarize yourself with the customs of your family and to connect with your personal heritage. Yak means you never give up, you see things in black and white, and you know there is always a means to an end. Yak reminds you to live in the moment. Yak doesn't rush and urges you to take your time. Yak is a social animal that lives in groups. In the harsh temperatures, it will huddle close together with the rest of the herd to combine body heat. It relies on the herd for its survival. This means while you like to do things your own way, sometimes you need the closeness of family or friends to see you through difficult times. Yak eats grass and will not eat grain like most bovine animals. Now is a good time to pay attention to your diet. If you have a layer of fat like yak and you want to lose weight, stay away from the grains and graze on fresh greens for sustenance.

Assists When: You need to gain control over your emotions. If your emotions are all over the place or out of sync with how you usually feel, yak can help you find balance by helping you see the positives and negatives you're dealing with. Once aware, you can reign in your emotions and get them under control. If you feel like crying, then cry. Release any negative feelings you're holding inside. They're holding you back and blocking your understanding. If you're happy, express your happiness and joy by sharing your feelings with others. Yak means productivity and accomplishments in life. If you are having problems staying on task or achieving your goals, yak can show you the clear and steady way to reach your desired results. Yak encourages you to consider multiple points of view on subjects in addition to your own.

Frequency: Yak energy sounds like a grunt that is clear in tone and medium in pitch. It is warm and feels soft yet rough to the touch. It moves in a steady *blump-blump-blump* pace.

See Also: Buffalo (Bison)

Imagine...

While vacationing in the Himalayan Mountains, you ride a yak to get to a remote destination. The yak wears a brightly colored saddle pad, a leather saddle, and another brightly colored pad on top. You sit in the saddle, which is different from a horse's saddle, and realize just how wide the yak's back is. After traveling for an hour, you switch one leg over to ride sidesaddle because you can already feel the soreness starting. You feel the animal's sides against your calves, the power in its walk, and his massive presence. You feel connected to this yak, as if you've known it all of your life. You have a vision of living in this area a couple of hundred years earlier, and in the vision, the yak you're riding was with you. When the day is over, you say goodbye to your old friend from a past life.

Part 3
Mythical
Animals

Amarok

Traits: The amarok, a figure in Inuit mythology, is a giant lone wolf that preyed upon hunters who went out at night. In one of the legends associated with the amarok, it is said a boy whose growth was stunted called out to the Lord of Strength and an amarok appeared. It wrestled with him and knocked several small bones out of his body that were stunting his growth. The amarok then trained the boy until he became strong enough to wrestle three large bears, which gained the boy the respect of his village. This means the amarok can guide you to discover your weaknesses and overcome them to become strong.

Talents: Courageous, guidance, hiding, hunter, independent, loner, self-reliance, solitude, strength, wildness

Challenges: Aggressive, demanding, isolation, reclusive, without conscience

Element(s): Earth

Primary Color(s): Gray

Appearances: When amarok appears, it means for you to be more self-reliant and independent. While the obstacles you face may be intimidating, you have the courage and strength of character to easily overcome them. Amarok encourages you to connect to your inner huntsman. If there is something you need or want in life, now is the time to go hunting. Seek it out, track it, and make it your own. If you're looking for a new job or a different vehicle or if you simply want more plants around your home, you will be successful in finding exactly what you need. Amarok is a loner who lives in solitude. While some of the legends surrounding amarok have positive outcomes, there are many other stories where amarok captures or kills people. This negativity causes fear of the ferocious beast that amarok becomes when in its dark state. These opposite sides of amarok represent the positive and negative situations that are encountered during a lifetime. You can choose to see a glass as half full or half empty, and your choices will be determined by which side of amarok is influencing you. When facing negativity, you can let it affect and influence you or you can be courageous and strong, choosing to walk away from it onto a path of light and positivity. Amarok encourages you to choose wisely and not to let darkness extinguish your light.

Assists When: You need to address negative emotions you are feeling. In legend it is believed nothing and no one can hide from the amarok. If it is out for revenge, it will find the one it seeks. Amarok acts and reacts without conscience. It will seek vengeance and retribution on those it believes have wronged it. In legend amarok will hunt down and devour men simply because they go hunting at night, which amarok thinks is foolish behavior. Amarok warns against harboring negative feelings toward another person just because you may not agree with what they are doing or saying. Each person has his or her own path and lessons to learn in life. It is not up to anyone else to pass judgment on how they live. You may not agree, but holding on to negative emotions about someone else's actions will only bring down your own frequency. Once you understand that you can't change people, you can only change yourself, then you will have understood amarok's warning.

Frequency: Amarok energy is dark and chilling. Its movement is low, deliberate, and slow. It feels hot with sharp points. It sounds like the crack of lightning and the roar of thunder during a storm.

See Also: Wolf

Imagine...

You're lost in the forest. The sun is setting, and you're starting to feel nervous. You wander into a clearing and sit down on a large rock in the center. You turn to see a giant gray wolf. This is the amarok you were warned about before your hike. The beast stills, walks toward you, and sniffs the air. It grabs your shirt in its teeth and pulls you to your feet. It pushes you forward with its large nose, walking at your side. After a while, you come to an open field high on a sloping hill. Down below you can see the lights of a town. You turn to thank the amarok, but it has vanished.

Amphisbaena

Traits: Amphisbaena is a winged serpent with the claws of an eagle and a second head at the end of its tail that eats ants. According to Greek mythology, Amphisbaena was created when Perseus flew over the Libyan desert with Medusa's head in his hand. Blood dripped from the head onto the land and Amphisbaena grew out of the blood. Amphisbaena moves by holding on to the tail head with the mouth of its primary head, creating a circle with its body and rolling backward or forward.

Talents: Aphrodisiac, childbirth, fearless, fertility, healing, lucky, medicine, power, pregnancy, regeneration, transformation, travel, two directional movements

Challenges: Poisonous, unlucky

Element(s): Earth

Primary Color(s): Brown, red

Appearances: When Amphisbaena appears, it means you're entering a time of renewal and transformation. If you're in a situation that feels as if you're being emotionally torn, or experiencing the deep cut of betrayal, Amphisbaena will help you heal quickly and come through the situation even stronger than before. Amphisbaena is believed to have amazing powers of regeneration. If it is cut in half, it can weld itself back together again as if the injury never happened. This means if you experience any kind of negativity that causes you emotional pain, you too can put yourself back together. Both of Amphisbaena's heads have a separate brain. This means you can look at situations from two points of view. It also means you can have more than one opinion on a topic, and these opinions may be differing or similar in nature. Amphisbaena's eyes are said to be powerful beams of light that penetrate the darkness. This means your inner light shines into the world. You connect to the light of the universe and the spiritual bond you have with all that is, all that was, and all that will be.

Assists When: You need to be able to move in two directions, backward or forward, in an instant. While the Amphisbaena can roll, it can also instantly move in opposite directions without having to turn around. If one head is moving forward but the Amphisbaena needs to go backward, the other head and legs take over, and it moves backward or vice versa. This means that you are not limited to only going one way in life. If you're making forward progress but realize you need to go back to relearn something or to do something you forgot to do, Amphisbaena can help you quickly achieve the goal. If you're stuck in the past, or backward motion, Amphisbaena can get you moving forward again. Amphisbaena means you're not held in one place and can go anywhere you choose simply by taking action. Amphisbaena is extremely poisonous, and it is said that if bitten by one, the wound never heals and will lead to death. But it is also believed to have medicinal properties. If a pregnant woman wore Amphisbaena around her neck, she would have a safe pregnancy. Its skin protected from colds and aided arthritis and rheumatism, and if you killed one and ate it, you would become pure of heart and attract a lover. So if you encounter situations or people who feel poisonous, you can turn their negativity into something positive and healing.

Frequency: Amphisbaena energy is hot and dry. It quickly moves forward then backward. It sounds like a low-toned *hiss-pop-hiss*. It rotates around you, pulling you along with its movement.

See Also: Snake (Viper)

> ### *Imagine…*
> It's hot in the desert. You take a drink of water, looking out into the distance. There is a tent of some sort, so you head that way. You're almost there when a two-headed snake holding its head in its other mouth rolls by. You're so astounded you stand still for a minute then hurry the rest of the distance to the tent. There are people inside who offer you food and drink. They can take you to your destination as well. You ask them about the snake, and they tell you the story of Amphisbaena, saying it's a good sign and congratulations on your upcoming transformation.

Basilisk

Traits: Basilisk is the legendary serpent with a white mark on its head that resembles a crown and was considered the king of all serpents. Most mythology describes the basilisk as a small snake that is extremely venomous. It is said that it can kill with its stare, its spit, and even its smell. It kills not only what it is aiming at but everything around it and leaves its venom behind as it moves forward. Other mythology says the basilisk is an enormous creature that walks on legs and can kill with its stare and breath. It is said to come from Africa and that it created the desert. Basilisk symbolizes leadership, self-confidence, and a positive self-esteem.

Talents: Faith, forward movement, independent, intense, leader, power, regal, self-confident, self-esteem, strength, visualization

Challenges: Aggression, destructive, overly prideful, vicious

Element(s): Air, earth

Primary Color(s): Black, green, yellow

Appearances: When basilisk appears, it means there is a new leadership opportunity coming your way. You have charisma, and people are drawn to your strength and intense personality. You are a natural leader filled with self-confidence and a high self-esteem (but not so much that you come across as a know-it-all). You lead by example and never ask others to do something you wouldn't do yourself. These qualities enable you to guide and direct people to do what needs to be done to accomplish goals. Basilisk means visualizing to gain insight into the best course of action. Basilisk is extremely venomous, so it is important to remember that your words and actions can cause harm if you strike out in anger. Basilisk warns to have pride in what you do but don't be arrogant about it. Basilisk gives the power, confidence, and faith to move obstacles out of your way. Just as the basilisk controls and rules through its venomous nature, you can control and rule your own life. When basilisk appears, it means to take a look at your personal hygiene and style. Basilisk caused fear in those who came across it. This is a warning that instead of causing fear, rise above and create inspiration in those you come into contact with during the course of your life. Little things often mean a lot and can be a great inspiration to others. Be careful of how you stare at people because your stare can be intimidating and make others uncomfortable even if you're not meaning it that way.

Assists When: You need to boost your self-confidence or raise your self-esteem. Everyone goes through times when they feel like they're not at 100 percent. If you're going through a time like this, basilisk can give you a big boost in both areas. Basilisk moves forward with its head and body held high. It looks above to see all that is in its path. This is a sign for you to do the same. Let go of any doubts you may have that are pulling you down so you can rise up and go forward with poise and self-assurance of your own worth. Visualize the powerful, positive spirit within you and let that part of you go forth into the world.

Frequency: Basilisk energy flows in strong, graceful, flowing currents around you. It moves forward with intention and purpose. It sounds like a deep hiss vibrating at a slow, steady tempo. It is hot, charged with electricity, and can burn with its touch.

See Also: Lizard (Gecko)

Imagine...

You're in an office, standing behind a desk and looking out the window at the city below. You're working your plans out in your mind when you hear a loud hissing noise. You turn and feel the ancient power of the basilisk flow through you when you look at it. You know the legend, that it can kill with its stare, but you stare right back, connecting with its energy and absorbing its strength. You reconsider your plan and see a new way to proceed that will remove the obstacles you were thinking about. You smile at the basilisk. It nods its head, knowing the message has been received, and then fades until it disappears.

Bigfoot

Traits: Bigfoot symbolizes invisibility, hiding, and the unknown. Bigfoot is believed to be a reclusive apelike being that is very difficult to encounter because it hides so well. It is as if it's invisible. Bigfoot represents an intense curiosity about the unknown and delving deep into the mysteries of the universe. For you this means you can easily disappear in a crowd or even if you're around a few people. It's as if they forget you're there for a moment and then discuss information that is unknown to you but beneficial to you at the same time.

Talents: Connection to the unknown, elusive, fast moving, hiding, invisible, mysterious, nature, secrets, spiritual awakening, unexplained, watching in silence, wildness

Challenges: Aggressive, destructive behavior, failure to communicate, fierceness, stalking

Element(s): Earth

Primary Color(s): Black, brown (depending on region), white

Appearances: When Bigfoot appears, it means you're going to face the unknown in some way. This could be a situation where things are happening at random, and you'll need to do some investigative work to get to the source. You enjoy a mystery and engaging in the search for something that others cannot find. Bigfoot means you may encounter some rather large obstacles crossing your path that you weren't expecting. Just as Bigfoot retains total control over who it allows to see it, you also retain control of your life path. Bigfoot represents fear of the dark and the things that live in the night. When you embrace the light of your being and release the fear that is confining you, then you can move forward into positivity. Bigfoot is an undiscovered creature, which means you've yet to discover all of your intuitive abilities, your life blessings, and your soul purpose. Keep looking because the more you look, the more you'll learn along the path. When Bigfoot appears, it is to remind you of the unexplained mysteries in life. Not everything in life can be seen, touched, or completely explained, but it still exists. Bigfoot warns to be aware of people who are dangerous to you but hide behind a façade of comfort and interest in your well-being. Bigfoot means you would rather be left alone but will engage in social events with those you feel closest to, just as Bigfoot interacts with its own kind.

Assists When: You need to get in touch with the animal part of yourself. Bigfoot is a being that embraces its wild side. It is thought to be intellectual, to have deep feelings but is reclusive and extremely shy. When you feel like something is missing in your life, Bigfoot encourages you to get in touch with the wildness within you. Find your inner cave man/woman; let yourself connect with images of the past so you can grow in the future. Do you need to be more aggressive at work? Bigfoot can show you how to obtain an increase in productivity on the job by connecting to the fierce beast within you. That beast isn't going to give up on what it wants and neither will you.

Frequency: Bigfoot energy is electric, sending prickles along your spine and goosebumps down your arms. It tingles with anticipation and feels dark and dangerous like something is stalking you in the night. It sounds like a loud, guttural roar that echoes around you.

Imagine...

You're camping when a loud, rasping bellow breaks the silence of night. Another roar fills the night. You grab your flashlight and go outside. You've never heard an animal make a sound like that. Feeling a sense of overwhelming danger, you decide to leave. You'll come back for the tent later because right now you just feel an urgency to get away from the campsite and to a safe location. As you're driving down the mountain, the beam of your headlights illuminates a beast on two legs that is standing in the road in front of you. It looks like a man but has hair all over its body, and when it looks in your direction, you see it has a face like an ape. Then it darts across the road and into the trees. Hands shaking, you drive until you're back in town with plans to return during daylight to see what clues you can discover that the beast may have left behind.

Bunyip

Traits: Bunyip is a water spirit monster from Australian Aboriginal mythology. It lives along rivers, in watering holes, and in swamps. It is said to have created so much fear in people that they couldn't really describe what it looked like. Descriptions vary greatly, but most often it is said to have a head and legs like a crocodile, long sharp teeth and claws, the tail of a horse, the face of a dog, horns or tusks, and a huge body with dark fur or scaly skin. It stayed in the water during the day and traveled the land at night, looking for food. Bunyip symbolizes supernatural power, disguise, and aggressive behavior.

Talents: Hiding, mysterious, supernatural powers, unique, vocal, works better at night

Challenges: Aggressive, disguise, imposter, monstrous, pretender

Element(s): Earth, water

Primary Color(s): Black, brown

Appearances: When bunyip appears, it means that someone around you is pretending to be something they're not. In mythology, the bunyip is also thought to be a shy creature who doesn't want to be around humans until it's hungry, then it will devour them. This means to be on the lookout for the same type of deception in your life. Be particularly aware of the intentions behind words or requests for you to do something. Is what you're being asked really in your best interest, or is there something menacing happening in the background? Bunyip means you work better at night than you do during the day. Your internal clock is set so you need less sleep, or you prefer sleeping in the daytime and being up at night like the bunyip. Some mythology says bunyip hugs its prey to death. This is a sign to examine your relationships. Are you being too clingy or aggressive in your affections because you fear losing the person you're involved with? Or are you not showing enough affection? If you're being too clingy and are holding on too tightly in your relationships, you could kill them because the other person feels smothered. If you're not showing enough affection, then bunyip encourages you to give hugs more often and let the other person know how much you love them.

Assists When: You need to seek clarity in your life. Bunyip lives in swampy, marshy, dirty water where it could drag a person under. It is thought that this story was told to keep children away from dangerous waters. This means if you're unclear about events in your life you can get trapped beneath them until you feel like you're drowning. Bunyip coming out of the water at night to hunt is a sign that you need to distance yourself from the events causing confusion. With a little distance comes clarity. Once you are able to see the situation through clear waters instead of murky ones, you'll know the direction to take and what decisions to make. Bunyip warns against making decisions without clear knowledge.

Frequency: Bunyip energy sounds like a low-pitched *boom* followed by a high-pitched *roar*. It moves around you in a lumbering gait, heavy yet swift. It smells like the dankness of decaying leaves near murky water. It feels hot, hard, and scaly.

See Also: Alligator (Crocodile)

Imagine…

While fishing in a pond near the edge of a swamp, you feel as if you're being watched. You decide it's your imagination running away with you. Then you hear water splashing and the sucking sound of feet being pulled out of mud. You quickly gather your supplies, ready to make a run for it, when you notice a deer standing near the trees to your right. You sit back down and ready your line when you realize the deer is looking at something else. You look over in the same direction. Moving slowly is a very large bunyip, walking deeper into the swamp. It turns its head and growls at you but keeps walking away. You follow the deer's lead and don't move at all. Once the bunyip is out of sight, the deer runs away. You throw the gear in the backseat, get in your car, and drive away, deciding it's time to find a new place to fish.

Cadmean Vixen

Traits: Cadmean vixen (aka Teumessian fox) was an enormous fox destined to never be caught. It was said to be one of the children of Echinda, the mother of monsters. Dionysus sent the Cadmean vixen to Thebes as punishment for an unpardonable crime. There it proceeded to wreak havoc on the city by preying on the children. Creon, the regent of Thebes, gave the task of capturing the Cadmean vixen to Amphitryon. To accomplish the feat, Amphitryon borrowed Prokris's immortal hound Laelaps, who was destined to catch everything it went after. Zeus couldn't believe the absurdity of the situation. The Cadmean vixen could never be caught by Laelaps, who would always catch whatever she pursued. Neither would ever win. They'd just go around and around forever. So Zeus turned both of them into stone and placed them in the stars, where they became the constellations Canis Major (Laelaps) and Canis Minor (Cadmean vixen).

Talents: Adaptable, chasing your dreams, cunning, escaping, intuitive, secretive, strategic, sure-footed, swift, wise

Challenges: Intimidating, predator, trickster

Element(s): Earth

Primary Color(s): Black, gray, red

Appearances: When Cadmean vixen appears, it means to stop running in circles. While there are times in life when you need to double back to revisit an area where you've already been, if you're continuously going to the past, then you're not making forward progress. Running in circles means you're spending time on aimless, nonproductive activities either because you're having difficulties coming to a solution or because you're procrastinating or putting off tasks that need to be completed. Cadmean vixen also means to pay more attention to the children in your life. Cadmean vixen had negative intentions toward children, which is a warning to you to make sure you're treating the children around you with love, honor, respect, and great care. The impression you make on them at a young age will last a lifetime. Cadmean vixen means that when you find yourself going around and around an issue, you need to stop, look at the pros and cons, and make a decision without letting others influence how you feel. You may believe they are chasing you into a corner, forcing you to do something you really may not want to do. If that's the case, Cadmean vixen will help you get away so you can think things through and come to your own decision.

Assists When: You need to get away with something and not get caught. Sometimes you have to do things secretly in order to surprise other people. In these instances, you don't want to get caught or it will ruin the surprise. Cadmean vixen can help you be secretive so no one finds out what you're doing. If you need to be cunning, wise, and adaptable in business, then call on Cadmean vixen for assistance. It will help you present yourself in a strong, authoritative position, which will lead to success. Once your business takes off it will be difficult for anyone to catch up with you. This especially applies to new ideas or inventions you may have. Make sure you keep your secrets close so they're not taken from you by unsavory people who might steal your ideas. Be careful who you trust right now as you lay the company's foundation.

Frequency: Cadmean vixen energy is swift moving and has a rapid beat. It feels silky and smooth. It sounds like a contradiction with its deep *yip, yip, yip* vocalization.

See Also: Fox

Imagine…

You're standing in a field when a large fox runs up to you. While petting its head, you wonder why it's out in the middle of the day. Soon a large dog runs into the field. The fox takes off and runs around you in a wide perimeter. The dog gives chase. Around and around they go. Day turns to night and still they chase each other. Soon you tire of watching them, but they don't stop. On and on they go, never tiring, never stopping. One day the fox and dog stop in their tracks and turn to stone. Then they rise up into the air and become stars.

Caladrius

Traits: Caladrius is a snow-white bird that lives in the houses of kings according to Roman mythology. It symbolizes life and death. Legends say the bird will not look at anyone who is ill unless they will make a full recovery. If a person will recover, caladrius will take the person's sickness into itself by putting its beak on the person's mouth, opening its mouth wide, and drawing in the illness like moisture. It then flies toward the sun so its heat will destroy the illness by burning it out of caladrius. Caladrius would then return home, having cured both the patient and itself of the disease. Because it drew illness into its body, it was considered an unclean bird that should never be eaten. It was believed that if caladrius refused to look at someone who was ill, that person was destined to die and caladrius would cry out in sorrow.

Talents: Casting off, cleansing, divine virtue, healing, renewal, spirituality

Challenges: Demise, taking on more than you can handle

Element(s): Air

Primary Color(s): White

Appearances: When caladrius appears, it means to look at your health. If anything has been worrying you, or if you haven't had a physical in a long time, now might be a good time to go to the doctor and get yourself checked out just to make sure all is well. Caladrius means you will be making emotional choices. In legends it is said that the caladrius wouldn't cure people with jaundice, which was believed to be caused by anger, because it would wound the bird. But, if a man had jaundice and the bird looked at him as if it were angry with him, then the act of gazing in anger would cure the person of jaundice. This means to consider your emotions. Are you only spurred into action when you get angry about something and have an *I'll show them* attitude? If so, is this negatively or positively affecting you? Think about it, and if it's a negative result, then decide how you can change the negativity into a positive and then make that change. The death associated with caladrius in the legend is physical, but when it appears to you it doesn't reflect physical death but instead means that something in your life will end and bring about something new.

Assists When: You need to see a situation clearly, especially if you have been turning a blind eye to it. In legend, it is believed that if a blind man put the bone marrow of a caladrius on his eyes, he would be healed and his eyesight would immediately return. This means to take off your blinders and see the situation for what it truly is, not what you want it to be. Consider the people involved to see them as they are. Look through any disguises they may be wearing or any actions covering their true intentions or feelings. Once you really look, you will see the truth of the matter of all those involved. Only then can you make decisions about your own involvement and how to progress forward. Caladrius warns against taking on more than you can handle. If you think something will harm you or cause you distress, then turn away from the situation just as caladrius turns away from what will harm it.

Frequency: Caladrius energy glows with a white radiance. It moves lightly, with an innate softness. It sounds like a soft, chirping birdsong floating in the wind.

> ### Imagine…
> You're lying in a bed. The walls of the castle look a bit blurry due to the fever raging through your body. You don't remember how long you've been here. The last thing you remember is eating dinner in the great hall. As you look around, you notice a white bird perched on a pedestal. It flies to your bed, lands at your feet, and then walks up to your chest. It leans close to your mouth, pushing your lips apart with its beak. Your total focus is on the bird staring into your eyes. It opens its mouth wide, and you feel energy pulling on your body. A white mist comes out of your mouth and moves into the bird. When the mist stops, the bird flies away. You realize you feel a lot better.

Cerastes

Traits: Cerastes, in Greek mythology, is a serpent that is so flexible it was considered spineless. It had either four moveable horns over its eyes or two ramlike horns on its head. It buried itself under the sand with only the horns exposed so that other animals would think the horns were worms or other type of food emerging from the sand when the serpent moved them. When animals got close, cerastes would spring out of the sand, strike, encircle, and kill its prey. If people investigated the horns, they were prey as well. Cerastes was used to ward off the evil eye and to detect poison. In modern culture, there is a venomous horned viper that lives in desert regions called *Cerastes cerastes* (named after the legendary serpent), which could have been the basis for the myth.

Talents: Awareness, change, concealment, creativity, cunning, elusive, intelligence, intuition, patience, protection, speed, stealth, transformation

Challenges: Betrayal, deceit, deception, trickery

Element(s): Earth

Primary Color(s): Brown

Appearances: When cerastes appears, it means there is falseness around you. There are people in your life who are concealing their true nature, which is hiding beneath the surface, while they're waiting to strike. Cerastes means to look for jealousy, envy, gossip, and dislike among those you come into contact with on a daily basis. Is someone treating you well and talking bad about you behind your back? This is cerastes's influence. Be aware so you're not the victim of deceit or deception. Awareness can always prevent problems because you're in the know. Cerastes means to use your intuition and trust in the information you're given to see to the heart of the matter. There are tricksters around you with negative intentions, so you need to be on your toes right now. Use stealth to find out what's really going on by being elusive and concealing your investigation. Protect yourself in whatever ways you feel are necessary at this time; especially build up a wall around your emotions so you're not hurt when someone betrays you. Cerastes means you may be able to stop betrayals before they happen by finding out information and confronting the other person before they can do something emotionally hurtful to you. If you can uncover the intention before the action takes place you can prevent disaster.

Assists When: You need to make a transformation. You carefully consider everything you do before taking action, even when you're being spontaneous, because you must remain in balance, even when at play. Cerastes can help you when you're transforming or making a transition in your life by giving you a sense of stability as you work through the changes. Cerastes means being flexible during times of change. Cerastes can hold still for a long time waiting for its prey. It's patient and will not move until it's necessary, and then it moves with lightning speed. Cerastes will lend you its speed to keep your life flowing smoothly.

Frequency: Cerastes's energy is dry, rough, gritty, pointy, and sharp. It moves in elastic motions, whipping around you with extreme momentum. It feels hot and dry to the touch and makes you feel thirsty.

See Also: Snake (Viper)

Imagine…

You're eating lunch in a gazebo outside of a desert hotel when you notice something moving in the sand. When you finish eating, you go over and poke at it with a long stick. Suddenly a large serpent with horns springs up out of the sand. It rises high above you, and then it circles its body around you, lifting you into the air. You've read about this beast in mythology class. You feel the hot, gritty texture of its energy surrounding you. Allowing your energy to merge with it, you feel its great transformational power weaving within your frequency and know you'll never be the same. You send pictures to let it know it's in the wrong time and needs to go back to its own dimension. It looks down at you, gently lowers you onto the sand, and uncoils. It leans close, nose to nose, and you hear *thank you* in your mind. It vanishes right in front of you. Your heart is beating rapidly as you hurry back to the hotel, filled with a new hope and positivity.

Cetan

Traits: In Lakota mythology, Cetan is a hawk spirit associated with the east. Cetan symbolizes inner stamina, dedication, swift speed, and intense vision. Cetan is a bringer of messages and warns of impending danger. Cetan means taking swift action. It is a fierce hunter that dives through the air with great speed to catch its prey. Cetan is a symbol of balance because hawks keep the population of mice, insects, and other small animals in check.

Talents: Awareness, connection to spirit, creative, cunning, decisive, guardian, inner stamina, insightful, intuition, leadership, maneuverability, messenger, observant, protection, speed, strategic, strength, truth, unique perspective, visionary

Challenges: Brutal, callous, insensitive, predator, too much focus, unsympathetic

Element(s): Air

Primary Color(s): Brown

Appearances: When Cetan appears, it means you are going to receive messages from the spiritual realm. If you've been working with your spirit guides, angels, or energy animals, you'll notice that the lines of communication will open wide and information starts to flow freely once cetan appears. Cetan removes any blockages that may have prevented you from being able to see or hear spirit clearly. Cetan indicates you will be experiencing changes. Its ability to make swift, spiraling turns like an acrobatic display as it flies through the air while making instantaneous decisions based on intuition will guide you to do the same. If opportunities are presented that need an immediate *yes, I'll do it* or *no, I'll pass* decision, Cetan can guide you to the right choice. Cetan means to be awake, present in your life, and aware. It is a connection to the earth, to your roots, and it is a symbol of the soul. Cetan means you're coming into a leadership role within your career or your community. This new position will also bring new responsibilities, change, and prosperity. Cetan warns against preying on the weak or taking advantage of others in order to succeed. Cetan reminds you to connect with the warrior spirit, the hero within you, to always move with grace and positivity and act from a place of love. You are a visionary, and it's important to retain your vision and goals for the future. Don't let them become clouded with negativity. Cetan means you will soar to great heights of success in all you attempt.

Assists When: You need to have more maneuverability in your life. If you've been feeling tied down or trapped, now is the time to spread your wings and fly. That doesn't mean to leave behind everything or everyone you know and love, it means to take some time for yourself, to do the things you enjoy doing while reconnecting to your true spiritual self. In this day and age it can be easy to get stuck in a busy *go, go, go* frame of mind. When this happens, you're often locked into a specific schedule without the opportunity to break free of the routine. Cetan opens the windows to the world so you can soar high in the sky, leaving the boring, hectic, or stagnant routine behind if only for a little while. Once you've maneuvered yourself out of the daily grind, you will be able to change things up more often and will let go of any negative feelings you may have been experiencing.

Frequency: Cetan energy moves erratically, as if it can't decide which way to go, and pulls you into its joyful, fast-moving currents. It sounds like a high-pitched screech echoing on the wind. It feels warm and free.

See Also: Hawk

Imagine…

The wind blows softly around you as you commune with nature. You hear the screech of a hawk and look up to see the large, majestic bird diving through the air. It flies close to you and lands on a tree branch. You walk closer to it, taking in the beauty of its feathers and the quick turn of its head. It preens its feathers and makes little soft sounds, and you hear, *I am Cetan.* A feeling of peace and serenity fills you along with awe at its majestic presence. It raises its wings and flaps them in the air as it flies away.

Chimera

Traits: In Greek mythology, Chimera is an immortal, unique, three-headed beast, the only one of its kind, and was considered to be of divine origin. It was usually thought of as a female. The three heads are a lioness, goat, and serpent/dragon, which look like they're stuck together with the lioness's head and paws in front, the goat head coming out of the back, and legs of a dragon in the rear. The tail had the head of a dragon (or sometimes serpent) at the end. The tail and its head arched over the back and looked forward. Each of the three heads could breathe fire. Sometimes it is described with wings and other times without. It ruined the area in which it lived by burning the land and destroying herds. This caused the people in the area to live in extreme fear. Chimera symbolizes perseverance, strength, and creativity.

Talents: Creativity, the Divine, life without limits, passionate, perseverance, speed, strength

Challenges: Aggressive, destruction, fire-breathing, instills fear, resistance

Element(s): Earth, fire

Primary Color(s): Brown, green

Appearances: When Chimera appears, it means that you can reach greater heights by combining your knowledge and abilities than by keeping them separated. Chimera was essentially three beings combined into one, but that one was far greater and more powerful than the three were separately. Chimera was killed by Bellerophon while riding Pegasus. He put lead on the end of his spear, and when Chimera breathed fire, it melted and went down Chimera's throat, killing it. Other legends say he speared it in the head with the lead while it was in the air, which resulted in the beast exploding. This is a warning not to go breathing fire to blow off steam or venting your frustrations without thinking about what you're saying. It might just come back on you and cause more damage. Chimera means by being persistent you can persevere over any obstacles in your path. Chimera enables you to live life without limits. This includes the limits others may try to place on you or those you place on yourself. Chimera means you are a creative individual who often thinks outside of the box. Your passion for life and the work you do enables you to excel in whatever areas interest you. Chimera warns that you become bored easily, and if you lose interest, it is as if the thing never existed to begin with. Chimera also warns of approaching natural disasters.

Assists When: You need to remain strong during chaotic times when your emotions are in turmoil. Chimera is of divine origin and had immense strength. When you're going through difficult times, Chimera urges you to return to your own divine source, to the beginnings of your spiritual self, in order to find the strength and fortitude to endure emotional difficulties. By doing this, you will be able to obtain emotional balance. You'll see what you couldn't when you were blinded by out-of-control emotions. Chimera has extreme speed. When you need to get something done quickly, Chimera can help you accomplish it in record time. Chimera warns against being too aggressive and instilling fear in those around you. This often happens when you lose your temper so try to keep it under control.

Frequency: Chimera energy is hot and fierce. It blows forward with ferocity and strength, swirling around you in such gusts that it causes you to stumble. It sounds like a strong stormy wind whistling as it blows across the land.

See Also: Goat, Lion, Snake (Viper)

Imagine...

A lion, goat, and dragon are looking at you, but the heads are all attached to one huge beast. It creeps closer to check you out. You maintain a quiet confidence without fear as the creature inspects and walks around you. After a few moments, the dragon head sniffs the air and stretches out to rub its head on your palm. Tentatively you stroke its head. It backs up and flies away. You passed the test.

Chupacabra

Traits: Chupacabra is a cryptid believed to inhabit the Americas. It is known for attacking livestock, primarily goats, and draining them of their blood through three holes in the shape of an inverted triangle. Other legends say there are only one or two holes. It is described as being three to four feet tall with a row of spines protruding from the base of its neck down its back to the base of its tail. Its skin is either scaly or leathery and is greenish gray in color. It is said to stand, hop, and move like a kangaroo. Chupacabra was first reported in Puerto Rico during March 1995, when eight sheep were discovered dead with three puncture wounds in each of their chests and all were thought to be drained of blood. Other reports say that the legend began in 1947 when two Puerto Rican newspapers started reporting deaths of local animals. It is believed to be a product of mass hysteria from sightings of dogs or coyotes who suffered from demodectic mange.

Talents: Endings, evasive, intuition, invisibility, nocturnal, quick reflexes, sensitivity, strength

Challenges: Aggressive, bad temper, predator, reclusive, strong-willed

Element(s): Earth

Primary Color(s): Gray, green

Appearances: When chupacabra appears, it means that something or someone is draining you. There may be someone in your life who is demanding a lot of your time, whether this is done on purpose or is unintentional. If you're caring for an ill family member, the task will pull on your energy, possibly leaving you exhausted, but it is not an intentional hardship instigated by the sick person. There may be strains on your finances at this time. You may encounter unexpected bills or expenses and need to tighten your spending patterns for a while. You could also be experiencing a situation where you feel your self-confidence is taking a hit. If you're experiencing a negative person who is putting you down, then you have to face this person, evade them, or become invisible around them in order for the behavior to stop. Chupacabra is symbolic of endings. But with endings come new beginnings. Look at the endings that chupacabra brings as a perfect opportunity to start over with a new beginning. You're entering a new phase of your life, step forward and embrace it.

Assists When: You need to learn to control your temper, be less of a predator, and not be so strong willed. Chupacabra can drive you forward so you are successful in all that you do; however, its predatory nature can cause you to be outspoken, inflexible, and have an out of control temper if things aren't going your way. When this happens, chupacabra encourages you to get away by yourself for a while and be as reclusive and hard to find as chupacabra. Focus on your internal challenges and address the struggles you're experiencing. You are sensitive and empathic, so make sure you're not drawing the emotions of others onto you.

Frequency: Chupacabra energy sounds like a loud chattering noise almost birdlike in quality. It slinks, moving in silence. It feels cool to the touch and smells dank and musky.

Imagine…

You're a police officer investigating a chupacabra report at a local farm where several cows have been killed. You discover three puncture wounds on the cattle that coincide with other chupacabra reports. You have the carcasses sent for a necropsy to see if they really have been drained of blood. As you finish at the scene and are returning to your vehicle, you notice a creature standing near the corner of a barn. It has large spines sticking out of its back and has leathery skin and looks scaly. You cautiously approach. As you get closer, it turns and runs behind the barn. Keeping your distance, you circle around so you can see from a safe range, but there's nothing back there. Still, you know what you saw.

Cockatrice

Traits: The mythical flying beast Cockatrice stands on two legs, has the head and feet of a cockerel (rooster), and has the body and tail of a dragon. Legend says it was born from the yolkless egg laid by a seven-year-old cockerel during a full moon and incubated by a toad or a snake for nine years. It was believed that if you threw the egg over your house and it landed on the ground on the other side without hitting the house, then the Cockatrice wouldn't be born. The Cockatrice can kill vegetation, animals, and people by turning them to stone with its touch, breath, or saliva, or if the animal or person looks directly into its eyes. Cockatrice can be killed by a venom-spitting weasel, seeing its reflection in the mirror (its own gaze kills it), or if it hears a rooster crow.

Talents: Adaptable, fearless, flight, impressive, independent, inner truth, maneuverability, mysterious, rarity, swift, transformation, transitions, unexplained, unique

Challenges: Deadly, destructive, ferocious, ill-tempered, intimidating, unpredictable

Element(s): Air, earth

Primary Color(s): Black, brown, green, red, white, multicolored

Appearances: When Cockatrice appears, it means you are independent and adaptable and have a unique perspective. You're a rare individual who often does things unexpected and out of the ordinary to make others happy just because you like seeing their faces light up with joy. You feel particularly drawn to anything that seems magical, inspirational, or enlightening. Cockatrice's ability to create endings means you are able to see when things are no longer needed in your life. You may donate material things to charity or give them to a family in need when you no longer want them. Cockatrice stands on two legs, which is a sign that you stand on your own and take care of yourself. You may be a bit superstitious (and throw that egg over the house *just in case*). Cockatrice means to enjoy the mornings, even if you're sometimes a night owl. Getting up when the rooster crows can give you new perspectives and fresh ideas as you watch the sun rise. It's a great time to get organized, evaluate your schedule, or get your exercise in before you really get going with your day. It will also boost your mood and enhance your productivity.

Assists When: You need to reflect upon your inner self and your spirituality. When Cockatrice sees itself in the mirror, its own gaze will kill it. This wouldn't ever happen to you, but if you looked into the mirror, what do you see? Are you in tune with your true spiritual essence and your higher self? Do you see doubt or negativity in your eyes? If so, now is a great time to analyze and eliminate it. Cockatrice can never look an animal or a person directly in the eyes without turning them to stone, but you can. When you're relating to others, give them your undivided attention by looking into their eyes. It might make some people uncomfortable, and if it does, you can adjust the intensity of your gaze. When you look someone in the eye, it lets them know you're really listening to what they have to say and you care about their opinion.

Frequency: Cockatrice energy moves in a smooth, gliding forward flow. It is bright and colorful. It sounds like a crackling, yodeling call that moves up and down in tone and pitch. It feels soft and silky yet prickly and sharp.

See Also: Chicken, Dragon

Imagine…

The Cockatrice has you pinned against a tree. It is confused because you didn't turn to stone when it looked at you. It stands a few feet away, scratching the ground with its claws and moving its head back and forth. You think it's going to jump on you. You tell it to calm down and that things aren't always as they seem. You hold out your hand, and magically a blue plume of smoke rises in front of the beast. You duck behind the tree. A large weasel is there and takes your place on the other side. When the smoke clears, the Cockatrice leaves in quite a hurry with the weasel following close behind.

Dragon

Traits: Dragon symbolizes strength, good luck, and financial growth. Dragon is a magical being that is physically strong, but it also has strength of character that is shown through its wisdom. Dragon is a symbol of good luck in many cultures because it collects gold and jewels, which it guards by sleeping on top of it, so it can also bring good fortune to you. Dragon signifies you are a strong, wise person. You're very lucky in all of your endeavors, especially when it comes to money and increasing your wealth.

Talents: Acceptance, adventure, beauty, dignified, ecstasy, enchantment, fearless, financial growth, fire, glory, good luck, guidance, higher purpose, impressive, inspiration, joy, leader, majestic, open-minded, passionate, presence, prosperity, protective, regality, spirituality, strength, transitions, wisdom

Challenges: Arrogant, deadly, destructive, ferocious, hoarding, impractical, intimidating, unpredictable

Element(s): Air, earth, water

Primary Color(s): Black, blue, gold, green, orange, red, white, yellow

Appearances: When dragon appears, it means this is a prosperous time for you. This prosperity can be connected to material possessions and brings an increase in the things you own or the amount of money you make. Spiritually you'll experience an increase in your intuition, growth along your spiritual path, and connection to your higher purpose. Dragon means you're open-minded and are drawn to all types of metaphysical and mystical topics. You're at one with your unique spirituality, are accepting of others, and see the beauty in all things. Dragon means you're a leader who has a great deal of presence. You are regal, dignified, and majestic in your approach to life. People are drawn to you because of these qualities. You are intuitively linked to ancient wisdom, which you willingly share with others. Dragon is fearless and passionate and has a high sense of adventure. Dragon can also be unpredictable and intimidating, and it is associated with death and destruction. It warns you to think before you act or react so you don't cause a good situation to go bad because you have intimidated or scared people off. This will lead to regret and be difficult to fix but can be avoided entirely if you maintain a steady course of action and keep your emotions positive and uplifting.

Assists When: You need to connect to your own inner dragon and the magical power it creates within you. Dragon means you are enthusiastic and filled with vitality. You have the fire of the dragon deep inside you, which means you are passionate about everything you do. Fire can forge beauty from clumps of metal. but it can also destroy all in its path. If your inner dragon has caused destruction, don't fall into despair about it. New growth happens even if fire has ravaged a forest. What can you learn from any destruction your inner dragon has caused? There are life lessons to be learned; rebirth and spiritual growth can come from destructive events. You just have to recognize them, forgive yourself, and move forward on your path. Dragon is a strong protector. Its wings will help you fly through transitions until you are once again soaring high on a fortunate path.

Frequency: Dragon energy is bold and heavy, and it burns with heat. It fills you with power and feels majestic, as if you're standing on top of the world. It moves with a slow, thumping rhythm but then flies in circles around you with speed, dips, and turns.

See Also: Cockatrice

Imagine...

You find yourself transported back to medieval times. An enormous dragon is flying above you in slow circles. You can't take your eyes off of the incredible beast. You move out into an open field as the dragon gets lower and lower. It sees you and lands in the field. You feel an affinity for it and walk closer. It regards you with curiosity. You talk to it and reach out to touch its nose. You can hear it speaking in your mind. It has been looking for you to take you back to your own time. You climb on its back and fly home.

Erymanthian Boar

Traits: The Erymanthian Boar, in Greek mythology, was a giant boar with very sharp teeth that lived on Mount Erymanthos. It was a very dangerous animal that inspired fear because it could easily destroy crops. It was also the fourth labor of Hercules's twelve labors. Hercules drove the Boar into the snow, bound it, and carried to back to Eurystheus, who was terrified of the beast. He told Hercules to get rid of it, so Hercules threw it into the sea. The Boar swam to Italy. Eventually its tusks were preserved in the Temple of Apollo at Cumae.

Talents: Approaching conflicts head on, closure, escape, finding what's hidden, new beginnings, persistent, personal and spiritual growth, prosperity, rooting, wealth

Challenges: Aggression, confrontations, procrastination, stubborn

Element(s): Earth

Primary Color(s): Brown

Appearances: When the Erymanthian Boar appears, you are about to escape from something that has been holding you back and start over, creating your own new beginning. When Hercules threw the Erymanthian Boar into the sea, the expectation was that it would drown. But the Boar, intent on survival, swam across the sea to Italy. This means, regardless of the conditions you find yourself thrown into, you will find a way to turn a negative into a positive and start again. The Erymanthian Boar gives you the courage to take on tasks you'd rather avoid by encouraging you to put your fear and doubts behind you so you can step up to the job at hand with a sense of determined resolve to see it through to a successful completion. This quality, of intuitively moving into the unknown, even when doubt is in the back of your mind, will bring success and wealth to you. The Erymanthian Boar means to look for what's hidden. This applies to both your personal life and your spirituality in order to experience growth in both areas. Is there new information that may change your point of view? You'll have to dig to find out by reading, researching, and investigating, but now is the perfect time to look. With new beginnings often come great amounts of growth and changes of perspective. What you once disbelieved you may now hold as truth. What was once unknown is now known. The Erymanthian Boar warns against procrastination. Work now to reap your rewards.

Assists When: You need to obtain closure to problems or sources of conflict in your life. If you feel you've been wrongly judged, or found guilty in the eyes of others when they don't know the whole story, now is the time to address the situation with the other people involved. Resolve it and leave it in the past. Unless the issue is directly addressed then it will be difficult for you to find closure. The Erymanthian Boar means to make the most of every opportunity that comes your way. Do what people aren't expecting you to do. Keep everyone guessing what you'll be up to next. Be a surprise waiting to happen. This enables you to live a full and joyful life filled with wonder and unpredictability.

Frequency: The Erymanthian Boar energy sounds like a low, rumbling roar that slowly turns into an intense squeal. It feels like a warm breath against your face. It moves at a medium pace with a *clump-clumpity-clump-clump* rhythm.

See Also: Boar, Pig

> ### Imagine...
> You're fishing at sea in a small boat when you see a huge boar swimming by you a short distance away. You know this beast. You don't want it to see you, so you pull in your line and wait. Even from this distance you can see its sharp teeth and feel the power and strength of the boar. It makes you tremble with fear, but you also feel excited to have seen it this close. You don't know why the Erymanthian Boar is in the sea instead of being on Mount Erymanthos, but its sheer power is something you'll never forget. Once the boar is out of sight you row back to shore.

Gargoyle

Traits: In legend, gargoyle is a mythological creature of a winged race that was once human but gave in to its more animalistic and negative basic behaviors. Its wings symbolize its ability to rise above and overcome these behaviors. Gargoyle was used in architecture as both roof rain spouts (the water ran off the roof through the gargoyle's mouth) and as protection from evil spirits. Gargoyle symbolizes the inherent ability to overcome negativity.

Talents: Cleansing, guardian, movement through shadows, protection, silence

Challenges: Coldness, creepy, frightening, motionlessness, standoffish

Element(s): Air, earth

Primary Color(s): Black, gray, green, white

Appearances: When gargoyle appears, it means you cannot let the conditions in which you find yourself affect your divine nature. Sometimes everything in life flows smoothly, is wonderful, and you're filled with joy. Other times the road is rocky or rough, and fills you with sadness. During the rough times, gargoyle reminds you to remember your divine origin. While the rocky road may hurt your bare feet, it can never hurt your spirit. Gargoyle means to take solace in the silence. Use it to connect to the divinity within you, embrace your inner self, and pull yourself up out of despair. Put on your shoes and move forward toward your bliss with a sense of purpose. Gargoyle reflects human potential and the ability to rise above negativity. Legend says the gargoyles on rooftops communicate when the rain or wind passes between their mouths. They can also manipulate water by purifying it, which prevented disease. This cleansing associated with water also applies to you. If you feel drawn to water, then spend time around it, drink more of it, and take a relaxing bath in it. These activities will cleanse you at a spiritual level just as the gargoyle cleanses the water passing through its mouth. Gargoyle also comes to life at night to protect the areas where it lives, but at sunrise it takes its position on the rooftop and waits for the sunlight to wash over it, turning it into stone. It is believed it can see through its stone eyes, even though it can't move. There it sleeps until nightfall when once again it transforms to monitor and protect humans. This means you may be more productive at night than you are during the daytime, have the ability to transform from negative to positive, and will defend those around you.

Assists When: You need to protect those you love and your belongings. Gargoyle can give you protection from the troubles in the world by keeping evil away from your door and away from your person. Not all gargoyles have wings. The ones that don't will scale the outside of buildings to reach their positions before dawn. They can help you overcome large obstacles by climbing over them. If you perceive a gargoyle as scary or coldhearted, that's a sign you're blocking your own spiritual growth. If this is the case, it is time to examine how you feel about yourself and how others perceive you. Do they see you as warm and caring or coldhearted? Make changes accordingly to turn coldness to warmth. Gargoyle can help you overcome any negative emotions you're holding within yourself.

Frequency: Gargoyle energy sounds like water gurgling. It is strong and feels rough to the touch. It glides smoothly, flowing from place to place with little effort. It is dark yet filled with the brilliance of light.

Imagine...

You're sitting on a bench in the park watching and waiting. You've heard that the gargoyles come alive at night in this town, and tonight you're determined to see it happen. After a while you think you see one of them move. Then again, maybe it's a trick of the moonlight. You blink and the stone creature is no longer on the building, but you didn't see it change or move. Moments later, it is sitting beside you on the bench. You carry on a short conversation before it disappears into the night.

Gremlin

Traits: Gremlin is the youngest creature in the monster mythology. Gremlin has its origins in Welsh folklore as creatures named Coranyeidd, spirit creatures who heard everything so no one could keep secrets. Two kings met on the English Channel to plan the elimination of the Coranyeidd so they wouldn't be overheard. During World War I, the Royal Navy kept having mechanical and technical problems. One of the Royal Air Force pilots experienced malfunctions and called the airport for a weather check. He was told there were gremlins over the channel. The name stuck. The pilot told the public they'd had problems with gremlins for months. It is believed gremlins are the modern-day version of the Coranyeidd. Gremlins are mischievous, use tools, and tamper with all kinds of machinery and technology, but they are said to have an affinity for aircrafts.

Talents: Builds morale, can fix things but prefers taking them apart, invisible, mechanically minded, silent, stealth

Challenges: Mischievous, sabotage, trickster, unpredictable

Element(s): Air, earth

Primary Color(s): Black, brown, green, red, multicolored

Appearances: When gremlin appears, it means to take responsibility for your own actions. Gremlins are often used as scapegoats for mistakes instead of the person taking responsibility for doing something wrong. If you've been blaming gremlins, or anyone else for that matter, for something you did incorrectly or you were supposed to do and didn't complete the task, now is the time to own up to your actions. If you can fix a past situation, then do it. If not, decide to start owning your actions beginning today. Gremlins have a mischievous and playful nature, which is a sign you need more fun in your life. You don't have to pull pranks or do negative things like gremlins are blamed for, but you should implement ways to find more enjoyment and pleasurable things to do on a daily basis. Gremlin means to give credit where credit is due. Legends say gremlins turned on humans when they took credit for what the gremlins did. Gremlins use stealth to sneak around and mess with machines. You often don't even know they've been there until the machine stops working properly.

Assists When: You need to lift your spirits or boost the confidence of someone who is feeling down or has low self-esteem. During World War I, gremlins helped boost the morale of airmen because they messed with planes on both sides of the war and didn't choose sides. Gremlins can help you get in a better frame of mind and have more confidence. They encourage you to tinker with something (preferably mechanical), and if you tear it all apart in the process, that's part of the fun. If you need to do something and you don't want anyone else to know what you're doing, gremlin will give you the invisible stealth you need to accomplish your goals.

Frequency: Gremlin energy radiates a glowing pulse of power that is invisible to the naked eye. It moves quickly, jumping from place to place in an instant. It feels cool to the touch. It sounds like the clanking thud of metal hitting metal.

Imagine…

It's one of those days when everything is weird. You toasted bread and it burned on the low setting. Your car wouldn't start and the television is constantly changing channels. You turn it off and it comes back on. You jump in the shower and the water goes from warm to super hot. The handle was turned so you put it back to warm. Now you feel like you're officially losing your mind and start talking to the room. *I don't know who's here, but you need to stop messing with me.* After your shower, you look in the mirror and see them run across the room behind you. *Gremlins!* That explains it. You go to the garage, open the door, and point to a car engine sitting in the middle of the bay. *That's for you! Have at it!* The rest of the day passes without incident. The gremlins are no longer bored, so they leave you alone.

Griffin

Traits: Griffin has the body of a lion and the head and wings of an eagle. Its front feet are eagle claws and its back feet are lion paws. Griffin symbolizes power, wisdom, and wealth. Griffin was known for finding and guarding gold and treasures. This means you have the power inside to be successful. You are knowledgeable, savvy, and smart. You thrive in business or any type of venture that deals with creating wealth for yourself or others. Griffin combines the qualities and characteristics of the lion and the eagle, which means you have great depth of character, high standards, and integrity.

Talents: Anonymity, balance of mind, body and spirit, digging, discovery, flexibility, flight, guardian, intelligence, kingly, knowledge, leader, mystery, persistence, physical strength, power, regal, respect, seeking, strength in battle, vigilance, wily, wise

Challenges: Boundaries that are too severe, conceit, greed, hoarding, inner conflict, spiritual arrogance, trickster

Element(s): Air, earth

Primary Color(s): Brown, gold, white

Appearances: When griffin appears, it means you're going to need to be strong in upcoming situations. Griffin represents strength in battle and was often used in coats of arms in ancient and medieval times. Whatever circumstances come your way, you have the ability to prevail and win due to your strength of character, wit, and charm. Griffin enables you to think quickly on your feet and come up with unique solutions to problems others may not see. Griffin means you live by your higher purpose and help others reach their own spiritual enlightenment. You are also a guardian of ancient knowledge and can access the Akashic Records. You have intuitive insight and a problem-solving mind, which aids in your ability to see situations from a different perspective. Griffin is a symbol of the Divine and is the guardian of sacred, mysterious libraries and also guards the path to spiritual enlightenment. It warns to keep negative emotions at bay as you travel your spiritual path. It will hold you back until you release any negative emotions. It is said that griffin feathers touching the eyelids heal the blind, which means griffin helps your intuitive sight.

Assists When: You need to command respect while protecting your inner self. In mythology, griffin was deeply respected for its regal appearance and mystical character. It has strong boundaries and only lets those who are pure of heart enter within sacred areas. This means you are a sacred being who puts restrictions on those you allow close to you. If you've been hurt in the past, these boundaries may be even stronger than before. Griffin reminds you not to make your boundaries so strong that you never let anyone in. It is easy to block everyone out due to past pain and the fear of getting hurt again. Griffin mated for life and was forever alone if their partner died. This warns that if you close yourself off too much, you'll end up alone and lonely. You can demand respect and protect yourself without becoming reclusive. You are a leader who inspires awe and respect in those around you.

Frequency: Griffin energy feels like powerful surges of electricity moving in a steady rhythm around you. It energizes you with its power, but you feel stable and calm. It sounds like *whoosh, zing, thump.* It feels warm, secure, and noble, as if you're waiting to see what will happen, knowing you can handle whatever comes your way.

See Also: Eagle, Lion, Snake (Viper)

Imagine…

Your crops aren't doing well because it has been a dry summer. While walking home from the fields, a large shadow looms over you from above. You look up to see a large griffin. It lands beside you and lifts up a claw, offering you a leather bag. You take the bag, look inside, and see many gold coins. You fling yourself against the griffin's chest and hug it. *Thank you, thank you, thank you!* It gently nuzzles your head with its beak before it steps back and flies away.

Hippogriff

Traits: Hippogriff is the offspring of a griffin and a horse. The front half looks like an eagle and the back half like a horse. It has lightning speed and was often tamed by sorcerers and knights to be ridden and become a companion, pet, and confidant. Hippogriff is a noble being filled with pride, and it demands respect from those it encounters. Hippogriff symbolizes achievement, love, and being grounded.

Talents: Achievement, beauty, grounded, love, new opportunities, noble, protection, quickness, respect, romance, spirituality, visualization, wealth

Challenges: Rarity, too prideful

Element(s): Air, earth

Primary Color(s): Brown

Appearances: When hippogriff appears, it means you will accomplish what seems impossible. Griffins view horses as prey, and they mate for life. So a griffin mating with a mare, who then foals out a hippogriff, would be an extremely rare event and is associated with love. This is a sign of an impossible situation coming to fruition. Hippogriff urges you to see extraordinary possibilities in your daily life, to see the Divine in everything around you, to believe nothing is impossible and you can achieve anything you set out to do. Hippogriff will remove barriers preventing forward movement as you strive toward your goals. Hippogriff means you are grounded and balanced, and when you love, you love with heart and soul. It is said the griffin was drawn to the mare because of her great beauty. This means for you to pay attention to your own beauty. Not just your exterior looks but the beauty within you. As a spiritual being filled with light and love, you are able to share these aspects of yourself with those you come into contact with on a daily basis. This allows them to see the same qualities within themselves. Hippogriff demands respect and urges you to do the same. It can be intimidating due to its large size, powerful body, and ability to move at great speeds. When not respected, hippogriff can lash out with aggression. They will fiercely protect their human companions from any threat.

Assists When: You need to bring your dreams to life. Hippogriff can help you achieve your dreams if you believe in what you want and actively pursue it. It will make your path easier by lending its energy to you. Hippogriff's calm, noble, and regal presence can help you remain calm in stressful situations. Hippogriff is a companion who comes to you of its own will. It is never owned by anyone, but it will be there for you if it feels you deserve its assistance. Hippogriff can help you love the life you have, embrace all that you are, and strive to achieve the impossible, which is always possible in hippogriff's eyes. Hippogriff is connected to spirituality and can help whatever you're manifesting appear sooner than you might expect.

Frequency: Hippogriff energy is calm and steady, but it can move quickly and with precision. It feels warm, light, and airy but can turn dark if a threat appears. It sounds like a low-pitched *whoosh, raaamm, whoosh*.

See Also: Eagle, Horse

Imagine…

You're feeling a bit depressed and stressed out, so you're sitting on a rocky ridge looking at the mountains. There is an early morning mist still lingering over the small town in the valley below. You need time to evaluate and plan, to pump yourself up, and to get out of this slump. You feel a gust of wind pass by you and then realize something is sitting nearby. Looking over you see an enormous hippogriff. It nods its head, acknowledging you, and then settles down, scooting a little closer to you. You're not surprised that it exists or afraid of it. Instead you feel calm and reassured by its nearness. Lost in your thoughts, you don't notice the hippogriff has moved closer until it wraps a wing around your back, giving you a hug. You sense everything will be okay. You draw strength and inner power from the hippogriff. You feel its concern and love, which makes you stronger.

Hydra of Lerna

Traits: Hydra, also called the Lernaean Hydra in Greek mythology, was a sea serpent with nine heads (the middle one was immortal, venomous, and had poison breath) that guarded the entrance to the underworld. In the twelve labors of Hercules, he was sent to destroy Hydra as his second labor. Each time Hercules cut off a head, Hydra would quickly regenerate two more in its place. He defeated Hydra with help from his nephew, Iolaos.

Talents: Abundant energy, formidable, persistence, protection, rejuvenation, relentless, resiliency, resolve, strength, success after failure, survival, unique perspective

Challenges: Aggressive, fierce, poisonous, violent

Element(s): Water

Primary Color(s): Black, brown, green, red

Appearances: When Hydra appears it means to look at situations from a different perspective. Hydra had nine heads. That's nine different points of view. When you analyze a situation from multiple perspectives and different possible viewpoints, you can see it in a unique way. What once may have seemed confusing may suddenly be clear. Hydra protected the gateway to the underworld, which means you have a protective nature as well. You can be fierce in the protection of those you care about or causes in which you're involved. Hydra encourages you to be flexible and not too rigid, just as its necks were flexible in the battle with Hercules. If you're too rigid and unmoving, you may encounter more difficulties in life than you would if you move with the flow of life. Hydra indicates you are a survivor, able to regenerate yourself and experience abundant energy in your life. People and situations don't usually get your spirits down for long. You're able to bounce back quickly because you see them from different perspectives.

Assists When: You need to control your temper. Hydra was violently aggressive, a formidable opponent who struck out again and again. This is a warning to you to remain calm and control your temper so you don't encounter any negative repercussions due to your actions. Hydra could regenerate itself at a rapid pace. This means if you're going through a hard time in which you're experiencing difficulties, you'll be able to resolve situations quickly and efficiently to come out ahead. During the battle with Hydra, Hercules never gave up but continued to fight toward his goal. When at first he failed, he kept trying, accepted the help of Iolaos, and was able to defeat Hydra. This means even though you might experience failures in your life, you will be successful in what you've set out to achieve. There's nothing wrong with accepting someone's help along the way, so don't let pride hold you back from taking help when it's offered.

Frequency: Hydra energy moves rapidly in all directions. It feels like it's lunging and slithering all around you. It is hot and burns if it touches you. It sounds like a deep, roaring growl that rumbles throughout the air.

Imagine...

You're exploring a lake in ancient Greece when suddenly serpent heads start rising out of the water. There are nine of them, and you realize that you're at the home of Hydra. You hide behind a tree, hoping it didn't see you. It climbs out of the water, shakes itself like a dog, and then walks to a field. It lies down, basking in the sun. Its heads take turns resting, while the others keep watch. You adjust your position and a branch breaks under your feet. The heads look in your direction and the beast rises. You tuck your head between your knees, making yourself as small as possible. Soon you feel its hot breath on your back. It pokes you with one of its noses, and you fall on your side, still in a ball. It loses interest and goes back into the lake. You hear the water splashing and turn to see it disappearing under the water. You look down at your feet to find a freshly picked yellow flower, a gift from Hydra.

Jackalope

Traits: In North American folklore, jackalope is a creature born from crossing a jackrabbit and antelope (or a killer rabbit and pygmy deer, depending on the legend) that looks like a rabbit with antlers. Jackalope is an intelligent creature that can get away from anything (or anyone) trying to catch it by imitating the human voice. It is believed to be a shy beast but so dangerous it would gore hunters in the legs, so it was advised to wear stovepipes on your legs when hunting jackalope. The jackalope loves whiskey, so it was believed that if you offered it to the creature it would be easier to capture. Cowboys in the Old West often heard jackalope singing along with them in the distance as they sat around their campfires. Jackalope only breeds during lightning flashes, and the antlers often get in the way. The originator of the jackalope legend (some say tall tale) is said to be Douglas Herrick (1920–2003) of Douglas, Wyoming, who was a taxidermist who created a rabbit with horns on a mounted plaque. Horned rabbits appear in early seventeenth-century history and five hundred years earlier in a Persian geographic dictionary. When rabbits or hares have horns, they are actually cancerous tumors growing on their faces.

Talents: Creative, diligent, fearless, fertility, flexible, independent, intuition, open-minded, quick thinking, sensitive, solitary, speed, strength, survival

Challenges: Bad attitude, impersonation, inconsistent, not social, reclusive, trickery, trust issues

Element(s): Air, earth

Primary Color(s): Brown

Appearances: When jackalope appears, it means to be fearless in competition. Use your intelligence and cunning to come up with ways to win that show you can think outside of the box. Jackalope imitates human voices to aid in its escape. This means you should listen closely to what others say because you might learn something you didn't know. Jackalope means people see you as shy when in fact you just keep quiet about a lot of things instead of being too talkative. You're really an outgoing person, but you tend to not say things unless you know that what you're saying is correct (because you don't want to be wrong). You're tough and can go the distance in any situation even if people don't see you that way. Your strong sense of purpose and inner confidence gives you an advantage in many different situations. You strive to be the best you can be but aren't above fighting back if necessary. Jackalope means you may be very good at doing impersonations of others.

Assists When: You need to think fast and be quick on your feet. Jackalope has never been caught because it always maneuvers itself out of tricky situations. It is a solitary creature, which means you enjoy being alone, but aren't reclusive like the jackalope. When someone is trying to trick you, your strong intuition often lets you see what's going on before it happens. You're very hard to surprise. Jackalope can help you get over trust issues by encouraging you to be more flexible and open-minded.

Frequency: Jackalope energy moves fast, spinning around you in a flurry of activity. It is warm and soft but has a hard edge to it. It sounds like lots of corks popping all at once.

See Also: Antelope (Pronghorn), Hare, Rabbit

Imagine…

You're participating in a five mile race, part of which goes through a large field on the outskirts of town. You're not the best runner, but you're doing this to raise money for a cause you support so you pace yourself. Soon you're bringing up the rear. When you get to the field, you slow down even more. That's when you see it—the jackalope. It's racing toward you and rams its horns right at your legs. The horns go on either side of your calf as its head butts your leg. You take off running with the jackalope right on your heels, goading you on. Soon you see the finish line up ahead, and it looks like you're in first place. You and the jackalope run through the tape at the same time.

Jersey Devil

Traits: According to legend, the Jersey Devil is a cryptid creature that lives in the Pine Barrens of Southern New Jersey. It has the head of a goat with horns, red eyes, small arms with claws, cloven hooves, wings like a bat, a forked tail, and the body of a kangaroo. The legend says that in 1735 a woman named Mother Leeds found out she was pregnant with her thirteenth child and swore it would be the devil. The child was born on a stormy night. At first it looked like a normal baby, but then it transformed into a beast. It killed the midwife then flew up the chimney. After circling the village, it flew into the pine trees. It was said to emit a bloodcurdling scream and could bark. Since its birth, it has destroyed farmer's crops, poisoned the water in the area, killed livestock, and would appear before ships wrecked along the New Jersey shore.

Talents: Creativity, curious, evasive, fearless, flight, indestructible, invisibility, moving through shadows, nocturnal, open-minded, practicality, quick reflexes, shyness, strength

Challenges: Arrogance, belligerent, destructive, impractical, intimidating, unpredictable

Element(s): Air, earth

Primary Color(s): Brown

Appearances: When Jersey Devil appears, it means you are fearless in the face of adversity. You have an inner strength you rely on to achieve what you want out of life and to get you through difficult situations. Jersey Devil has quick reflexes, can be invisible to humans, and moves silently through the shadows. You also rely on your quick wit and reflexes to get yourself out of tight spots, you can become invisible to others when it suits your needs, hearing what you need to know without others being aware of your presence, and you easily move within the shadows if necessary. These qualities make you a great detective whether or not it is your career. When confronted, you have the knack of evading questions you don't want to answer and are able to hold your own if someone is antagonizing you. It's easy for you to turn a negative situation into a positive one because you're connected to the universal flow. People see you as a quiet but powerful person who gleans great insights from little things that often go unnoticed by others. You may enjoy flying, hang gliding, rappelling, and other outdoor sports.

Assists When: You need to move quickly or change directions at a moment's notice. You tend to be practical, handy, and creative. If something needs to be fixed, you take on the task instead of waiting for someone else to do it. Jersey Devil can help you be more open-minded and not locked into one train of thought. It has a curious nature but is shy about being seen, so it prefers nighttime over daylight. Jersey Devil can help you overcome any destructive behaviors you have by making you more aware of those actions so you can change them. Jersey Devil warns against being too unpredictable, intimidating to others, and arrogant about your accomplishments.

Frequency: Jersey Devil energy sounds like a loud, heart-wrenching scream. It moves with great speed as it flies around you. It is harsh, tough, and flaps in long, slow beats. It feels cold to the touch, dry, and rough.

See Also: Bat, Goat, Kangaroo

> ### Imagine…
> You've recently moved to New Jersey and have heard the story of the Jersey Devil several times now. After work you have a meeting at a local restaurant for dinner. It's not far from your house, so you walk over. It's dark, but the streets and sidewalks are well lit. You're about halfway there when you hear an odd sound from the forest on the other side of the street. Startled, you jump and stare over there. The next thing you know, a beast with a goat head and wings is walking on two hoofed feet out of the forest. It sees you and, taking flight, heads your way. Frozen in place, you send it thoughts of peace, love, and serenity. After a few minutes, it turns and flies away.

Jormungand

Traits: Jormungand, according to Old Norse mythology, is a huge serpent with large fangs and a flat tail that lives in the ocean surrounding Midgard, the realm of human civilization. He grows to be so huge he can wrap himself in a circle around Midgard and grasp his tail in his mouth. Called an ouroboros, this is a symbol of cycles, of recreating itself as soon as it's destroyed, similar to the phoenix. It is said if the Jormungand ever lets go of its tail the world would end but it would be reborn again. Thor had several battles with Jormungand, as they were enemies, and in the last battle they killed each other, bringing on the end of the world and the land sunk into the sea. Soon thereafter, the land rose up again and life started over.

Talents: Change, conviction, cycles, determination, intuition, invisibility, life, mystery, mystical, rebirth, regeneration, silence, spiritual growth, strength

Challenges: Endings, evasive, negative attitude, reclusive

Element(s): Water

Primary Color(s): Black, green

Appearances: When Jormungand appears, it means to get ready for major positive changes in your life. You may be moving to a new location, starting a new job, or beginning a family. Whatever situation you find yourself in, Jormungand means that life as you know it will never be the same after the coming events. This is a time to hold on to your faith, positivity, and cheery attitude. While Jormungand and Thor were enemies and caused the end of the world in mythology, this means that the world as you know it will change so dramatically it will feel as if it ended. The new world you find yourself in will be filled with love, delight, and spectacular events. This is a time of rebirth, of growth, and of lifting your expectations. Listen to your higher self, experience the regeneration of your spirituality, connect with your bliss and joy, and live in happiness and love. Jormungand means to live your life with conviction. Stand by what you believe in and those you love. Your support means the world to them. Jormungand warns against stepping back from life and becoming reclusive as you adjust to the changes you'll experience. You can adjust to changes easier when you have support from others.

Assists When: You need to keep an aura of mystery around yourself. If you have secrets you aren't ready to reveal, or if there are life changes happening for you but you want them to be a surprise to others, Jormungand can help you keep things quiet. It can also help you be more determined and resolute as you reach for your goals. If you need to remain hidden in order to uncover information you need, Jormungand will help you remain invisible during your search. Jormungand warns against letting others get under your skin and annoy you. It urges you to keep a positive attitude and warns against allowing negativity to influence you. All will work out, just hang in there.

Frequency: Jormungand energy is sleek, fast, and powerful. It moves around you like a tornado, spinning with speed. It feels cold, distant, and calculating. It sounds like a long bleating groan of a monster.

See Also: Snake (Viper)

Imagine…

You're in a store when you see a pendant of a snake holding its tail. You feel drawn to it, so you buy it. That night you sleep with the pendant on and dream of a faraway land, a large island surrounded by water. The creature from your pendant lives under the sea, surrounding the island. You see it let go of its tail and slither onto the land. Its weight pushes it down into the ocean. The serpent encircles the area again and grasps its tail. You watch the land rise up out of the water and, as if moving in fast forward, the trees grow and the land comes back to life. Soon you see people on the land again, and time slows to normal speed. You wake up, determined to make positive changes so you can experience the same type of renewal.

Kelpie

Traits: Kelpie is a cross between a horse and a fish. The front of the kelpie looks like a horse and has two front hooves, the back is the tail of a fish. In Celtic mythology, kelpie could transform into human shape to lure victims into the water to drown them. They kept their hooves in human form and often gave themselves away because they had water plants in their hair. This legend was used to keep children away from bodies of water in case of accidental drowning. Kelpie means if you feel like you're drowning, due to stress or being overwhelmed, you can call upon kelpie to help you keep your head above water. Kelpie could be controlled by obtaining its bridle, which contained its shapeshifting abilities and was worn as a necklace when kelpie was in human form. This means you can maintain self-control during difficult situations.

Talents: Overcoming difficulties, spirituality, transformation, warning

Challenges: Disguise, duality, negative intentions

Element(s): Water

Primary Color(s): Black, white

Appearances: When kelpie appears, it means there are storms coming your way, so prepare for rough waters. Kelpie would howl and wail when storms were coming and for the duration. While things may be rough for a while, the storm will eventually pass and life will return to calmness. If a kelpie appears, it means you are connecting with your own spiritual nature, your thoughts and beliefs, to get you through a difficult emotional time. By looking within, you will be able to change any negative emotions you're feeling into positive ones. It may be difficult at times because kelpie is known to be a malicious being, but you will get through the storm with patience and by relying on your spiritual beliefs. Kelpie warns against blaming others for your problems. It's time to break free from anything holding you back, of being emotionally controlled by someone else, and any restraints you've placed upon yourself. Kelpie is known to misrepresent itself to deceive unsuspecting humans and put them in harm's way. Are you deceiving yourself by thinking that someone will change when you know they will only change when *they* want to, not because *you* want them to? Or maybe you keep saying things will be different at work when this happens or that happens, when those things may never happen? Look at all areas of your life to see if you're looking with blinders on instead of seeing situations and people as they truly are.

Assists When: You need to uncover duality in your life. The kelpie lives in rivers, streams, and lochs. Water is necessary for life, but it can also take life away. Kelpie can help you uncover instances and people that aren't what they at first appear to be. You may be involved in a situation you believe to be positive in nature when in actuality there are ulterior, negative motivations taking place behind the scenes. Kelpie can help you see this duality and take the appropriate steps. Kelpie warns to only make transformations in your life for positive and not negative reasons. Only transform yourself because it is what *you need* for your own personal or spiritual growth, and not because someone wants you to change to fit what they want or believe you should be.

Frequency: Kelpie energy is cold, fast, and unpredictable. It feels like ice touching your skin and makes you instantly alert, gasping for air. It sounds like a low-pitched splash into water followed by a gurgling noise.

See Also: Horse

Imagine…

You're walking along a road next to the ocean when you see a beautiful white horse approaching. When it gets closer, you notice the ocean weeds in its hair and recognize it as a kelpie. You know the tales and walk a wide circle around the beast, telling it to go back into the sea from whence it came. When you call it by name, it jumps into the sea, rising up again in its true form, then diving down and splashing the water with its large fish tail, soaking you with the spray.

Kongamato

Traits: Kongamato is a creature similar to a pterodactyl that lives in the Jiundu swamps in western Zambia near the Congo and Angola borders. It is an enormous red bird with leathery skin instead of feathers. Its wingspread was up to seven feet and looked like bat wings. It had a long tail, narrow head, and sharp teeth inside its beak. People in the area who have seen the Kongamato identified it as a pterodactyl, but they couldn't identify any of the other prehistoric dinosaur pictures. The people believed it to be a part of the natural world and not a demon of any kind. Kongamato often capsized canoes, so the villagers would take it an offering of some kind of food when they had to cross areas where it was known to attack.

Talents: Bioluminescent, calmness, mischievous, mysterious, reaching new heights, spiritual development, strategies

Challenges: Aggressive, external struggles, internal struggles, outdated or old ways of thinking

Element(s): Air

Primary Color(s): Black, red

Appearances: When Kongamato appears, it means that it is time for you to reach new heights. In order to soar through the sky you have to be released from the ropes holding you down. This means to look to your past and let go of old habits or fears that are no longer necessary. Kongamato means someone from your past may reappear. It also means you have an interest in history. You may even have a secret desire for things to be how they once were in your life instead of how they are now. Kongamato urges you to seek out the truth so you will gain a better understanding of yourself. That way you can move out of idealizing the past to live in the present. Kongamato is said to glow at night due to its bioluminescence. This signifies you should let your own inner light shine brightly into the night for all to see. You can be a guiding light to others. Kongamato urges you to deal with any old issues that show up as quickly as you can so they don't pull you down. Fix it and let it go. It also urges you to never give up on your dreams. Fly high, glide at a slow pace, and feel the wind above and beneath you. When you can appreciate the simplicities in every moment, then you can truly soar.

Assists When: You need to adjust the way you think about things. The world is constantly changing around you. If you're stuck thinking about things as they used to be, then you're blocking yourself in enjoying how things are now. It's like listening to music on an 8-track tape player when you could be listening to it via a digital download on your cell phone. Kongamato urges you to learn how to make better decisions by considering possible outcomes before taking action. While you shouldn't fear living your life to the fullest, you also shouldn't make rash decisions that you haven't thought out. Kongamato reminds you to remain calm, create a strategy, and then make a move. Kongamato means you're entering a time of spiritual development even if you don't realize it yet. Listen, absorb, and hold on to new knowledge.

Frequency: Kongamato energy is swift and navigates side to side as it angles through the treetops. It is slick, hot, damp, and smells like the dankness of dirt. It sounds like a high-pitched squall.

Imagine...

You're trudging through the swamps in Zambia. The mosquitoes are eating you up, it's hot, and you didn't want to come on this assignment in the first place. You hear a loud bird call above you just as you feel something clasp both of your shoulders. Claws grip you tightly, and you look up into the face of a huge pterodactyl. It flies away with you, taking you to its nest. There are two babies, and you get the feeling you're the babysitter. The mother leaves you with the babies for three days. They happily munch on the meal their mother left behind, and you eat food from your backpack. When you're bored, you play peekaboo with them. When the mother returns, she picks you up and takes you back to your camp. You don't understand it at all, but you *are* thinking differently now.

Kraken

Traits: Kraken, in Scandinavian mythology, was a giant sea creature with a body so big (about one mile long) it looked like an island if it was floating near the surface. It had many long tentacles and fins, and its favorite pastime was wrapping its enormous tentacles over ships and sinking them into the sea. Kraken created a large whirlpool as the ship sunk, which sucked under anything that may have been floating on the sea's surface. It slept on the bottom of the sea in very deep waters but awakened to feed or when a ship disturbed it. Legend says only two existed, and they could not reproduce because they would need so much food they wouldn't survive as a species. Kraken symbolizes a solitary existence and being present but rarely seen.

Talents: Abundance, ancient knowledge, bravery, courage, disguise, elusive, hiding in plain sight, hunting, manifestation, rest, self-reliance, spiritual awakening, strength, wealth, wildness

Challenges: Aggression, awakening the monster, destructive, evokes fear, fierce, lack of conscience, loneliness

Element(s): Water

Primary Color(s): Black, gray, green

Appearances: When Kraken appears to you, it is a sign of upcoming abundance and an increase in wealth in all areas of your life. Kraken would trap fish by belching and releasing food into the water. This attracted other fish that would swim right into the Kraken's mouth, where they'd be eaten. This is symbolic of manifestation and bringing what you desire to you. Kraken desired a meal, so it brought the fish to it. What do you desire? What are your goals and dreams? What can you do to bring the things you want to you? Begin by practicing creative visualization and manifestation to create abundance in your life. Kraken means to be brave and courageous in all that you do. Face situations head on instead of backing away from them. You are self-reliant just like Kraken and usually don't depend on anyone but yourself. Kraken urges you to access the ancient knowledge within you because it will lead to a spiritual awakening. Kraken means to make sure you're getting enough sleep and resting whenever you can. You tend to do a lot in your life and can get run down if you're not resting enough.

Assists When: You need to be in attendance but don't want to get too involved in the event. Kraken often hides right in plain sight, making others believe it is an island in the sea. When you want to remain unnoticed in any given circumstances, Kraken can help you. If you're bored or need a change of pace, Kraken can connect you to the wildness of nature. Take a walk or participate in any outdoor event to get in tune with the wild part of your inner spirit and link your energy to that of the land or sea. Kraken warns against stirring up or harboring any negativity inside yourself (awakening the monster) and instead urges you to maintain control while letting go of the negative emotions that can cause you to act out of character or cause fear in others. Kraken lends you its strength in any situation if you need it.

Frequency: Kraken energy is extremely hot at the center but chilled around the edges. When sleeping, it is completely still, but when awakened, it moves with speed and precision. It sounds like a very loud boom followed by splashes and a deep whirring noise.

See Also: Octopus (Squid)

Imagine...

You're cruising across the ocean in a speedboat when the sky darkens and the waves get rough and turbulent. You look back from your place on the helm to see Kraken rising up out of the water. A tentacle grabs the boat and lifts it up into the air, and Kraken stares right at you. Its words boom like thunder when it speaks. *You are seen and heard. All you want is yours if you'll only ask for it.* You yell over the din, *Thank you! Please let me go!* The turbulence stills, the storm clouds dissipate, and the Kraken disappears beneath the water, steadying the boat as it puts it back in the water.

Ladon (Python)

Traits: Ladon, in Greek mythology, was a hundred-headed serpent dragon that guarded the golden apples of the Hesperides. Because of its many heads, some of Ladon's eyes were always on alert if anyone tried to take the sacred apples. Hercules killed Ladon by shooting him with an arrow that had been dipped in the Hydra's poisoned blood and then decapitating the heads. He then stole the sacred golden apples to complete his eleventh labor. Hera turned Ladon into the constellation Draco. It is said that after Ladon died the Hesperides were so wrought with grief that they turned themselves into a black poplar, an elm, and a willow tree.

Talents: Adventure, assertive, different perspectives, fearless, fluidity, formidable, passionate, persistence, prosperity, protection, regal, relentless, resiliency, riches, strength, survival

Challenges: Deadly, fierce, hoarding, intimidating, possessive, unpredictable

Element(s): Earth

Primary Color(s): Black, brown, green

Appearances: When Ladon appears, it means to be on guard because someone may try to take something that is yours. This could be as simple as someone taking an ink pen off of your desk or taking your lunch from the refrigerator, or it could be very complicated. Ladon means to watch your back and be extra diligent about safety for the next few weeks. Ladon will protect you but you should also heighten your awareness. Landon means you will have new opportunities coming your way that will increase your financial status. The golden apples Ladon protected were sacred and valuable. This means your own financial value will increase. Make sure you're looking for these opportunities so you don't miss them. Ladon means you're a formidable opponent at work. You enjoy the competitiveness of a business environment and fearlessly work to be successful. You may even own your own company. Ladon was passionate about its job of protecting the golden apples and fought to the end to keep them safe. You're just as passionate in every aspect of your life. You don't hide your feelings but express them as you feel them. You are a great debater because you have many different points of view and the strength and determination to get others to see your views.

Assists When: You need to be more flexible. There are times when you can get stuck in your ways and be somewhat inflexible. Ladon can help you let go of any rigidity, so you're suppler in how you think and feel. Ladon can help you be more assertive in situations when someone else is always talking over you or never letting you get a word in the conversation. With a hundred heads, Ladon can have a lot to say and can take the attention away from others who are trying to be controlling. Ladon warns against being too intimidating, so you have to handle yourself with grace and in a regal manner. Ladon is unpredictable and encourages you to shake things up in your life sometimes.

Frequency: Ladon energy sounds like hundreds of separate screeches happening all at the same time. It is cool and feels like thick leather. It's rough yet smooth. It moves all around you in undulating, waving motions.

See Also: Snake (Viper)

Imagine...

Swirling around you are the many heads of the beast and they're all talking at once. You're the only one who can hear the words within their roars, so they all have things they want to tell you. This head is bickering with that head, two other heads are mad at each other, and they're bored if there's no one trying to steal the golden apples. You look up and tell them to be quiet. They stop talking and you rub the top of each head, sending positive, calming energy to it. When you're finished, you tell the heads to please get along so they can do a good job protecting the apples. You explain that when they're divided or upset at one another, that can affect their overall efforts. They agree, so you leave. As you're walking away you hear, *See, I told you I was right... No, you weren't. ...*

Loch Ness Monster

Traits: The Loch Ness Monster, commonly referred to as Nessie, is a cryptid lake monster that lives in Loch Ness in the Scottish Highlands. It is thought that Nessie could be a prehistoric plesiosaur that somehow survived. Sightings of the Loch Ness Monster date back to the sixth century. The Loch Ness Monster symbolizes ancient knowledge, intuitive insight, and universal connections.

Talents: Ancient knowledge, awareness, continuation of life, conviction, enchanted, eternal life, existence, faith, hardiness, hope, illumination, inspiration, intuition, invisibility, magical, mystery, purity, reemergence, speed, spiritual awareness, strength, transformation, wisdom

Challenges: Evasive, lethargy, living in the past, reclusive

Element(s): Earth, water

Primary Color(s): Gray

Appearances: When the Loch Ness Monster appears, it means to pay attention to the natural world around you. You are intuitively connected to the elements at this time, especially anything to do with water. Since the Loch Ness Monster is rarely seen, this is a sign to connect to the part of your inner self that you often avoid. In order to reach spiritual enlightenment, you must consider every part of yourself—your faults as well as your gifts. If you are only aware of your gifts then you're blocking yourself from further growth. Analyzing your faults will enable you to find ways to turn them into gifts, furthering your spiritual growth. The Loch Ness Monster encourages you to use your intuitive insightfulness to connect to deeper, more ancient knowledge. Just as Nessie can dive to great depths and stay out of sight, this knowledge is hidden deep within you and will only appear when you really look for it. Even then it can be elusive, so you must look to your inner essence and higher self with awareness, conviction, and purity of heart. The Loch Ness Monster is an inspirational hope that, once seen and acknowledged, can lead to great positive transformation. Those who have seen the Loch Ness Monster are forever changed in a positive way. Once you see your own inner truth and discover your own ancient knowledge, which has been with you since the birth of your soul, you too will be forever changed in a positive way.

Assists When: You need inspiration, hope, and strength. Loch Ness Monster represents the uplifting of spirit. It is a magical, mystical, enchanted being that touches a chord of optimistic expectation within you. These qualities can inspire you to reach for greater heights. Loch Ness Monster is a reminder that you are a strong person with great wisdom. Like Nessie, you can find the best ways to inspire those around you. Loch Ness Monster is reflective of the continuation of life and eternal life. It warns against living in the past, being too evasive with others and of becoming a recluse. If you find yourself fitting with any of these qualities, now is the time to get out and about, let go of past events, and move forward, making new friends along the way.

Frequency: Loch Ness Monster energy is cool and crisp. It moves at a medium pace with a *slish-splash-slish* sound. It feels heavy yet light, is hidden yet seen. It has a medium-pitched, fluctuating tone.

See Also: Ogopogo

Imagine…

While visiting the Scottish Highlands, you make a point to spend a day at Loch Ness looking for Nessie. After a boat tour you decide to go off of the beaten path and drive to a remote area of the loch. You make your way down to the water's edge and sit down, staring out across the loch. After a while you see a ripple in the water that gets bigger and bigger. A small head comes up, followed by a long arched neck. It's Nessie! You take a video as the creature swims around, rolling and playing in the water. Then you put the camera down. Nessie's large flippers splash against the top of the water as she rolls. For a moment she disappears only to resurface facing you. You think you see her smile, then she disappears beneath the surface, one flipper waving goodbye.

Nandi Bear

Traits: Nandi Bear in legend was a cryptid that lived in East Africa. It was a carnivore with shoulders more than four feet tall, the face of a bear, and the sloping back of a hyena. It had long, thick fur, large teeth, and claws that it used for digging or as a weapon during an attack. It would stand on its back legs and had the shuffling walk of modern-day bears. Legend says the Nandi Bear only came out on moonless nights, and its mouth glowed red. When it killed, it only ate the brains of its victims. Local folklore from 1919 reports a farmer who had more than fifty-seven goats and sheep killed over a period of ten days by having their brains eaten, but the bodies were left untouched.

Talents: Ability to hide, balance, confidence, courage, digging, freedom, harmony, power, resourceful, strength, victory, warrior

Challenges: Aggressive, ferocious, overconfident, unpredictable, violent

Element(s): Earth

Primary Color(s): Brown, red

Appearances: When Nandi Bear appears, it means to use your brain and your intelligence to come to reasonable decisions. The Nandi Bear was known to only eat the brains of its victims. This also indicates you are connected to ancient knowledge. By accessing this knowledge you can understand more about human nature, life, and the spiritual. It is your divine right to grow in spirit. According to lore, Nandi Bear terrorized local villagers. This is a sign for you to look around your community or workplace at those who seem negative. Are there reasons for their feelings, or are they just miserable people who never look at the bright side of life? If you understand the reasons for their behavior, can you help them? Maybe they lost a loved one recently and are going through grief. Maybe they are experiencing financial difficulties. Nandi Bear has the ability to hide where no one will find it, but it also has a warrior spirit. It is filled with power, is resourceful, and is confident that it will succeed. While it does have the brain-eating zombie thing going on and is an unpredictable, violent beast, it also lives in harmony within its own world and finds balance within itself. You too are resourceful, filled with confidence in your abilities, and have the spirit of a hero. You will fight for those who need your help. Just leave the brain eating to the Nandi Bear.

Assists When: You need to connect with your inner courage to be victorious. You may be in a situation where you don't feel comfortable with what's going on. Nandi Bear can help you connect with the strength of the warrior within you so you have the courage and fortitude to see the situation through to the end. There are life lessons to be learned from all events you're involved in. Nandi Bear means to be aware and take advantage of the growth you will experience. Sometimes uncomfortable situations will help you find balance and harmony within yourself.

Frequency: Nandi Bear energy moves at a medium, lumbering pace. It sounds like a howling roar. It is hot and feels furry against your skin.

Imagine...

You've been trying to resolve a problem at work, but nothing you've come up with has worked. Before you go to sleep, you ask your guides to help you resolve the issue in your dreams and to let you remember them in the morning. You dream that you're in Africa and a large bearlike hyena is chasing you. When it catches you, it grabs your head in its mouth and sucks out your thoughts until there's nothing left except the solution to your problem. It lets you go, and you touch your head, but there's no blood. You ask why it didn't eat your brain. *Not hungry,* it says, *just helping.*

Nemean Lion

Traits: In Greek mythology, the Nemean Lion was a shapeshifter that took women from the towns as hostages. Killing the Nemean Lion was the first labor of Hercules set forth by Eurystheus. Barehanded, using only his own strength, he strangled it to death. It was believed that Hercules's armor was the coat of the Nemean Lion. Hercules carried the Nemean Lion to Eurystheus, who freaked out and said Hercules could never enter the city again and had to display the results of his labors outside the city walls. Hera transformed the Nemean Lion into the constellation Leo. The Nemean Lion symbolizes disguise, transformation, and hidden truths.

Talents: Assertiveness, bravery, courage, decision-making skills, fortitude, leadership, organization, personal power, resolve, ruling, strength, tenacity, valor

Challenges: Aggression, personal struggles, predatory feelings, strong-willed, too controlling

Element(s): Earth

Primary Color(s): Gold

Appearances: When Nemean Lion appears, it is a warning that a threat is nearby. This could be a situation at work or in your personal life. Nemean Lion means to be alert, pay attention, and be ready to fight for what you want or believe in if necessary. This threat could come in the form of a person who disguises their intentions, just as the Nemean Lion pretended to be something it wasn't in order to obtain its predatory goals. The Nemean Lion represents your own inner strength and bravery. You're not afraid to be assertive in order to obtain what you want. You are courageous and will step forward in situations where others cower. There is valor and fortitude within you. People look up to you for your strength and wisdom. Nemean Lion warns against being too aggressive or presenting yourself as something you're not. Be true to yourself to achieve all that you want. When you purposefully deceive others to gain your own ends, that's when you'll experience defeat. It takes bravery to be honest and forthright.

Assists When: You need to deal with an overpowering authority figure in your life or handle a personal struggle. Just as the Nemean Lion terrorized the local towns, you may be dealing with someone at work who is driving you nuts by causing you to feel inner conflict. Now is the time to be quietly assertive and use your own personal power and inner strength to handle the situation so this person will no longer negatively affect you. This may mean confronting the person or even removing yourself from their presence by changing jobs. You have the innate ability to always know the right path to take. Sometimes you must stand your ground and fight, while other times it means walking away and finding a new territory to claim as your own. Nemean Lion helps you with any personal struggles you are involved in. It can also help you get more organized or step into a leadership position where you'll use your decision-making skills. Nemean Lion warns against being too strong-willed or controlling.

Frequency: Nemean Lion energy moves slowly around you with the *thump, plop, thump* of its feet. It is warm, flows like silk, and can wrap you tightly in its grasp as it lifts you up or protects you. It sounds like the crack and crash of a large tree being felled.

See Also: Lion

Imagine...

The beast stalks you, circling around you, as if it's about to pounce. It walks behind you, and when it comes back around, it's no longer a large lion but is now a woman. You know the story of the Nemean Lion, so you know it has shifted into the woman. She says, *What do you fear?* The first thing that comes to mind is *You!* but you say, *I fear nothing.* The woman laughs. *I like your bravery, so here's some advice. That which is hidden transforms when the pretense is removed. Now go. Get out of here.* You don't have to be told twice. Once you're a distance away, you look back to see the lion watching you. Thinking about its words, you decide to look for what is hidden in your life.

Ogopogo

Traits: Ogopogo is a sea serpent that lived in Okanagan Lake in British Columbia, Canada. Ogopogo was originally named N'ha-a-tik (lake demon) or Na-ha-ha-itk (snake in the lake) by the First Nations Aboriginal people before the arrival of European settlers. If they had to cross the lake, they took a sacrifice of a small animal to appease the creature because it had attacked in the past. Ogopogo is said to have multiple humps, is snakelike in appearance with a horse-shaped head, horns, and a flipper like a whale at the end of its tail. It moved in an undulating motion similar to a snake. Ogopogo symbolizes spirituality, new beginnings, and transformation.

Talents: Divination, facing fear, hiding, insightful, meditation, memories, new beginnings, planning, recuperation, rejuvenation, rest, spirituality, starting over, transformation, wisdom

Challenges: Reclusiveness, repressed emotions, unpredictable

Element(s): Water

Primary Color(s): Green

Appearances: When Ogopogo appears, it's a sign of transformation and to look for deeper meanings in your life. In First Nations mythology, a native possessed by demons killed Kan-He-Kan, a local wise man. The gods captured the murderer and transformed him into a serpent as punishment. They threw the serpent into the lake, condemning him to remain there forever. Since that time, there have been many sightings of the beast that quite often appears like a log but moves against the water currents. In 1989, Ogopogo was given protected wildlife status, which makes it illegal to harm it. This means to protect yourself from negativity as you discover new ideals and how to use latent abilities on your spiritual path. There is always negativity in the world. It is how you handle it that either blocks your path or allows you to move along without interruption. Ogopogo's transformation from man to beast indicates you too will change as you walk your path. How you transform will depend on your outlook, intention, and connection to the truth within your soul. Is that truth positive or negative? Do you harbor resentments or let go of negative feelings? Do you act and react with love in your heart, or are you angry and feel entitled? Think of these things and know that true spiritual growth is found through love, light, and positivity, all of which are within you.

Assists When: You need to rest so you can come back stronger than before. Ogopogo means new beginnings. If you've been working hard for a while, it's time to take a vacation, rest, and relax so you rejuvenate both physically and at a soul level so you can begin again.

Frequency: Ogopogo energy is smooth, flowing, and moves with a rising and falling motion. It surges upward, then dips downward. It is hot and can strike out without notice. It feels dark and creaks and groans in a rolling movement of sound.

See Also: Loch Ness Monster

Imagine...

While visiting Canada, you drive along Okanagan Lake in British Colombia. It's beautiful in this area, and you're taking in the sights when you see movement on the lake. You glance over, but this isn't a boat. You find a place to pull over. Outside of the car you watch as several large humps appear in the water. It looks like a long snake of some sort. Maybe it's an enormous anaconda. The creature suddenly rises up from the lake and then dives under the water. As its tail emerges you notice it looks like a whale's fluke. It hits the water with a large splash, and then the lake is quiet again.

Owlman

Traits: Owlman is an oversized owl with red, glowing, slanted eyes, pointy ears, a beak-shaped mouth, large wings, sharp talons, and a seven-foot-tall body. It is found in Mawnan village in Cornwall County, England, near the old churches in the area. It is nocturnal and often appears to young girls at dusk. Eye witnesses say it would suddenly appear in front of them. It is thought to live inside the church towers. Legend says if Owlman looks in your eyes, you will be unable to speak for days or weeks afterward due to the extreme fear it causes. It was first seen flying around the Mawnan church towers in April 1976 by two sisters as they walked nearby. The family was on vacation and the father took the girls to the police to report the creature but would only let the girls draw it. They immediately cut their vacation short and returned home out of fear. The latest sighting was in 2009.

Talents: Can see in the dark, flight, illusions, mysterious, pursues, rising above, strength, transitions, unexplained

Challenges: Aggressive, attacks the weak, causes lightheadedness, stalking, terrifying

Element(s): Air, earth

Primary Color(s): Brown, gray

Appearances: When Owlman appears, it is a sign to rise above negativity. People saw Owlman suddenly appear standing right in front of them, up in the trees, or flying around the top of church towers. Once seen, Owlman would often rise up in the air and fly out of sight. This signifies being able to lift yourself up with your own inner strength to rise above obstacles appearing along your path. Owlman would pursue people, quietly and unseen, before it appeared. This is a sign for you to pursue your dreams. You don't have to tell everyone what you're doing, but, like Owlman, you can be silent in your pursuit until you've realized your dreams. Owlman sees in the dark. You too can see what is hidden when you're paying attention. Owlman is often considered an illusion, a being that was made up out of fear of the unknown. This means to look for illusions in your life. Did you misunderstand a situation or make an innocent action into something that it's not? Look with clarity to be sure before taking a stand.

Assists When: You need to find your way. Owlman, while known to frighten, can also lead you in a different direction. If you've been pursuing an activity or person that's not exactly right for you, Owlman can help you rise above and see the situation from a different perspective while also showing you new opportunities or a different possible path. In legend, owls know the truth of your soul and can see unseen truths. Owlman also sees the same, as it looks through the shadows to see you for who you really are. If you are weak, he considers you prey, but if you are strong, you can fight him away. This means to connect with your inner strength and confidence. Legend says when Owlman is in your presence, you will suddenly feel lightheaded. If you experience lightheadedness, Owlman may have a message for you.

Frequency: Owlman energy pulses. It feels like your heartbeat pounding through a minor injury, a bit painful and rhythmic. It sounds like a high-pitched hiss and feels as if a presence you can't see is towering above you.

See Also: Owl

Imagine…

You've always been interested in the architecture of old buildings. Today you're exploring the Mawnan Village churches. You've heard the story of Owlman, who supposedly lives in the area, but you think it's just someone's wild imagination. You're inside the church looking out of the tower when you see something flutter in your peripheral vision. Nothing's there. You're walking around the back of the church to get to your car when you run into a man. You mutter your apologies and back up only to realize it's Owlman. His slanted eyes are glowing red, his beak is large and hooked, his claws are long and sharp. His energy is thick and heavy as if he came from another dimension. As you watch, he rises into the air and flies away.

Pegasus

Traits: Pegasus is a divine stallion with wings that brought lightning and thunderbolts from Olympus to Zeus. His sire was Poseidon (as horse god) and his dam was Medusa. He was born, along with his brother Chrysaor (who is depicted as a human boy) at the moment Perseus decapitated Medusa. Pegasus immediately escaped to Mount Helicon and was taken in by the Muses. He is associated with the arts and creativity. Upon his death, Zeus honored Pegasus by transforming him into a constellation for his faithful service. Pegasus symbolizes being in service to others, spirituality, and travel.

Talents: Beauty, emotional stability, gentleness, graceful, inspiration, messenger, purity, speed, spirituality, travel, wisdom

Challenges: Feelings of intellectual or spiritual superiority, manipulating others emotions, snobbish behavior

Element(s): Air, earth

Primary Color(s): White

Appearances: When Pegasus appears, it means you desire to rise above your ordinary way of life in the physical realm to seek knowledge in the spiritual realm and attain soul growth. It was believed that each time Pegasus struck his hoof on the ground an inspirational spring was born. Pegasus means you have the innate ability to transform negativity into positivity through your connection to the spiritual. Pegasus is a beautiful, pure being filled with gentleness and grace. This means you have the same qualities within you, which draws people to you. They sense you are down to earth, transparent, and willing to listen and help them with their problems. Your emotional stability helps you give them unbiased guidance that inspires and elevates their own spiritual nature. Pegasus warns against purposefully manipulating situations or other people to get your own way, blaming others for your actions, or playing on another's emotions. These types of actions are negative, and Pegasus encourages you to own up to your faults, turn negatives into positives, and be strong in your service.

Assists When: You need inspiration. Pegasus can show you how to be more creative and get in touch with your inner muse. If you're working on your spirituality, which involves travel to the astral realms, Pegasus will keep you safe from danger during your travels and help you quickly return to the physical realm if you feel insecure or uneasy during the journey. Pegasus helped Bellerophon slay the Chimera, but then Bellerophon tried to ride him into the realm of the gods. Bellerophon was killed when Pegasus threw him after being stung by a gadfly sent by Zeus to stop them from entering the realm. This is a warning not to let others control you or make you do something you're not comfortable doing. It means to be true to yourself or you may experience the sting of their manipulations.

Frequency: Pegasus energy moves in a soaring wave of motion, a gentle undulation with each flap of its wings. It is a smooth four-beat cadence that lifts upward. It feels warm, calm, and steady. It sounds like a low-toned *whoosh* followed by a sweeping roll of wind.

See Also: Horse

Imagine…

You happen upon Pegasus grazing in a field. Awestruck, you watch for a few moments before calling his name. He looks over at you then goes back to grazing. Feeling brave, you walk over to him and rub his neck and feathers. He isn't bothered by your presence at all but softly nickers as you pet him. He's the most beautiful creature you've ever seen. Touching him sends powerful energy from your fingertips to your core spiritual self. You are humbled by his gentle and kind nature. You start to leave, and he walks along beside you, stops you with his nose against your stomach, and pushes you toward his back. *Could it be?* Is he willing to give you a ride? You ask, *Are you sure?* Pegasus nods and bows down so you can get on. Moments later you're flying through the sky, holding on to his mane. After a while, he takes you back to the field. You whisper your thanks, he nuzzles your face, and then he returns to grazing.

Phoenix

Traits: Phoenix symbolizes birth, living life, death, and rebirth. It is the ability to overcome hard times and loss to bounce back better than before. People often say they will rise from the ashes like a phoenix, meaning they'll get through whatever tough experience they're involved with and will rise out of it better than before. It's survival at its finest through internal transformation and regeneration. A heightened sense of spiritual awareness, intuition and sense of being, feeling connected to the universe and all within it are traits of phoenix.

Talents: Clarity, consumption, continuation of life, conviction, creativity, eternal life, existence, expression, faith, growth, hardiness, hope, illumination, intuition, longevity, power, protection, purification, rebirth, reemergence, rejuvenation, renewal, resurrection, spiritual awareness, strength, transformation

Challenges: Being too assertive, depression, destruction, lethargy, living in the past, overexertion, physical illness

Element(s): Air, fire

Primary Color(s): Orange, purple, red, yellow

Appearances: Phoenix often appears during times of transition. Doors may shut but keep watch for the opening windows. You are about to experience a time of rebirth, letting go of the old and embracing the new. It means to rise above difficulties, remain true to your inner essence, and look at situations using your intuition. Keep the faith that everything will work out the way it is supposed to and light will result from any darkness you are experiencing. Stay strong with your convictions and remain true to your inner self and your beliefs. There is purity and strength associated with your transformation. Remain present in daily activities and pay particular attention to the moments of your life.

Assists When: You are experiencing situations where you must overcome difficult circumstances. This includes times of change, when you feel like your life is falling apart or you're being held back and unable to move forward. Phoenix helps you to keep your faith that you will rise above hard times. In the end, the situation will be better than before. Phoenix assists with fresh starts because every ending must have a new beginning. Phoenix enhances your sense of self and your spirituality and reminds that you will reemerge even stronger. This too shall pass, and the transformation will give you clarity.

Frequency: Phoenix's frequency is hot, fiery, and all-encompassing. It shimmers with brilliant radiance. It moves quickly, sparks flying, completely engulfing you in its heat, leaving you filled with positive passion and feelings of rejuvenation.

Imagine…

You're in the desert. The heat is bearing down on you, sweltering and humid, and you're sweating, desperate for a drink of water. You see a mirage and struggle to reach the water just within your reach. As you move forward, you happen upon a nest built upon a rocky structure. Within the nest sits the most magnificent bird you've ever seen. Its piercing blue eyes seem to look straight into your soul, as if it knows you better than you know yourself. You move closer, drawn to it as if mesmerized. You sit down on a rock beside the nest, your thirst forgotten. You reach out your hand to touch the soft feathers. Phoenix wraps its wings around your hand in an embrace. Suddenly, fire explodes around your hands, but you're not burned. Phoenix arches its head back and cries out like a warrior and disappears. When the flames die down, you search frantically through the ashes. The white hot energy enters through your fingertips and fills you with a sense of purpose and strength. And then you uncover a new, young bird. It tentatively steps into your cupped hands, opens its wings wide, and sings the most beautiful song you've ever heard. Joy radiates through you as the tiny bird wraps its wings around your hand once again.

Sea-Goat

Traits: Sea-goat mythology says that the god Chronos created Pricus, the first sea-goat from which all of the others came. The sea-goat is half goat and half fish, is very intelligent, can speak, and was favored by the gods. Young sea-goats are drawn to the shore. Using their goat legs, they pull themselves out of the water and bask in the sun. The longer they are on shore the more they transform into regular goats, until one day, their tail completely changes into hind legs and they lose their ability to talk and think. Pricus uses his ability to turn back time and revert his lost children back into sea-goats, which also reverses everything on earth, so Pricus is the only one who knows what will happen. After reversing time on several occasions, Pricus finally realizes he can't control his children. When Pricus is the only sea-goat left, he begs Chronos to let him die because he can't stand being the only one. Chronos lets Pricus live out his immortality in the sky by transforming him into the constellation Capricorn. Now he can watch over his children the world over. Sea-goat symbolizes letting go and allowing others to live their own lives.

Talents: Ambitious, careful, disciplined, faithful, loyal, patient, practical, prudent, sense of humor

Challenges: Careless, fatalistic, holds grudges, miserly, overly conventional, pessimistic, rigid, tactless

Element(s): Water

Primary Color(s): Brown, green

Appearances: When sea-goat appears, it means to let go of something or someone you've been trying to control. This means you may think you have the best interest of someone at heart when you try to control their actions, but you can't control someone else. Once they reach adulthood, each person has to be free to make their own decisions and to follow their own path of spiritual growth and enlightenment. There will be mistakes made along the way, but that's when the most spiritual growth happens. When you try to control someone else, it is usually due to your own fears and insecurities. Once you recognize these traits in yourself, as Pricus did, then you can stop being controlling and allow things to move forward as the universe intended.

Assists When: You need to have patience, be disciplined, and be loyal. Pricus was patient as he tried time and again to keep his children from leaving the sea. He practiced discipline as he repeatedly turned back time to give them another chance to stay. He was loyal in his devotion to them even though he was trying to control their actions. This means now is a time to be patient with others to give them a chance to make up their own minds. Even if you don't agree with their decision, your loyalty is needed as you stand by those you love. Maintain discipline over your own actions so that you don't negatively influence those you are trying to help. Keep your sense of humor; be faithful to your cause and practical in your plans.

Frequency: Sea-goat energy moves with a sleek twisting and turning motion. It is warm but can be chilly at times. It feels slick and wet and smells like a dog that has gotten caught in the rain.

See Also: Goat

Imagine...

You're rowing a small boat across part of the sea inlet when a goat emerges from the water. You're even more shocked when it starts up a conversation with you. It appears to be very intelligent and has a broad understanding of universal knowledge. When you reach the shore, you pull the boat up onto the beach. The sea-goat climbs out of the water, and that's when you see the back half of it is a fish tail. Once on land, he stops speaking and you get the sinking feeling that he's not supposed to be out of the water. You grab him by his hooves and pull him back into the ocean, telling him that he can't be on the beach. *But the beach is so warm and beckoning*, he says. You watch him swim away but know in your heart that he'll come back to the beach one day.

Shisa

Traits: Shisa are wards symbolizing protection and keeping evil spirits away. In Okinawan mythology, these beasts are lions, although some say they're a cross between a lion with a curly mane and a dog. In Okinawan traditional culture, people use shisa as symbols of protection. Shisa are traditionally positioned with the closemouthed one on the left and the openmouthed one on the right. It is considered bad luck to reverse the positions.

Talents: Caring, connection to universal knowledge, good luck, goodness, nurturing, protection, spirituality

Challenges: Anger, indifferent, wary

Element(s): Earth

Primary Color(s): Black, blue, brown, gold, gray, green, indigo, orange, pink, purple, red, silver, turquoise, white, yellow, multitude of color combinations

Appearances: When shisa appears, it means now is the time to deepen your connection to universal knowledge and your higher self. The shisa represents Buddhist symbolism in that the shisa with the open mouth is meant to be shaping the "a" sound while the shisa with the closed mouth is meant to be shaping the "un" sound. Separately, these two sounds are symbolic of beginnings and endings. When said together they create *a-un*, which when translated from Hindu to Indian is the word *om*. In Buddhism, *om* represents the sound of universal vibration. *Om* is often used in meditation and in yoga because it is a highly spiritual sound that helps connect your creative inner power to the frequency of the universe and, in turn, universal knowledge. In Okinawan mythology, it is said that a nobleman gave a boy a shisa as a gift. The boy sensed the shisa was mystical, so he took very good care of it. One day a dragon traveled through the boy's village, causing a lot of destruction. The shisa came to life and saved the village. In another version, the dragon had been tormenting the villagers for a while, so the king asked the shisa to help. It confronted the dragon, who laughed at its small size. The shisa became very angry and roared so loud that a boulder fell and landed on the dragon's tail so it couldn't move. After a while, the dragon died and the dragon and boulder are now known as Ganna-mui Woods near Naha Ohashi Bridge.

These legends mean that when you're facing an obstacle that is much larger than you are, reach inside, gather your voice and courage, and face the obstacle head on to overcome it. Shisa warns against acting in anger but the emotion of anger can spur you to accomplish your goal.

Assists When: You want to increase your wealth or positivity or are trying to achieve success in any way. A shisa that has a golden sphere under its pad is symbolic of wealth, bountiful crops, intense goodness, and can help you achieve your goals. Shisa is known for its ability to protect and ward off evil, so if you feel unsafe or threatened, call on shisa for assistance. Shisa also protects from fire. According to mythology, the people of Tomimori Village in Southern Okinawa were encountering many fires. A feng shui master told them to build a stone shisa facing Mt. Yaese. Once built, the fires stopped and the village was protected thereafter. If you fear fire, or feel a threat from fire, ask shisa to help ward it away.

Frequency: Shisa energy feels solid, hard, and concrete. It moves extremely slowly and often stops, remaining in one place for a long time. It sounds like an extremely loud roar like a sonic boom.

See Also: Dog, Lion

> ### *Imagine…*
> You're shopping when you see a cute pair of shisa in beautiful colors and put them in your cart. Later you change your mind and put them back on the shelf. You can't stop thinking about them and wonder if this is a sign that you need more spiritual protection in your home. You start back toward them but then change your mind again and head to the checkout. You're putting the purchases on the belt when you see the shisa sitting in your cart. *What? How in the world did they get back in there?* You don't know, but you do know you're buying them.

Sleipnir

Traits: Sleipnir is an enormous enchanted horse with eight legs in Norse mythology. He was Odin's personal mount that carried him from Asgard to Earth, throughout the Nine Worlds, and on other journeys looking for fallen Viking warriors to return to the burial grounds of Valhalla in the Realms of the Dead. Sleipnir was the most powerful, fastest, and largest horse in the universe. He could run with extreme speed in the air, over the sea, and on land. He was enchanted by symbols that were carved into his teeth, giving him these abilities. Sleipnir symbolizes safe passage, the wind, and speed.

Talents: Adventure, awareness, capable, competence, creativity, enchanted, fearless, honor, inspiration, intelligence, noble, prestige, protection, quests, service, shamanism, speed, strength, wisdom

Challenges: Fury, relentless, ruthless pursuit

Element(s): Air, earth, water

Primary Color(s): Gray

Appearances: When Sleipnir appears, it means you will be very busy doing a lot of things at once, so you feel as if you're moving at a great rate of speed, or you will be traveling. Sleipnir also means that you are on a quest of spiritual enlightenment and will receive assistance from many helping spirits on your journey. Sleipnir reminds you to be aware, so you acknowledge them when they appear to you. Sleipnir warns against being ruthless in your search for more knowledge or wisdom. Don't be cold or unfeeling in your pursuits but instead seek the truth by connecting to your emotions. Odin gave his eye for more wisdom. This warns you can seek and find without causing yourself pain and suffering. The spiritual journey is one filled with wonder, awe, and inspiration. If you're feeling negative emotions or darkness on your search, then you're on the wrong path. Look for the light and follow Sleipnir out of darkness.

Assists When: You need to find inspiration to be more creative. If you feel blocked, just thinking about Sleipnir can boost your creativity. Think of its large size, eight legs, magical markings on its teeth, and the ability to practically fly between worlds. How can Sleipnir's qualities inspire you? If you're seeking adventure, Sleipnir can help you find places and exciting activities that will engage and fulfill you. If you need safe passage on a trip, ask Sleipnir to assist you. He will take you on the fastest and safest route, protecting you along the way. When you're in a delicate situation that requires honorable wisdom, Sleipnir will help you make the right choices or urge you to pass your wise knowledge to someone else in order for them to take the best course of action. Sleipnir will bring other helping spirits to you on your quest for spiritual enlightenment. He will help you be aware of these spirits when they come to you and urge you to accept their assistance as you accept him. No man walks the path of enlightenment alone. Many walk with you to light your way.

Frequency: Sleipnir energy feels smooth, as if you're leaning into the wind while traveling at a high rate of speed. It buzzes with electric pulses, stimulating and urging you to move faster still. It has a quick, rhythmic, eight-beat cadence.

See Also: Horse

Imagine...

You're stuck. Where, you don't know. It feels like you're in limbo somewhere in space. You're just floating along when you see a giant horse running toward you, which is weird because it looks like it's flying. It stops and you realize it has eight legs. The horse nuzzles your arm, so you grab its mane and swing yourself onto its back. As soon as you sit, you no longer feel like you're floating. It's as if it has a strong magnetic pull that's holding you in place. When it takes off, you know why. It moves at tremendous speeds. The next thing you know you're standing in front of your house. You climb down and scratch its neck, and then it runs away, disappearing into the sky.

Stymphalian Bird (Roc)

Traits: Stymphalian bird has sharp metallic feathers, poisonous feces, and a bronze beak. It is about the size of an Ibis bird but with a straight beak. In Greek mythology, it was considered a man-eater who threw its feathers at victims. Ares, the god of war, kept Stymphalian birds as pets. While escaping a pack of wolves, the flock of Stymphalian birds ended up in Arcadia, where they quickly reproduced. They destroyed crops, trees, and the townspeople. Stymphalian bird symbolizes destruction and renewal.

Talents: Creativity, fertility, renewal, teamwork

Challenges: Aggression, destruction

Element(s): Air

Primary Color(s): Gold

Appearances: When Stymphalian bird appears, it means to think of unique ways to achieve your goals. Its bronze beak could pierce through the toughest armor of bronze or iron. In order to win against the Stymphalian bird, men created a suit of armor woven out of thick cork. When it attacked with its beak, it would get stuck in the cork. By being creative, the villagers were able to avoid being hurt by the bird. When you apply creative thinking to your life, you can achieve things that others think are impossible while keeping negativity at bay. Using unique creative visualization will also enable you during manifestation. In Hercules's sixth labor for Eurystheus, he had to drive the flock of Stymphalian birds away from a lake at Stymphalos, where they were causing havoc. Upon arrival, he discovered that the forest was too dense and dark to see through, and the marsh couldn't support his weight. The goddess Athena came and gave Hercules a krotala (noisemaking clapper) made by Hephaestus, the god of the forge. Hercules climbed to a nearby mountain, clapped the krotala together, and scared the birds from the trees. As they flew, Hercules shot them with a bow and arrows and with a slingshot. The ones who escaped never returned to Greece. This legend means there are times when you need to accept help from others even when you are tasked to do something on your own. Your ultimate success may just rely on the unexpected help of a friend or even someone you've never met before. If you find yourself in a situation where someone is offering help, consider the offer in a positive way and not negatively (as in thinking of what the person wants in return) to ensure your success.

Assists When: You need to purposefully put an end to something so new opportunities and people can enter your life. Stymphalian bird was the ultimate destructive machine (as it was made out of metal). It made a mess of everything it touched. If you've been feeling as if your life is upside down and you're making a mess of everything you touch, then you may be receiving a message from Stymphalian bird to take a closer look around you. In order for renewal to occur, there first has to be some kind of ending, whether it's in the form of destroying any negativity that's holding you back, ending a relationship, or letting go of something that's no longer serving you. Stymphalian bird is with you to help with the ending so you can move forward into renewal, meeting new people, and experiencing new opportunities.

Frequency: Stymphalian bird energy flows in a choppy, up-and-down rhythm. It is hard, pointy, and sharp. It feels as if you're drawing a small piece of metal down your arm. It is hot and sounds like metal grinding on metal.

Imagine...

You're looking out of your window when you hear a strange noise. Then a huge flock of glittering metallic birds fly into view. The sun glitters off of the metal, making it difficult to look at them. You've never seen anything like this before, so you walk outside to get a closer look. They land in a large tree in your yard. Their rustling movements sound like music. You begin to hum along. Suddenly they stop moving and you stop humming. You realize that there are hundreds of eyes staring at you. It makes you a little nervous, so you start humming the tune again. They lift off in flight, circle around you three times, then take to the sky.

Thunderbird

Traits: In Native North American mythology, thunderbird is a supernatural being that carries around glowing snakes and creates thunderstorms at will when it flies. When it beats its wings, it causes a thunderclap, and the movement of the air around it creates clouds. When it blinks, cloud to cloud lightning happens, and bolts of lightning are caused by the glowing snakes. Thunderbird would also make it rain. It created war and fighting in the earth's waters, especially with the horned serpents and water snakes. It most often takes the form of an eagle with outspread wings but with two curling horns and teeth inside its beak. Thunderbird symbolizes protection, power, and strength.

Talents: Illumination, intelligence, power, protection, spirituality, strength

Challenges: Angry, easily enraged, instigator, vengeance, war

Element(s): Air

Primary Color(s): Black, blue, green, orange, red, yellow, all arranged so it's multicolored

Appearances: When thunderbird appears, it means you will be going through a time of transition, shifting from your present form to another in regard to your spirituality and beliefs. Depending on the legend, thunderbird can be either a single entity that lived at the top of a mountain or a species that could shapeshift into human form by pushing their beaks back on their head and removing their feathers like a blanket. They were said to marry humans. Thunderbird is a sign of war because it raged war against the great horned snake that attempted to devour man and take over the world, thus protecting mankind and the earth from destruction. Thunderbird is revered because it would guard a sacred fire or carry dew on its back that, when released, would restore fertility to the earth. Thunderbird has a dual nature. While it is protective and will fight other supernatural beings on behalf of man, it can also be destructive due to the storms it creates. When thunderbird appears, it means you are protected from negative energy, but you also need to be careful of instigating change that comes from a place of negativity. When this happens, you will experience delays and possibly regrets for your actions. Cling to the positive during your transformations.

Assists When: You need to conceal yourself, a project you're working on, or a secret you're keeping. Thunderbird is described in many different ways because it is a difficult being to see. When it is in flight, it is surrounded by thick cloud cover which makes it impossible to see. This means you have the ability to keep things hidden. When the time is right to reveal what you've been hiding, the clouds will open up and there will be clear skies. You'll feel this more than see it. You'll intuitively know the time is right to tell your secret or that you've be finished with the project and it's time to present it. Thunderbird also brings illumination so it will be easier for you to see and learn what you need as you follow your spiritual path.

Frequency: Thunderbird energy swirls around you in intense, powerful gales with bright bolts of lightning striking near you. It is loud and sounds like you've stepped into the middle of an intense thunderstorm. It feels hot at first but quickly cools.

> ## Imagine…
> A storm is brewing on the horizon. You feel its power in the wind and its strength in the lightning flashing through the sky. You know the thunderbird is coming in this storm, so you wait patiently for it to appear. The thunder claps loudly around you, and the wind is really blowing now. The rain begins, and soon you're soaked. And then you see the thunderbird. It is enormous, filling the sky with its broad wings as it screeches into the storm. You wave and catch its attention. You two are kindred spirits. You love thunderstorms as much as the thunderbird loves making them. It flies closer to you, and you hear it say your name on the wind. You feel protected, powerful, and recharged from the thunderbird's acknowledgment of your presence in its storm.

Unicorn

Traits: Unicorn symbolizes purity, innocence, faith, intuition, and enchantment. It is all that is right within the universe and is a connection to the higher realms of spirituality. It signifies the higher self, a gentle nature, a pure heart, and a loving and giving nature. Peace and inner calm, righteousness, and belief in things others may not see.

Talents: A connection to all that is, a giving heart, beauty, innocence, kindness, patience, perfection, positive beliefs, purity, spirituality, unity, virtue, wisdom

Challenges: Being ditzy, being naïve, flighty, impractical expectations, tendency to live in a fantasy world

Element(s): Earth, water

Primary Color(s): White

Appearances: Unicorns often appear when it's time to connect to your core essence, inner being, and higher self. It can mean your spirit guides are trying to reach you, but you're not listening. When you see unicorn, stop what you're doing and listen telepathically for unique messages. It means to believe in yourself and have faith that everything will work out how the universe intends. Connecting with unicorn means to delve into your own exceptional creativity and to open yourself to the enchanting ways of the mystical realms, to believe in your intuition and psychic abilities. It means it's time to experience spiritual growth and to discover the mysteries of the universe. You are pure of heart and connected to the Divine.

Assists When: You are experiencing spiritual growth, are working on developing your intuition or psychic abilities, are connecting with your spirit guides, and are searching for the meaning of your life. Unicorn helps you learn patience and to have faith in that which you cannot see. If you've been feeling out of sorts or stressed out, unicorn helps you to see the miracles in your life. If you've lost touch with the beauty of your relationship with the world around you, unicorn helps you see with a sense of wonder and awe. If you feel burdened with too much responsibility, or are feeling depressed or anxious, unicorn helps to clear away the negativity, release judgmental tendencies, and replace these with a positive lightness of being. Unicorn can travel throughout the universe, so it can guide you during your own travels. Seeing unicorn means to trust in your instincts and soul essence, your true nature. Unicorn allows you to see purity and beauty in everything.

Frequency: Unicorn's frequency is magical like the tinkling sound of chimes or small high-pitched bells. It is light and airy and flows like a gentle breeze. It is reflective like the light of the moon and when connected to your frequency can inspire and raise you to even higher frequencies.

See Also: Horse, Pegasus

Imagine...

You find yourself walking through a beautiful forest filled with greenery, moss, and the shade of a canopy of trees. You come upon a waterfall, and there at the edge of the pool of water at its base stands a unicorn. Its energy flows across the water toward you and dances around you as if filled with stardust. It is light yet extremely powerful, so much so that it takes your breath away. You stare at this majestic creature in wonder and awe. You feel such a strong connection to the unicorn that you step into the pool of water and begin to swim toward it. As you do, the unicorn enters the water, where you meet. The unicorn nuzzles your face and then tips its head to guide you toward its back. You climb on and hold on to its neck as it swims back to its side of the pool. The unicorn slowly walks into the forest and finds a large bed of moss, where it lies down. You slip off of its back and rest your head against its withers. You're filled with song and start to sing to the unicorn. It turns to look at you and touches its horn to your chest above your heart. You're instantly filled with love and a sense that all is right within the universe.

White Stag

Traits: White stag symbolizes spiritual growth, prophecy, and the beginning of a quest. In Celtic myth, the white stag appears when the otherworld is close by or when someone is doing something that is improper and unacceptable. In King Arthur's court, the appearance of the white stag meant that the knights would begin a quest against the gods or the fairy realm. In other mythology, the white stag led people to settle specific places or to fall in love. It is symbolic of the universal life forces of creation. This means as you travel your spiritual path white stag can guide you to the information you seek and can enable you to have prophetic visions and dreams so you experience spiritual growth.

Talents: Abundance, alternate dimensions, ancient knowledge, awareness, cleansing, creativity, dignity, dreams, endurance, fertility, grounding, higher thoughts and ideals, journey, kindness, magical, messages, mystery, nobility, perception, power, prophecy, protection, purity, regeneration, renewal, sensitivity, shifts, spirituality, strength, transitions, vitality

Challenges: Arrogance, escapism, lack of clarity in its message, overthinking, reclusive, too elusive, too prideful, unrealistic goals

Element(s): Earth

Primary Color(s): White

Appearances: When white stag appears, it means you're about to experience extreme spiritual growth. What was unknown will become known. You will experience a leap in your intuition, an expansion of your abilities, and access to ancient knowledge. Like a sponge, you will soak it all in, making it your own. This allows you a deeper connection to your inner essence and higher self. White stag appears during times of transitions to lend you its power, protection, and sense of perception. It will also keep you grounded as you acclimate to your newfound connection to higher thoughts and ideals. White stag means to keep your sense of purity, sensitivity, and kindness. For if you maintain these qualities, you will be rewarded with great abundance, renewal, and an increased sensitivity that all is connected. White stag means you will have the endurance and strength needed as you adjust to your acknowledgment of universal life forces. White stag means to remain kind and pure of heart. When white stag appears, expect to receive a powerful message in the near future.

Assists When: You need to be more aware and have more endurance and strength. White stag enables you to see even the smallest nuances of your life. White stag helps you become stronger and have more endurance in trying times. It will give you more vitality, like a second wind, so you can make it through the day energized and with eager anticipation. If you feel like you're lacking purpose or aren't connected to your inner self, white stag can help you become more grounded and show you the path to take to become closer to your life quest and spirituality. It will also show you how much others hold you in high esteem, appreciate you, and look up to you for advice and leadership. You're well loved by those around you. White stag warns some journeys may be lonely and difficult but you will endure to learn these great lessons.

Frequency: White stag energy moves at a slow pace. It stops and starts, always swirling around before moving forward. It sounds like steps on newly fallen snow with the soft twinkling of chimes in the air. It is a softly glowing white light leading the way on a long journey.

See Also: Deer

Imagine…
You're taking a walk on a nature trail to regain your balance, to feel grounded and connected to the earth. You round a curve on the path, and standing a short distance away is a white stag. You feel an overwhelming spiritual presence filled with positivity as you gaze at the stag. It walks up to you, nuzzles your arm, and starts to walk away. It looks back, so you follow it to a natural spring. It drinks so you do, too. You feel rejuvenated and as if you've moved to a higher level of consciousness. The stag bows down on one leg and then rises and disappears into the forest.

Conclusion

I hope you've enjoyed reading about energy animals and that the imagine sections have helped you connect with them on a deep level. It's important to remember to honor your energy animals as often as you can. Here are some ideas to get you started.

Honor Your Energy Animal

It is a blessing to be able to connect with your energy animal's frequency, so it only makes sense that you should want to express your gratitude to them for their shared energy connection. There are many ways you can do this, and it is a unique expression of gratitude for their part in your life. Here are some of the things I do that you can also do, or use these as ideas to jump-start your creativity.

Share Your Frequency by Sending Energy: One of the easiest and best ways you can honor your energy animal is to send it positive vibrations from your core soul essence. Imagine these vibrations as two beams of light moving from the center of your chest and from your head to the animal's heart and head. Send them love from your heart and positive thoughts to let them know you respect and care about them and that they can trust you. Thank them for sharing this sacred part of their spiritual being with you. Your appreciation for their gift is powerful energy. They want to help us, and knowing we are thankful for their advice and presence in our lives brings balance between our energy animals and our spiritual selves. It's always amazing to me how easily energy animals (and animals in the physical realm) pick up on this sharing of frequency and will feel drawn to you.

Collecting Statues and Figurines: My lifetime energy animal is the horse. As a child, I had horse statues all over my room. As an adult, I no longer collect the large figures that I did as a child but instead collect the small figurines. I have them all on the top of three bookshelves where I can see them every day. I also have several larger horse statues that are displayed prominently in my home. You can collect figurines of your energy animal and also create your own sculptures of them.

Sharing Life: When I go out to my barn, I enjoy a physical connection with my energy animal because I have lots of horses in my life. As I visit with each of them, I connect with their unique frequencies and personalities. If your energy animal is one you can have in your life, then by all means do it! If your energy animal is a wild animal instead of a domesticated one, then you'll have to engage with its energy from afar, but if you can see it in person, you'll get the same *in the flesh* effect. You can also go to a wildlife sanctuary, zoo, or any other place where you'll encounter the animal.

Support: There are many charitable organizations that work with specific types of animals and their habitat. There are fish, wildlife, and bird refuges and sanctuaries; animal rights, welfare, and service organizations; and zoos, aquariums, and zoological societies. Find one that works with your energy animal and offer a monetary donation to support the cause or volunteer your time at the facility.

Images: Can you draw or paint? If you can, create drawings or paintings of your energy animal. You can keep them in a private sketchbook or create large canvas images to display on your wall. If you use a computer, then make your screen saver an image of your energy animal. Take photographs of the animal and create a physical photo album or save the images on your computer so you can look at the animal often.

Vision Board: You can find pictures in magazines and create an image montage of your energy animal and then hang it on the wall for easy viewing. These images can be pictures of your energy animal and ones that depict its appealing qualities such as wisdom, strength, patience, or courage. Have you noticed the qualities you admire in your energy animal are often qualities you also possess? A vision board will strengthen your connection to your energy animal and remind you of your own positive characteristics.

Write: As an author, I often include stories about my experiences with my energy animals in my nonfiction books and include my energy animals in my novels. It's a way to share my energy animals with you, my readers, and to honor the energy animals at the same time. You can write stories or poems about your energy animal or keep a diary about them.

Jewelry and Clothing: I have lots of pendants of my energy animals. You can also wear pendants, bracelets, necklaces, earrings, and other jewelry in the shape of your energy animal. Wearing hats, shirts, jackets, and other clothing that have pictures of the energy animal on it is also a way to honor that animal.

Movies and TV: Enjoying a movie or television show about your energy animal is a great way to honor it. You can rent the movie and watch it at home or visit a theater. You could even have friends over to watch the movie or television show with you, especially if their energy animal is the same as yours.

Tattoo: If you're a fan of tattoos, consider getting one of your energy animal. If you're unsure about the permanence of getting a tattoo, then get a temporary tattoo. That way it's not permanent, and you're honoring your energy animal.

Research: The more you know about your energy animal, the more you will understand its messages and the easier it will be to connect to its frequency. Read as much as you can about the animal and watch nature videos so you can see it living in its habitat. Learn about medical conditions it can have, what it likes to do for playtime, how it interacts with other animals, how it cares for its young, what it eats, and how it feeds. Become an expert on your energy animal.

Commune: Sometimes the best way to interact with your energy animal is to just sit silently and feel its personality and energy. Oftentimes, you'll find that the energy animal will seek you out. For example, the other day there was a red-tailed hawk flying around the barn. I'm pretty sure it was hunting. I started to commune with it by wondering what it was doing and then how it felt to fly in circles like that. The next thing I knew, the hawk was sitting on the fence about ten feet away staring at me. It was an amazing moment with an energy animal.

Gifts: Giving gifts to or leaving gifts out for energy animals was common practice throughout history by many different cultures as a way to express gratitude to the animal for its help. You could give the animal a food treat if it is a dog, horse, or other domesticated animal. If it is wild, you can burn incense for it or leave something on the ground for it. Native Americans often left tobacco as a gift of gratitude for the animals.

As I've discussed throughout this book, animal frequency is a divine connection to the animal kingdom. It's important to trust in your abilities when combining your frequency to that of your energy animals. Empathy, telepathy, and intuition are especially important so you can feel the deepest connection possible. Your energy animals *want* to share their frequency with you; they want to guide and assist you on your spiritual path. You must believe in yourself and trust that what you hear, see, and feel are messages from your energy animal. Don't doubt or second-guess yourself. Instead trust in your first impression; it will always be correct. There is no limit to the success you will attain when connecting your energy to the animal kingdom. I hope you enjoy your journey into animal frequency.

Appendix A
Color Meanings

Have you ever considered what a gift color is to us? What if we could only view the world in black and white as it is with some animals? We'd really miss out on the richness, depth, and joy that color brings to our lives. Even though some only see in black and white, energy animals can give us messages through color. As spirit, we are continually shifting colors based upon our vibrational level at any given time, which also enables us to connect with the color and energy vibrations of our energy animals.

In animal frequency you often seek animal connections when you're dealing with specific situations in order to obtain guidance from the energy animal. Considering colors during this process can give you insight into the energy animal and can help clarify the message it gives you. You'll consider both the color of the animal's energy and any colors you see or feel during the connection. For example, you may be sharing frequency with a black bear, but suddenly you see it surrounded by a blue cloud. While black can indicate a secretive nature, the blue represents calmness and truth. In interpreting this connection and situation, the message might be to keep calm and quiet until the truth is revealed.

Look at the animal's actions, the way it looks at the world, how it acts and reacts to situations it's involved in, and any colors that are associated with these activities. When you consider color as part of the whole experience, it can help you view a broader spectrum about your energy animals and the message they're sending to you. I've included this list as an easy reference to the meanings of colors when doing an animal frequency session.

Black: Assertive, being in control, birth, daring, independent, inner control, mystery and magic, powerful, protection, the unconscious. Warns of being controlling, fear, indecisiveness, inflexible, lack of self-confidence, panic attacks, refusal to give up control, secretive, too opinionated, worry.

Blue: A search for truth, affection, analytical, calmness, creativity, feeling things deeply, good problem solver, happiness, highly intelligent, imagination, insightful and peaceful spirituality that has a soothing effect on others, logical thinker, love, perceptive, rational outlook, responsible, tenderness, tranquility. Warns of a suspicious nature, the inability to trust easily, worry, being overly cautious, loss of control, obsessive behavior, fears, depression, loneliness, and carrying too much responsibility.

Brown: Being grounded and drawn to nature, honesty, new growth, practicality, protectiveness, sensuality, stability. Warns against hiding secrets and emotional insecurity. Acceptance is important and isolation is feared. Brown also gives warning of bad moods, experiencing difficulties in life or lack of discrimination, a negative outlook, and the inability to focus on the positive.

Gold: Dependability, high ideals, influence, trustworthiness. Contains masculine energy. Gold radiates power. It means being balanced with determined focus, enlightening others without even trying, fearless and self-assured, looking for the good in every situation, inspiring others, spirituality, wisdom and understanding, mentors and guides who are good-hearted and who put their own welfare behind their concern for others. Gold is also a sign of wealth and good luck. Warns of self-esteem issues and rejecting material or spiritual wealth.

Gray: Being in control, getting what you want instead of waiting for someone to give it to you, good judgment, great imagination, hard work, living life the way you want to, quick thinking, taking care of yourself. Warns against working too much, anxiety, depression, difficulties coping with life, fears and antisocial behavior, illness, imbalance, isolation, loneliness, low energy, and passivity.

Green: Ability to soothe others, abundance, balance, caring, clear judgment, control, deep-seated calmness, even focus, happiness, health, gentleness, good decision-making skills, good health, growth, healing, keen observation, keen sense of balance and harmony, kindness, overly cautious, prosperity, rejuvenation, relaxation, sensitivity, solid foundation of spirit, untrusting, without conflict and stress. Warns against greed, jealousy, miserly tendencies, muddy thinking, and oversensitivity.

Indigo: All things are possible, high aspirations, inspiration, love of animals, patience, permanent relationships, security, spirituality and wisdom, staying in control of yourself even if you can't control what is happening around you, trust and sensitivity, wise beyond your years. Warns against believing you're better than other people and looking down at them because you feel you're more spiritually advanced or because you're in a better position in your career or life than they are.

Orange: Agitation, competitiveness, confidence, correlates to self-motivation, creativity, enthusiasm, happiness, high levels of activity, impatience, joy, prideful, quick action, restlessness, warmth, worry. Warns of being dominant, frustrated, and strongly opinionated.

Pink: A gentle nature, a good listener, affection, at ease, being modest/shy, calming, compassionate, friendship, high ideals, joy, loving and caring, nonaggressive, nurturing, protectiveness, relaxed, romantic notions, soothing, unconditional love, understanding, unselfish. Warns of anger, having your feelings easily hurt, irritability, needing more support from others than you let on, violent behavior.

Purple: Concern, great depth of feeling, high ideals and standards, humility, increasing your expectations, leadership, mystic qualities and clairvoyance, open-minded, royalty, spirituality, wisdom. Warns of arrogance, blocking your creativity, feeling others are holding you back, ignoring those you don't feel are worthy of your attention, are self-serving, or are trying to make you conform to their belief system.

Red: Control, courageous, creativity, elevates energy, extrovert, fun-loving, loyalty, over-achievers, passion, sexuality, strength, symbolic of ambitions, vitality. Warns of aggression, anger, and impulsiveness.

Silver: Balance, calm and confident, communication, dependability and responsibility, good fortune, high ideals, intuition, mental, physical and emotional harmony, time for reflection, and changes in direction by seeking truth, honesty, and clear understanding. Warns against being too introspective as to appear aloof to others, despair, destruction, extreme moodiness, fear, living in a fantasy world, negativity accumulating in the body, repentance, and weakness.

Turquoise: Abundant energy, being in tune with your feelings, considering new ideas, creativity, efficient and productive, is invigorating but brings calmness at the same time, making plans, moving forward to attain goals instead of waiting to make a decision, sensitivity, taking charge and leading the way, talkative, talking things out, tranquility. Warns of avoiding true feelings, being in a rut, fearing change, despondence, and shutting down.

White: A leader others look up to, change, innocence, new direction, new opportunity, positive energy, protection, purity, sharing, truth, unique standards that set them apart, well-balanced optimism. Reclaim your positive energy through purity and truth. Look for new opportunities and seek direction in your life. Warns of being overextended and overwhelmed, feeling scattered and frayed without direction.

Yellow: Activity, communication, conquering conflicts, creativity, facing challenges, fun, gaining clarification, happiness, high motivation, increasing energy, inspiration, optimism, overcoming disappointments, risk-taking, spontaneity. Warns of being overly critical, suspicious, or untrusting and deep pain or hidden anger that needs to be addressed.

Appendix B:
Elemental Meanings

When you're working with animal frequency and energy animals, it's only natural that the elements are part of the process to help you understand the significance of their messages. Just as we inhabit the earth, move through the air, swim in the water, and experience fire, so do animals. Some animals have a primary element where they spend the majority of their time. Others spend their time equally in two or more elements, so you'd want to consider each of the elements. Think of where your energy animal spends most of its time. For example, horses spend the majority of their time on land, but they also like to swim. Since the time spent swimming and being on land isn't equal, then the horse's element would be earth. Ducks, on the other hand, spend their time equally on land, in the water, and in the air, so they would share all three. Animals that live in the trees would have the element of air if they spend more time in the trees than on the ground. The better you understand the nature of your energy animal and its environment, the better your frequency connection with it will be.

Air: Adapts well to changes, carries away troubles, communication, concepts, connected to the soul, creativity, flowing and evolving, forward thinking, high mental activity, intelligence, observant, open-minded, power of the mind, reasoning, seeking new opportunities, simple and straightforward thinking, thoughtfulness, tolerance, travel, wisdom. Warns against stagnation and becoming too studious without taking action, of being overly analytical and too much of a perfectionist, and of feeling too much negativity and strife.

Earth: The ability to find and use resources, absorbs excesses of the other elements, adventure, being grounded, caring, compassion, death, endurance, feeling, fertility, forgiving, friendly, great disposition, great listener, life, non-judgmental, nurturing, obtaining what you desire, outgoing personality, patient, peacekeeper, practicality, rebirth, seeking opportunities, sensation, solid, stability, sympathetic, tolerant, touching, using the senses. Warns against being hypersensitive, emotional insecurities, fear of abandonment, fear of consequences of not saying yes and saying no instead, overprotectiveness, suffocating, a worrywart.

Fire: Astounding depth of emotions, attracts others, cleansing, cognitive thinking, energy levels are unparalleled, empathic, enthusiasm for life, fertility, insights, inspiration, intuition, not going to extremes, passion, purification, rebirth, relationships hold great importance, sensitive, spirituality, strong will, taking action. Warns against being anxious, disconnected from people and activities, fears, feeling overwhelmed, irrational thoughts, losing direction, losing yourself in relationships, nervous, overload of the senses, overstimulation, panic attacks, restlessness.

Water: Active imagination, cleansing, creativity, curious about spirituality, darkness and heaviness, emotions, enjoys quiet places, healing, how things work, intuition, the meaning of life, memory, passion, psychic abilities, purification, senses of smell and taste, strong opinions, strong sense of self and purpose. Warns against being absent-minded, being distant, coldhearted, difficulties coping with problems, feeling cheated, isolation, lazy, loneliness, melancholy, paranoia, persecuted, sadness.

Have lots of fun practicing animal frequency to become closer to your energy animals!

Bibliography

Alderton, David. *The Encyclopedia of Animals.* New York: Chartwell Books, 2013.

Alexander, Skye. *The Secret Power of Spirit Animals.* Avon, MA: Adams Media, 2013.

Allen, Judy. *Fantasy Encyclopedia.* Boston: Kingfisher, 2005.

Alvarez, Melissa. *365 Ways to Raise Your Frequency.* Woodbury, MN: Llewellyn Worldwide, 2012.

Andrews, Ted. *Animal-Speak: The Spiritual & Magical Powers of Creatures Great & Small.* Woodbury, MN: Llewellyn Publications, 2004.

———. *Animal-Wise: The Spirit Language and Signs of Nature.* Jackson, TN: Dragonhawk Publishing, 1999.

Angell, Madeline. *America's Best Loved Wild Animals.* New York: Bobbs-Merrill Company, 1975.

Austin, Elizabeth, and Oliver Austin. *Random House Book of Birds.* New York: Random House, 1990.

Baring-Gould, Sabine. *Curious Mythos of the Middle Ages.* New York: University Books, 1967.

Barnum, Melanie. *The Book of Psychic Symbols.* Woodbury, MN: Llewellyn Worldwide, 2012.

Baumgartner, Anne S. *A Comprehensive Dictionary of the Gods.* New York: University Books, 1984.

Bulfinch, Thomas. *Bulfinch's Mythology: The Age of Fable / The Age of Chivalry / Legends of Charlemagne.* New York: Didactic Press, 2015.

Burnie, David, and Don E. Wilson. *Animal: The Definitive Visual Guide to the World's Wildlife.* New York: Dorling Kindersley, 2001.

Caras, Roger A. *Panther.* Lincoln, NE: University of Nebraska Press, 1969.

Cheung, Theresa. *The Element Encyclopedia of 20,000 Dreams.* New York: Barnes and Noble, by arrangement with HarperElement, 2006.

Chevalier, Jean, and Alain Gheerbrant. *A Dictionary of Symbols.* London: Penguin Books, 1996.

Clark, Jerome. *Unexplained!: Strange Sightings, Incredible Occurrences, and Puzzling Physical Phenomena.* Canton, MI: Visible Ink Press, 2013.

Clark, Jerome, and Loren Coleman. *Cryptozoology A To Z: The Encyclopedia of Loch Monsters, Sasquatch, Chupacabras, and Other Authentic Mysteries of Nature.* New York: Simon & Schuster, 1999.

Cohen, Daniel. *The Encyclopedia of Monsters.* New York: Dodd, Mead & Company, 1982.

Coleman, Jerry D. *Strange Highways: A Guidebook to American Mysteries & the Unexplained.* Alton, IL: Whitechapel Productions Press, 2003.

Coleman, Loren. *The Field Guide to Bigfoot, Yeti, and Other Mystery Primates Worldwide.* New York: Avon Books, 1999.

———. *Mysterious America: The Revised Edition.* New York: Paraview Press, 2001.

———. *Tom Slick and the Search for the Yeti.* Boston: Faber and Faber, 1989.

Conant, Roger, and Joseph T. Collins. *A Field Guide to Reptiles and Amphibians: Eastern and Central North America.* New York: Houghton Mifflin Company, 1998.

Conway, D. J. *Animal Magick: the Art of Recognizing & Working with Familiars.* Woodbury, MN: Llewellyn Publications, 2003.

———. *Magickal, Mystical Creatures.* St. Paul, MN: Llewellyn Publications, 1996.

Cotterell, Arthur. *World Mythology.* United Kingdom: Parragon Publishing, 2005.

Cotterell, Arthur, and Rachel Storm. *The Ultimate Encyclopedia of Mythology.* London: Hermes House, 2005.

Courage, Katherine Harmon. *Octopus.* New York: Penguin Group, 2013.

Dempsey, Colin. *The Ultimate Encyclopedia of Mythical Creatures.* United Kingdom: Kandour Ltd, USA: Barnes & Noble Books, 2006.

Edmonds, Margot, and Ella E. Clark. *Voices of the Winds: Native American Legends.* New York: Facts on File, 1989.

Erdoes, Richard, and Alfonso Ortiz, eds. *American Indian Myths and Legends.* New York: Pantheon Books, 1984.

Evans, Bergen. *Dictionary of Mythology*. New York: Dell Publishing, 1970.

Farkas, Ann, et al. *Monsters and Demons in the Ancient and Medieval Worlds*. Mainz am Rhein: Philipe von Zabern, 1987.

Farmer, Steven D. *Animal Spirit Guides*. Carlsbad, CA: Hay House, 2006.

———. *Power Animals: How to Connect with Your Animal Spirit Guide*. Carlsbad, CA: Hay House, 2004.

Fire, John, and Richard Erdoes. *Lame Deer: Seeker of Visions*. New York: Washington Square Press, 1972.

Fleming, Fergus, et al. *Myth and Mankind: Heroes of the Dawn: Celtic Myth*. London: Duncan Baird Publishers, 1996.

Gabb, Michael H. *Creatures Great and Small*. Minneapolis, MN: Lerner Publishing, 1980.

Gill, Sam D., and Irene F. Sullivan. *Dictionary of Native American Mythology*. New York: Oxford University Press, 1992.

Gilpin, Daniel. *The Complete Illustrated World Guide to Freshwater Fish & River Creatures*. London: Lorenz Books, 2014.

Goldworthy, Brigit. *Totem Animal Messages: Channelled Messages from the Animal Kingdom*. Bloomington, IN: Balboa Press, 2013.

Grandin, Temple, and Catherine Johnson. *Animals in Translation: Using the Mysteries of Autism to Decode Animal Behavior*. New York: Harcourt Books, 2005.

———. *Animals Make Us Human: Creating the Best Life for Animals*. New York: First Mariner Books, 2010.

Hall, Derek. *The Ultimate Illustrated Guide to Marine & Freshwater Fish of the World*. London: Lorenz Books, 2012.

Hall, Mark A. *Thunderbirds: The Living Legend of Giant Birds*. Minneapolis, MN: Fortean Publications,1988.

Henderson, Kelly. *Your Mythic Spirit Guide*. Indie Published, 2012.

Hines, Donald M. *Ghost Voices: Yakima Indian Myths, Legends, Humor, and Hunting Stories*. Issaquah, WA: Great Eagle Publishing, 1992.

Hultkrantz, Ake. *Native Religions of North America*. San Francisco: Harper & Row Publishers, 1987.

Jackson, Tom. *Animals of the World*. London: Anness Publishing, 2014.

———. *The Illustrated Encyclopedia of Animals, Birds & Fish of North America*. London: Lorenz Books, 2012.

Johnson, Sylvia A. *The Wildlife Atlas*. Minneapolis, MN: Lerner Publishing, 1977.

Kays, Roland W., and Don E. Wilson. *Mammals of North America*. Princeton, NJ: Princeton University Press, 2002.

Keel, John A. *The Complete Guide to Mysterious Beings*. New York: Doubleday, 1994.

King, Scott Alexander. *Animal Dreaming Book: The Symbolic and Spiritual Language of the Australian Animals*. Woodbury, MN: Llewellyn Worldwide, 2014.

Levy, Joel. *Fabulous Creatures and Other Magical Beings*. London: Carroll & Brown Publishers, 2004.

Lloyd-Jones, Hugh. *Mythical Beasts*. London: Gerold Duckworth & Co., 1980.

Matthews, John and Caitlin Matthews. *The Element Encyclopedia of Magical Creatures*. New York: HarperCollins, 2005.

Meyer, Regula. *Animal Messengers: An A-Z Guide to Signs and Omens in the Natural World*. Rochester, VT: Bear & Company, 2015.

Murphy-Hiscock, Arin. *Birds: A Spiritual Field Guide: Explore the Symbology and Significance of These Divine Winged Messengers*. Avon, MA: Adams Media, 2012.

Neihardt, John G. *Black Elk Speaks*. New York: Simon & Schuster, 1959.

Newton, Michael. *Encyclopedia of Cryptozoology: A Global Guide to Hidden Animals and Their Pursuers*. Jefferson, NC: McFarland & Company, 2005.

Nigg, Joseph, ed. *The Book of Fabulous Beasts*. Oxford: Oxford University Press, 1999.

Nozedar, Adele. *The Element Encyclopedia of Native Americans*. New York: HarperElement, 2012.

———. *The Illustrated Signs & Symbols Sourcebook: An A to Z Compendium of Over 1000 Designs*. New York: Metro Books, 2010.

O'Connell, Mark, Raje Airey, and Richard Craze. *The Illustrated Encyclopedia of Symbols, Signs & Dream Interpretation*. New York: Anness Publishing, 2009.

Page, Michael, and Robert Ingpen. *Encyclopedia of Things That Never Were*. New York: Penguin Putnam, 1985.

Payne, Ann. *Medieval Beasts*. London: The British Library Board, 1990.

Perez, Daniel Edward. *Big Footnotes: A Comprehensive Bibliography Concerning Bigfoot, the Abominable Snowmen and Related Beings*. Los Angeles, CA: D. Perez Publishing, 1988.

Radin, Paul. *The Trickster: A Study in American Indian Mythology*. Westport, CT: Greenwood Press, 1956.

Sams, Jamie, and David Carson. *Medicine Cards*. New York: St. Martin's Press, 1999.

Seidelmann, Sarah Bamford. *What the Walrus Knows*. Sarah Seidelmann LLC, 2013.

Shackley, Myra. *Still Living? Yeti, Sasquatch and the Neandertal Enigma*. New York: Thames and Hudson, 1983.

South, Malcom, ed. *Mythical and Fabulous Creatures: A Source Book and Research Guide*. New York: Greenwood Press, 1987.

Steiger, Brad. *Medicine Power*. New York: Doubleday & Company, 1974.

———. *Real Monsters, Gruesome Critters, and Beasts from the Darkside*. Canton, MI: Visible Ink Press, 2011.

Stevens, Jose, and Lena Stevens. *Secrets of Shamanism*. New York: Avalon Books, 1988.

Steward, Julian Haynes. *The Clown in Native North America*. New York: Garland Publishing, 1991.

Walters, Martin. *The Illustrated World Encyclopedia of Insects*. London: Lorenz Books, 2011.

Zolar. *Zolar's Encyclopedia of Omens, Signs and Superstitions*. New York: Prentice Hall Press, 1989.

Websites

www.ancient.eu/mythology/

www.ancientgreece.com/s/Mythology/

www.ancient-origins.net

www.animalplanet.com

www.animals.nationalgeographic.com/animals

www.animalspirits.com

www.animaltotem.com

www.ansci.cals.cornell.edu

www.arkive.org

www.audubon.org/field-guide

www.bbc.co.uk/nature/animals

www.birds.cornell.edu

www.crystalwind.ca/animal-totems

www.desertusa.com/animals.html

www.dreammoods.com/dreamthemes/animals.htm

www.egyptianmyths.net

www.gods-and-monsters.com/list-of-mythical-creatures.html

www.greekmythology.com

www.healing.about.com/od/animaltotems/tp/animal-totems.htm

www.in5d.com/animal-symbolism-totems-dream-analysis-from-a-to-z

www.infoplease.com/ipa/A0900731.html

www.legendsofamerica.com/na-totems.html

www.linsdomain.com/totems/pages/

www.visualdictionaryonline.com/animal-kingdom/insects-arachnids.php

www.mythicalcreaturesguide.com/page/List+of+Mythical+Creatures

www.nwf.org/Wildlife.aspx

www.pantheon.org

www.primalastrology.com

www.psychiclibrary.com/beyondBooks/animal-spirit-guides

www.seaworld.org

www.shamanicjourney.com/category/power-animals-totems-spirit-guides

www.spiritanimal.info

www.spirit-animals.com

www.spiritlodge.yuku.com

www.spiritwalkministry.com/spirit_guides/animal_spirit_guides

www.starstuffs.com/animal_totems/

www.sunsigns.org

www.thehellenictimes.com/beasts.html

www.universeofsymbolism.com/animal-totems.html

www.warpaths2peacepipes.com/native-american-culture/animal-totems.htm

www.whats-your-sign.com/animal-totems.html

www.wildspeak.com/animaldictionary.html

www.windows2universe.org/mythology/mythology.html

www.openherd.com

To Write to the Author

If you wish to contact the author or would like more information about this book, please write to the author in care of Llewellyn Worldwide Ltd. and we will forward your request. Both the author and publisher appreciate hearing from you and learning of your enjoyment of this book and how it has helped you. Llewellyn Worldwide Ltd. cannot guarantee that every letter written to the author can be answered, but all will be forwarded. Please write to:

Melissa Alvarez
℅ Llewellyn Worldwide
2143 Wooddale Drive
Woodbury, MN 55125-2989
Please enclose a self-addressed stamped envelope for reply,
or $1.00 to cover costs. If outside the U.S.A., enclose
an international postal reply coupon.

Many of Llewellyn's authors have websites with additional information and resources. For more information, please visit our website at http://www.llewellyn.com

365 WAYS to RAISE YOUR FREQUENCY

Simple Tools to Increase Your Spiritual Energy for Balance, Purpose, and Joy

MELISSA ALVAREZ

365 Ways to Raise Your Frequency
Simple Tools to Increase Your Spiritual Energy
for Balance, Purpose, and Joy
Melissa Alvarez

The soul's vibrational rate, our spiritual frequency, has a huge impact on our lives. As it increases, so does our capacity to calm the mind, connect with angels and spirit guides, find joy and enlightenment, and achieve what we want in life.

This simple and inspiring guide makes it easy to elevate your spiritual frequency every day. Choose from a variety of ordinary activities, such as singing and cooking. Practice visualization exercises and techniques for reducing negativity, manifesting abundance, tapping into Universal Energy, and connecting with your higher self. Discover how generous actions and a positive attitude can make a difference. You'll also find long-term projects and guidance for boosting your spiritual energy to new heights over a lifetime.

978-0-7387-2740-0, 432 pp., 5 x 7 $16.95

Melissa Alvarez

Your Psychic Self

A Quick and Easy Guide to
Discovering Your Intuitive Talents

Your Psychic Self
A Quick and Easy Guide to
Discovering Your Intuitive Talents
Melissa Alvarez

Ever wondered if you were psychic? *Your Psychic Self* is designed to help you recognize your natural intuitive abilities and strengthen them to enhance your daily life.

In an easy, conversational tone, professional intuitive Melissa Alvarez shares her own experiences and offers direction for discovering where your skills and interests lie within the psychic and metaphysical worlds.

Good for beginners or as an all-around reference, this guide gives you an overview of the signs of intuition, different kinds of abilities, psychic experiences, and forms of intuitive communication. Understand the types of readers—from psychic detectives to animal communicators—and explore your own connection with spirit beings. Use the practice exercises to develop your abilities and learn how to protect yourself from negative influences.

978-0-7387-3189-6, 264 pp., 6 x 9   **$14.99**

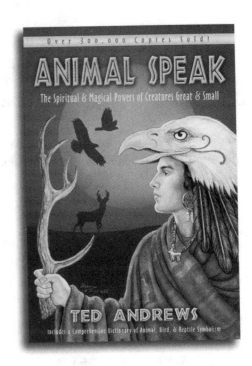

Animal Speak
The Spiritual & Magical Powers of Creatures Great and Small
TED ANDREWS

Open your heart and mind to the wisdom of the animal world.

Animal Speak provides techniques for recognizing and interpreting the signs and omens of nature. Meet and work with animals as totems and spirit guides by learning the language of their behaviors within the physical world.

Animal Speak shows you how to: identify, meet, and attune to your spirit animals; discover the power and spiritual significance of more than 100 different animals, birds, insects, and reptiles; call upon the protective powers of your animal totem; and create and use five magical animal rites, including shapeshifting and sacred dance.

This beloved, bestselling guide has become a classic reference for anyone wishing to forge a spiritual connection with the majesty and mystery of the animal world.

978-0-87542-028-8, 400 pp., 7 x 10   **$22.99**
